Strategic Development:
Methods and
Models

Strategic Development: Methods and Models

Edited by

Robert G. Dyson and Frances A. O'Brien

University of Warwick

JOHN WILEY & SONS

Chichester · New York · Weinheim · Brisbane · Singapore · Toronto

Other Wiley Editorial Offices

John Wiley & Sons, Inc., 605 Third Avenue,
New York, NY 10158-0012, USA

WILEY-VCH Verlag GmbH, Pappelallee 3,
D-69469 Weinheim, Germany

Jacaranda Wiley Ltd, 33 Park Road, Milton,
Queensland 4064, Australia

John Wiley & Sons (Asia) Pte Ltd, 2 Clementi Loop #02-01,
Jin Xing Distripark, Singapore 129809

John Wiley & Sons (Canada) Ltd, 22 Worcester Road,
Rexdale, Ontario M9W 1L1, Canada

1189475 ✗

Library of Congress Cataloging-in-Publication Data

Strategic development : methods and models / edited by Robert G. Dyson
    and Francis A. O'Brien.
        p.   cm.
    Includes bibliographical references and index.
    ISBN 0-471-97495-1 (pbk. : alk. paper)
    1. Strategic planning—Mathematical models.   I. Dyson, Robert G.
    II. O'Brien, Francis A.
    HD30.28.S729234   1998
    658.4'012—dc21   97–45636
                                                          CIP

British Library Cataloguing in Publication Data

A catalogue record for this book is available from the British Library

ISBN 0-471-97495-1

Typeset in 10/12pt Times by Dorwyn Ltd, Rowlands Castle, Hampshire.
Printed and bound in Great Britain by Bookcraft (Bath) Ltd, Midsomer Norton, Somerset.
This book is printed on acid-free paper responsibly manufactured from sustainable forestry, in which at
least two trees are planted for each one used for paper production.

Contents

About the Editors

Robert Dyson graduated from Liverpool University in mathematical statistics and from Lancaster University with a Ph.D. in operational research. He worked for Pilkington PLC from 1964–70 on cutting stock problems, forecasting and risk analysis. In 1970 he joined the University of Warwick and was appointed a professor in the Warwick Business School in 1984. He was Chair of the Business School from 1978–81, and a Pro-Vice-Chancellor of the University from 1989–95. His research interests include strategic planning/development, capital investment appraisal, organisational performance measurement and data envelopment analysis. He has published in a number of journals including the *Strategic Management Journal*, *Long Range Planning*, the *Journal of the Operational Research Society*, the *European Journal of Operational Research*, *Omega*, *Annals of Operational Research* and the *Journal of Business Finance and Accounting*, and is author/editor of *Strategic Planning: Models and Analytical Techniques*, published by Wiley. He is President of the UK Operational Research Society for 1998–9, and a member of the British Academy of Management.

Frances O'Brien graduated from Surrey University in mathematics and classical studies and Southampton University in operational research. She worked for the Operational Research group with Ford of Europe on simulation, manpower planning and allocation problems. In 1990 she joined the University of Warwick as an ESRC Management Teaching Fellow and was appointed as a lecturer in 1992. Her research interests include heuristic algorithms for allocating problems, and the use of scenarios for the assessment of uncertainty and for supporting visioning exercises. She has published in *Omega* and *OR Insight*. She is actively involved in the UK Operational Research Society in the organisation of annual conferences and as a member of Council.

Part I

Introduction

This book presents a conceptual model of the strategic development process. Views of the strategic development process in organisations range from it being seen as purely creative with little or no scope for analysis to one that is over formalised, static and focusing on producing a strategic plan rather than on actions. The approach here is to argue that effective strategic decision making requires a mixture of creativity and structured methods. The book should be of interest to both academics and practitioners interested in strategic development and to those teaching and researching in the fields of strategic management, management science and operational research. This book is developed from a previous text *Strategic Planning: Models and Analytical Techniques*, following a similar approach and including some of the same methods and models but incorporating an entirely new set of articles.

The strategic development process consists of a series of elements which need to be working effectively for the process to ensure the successful development of the organisation. These elements include objective setting and performance measurement, strategic initiative formulation, strategic evaluation and a process for modelling uncertain/ uncontrollable factors. Having identified the elements, the book then presents a range of hard and soft methods and models capable of supporting them. These include the balanced scorecard, visioning, the TOWS matrix, cognitive mapping, scenario development, system dynamics modelling, transformation methods such as reengineering, strategic investment appraisal and real option theory. The methods and models are structured into sections covering objectives, performance measurement and strategy creation; strategy formulation; modelling uncertainty; corporate modelling and evaluation and selection.

Chapter 1

Strategic Development

Robert G. Dyson and Frances A. O'Brien

University of Warwick

This book develops from the 1990 book *Strategic Planning: Models and Analytical Techniques*[1]. The stated aim of that book was to consider the use of models and analytical techniques to support the strategic planning process. Strategic planning was seen as 'a management process involving consultation, negotiation and analysis which is aimed at facilitating effective strategic decision making.' Decisions in organisations can range from short term operational and tactical through to strategic. There are no sharp divisions between different categories of decisions, but it was argued that strategic decisions can be characterised by the extent to which they have enduring effects, are broad in scope and are difficult to reverse. They typically involve large resource commitments and significant time lags from inception to full implementation.

It is fashionable to classify strategic decisions, although fashions by their nature inevitably change. Vertical integration and diversification were the fashions of the 1970s, to be replaced in the 1990s by focusing, single sourcing and reputation. Product, process and market strategies are more persistent, whilst mergers and demergers come and go. Examples of strategies include the reputation strategy of Mitsubishi who produce food, electrical goods and cards. A more flamboyant example is Richard Branson's Virgin, with its airline, rail companies, cola, financial services and hotels. The Korean company Daewoo represents a good example of market development and innovative selling with its entry to new markets and its novel approach to sales by direct selling, rather than through the typical agencies using commissioned sales staff. Chrysler has recently attempted to re-enter the UK market having ceased production there some years ago. (In fact they sold their UK plant to Peugeot who have since developed a significant presence.) In the financial sector a building society (savings and loan) might diversify its services and indeed convert to a bank to facilitate that diversity rather than retain the more restrictive mutuality condition. In the USA the numbers of banks has shrunk by thirty percent through mergers and insolvency, also as a result of deregulation. In transport, the decision to build the Channel Tunnel is about as strategic as you can get, whilst another example would be the diversification of Stagecoach, originally a bus company which took advantage of bus deregulation to become the largest private bus company in the world, into rail transportation. Pepsi-Cola decided to paint its cans blue! Companies might also seek to merge as BA and American Airways are wishing to do at the time of writing, or they might de-merge, ICI being a recent example.

Finally, a strategic transformation of the organisation may be sought through the application of business process reengineering, benchmarking or total quality management, or through resourced based planning with a focus on core competencies. Porter[2] argues that these strategies are necessary for superior performance, but are easy to imitate and therefore not sustainable and are thus in support of, but not a substitute for, activity based strategies. Doyle[3] argues that sustainable strategies (robust growth strategies) appear to base their development on four principles: delivering superior value, the recognition that no specific advantage is sustainable, learning and continuous innovation, and building relationships with customers, employees, suppliers and other stakeholders.

Strategic developments such as these all have a broad impact on the organisations affecting personnel, plant and equipment, are difficult to reverse (what else can you do with an uneconomic tunnel, convert it to a mushroom farm?), involve considerable human and capital resources, and have consequences that endure for many years which might be physical, organisational or a culture change.

The 1990 book started with the development of a model of the strategic decision making process with foundations in control theory, and then identified the essential elements of an effective process and used this framework to organise a collection of articles on the theme of the book. These articles were taken from both the strategic management and management science/operational research literatures, involved hard (e.g. risk analysis) and soft (e.g. cognitive mapping) methods, and both classic and contemporary (future classic?) articles. The book was reprinted five times, and a softback version produced although originally it was felt that it was too specialised and only a library hardback version was warranted. As it came to the end of its commercial life a new edition was considered, but for a variety of reasons it was decided to produce a more or less completely new book with a different title, but retaining the same approach.

Since its publication the book has been used as a text on courses at undergraduate (Operational Research for Strategic Planning—the original title predating the book was *Analytical Aids to Strategic Planning*, known as 'Aids' for short, but that title was overtaken by a new meaning to the word 'Aids'), specialist master's (Strategic Planning Systems), and at post-experience MBA levels (Strategic Planning Models). The contents have thus been road tested for educational purposes with approaching a thousand students. Frances O'Brien joined the Business School from the Ford Motor Company and became a key member of the teaching teams, additionally pursuing research into the impact of uncertainty on strategy development, and more recently researching into the use of scenarios for visioning. On completion of the book the author spent six years from 1989 to 1995 as a Pro-Vice-Chancellor of the University of Warwick, and being a member of all the key strategic committees including the Strategy Committee was able both to contribute to, and observe and reflect on, the strategic development of the University. This followed a period of close involvement in the 1980s in the strategic development of the Warwick Business School led by George Bain, lately the Principal of the London Business School.

When discussions began about a new version of the book, we were influenced by our experiences, and aimed to produce a new version that would involve a completely new set of articles as we felt that the previous articles were looking dated. Our search of the literature of the 1990s initially proved disappointing, and we wondered whether perhaps the modelling approach really was past its sell-by date. We were however convinced of the efficacy of incorporating uncertainty into strategic decision making, and the pervasiveness of scenario planning. Additionally our experiences confirmed the validity of the conceptual model of the strategic decision making process which we wished to retain with modifications, and although there was little evidence that corporate models other than simple financial ones seemed to have much of a role to play in the current practice of strategy evaluation, the evidence of their potential value as a learning tool was persuasive. We therefore remained convinced that modelling and analysis indeed had a valuable role to play in supporting the strategic decision making process and hence the strategic development of the organisation.

We had some difficulty with the title also as although we used the term 'strategic planning' in a deliberately loose way, Mintzberg had effectively discredited the term in his book *The Rise and Fall of Strategic Planning*[4]. The title 'Strategic Planning Revisited' was suggested, but in the end we argued that strategic planning, strategic management, strategic thinking, strategy formulation and strategic decision making were all concerned with the 'strategic development' of the organisation so we would use that as our generic term.

The organising framework for this book is a conceptual model of the strategic development process. The origins of the model lie in control theory. A simple control system model is shown in Figure 1.1. (See for example Eilon.[5])

An example of such a simple control system would be a heating system in a room. A target room temperature is required, and the current temperature (performance) of the room (system) measured by a thermostat. This is fed back to the control procedure which compares the temperature with the target, and if there is a gap, with the temperature below the target, then the heat source is called on by the control procedure to input heat into the room and thus raise the temperature. There may also be uncontrolled heat inputs from appliances such as lights or cookers, or from human activity, and heat losses through the walls, floor or ceiling. In hot weather an air conditioning system would work in a similar but reverse way.

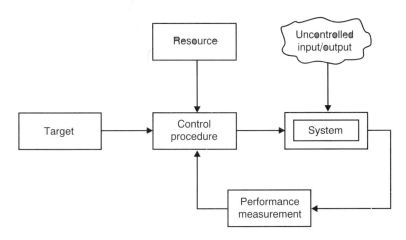

Figure 1.1. A Simple Control System

For such a system to work effectively there are a number of essential elements which must all be in place. These are:

- a target or standard
- a measurement task
- a feedback signal
- a control procedure
- a corrective action
- an adequate resource source.

Central heating or air conditioning systems are good examples of cases where a simple control system can work effectively. The occupant(s) of the room can set a required temperature; a room thermostat is usually an adequate measurement device; control procedures are available to receive the feedback on the temperature and determine whether corrective action is required; the heat source can be activated; and provided that there is an adequate supply of heat (or cool air) the desired temperature can be maintained. If any one of the above elements is missing however the system fails, and like a chain is only as effective as its weakest link.

The system is also essentially tactical and reactive. The control procedure can only respond to measures of the current performance of the system and is unable to anticipate future performance. As it stands it is therefore not a useful model for strategic decision making but the principles of the system and its purpose can form the basis of a strategic model. It should be observed though that control is being interpreted actively as concerned with effectiveness, and not passively as a constraining mechanism.

MODELS OF THE STRATEGIC DECISION MAKING PROCESS

It has been argued that strategic decisions amongst other characteristics have enduring effects and typically involve significant time lags from inception to full implementation. To allow for these, a model needs to be proactive rather than reactive. As there are usually no strategic quick fixes, only initiating strategic action when a deterioration in performance has been detected can have catastrophic consequences such as bankruptcy in the private sector or loss of public confidence. Tomlinson and Dyson[6], and Dyson[7], proposed a development of the simple control model involving an additional forward loop enabling the possible future performance of the organisation to be anticipated, hence facilitating timely strategic action, and also allowing proposed strategies to be tested so that their future impact can be estimated. The model is shown in Figure 1.2.

The model retains the feedback system of the simple control model in its outer loop, although the elements are necessarily more elaborate. The objectives will be multidimensional and focused sufficiently far into the future to allow for the time lags in the full implementation of new strategies. The control procedure receives the feedback on current and possible future performance, compares this with the objectives (gap analysis), selects or rejects trial strategies (strategic options) depending on the extent to

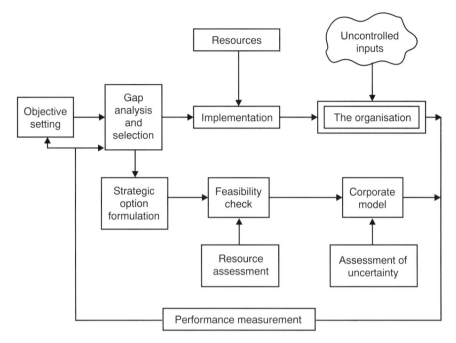

Figure 1.2. Model of the Strategic Decision Making Process

which they support the objectives, and may seek to step up the strategic option formulation process if the anticipated gaps are too large. Strategies requiring formal approval will then move to the final implementation stage thus changing the nature and performance of the organisation.

The key difference between the two models however is the addition of a forward limb. This is necessary to represent the process of anticipating the future performance of the organisation, and evaluating proposed strategies at the early stages of their development. The limb includes the strategic option formulation process; checks on feasibility (can planning permission be obtained?); an assessment of resources required; a model of the organisation; and an assessment, description or model of the uncontrolled, usually environmental, inputs. The corporate model combines the strategies and environmental uncertainties to assess the future implications of a no change strategy (sometimes referred to as the base case), or of any proposals. The future anticipated performance is then fed back to the control procedures and may also influence the review of the mission and objectives of the organisation.

This new limb can be thought of as representing the strategic planning processes of the organisation in the sense that it represents the process of reflection before action (Boothroyd[8]). Its existence is based on the assumption that strategic development is not simply based on hunch and hope, but that new strategies are articulated and tested and that those that stand up to rigorous testing are more likely to prove viable in the long run. In his demolition of strategic planning Mintzberg[4] (Chapter 5) characterises it as a formal process staffed by specialists, detached from action, driven by hard data, and assuming a predictable environment. In our view strategic planning, perhaps better described as strategic development, is a process that will indeed have some formality, but not at the exclusion of informal strategic thinking; there is no necessity for a separate strategic planning function although there will be a need for experts and facilitators; data and indeed techniques can be hard or soft; but most importantly a fundamental assumption is that the future cannot be forecast. In claiming that strategic planning assumes a predictable environment, Mintzberg quotes Allaire and Firsirotu[9] as noting that 'uncertainty is the Achilles' heel of strategic planning', but David Hertz[10] had used the term twenty-five years earlier in his seminal paper on risk analysis, stating that uncertainty is the Achilles' heel of capital investment appraisal, which is surely a part of all strategic planning processes. Scenario planning accepted uncertainty as a fact of life as developed in Shell in the 1970s (Beck[11], Wack[12,13]), and O'Brien[14] found that strategic planners were systematically recognising the uncertainty of the future. Mintzberg seems to be attacking just over-formalised inflexible strategic planning, and Ansoff[15] suggests his understanding of planning was frozen in 1964.

STRATEGIC DEVELOPMENT AT THE UNIVERSITY OF WARWICK

The model of the strategic decision making process (Figure 1.2) is a conceptual model containing a set of elements or sub-processes such as strategic option formulation which must be in place and operating effectively for the entire process to operate effectively. One test of the model is to compare it with the strategic decision making process of the University of Warwick. The University had a turnover of some £130m. in 1996, and had undertaken a period of development and growth during the 1980s and early 1990s which had placed it in the top ten UK universities for research quality, had performed equally well in teaching quality assessments, and was recognised as one of the more entrepreneurial universities due to its development of non-governmental income streams from conferences and full cost education programmes often in partnership with industry and business. This period stems from the reduction in government funding to universities in 1981. Warwick adopted a make half, save half policy as its response and as a result the 1980s became a significant period in the University's development.

If the elements of Figure 1.2 are seen as being essential to an effective strategic decision making process then it is instructive to see how they manifested themselves at Warwick. It is worth noting that the university operated through a committee structure with the Council being the governing body, the Senate responsible for purely academic matters, a Steering Committee of senior academics and administrators which met on a weekly basis for some forty weeks of the year, and the (Joint Council and Senate) Strategy Committee which consisted of the Steering Committee plus the lay members of Council who chaired Council, Finance Committee and Buildings Committee. There was no-one with the title of strategic planner.

The University had a formal set of *objectives* and a mission statement, and the formulation and review of these was addressed periodically by the Strategy Committee. These were broad and related to research and teaching, the development of science and engineering (formally recognised to ensure a balance in the university which might disappear if growth were organic), and to the earned income, i.e. non-governmental funding, activities.

Strategic option formulation was a distributed activity with strategic initiatives being taken centrally such as the building of two new residential post-experience education and training centres, and the introduction of the Warwick Research Fellows scheme which led to the appointment of some forty new academic staff selected for their outstanding research potential. Strategic initiatives also stemmed from academic departments with examples being the growth of MBA programmes in the Warwick Business School, and the Integrated Graduate Development Scheme in the Warwick Manufacturing Group involving industrial partners initially in the UK, and later leading to overseas bases.

A further successful strategy involved overseas students. These had originally been funded in the same way as UK students, but again in the early 1980s government funding was withdrawn and universities had to charge full cost fees. A decision was taken centrally at Warwick to remove overseas students from the normal resource allocation system and fund departments who recruited overseas students separately with a cash stream related to the number of students which could be used to appoint staff, purchase equipment or for other academic purposes. Departments thus saw the recruitment of overseas students as a way of developing and as a result there was a considerable growth in the number of overseas students throughout the university. This is a good example of an initiative taken centrally leading to distributed initiatives which collectively contributed strongly to the growth and development of the University.

Feasibility checking and *resource assessment* of new strategic initiatives would occur in a variety of ways. If buildings were involved any proposals would be considered by the Buildings Committee who were concerned with the physical aspects of the buildings and the site. This committee was serviced by the Estates Office, and the Estates Officer would seek planning permission and cost the proposal. Overall financial assessments of proposals would be carried out by the Finance Office and considered at the Finance Committee. The assessment of human resources required was usually limited on the assumption that Warwick would be attractive to potential employees. This was generally the case, although it was sometimes difficult to recruit some categories of specialist staff such as finance academics in the Business School, or practitioners in the Finance Office.

A *corporate model* has the purpose of evaluating the future performance of the enterprise. At Warwick this was a five year financial model developed by the Finance Office, which was reviewed each year by the Strategy Committee, and the impact of any new strategic initiatives were considered with a view to their adoption or not. The Strategy Committee would typically meet two or three times in the Spring to agree on a financial plan and select new initiatives in the process. This procedure has the potential to stifle initiatives throughout the rest of the year, but decisions beyond the first year were seen as trial decisions only, and strategic initiatives were considered at any time during the year with decisions not being tied rigidly to the annual review. If necessary the financial model would be used during the year to evaluate proposals.

The *assessment of uncertainty* was not well developed although the inherent uncertainty of the future was recognised. The approach adopted was to make the best estimates, perhaps with a slight pessimistic bias, of cash streams which were seen as reasonably predictable such as the salary bill (although an academic staff model was under development to improve predictions), or the income from home students. The earned income activities were seen as more volatile and this was allowed for by depressing the contribution from that source by an increasing factor throughout the planning period. Overall the approach tended to lead to end of year balances more favourable than in the plan, providing a cushion against short term shocks, although it could also lead to unnecessary cutbacks on occasion. This prudent approach however leads to a robust strategy and is arguably not inappropriate for a not for profit organisation.

The *performance measurement* function was also distributed. Financial performance measures were generated by the financial plan which was used to set budgets. Additionally there were financial indicators available to allow comparisons with other universities. These were discussed at Finance Committee, and sometimes led on to investigations into for example funding of the library. The relatively unique financial structure of the University (due to its high earned income) often made comparisons difficult. The University also produced an academic data base of performance measures and indicators covering such items as numbers of applications to programmes, entry qualifications of entrants, ethnic and gender mixes, PhD completion submission rates, and staff publications. This was a comprehensive document of 178 pages (1996/7). This document would be considered each year by various academic committees, and lead to specific investigations perhaps related to the quality of intake or the research income of a department. The document would also influence discussion on issues such as the placement of additional student numbers. The Warwick experience indicates a more pervasive impact of performance measures than may be apparent from a cursory study of Figure 1.2. This role of performance measures in affecting strategic development is illustrated in Figure 1.3.

Gap analysis and selection is concerned with the adoption of strategies which move the organisation in the desired direction. At Warwick selection or confirmation of strategies would be the concern of the Strategy Committee as indicated previously. As objectives were often not converted into explicit targets and hence there were no explicit gaps to close, selection criteria related to the extent to which a strategic initiative moved the University in the direction indicated by the objectives.

Implementation of strategic initiatives is of course a process that begins at the initiation stage, but would normally be carried out by a departmental or central team depending on the nature of the initiative. For example to implement a major project to implant a computer network in all the campus buildings a special project team was set

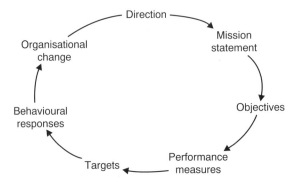

Figure 1.3. Performance Measures and Strategic Development

up using outside contractors operating under the supervision of a project manager and the Director of Information Technology. In the growth and development of the Business School a key factor in successful implementation was the identification of a product champion to lead any implementation team.

Although the University had a successful period of growth and development not all strategic initiatives which received formal support were successful. An interdisciplinary research/consulting centre, the Warwick Research Institute, was established, but eventually closed. The Institute lacked clear *objectives* and failed to contribute sufficiently either to the University's earned income objective, or to its objective of producing quality research output. A rather different initiative involved moving the playing fields to a new location on the green-belt side of the campus to free up the existing land for future academic buildings. After the move was already underway, planning permission for floodlit all-weather pitches could not be obtained—a thorough *feasibility check* had not been carried out. Fortunately land was available on another part of the campus which already contained a floodlit running track and tennis courts and the all-weather pitches were located alongside. This move was rationalised as resulting in grass pitches in the green belt, with all-weather facilities concentrated in a separate more urban location—an emergent strategy perhaps?

THE STRATEGIC DEVELOPMENT PROCESS

In reviewing Figure 1.2 then, a development of the model would need to make explicit the distributed nature of the *strategic option formulation* process and the pervasive nature of the role of *performance measures*. The former has similarities with Mintzberg's combination of intended and emergent strategies, but the combination here is of centrally driven and locally driven strategic initiatives all of which may be intended in the sense that they support the objectives of the University, may be stimulated by formal performance measures and are encouraged and supported by the centre. Other initiatives may occur unknown to or not supported by the centre, which may subsequently affect the strategic direction of the University, and these may be considered as part of the *uncontrolled inputs* to the development of the organisation.

The increasing use of formal performance measures at its best can lead to the desirable strategic development of the organisation, but at worst to short-termism and undesirable developments (Kaplan and Norton (Chapter 4), Smith[16]), so the design of formal performance measurement systems becomes a key feature in engineering effective strategic decision making processes (Dyson and Foster[17]). Taking these issues into account Figure 1.2 can be developed into Figure 1.4, a model of the strategic development process of an organisation.

The model retains the same basic structure as Figure 1.2. The changes include the separation of mission, objectives and performance measures and the fuzzy boundary round the mission is intended to indicate the general broad nature of typical mission statements which becomes sharper and more precise as objectives and performance measures are articulated. Strategic initiative development is also given a fuzzy boundary to indicate its distributed nature. The influences stimulating strategic initiative development are not just from the central strategic control function, but also from the

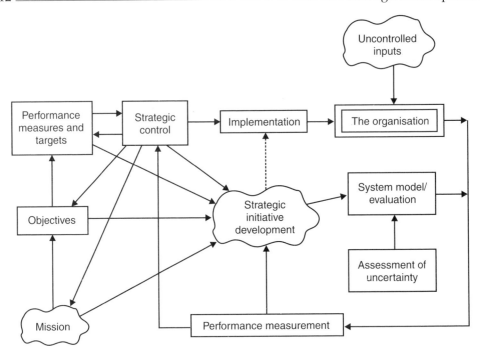

Figure 1.4. The Strategic Development Process

performance measurement system. The broken line represents unintended (by the centre) activities which affect the strategic development of the organisation. The gap analysis and selection element of the process has been replaced by the more general *strategic control* function, which represents the central function responsible for the formulation of the mission and objectives, the formal adoption of strategies and for the central contribution to strategic initiative development. *Evaluation* is a shorthand encompassing the feasibility checking, resource assessment, corporate modelling and uncertainty assessment elements of the original model. The feedback loop from evaluation to the strategic initiative development process and to the strategic control function represents organisational learning.

The strategic development process as conceptualised in Figure 1.4 is more complex than the tactical system of Figure 1.1. However in common with the tactical system for the process to work effectively all the elements or sub-processes must be in place and working effectively themselves. This process view of effectiveness was also put forward by Dyson and Foster[17]. The usual definition of effectiveness relates to the extent to which goals or targets are achieved. Strategic decision making takes place in a changing and uncertain environment, and the setting of goals takes place within the process itself. With regard to the former, as there is often a significant time lag between commitment to a decision and the realisation of the outcomes, there may be significant changes in the environment beyond the control of the organisation. As in principle there is an infinity of possible futures and therefore outcomes, deciding whether targets have been achieved is complex and can be done only after a considerable time has elapsed. The fact that goals and targets are set internal to the process also allows for the possibility of only modest short-term goals being set if their achievement is seen as a measure of success of the decision making process. These arguments support the view that the concept of effectiveness must relate to the strategic development process itself rather than to the achievement of goals.

The elements and sub-processes of the strategic development process as illustrated in Figure 1.4 are as follows:

- Mission, setting and review
- Objectives, setting and review
- Performance measures and targets, setting and review
- Strategic initiative formulation process
- Evaluation process including:
  —feasibility checking
  —resource assessment
  —assessment/modelling of uncertainty
  —corporate model
- Feedback system
- Strategic control function
- Implementation process
- Resources.

Having established the set of essential elements or sub-processes, the concern now is with the range of techniques (models, problem structuring methods and analytical tools) available to support those elements. There is not a simple one-to-one mapping between techniques and elements. For example corporate modelling, possibly in the form of a financial model, is a key component of the evaluation process, but recent work suggests the potential for corporate models to be an aid to learning and understanding the organisation and thus contributing more generally to the strategic development process. Similarly scenario development has a key role in evaluation through modelling uncertainty, but the environmental assessment required can support strategic initiative formulation through the identification of opportunities and threats. Cognitive mapping, a problem structuring method, can aid strategic initiative formulation, support the objective setting process, and also assist in the construction of a corporate model. Finally, risk analysis, scenario development and capital investment appraisal can all contribute to evaluation.

Examples of these one-to-many, and many-to-one relationships between process elements and techniques are illustrated in Figure 1.5.

Figure 1.5. Support of the Strategic Development Process

STRATEGIC DEVELOPMENT: METHODS AND MODELS

The articles selected cover a range of methods and models which have either demonstrably been of benefit in supporting the strategic development process, or are relatively untested but show clear potential. Many of the techniques have stood the test of time, but even for them recent articles have been included to give a contemporary perspective. Although it has been demonstrated that there is not a one-to-one relationship between techniques and process elements, the ordering of articles follows roughly an objective setting and performance measurement, strategy formulation, evaluation, selection/adoption sequence with the techniques also broadly ordered along a soft to hard continuum.

Part II of the book brings together a set of papers focusing on the way objectives are identified, their link to performance measurement and benchmarking, and their role in strategy creation. Chapter 2, by Gregory and Keeney, is concerned with the issue of multiple and conflicting objectives arising from an explicit recognition of multiple stakeholders, and proposes an approach to identification of objectives and the creation of policy alternatives (strategic initiatives). This is perhaps of greatest relevance in the public sector, but the role of stakeholders in private organisations is a matter of continuing debate. O'Brien and Meadows, Chapter 3, also addresses the linked issues of objective setting and strategy formulation through the approach of visioning, a development of normative scenario formulation.

The explicit role of performance measurement for strategic development is the concern of Chapter 4. The contemporary classic paper by Kaplan and Norton on the balanced scorecard is concerned with the design of effective performance measurement systems. This is a broad based model focusing on strategy rather than control (restraint), emphasising the pervasive nature of performance measurement systems and their potential to keep companies forward looking.

In Part III a collection of papers focusing on strategy formulation is included. Both long standing and contemporary methods are included, although no space has been found for product portfolio models where there appears to have been little advancement since the exposition of the previous book[1]. In Chapter 5 Weihrich illustrates the use of the TOWS matrix for strategy formulation at Daimler-Benz. The TOWS matrix, more commonly known as SWOT analysis (strengths, weaknesses, opportunities, threats), is a well structured approach that has stood the test of time and is the foundation of many contemporary approaches to strategy formulation. Porter, Chapter 6, reviews the progress of the strategy formulation field including his seminal five forces model. He considers the role of the static cross-sectional approaches and then advocates the need for research leading to a dynamic theory of strategy formulation.

The following three chapters describe alternative, complementary approaches to strategic development by organisational transformation. Black and Boal introduce resourced based planning and develop networks of strategic resource factors aimed at delivering sustainable competitive advantage. This internal approach emphasises the importance of the organisation's resources in sustaining viable strategies, and can be considered in contrast to the externally driven approach of scenario planning. A complementary approach from the human resource school, that of competency based approaches to strategic development, appears in the chapter by Kochanski and Ruse. The chapter by Edwards and Peppard describes the potentially pervasive approach of business process reengineering, and the article focuses particularly on its contribution to strategy implementation. In Chapter 10 Ormerod, focusing on information systems strategy, introduces a range of soft OR approaches including cognitive mapping and soft systems methodology, and advocates mixing and linking methods to support various phases of the strategy development process.

Part IV focuses on the fundamental issue of strategy development—that of describing uncertainty and incorporating it in the strategic development process. Strategic development with its long term orientation, and the uncertainty of external factors and some internal ones, are inextricably linked. The development of scenario planning at Shell has already been mentioned (Beck[11], Wack[12,13]), and a leading contemporary exponent, Schoemaker, although an academic also spent time with Shell. In Chapter 11, the steps in scenario development are explained and the role of scenarios in strategy formulation and evaluation discussed. Warren explores the use of cognitive maps to build credible scenarios to inform strategy development.

Central to the evaluation of strategic initiatives is a corporate model of some kind, and this topic is addressed in Part V. This may be a simple financial model, or a more

	Objective setting and performance measurement	Strategy formulation	Modelling uncertainty	Corporate modelling	Evaluation and selection
Stakeholder analysis	X	X			
Balanced scorecard	X	X			X
Visioning	X	X			
TOWS matrix		X			
Five forces		X			
Resourced-based planning		X			
Transformation methods [1]		X			
Soft operational research	X	X			
Cognitive mapping	X	X	X	X	
Scenario planning		X	X		X
System dynamics				X	X
Risk analysis			X	X	X
Real options theory		X	X	X	X
Capital investment appraisal					X

[1] Transformation methods include competency-based design and reengineering.

Figure 1.6. Strategic Techniques/Process Elements Matrix

complex dynamic one. The development of standard spreadsheet based financial models is not included here, but rather the focus is on the potential for more sophisticated modelling. Eden advocates the ubiquitous cognitive mapping to guide policy making and to facilitate the construction of analytical models for analysis and evaluation. Ford explains the construction of a simulation model to aid in the policy evaluation of the transport system in Southern California.

The final part (VI) advances from the evaluation of strategy to methods of selection. Berry and Dyson (Chapter 15) review the approaches to the financial appraisal of strategic initiatives covering shareholder value approaches, risk analysis, the issue of interdependencies and real option theory. The latter is increasingly advocated as the appropriate approach to a range of strategic investment decisions, and Trigeorgis presents a detailed exposition in Chapter 16. Chapter 15 also develops a framework for strategic evaluation.

Finally the interlinkages between the methods and models on the one hand, and the elements of the strategic development process on the other were mentioned earlier. The matrix in Figure 1.6 shows in detail how the techniques can support the strategic development process.

REFERENCES

1. Dyson R. G., 'Strategic Planning: Models and Analytical Techniques', Wiley, Chichester, 1990.
2. Porter M. E., 'What is Strategy?', Harvard Business Review, Nov–Dec 1996.
3. Doyle, P., 'Radical Strategies for Profitable Growth', Warwick Business School Working Paper, 1997.
4. Mintzberg H., 'The Rise and Fall of Strategic Planning', Prentice Hall International and Free Press, 1994.
5. Eilon S., 'Management Control', Pergamon, 1979.
6. Tomlinson R. C. and Dyson R. G., 'Some systems aspects of strategic planning', Journal of the Operational Research Society, 34, 765–778, 1983.
7. Dyson R. G., 'Strategic decision making a control system perspective', Working Paper 81/82-4-27, Graduate School of Business, University of Texas at Austin, 1982.
8. Boothroyd H., 'Articulate Intervention: the Interface of Science, Mathematics and Administration', Taylor and Frances, London, 1978.
9. Allaire Y. and Firsirotu M., 'Coping with strategic uncertainty', Sloan Management Review, XXX 3, 7–16, Spring 1989.
10. Hertz D. B., 'Risk Analysis in Capital Investment', Harvard Business Review, Sep–Oct 1979, 169–181, reprinted from HBR, 1964.
11. Beck P. W., 'Corporate planning for an uncertain future', Long Range Planning 15, 4, 12–21, 1982.
12. Wack P., 'Scenarios: shooting the rapids', Harvard Business Review, Nov–Dec, 139–150, 1985.
13. Wack P., 'Scenarios: uncharted waters ahead', Harvard Business Review, Sep–Oct, 73–89, 1985.
14. O'Brien F., 'Understanding future uncertainty', OR Insight, 8, 3, 9–14, 1995.
15. Ansoff H. I., 'Comment on Henry Mintzgerg's Rethinking Strategic Planning', Long Range Planning, 27, 3, 31–32, 1994.
16. Smith P., 'Outcome-related performance indicators and organizational control in the public sector', British Journal of Management, 4, 135–151, 1993.
17. Dyson R. G. and Foster M. J., 'Effectiveness in strategic planning', European Journal of Operational Research, 5, 3, 163–170, 1980.

Part II

Objectives, Performance Measurement and Strategy Creation

Chapter 2

Creating Policy Alternatives Using Stakeholder Values

Robin Gregory and Ralph L. Keeney
Decision Research, Eugene, Oregon
University of Southern California, Los Angeles, California

INTRODUCTION

Important public decisions incite controversy because they require difficult tradeoffs among objectives stressed by different stakeholders. The decision to develop a port facility may result in the loss of fishing opportunities, or the decision to increase production at a factory may result in a corresponding increase in pollution from the site. Such tradeoffs are not easy for an individual to make, because they require giving up something that is valuable. These decisions are particularly complex because of disagreements among stakeholders about the key objectives and their relative importance.

Decision makers are not known for their willingness to address difficult tradeoffs explicitly. In recent years, however, the growth of public-interest and advocacy organizations has resulted in demands for a higher level of accountability on the part of politicians and social decision makers. As a result, decisions that once were discussed behind closed doors now must be debated in front of appointed committees or television cameras, and decisions that once were made on an ad hoc basis now must be defended with reference to explicit criteria and a logical approach.

An important class of problems facing societal decision makers involve choices between economic and environmental objectives. These decisions are often controversial because of what appear to be sharply conflicting stories about the economic impacts, environmental effects, and social implications of the leading options. Examples of controversial economic/environmental tradeoffs include management of old-growth forests in the western U.S., reductions in CO_2 emissions from midwest coal plants, offshore drilling for oil and gas in Alaska, and development of the Amazon rain forest in Brazil. The adversarial tone of these debates and the confusing nature of

Reprinted by permission, Gregory, R. and Keeney, R. L., Creating Policy Alternatives Using Stakeholder Values from *Management Science*, Volume 40, No. 8, August 1994, The Institute of Management Sciences (Currently INFORMS), 2 Charles Street, Suite 300, Providence, RI 02904 USA.

the information has baffled the decision makers, alienated the public, and encouraged a lack of trust in both the analysts and the managers participating in the public decision-making process.

This paper presents and illustrates an approach to guide social tradeoff decisions that uses a logically sound methodological framework which complements and builds on common sense. We first describe the general approach and then discuss its implementation to examine whether to permit development of a coal mine within an isolated pristine tropical rain forest. The discussion does not address methods for choosing among projects but instead focuses on clearly articulating stakeholder values and using them as the basis for creating an improved set of policy alternatives.

STRUCTURING A PUBLIC DECISION

Tradeoffs between economic and environmental objectives are present in significant public decisions that, by their inherent nature, are of interest to a diverse set of stakeholders (Wathern 1988). These stakeholders have a right to be involved in the decision process, because they will be among those affected by the ultimate policy choice. To be most useful, we believe that stakeholders should have substantial early input, helping to specify and guide the entire decision process as well as identifying objectives that should be considered.

We use three interdependent steps to structure a decision with stakeholders. These are:

(1) setting the decision context,
(2) specifying the objectives to be achieved, and
(3) identifying alternatives to achieve these objectives.

Each step involves meetings between stakeholders and the analysts chosen to provide guidance to the decision makers. Such meetings may be held separately although, as the case-study presented here illustrates, there are important advantages of jointly meeting with stakeholders. After each step, there is a need to obtain agreement that the issues explicitly outlined represent the substance of the problem.

How are these three steps achieved? The decision context typically is set by those facing the decision and those with factual knowledge about the decision. In the usual case, a government agency must decide whether a proposed activity should go ahead. The decision context is outlined by the agency, by the proponent (often a private resource-development company), and by community or environmental groups. As analysts, we find that our key role in the process is insuring that the decision context is cast broadly enough so that all stakeholders can agree on the context (Brown 1984). Disagreements tend to occur when the initial statement of the decision context explicitly or implicitly rules out either objectives or alternatives that certain stakeholders consider important. To reach a consensus, we try to obtain agreement on removing the constraint on excluded objectives or alternatives. For example, with respect to offshore oil exploration in northern California, a decision context that only considered alternatives of when and where to drill exploratory wells and omitted the alternative of not drilling would likely not be acceptable to certain environmental stakeholders.

Operationally, we form the basis for a stakeholder consensus on the decision context by agreeing to accept the union of all stakeholders' objectives as the set of objectives for the decision context and the union of all alternatives that any stakeholder wants considered as the set of alternatives. These sets of objectives and alternatives may then be refined to provide a consensus decision context.

With the mutual understanding of the decision context, each stakeholder is then asked to articulate objectives for the decision. Techniques have been developed to help the stakeholders probe their values (Keeney, 1988, 1992). Once objectives are listed, they are organized into structures that distinguish means and end objectives and identify the fundamental (i.e., the ultimate ends) objectives for the decision being faced. The fundamental objectives of the various stakeholders are then combined in a process that could simply be described as combining lists. Since the combined list has all the objectives of each stakeholder and since no prioritization of objectives is to occur at this stage, it is not difficult to obtain stakeholder agreement on the fundamental objectives.

Next, we help the stakeholders identify alternatives that are legitimate contenders to achieve the stated objectives in the decision context. Often some alternatives are obvious from the decision context alone. Once these obvious 'standard' alternatives are on the table, it is useful to use the stated objectives to create innovative alternatives and to enhance and better define existing alternatives (Keeney 1992, Keller and Ho 1988). The final list of alternatives should include any alternative identified by a stakeholder. At this stage in the process most stakeholders will feel that each group has a right to include its favored alternatives for consideration. Hence, it may not be difficult to reach an initial consensus agreement on the list of alternatives. On the other hand, if stakeholders are not allowed to include their favorite alternatives, then an agreement on the set of alternatives is unlikely to occur.

Fundamental and means objectives are each relevant to the identification of alternatives. Both fundamental and means objectives represent a starting point for thinking about mitigation and other improvements in the design of alternatives and can be used as the basis for thinking creatively about the generation of new project options. With more and better specified objectives, experimental evidence suggests that more policy alternatives will be created (Jungermann, von Ulardt, and Hausmann 1983, Pitz, Sachs, and Heerboth, 1980). The proposed approach to structuring social policy decisions, therefore, provides the basis for including alternatives that might well have been ignored had less attention been given to identifying and articulating stakeholder values.

Once stakeholders agree that alternatives should be linked to values, we think that it makes sense to create several alternatives to address any multiple-objective policy problem. This is an important step for developing acceptable policy alternatives for a large class of decisions that require value tradeoffs to be made between the expected economic and environmental benefits of alternative actions (Peters, Gentry, and Mendelsohn 1989, Smith, Williams, and Plucknett 1991). Inter-agency as well as public debate in these situations is often highly polarized because the decision is viewed as a choice between dramatically different end-states, framed in terms of economics vs. the environment or jobs vs. habitat preservation.

In many such situations a balanced compromise, built from the key objectives of the competing stakeholders, can be created through negotiations. As noted by Raiffa (1982) and others, the difference in values which accounts for the acrimonious tone of the debate also can provide an excellent basis for negotiator success because of the sharp differences in priorities given to specific objectives (i.e., their weights) across the different stakeholder groups.

Another of the important advantages of the proposed approach, therefore, is its role in defusing the 'we versus them' framing which often is encouraged both by the media and by the litigation process. This framing implies that key stakeholder groups hold very different, and fundamentally incompatible, objectives. In our experience, this is rarely the case. Rather, we anticipate that the classes of values held by different stakeholders, made explicit by their objectives, will be quite similar: when other things are equal, nobody prefers more environmental damage, fewer jobs, higher-priced products, or greater health risks. Instead, the disagreements between stakeholders are often due to different priorities for the objectives or different beliefs about the degree to which specific alternatives measure up in terms of the objectives (Keeney, von Winterfeldt, and Eppel 1990). These disagreements, which can be substantial, can be addressed systematically in the context of a structured discussion that permits the stakeholder groups to realize that, despite their years of battle and accumulated misunderstandings, much of what each wants also is desired by everyone else.

THE SABAH DECISION CONTEXT

Sabah is one of two states in East Malaysia, located at the northern tip of the island of Borneo. Early in 1991 the government of Sabah decided to contract a preliminary environmental impact assessment of a proposed coal mine. The proposed mine site is located in south-central Sabah (Figure 2.1), within a pristine and largely unexplored wilderness forest reserve known as the Maliau Basin. The Basin is marked by an unusual diversity of plant and animal species and it is home to several animals and plants, such as the Sumatran Rhino and the Rafflessia, that command international attention (Marsh 1989). Initial reconnaissance of the area by Broken Hills Proprietary (BHP), a large Australian mining company, has revealed substantial deposits of high-grade coal. The decision facing the state government of Sabah is whether BHP should be issued a drilling permit allowing it to explore the coal reserves within the Basin, thus setting in motion actions likely to lead to the development of a coal mine within the Maliau Basin area.

The problem is intriguing and difficult. Neither of the two obvious alternatives, which are to grant or forbid coal development in the area, were well defined. Ecologists know little about the natural resources within the Maliau Basin and there exists substantial disagreement regarding the best means for preserving the area in its current pristine natural state. Geologists know little about the extent of the coal resources and there are several different ways for the coal to be extracted and transported. The proposed project is controversial and no matter what decision ultimately is made, several citizen and government groups within Sabah will be affected. Each of these stakeholders has its own reasons for caring about the future of the Basin.

There is no well-defined process in Sabah or in Malaysia for making decisions of this type, either for deciding on the different parties that should have a voice in the decision process or for weighting their objectives as part of the process of deciding among alternative policy and project options. To provide better information for decision makers within the state and federal governments, the Sabah state government

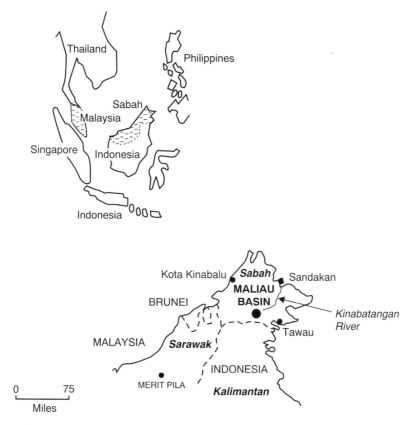

Figure 2.1. Map Showing Location of the Proposed Coal Mine in Sabah

hired a Canadian consulting firm to conduct the preliminary environmental impact assessment. We were hired as consultants to the Canadian firm to structure the problem in order to define the focus for the ensuing impact assessment. In July 1991, we designed and led a three-day workshop in Kota Kinabalu, the capital city of Sabah, to accomplish three principal tasks of this structuring (Gregory, Keeney, and von Winterfeldt 1992). One task was to establish a mechanism for bringing the concerns of the key stakeholders into the project planning and evaluation process. The second task was to identify stakeholder objectives important to the decision. The third task was to identify alternative uses of the Basin's resources over time and to define these alternatives clearly in terms of their required support, infrastructure, and action.

INVOLVING STAKEHOLDERS IN THE DECISION PROCESS

Stakeholder Selection

A first step in setting up the workshop was to define an appropriate set of stakeholders. Based on conversation with state government officials and our general knowledge of the problem, it was decided that five groups should be involved:

proponents of the mine development (BHP), local government officials (town mayors or forestry officers), key state government development representatives (Economic Development, Geological Surveys), spokespersons for environmental and social interests (Sabah Wildlife Department, Sabah Foundation, Institute for Development Studies), and representatives of the international conservation movement (World Wildlife Fund, United Nations). We encouraged the attendance of more than one representative from each of the groups, so as to allow for a broad-based discussion of the group's perspective. At the same time, we wanted to keep the total number of participants at 25 or less in order to facilitate discussion among stakeholder groups.

Before the start of the workshop, we drafted a letter that was sent to each of the designated groups by the Department of Mines. The letter explained the purpose of the stakeholders workshop, indicated the importance of participation by the group, and asked for the names of representatives. The workshop was described as a Public Values Forum, that would not itself be making any decisions but instead would provide information about stakeholder objectives and project alternatives. The letter also described the location of the workshop (at a convenient hotel), its duration (three days), and essential logistical information.

Workshop Organization

At least two representatives of each of the five groups identified above attended the workshop. Altogether there were approximately 25 participants. At the beginning of the workshop, we told the participants that they would be asked to develop objectives to help answer the question 'What use of the Maliau Basin is best for Sabah?' They were asked to address this question from three viewpoints: their own individual perspective, the perspective of the organization that they represented, and what they felt was appropriate for the Sabah government. Objectives were defined in terms of what the participants would want to know to compare alternative uses of the Maliau Basin in a logical and defensible manner.

The first morning of the workshop was taken up by three presentations that provided participants with a common factual base about the decision context. A first speaker provided an overview of federal and state economic policies. Development of coal resources, for export or for electricity generation within Sabah, was discussed as a possible catalyst for economic development, including the creation of an industrial base for manufacture of cement or steel. A second speaker, the executive in charge of BHP in Sabah, noted the high quality of mineral resources within the Basin. Although surface outcrops suggest the presence of a deposit of high-grade thermal coal, he reported that plans for development would remain uncertain pending the results of additional tests (e.g., drilling) and the securing of a long-term contract with an overseas purchaser (e.g., a designated power plant). He also noted that getting the coal to international markets would require development within the Basin as well as construction of a rail line from the Basin to the coast. A third speaker was the leader of the first organized (in 1988) expedition into the Maliau Basin by ecologists, biologists, geologists, and zoologists. He stated that the Basin is the least explored area in Sabah and that less is known about its plant and animal species than anywhere else in Malaysia and, perhaps, anywhere in Southeast Asia. As evidence of this claim the speaker cited the diversity of breeding habitats, abundant speciation, and the existence of several rare species such as the Sumatran Rhino and the Rafflessia, the world's largest flower. Although the Basin itself is uninhabited, the expedition found evidence for occasional use of the area by both poachers and indigenous peoples (known as Murut) living in nearby areas of Sarawak and Sabah, as well as occasional visits by hunters from the adjacent Indonesian state of Kalimantan.

SPECIFYING OBJECTIVES

Assignment of Stakeholder Groups

The first afternoon and second morning of the workshop were designed to obtain the objectives of the various stakeholders. Initial lists of objectives were developed in four small group sessions. This division into small groups, each including between five and seven participants, served two purposes. First, the small groups were designed to allow each participant adequate time to define and explain those objectives important to them. Second, the division into four groups provided an effective means for utilizing the time of the participants.

Our placement of participants into the groups was based on the primary expressed interests of participants, with minor adjustments due to timing and schedule conflicts. Those participants with strong environmental interests were placed in Group 1; local and tourism interests formed Group 2; forestry and mining interests were in Group 3; and state government representatives comprised Group 4. These divisions covered the range of stakeholder interests without requiring an unwarranted precision in the definition of the groups. Our goals in distinguishing these general interest areas were to achieve a comprehensive set of objectives and to avoid, both in reality and in appearance, having any one perspective dominate the discussions of each of the groups.

Elicitation of Objectives

At the beginning of each group meeting, we reminded the participants that the purpose of the session was to develop a comprehensive list of their objectives; anything important to the participants was considered to be a legitimate objective. Then we asked each participant to take 5–10 minutes to write down everything he or she believed to be important for consideration as part of the Environmental Impact Assessment (EIA). This insured that each participant recorded his or her individual thoughts to bring to the subsequent group discussion.

The group discussion recorded each individual's objectives and formed the basis for a combined listing of objectives. The session included a probing discussion of the reasons why an objective appeared on someone's list. The participants' responses helped to articulate additional objectives, recognize means–ends relationships of objectives, and identify the set of fundamental objectives.

Three general categories of objectives—environmental, economic, and social—appeared on most individual lists and in all four groups. Environmental objectives were noted that reflect the special qualities of the Maliau Basin: rare and endangered species, river quality, biological diversity, and the importance of undiscovered plant or animal species. Economic objectives concerned jobs, income, and economic diversity, and were noted in terms of their impact on local populations, the region, the state of Sabah, and Malaysia. The tourism potential of the Basin as a conservation area of international reputation was discussed by each of the groups. Social objectives, related directly to development of the Basin and the proposed rail line as well as indirectly to the long-term implications of increased access, also were noted; special emphasis was given to impacts on the regional population and to the effects of any development on in-migration, both legal and illegal.

Important differences also were found in the objectives noted by each of the four groups. As a general comment, the small groups spent considerably more time and developed more detailed lists of objectives when discussing the topic areas in which they possessed special expertise. For example, the Environment group was the only one to note specific species of animals and plants when discussing the objective reflecting the value of endangered species. Similarly, the Government group was the most specific when describing geopolitical factors arising from effects of the different development options on relations between Sabah and the Philippines or Indonesia.

Combined Structure of Objectives

The participants reconvened as a single group to develop a combined list of fundamental objectives for the EIA and, in this process, identify and separately list all of the means objectives articulated by the groups. This difference between fundamental objectives and means objectives was introduced in terms of a distinction between those things that participants fundamentally care about, such as environmental quality, and those that matter only through their effect on these fundamental concerns, such as waste disposal (which affects water quality and, in turn, the environment). Note that this does not imply that means objectives are any less important than are fundamental objectives. As a simple example, if one means objective accounted for one-half the impact on each of five equally weighted fundamental objectives, then the de facto weight on that means objective would be 50% whereas each fundamental objective would count only 20%.

The distinction between fundamental and means objectives is important because a listing of only the fundamental objectives is appropriate to evaluate alternatives. Otherwise, double-counting will distort the evaluation. On the other hand, means objectives are important to articulate and appraise alternatives and to indicate how some stakeholder concerns that were stated as means objectives are accounted for in an evaluation.

To structure fundamental objectives, we began the session by reviewing all the objectives generated by each of the four groups. We combined redundancies, meaning those for which the groups used different words to describe the same objective. Next, for each objective, we asked the participants 'why is this objective important?' If the response was that it contributes to achieving other objectives on the list, it was categorized as a mean objective. Otherwise it was categorized as a fundamental objective. By grouping objectives from the resulting list of fundamental objectives, we constructed five major categories: environmental impacts, economic benefits and costs, social impacts, political impacts, and international prestige. These results are shown in Table 2.1.

Table 2.1. Categories of Fundamental Objectives Appropriate to Evaluate
Sabah's Maliau Basin Alternatives

1. Environmental Impacts
   A. Species (rare, endangered, and threatened)
      a. flora
      b. fauna (clouded leopard, sumatran rhino)
   B. Biodiversity
   C. Human experience
      a. scenic beauty
      b. wilderness (option/existence demands)
      c. noise
2. Economic Impacts (Direct: Indirect)
   A. Local (within 25 kms)
   B. Kalabakan Region
   C. Kinabatangan Basin
   D. Sabah
   E. Malaysia
3. Social Impacts (Local: Kalabakan Region; Kinabatangan Basin; Sabah)
   A. Health
   B. Culture
   C. Education
   D. Crime
   E. Standard of living
4. Political Impacts
   A. Public opinion
   B. Political stability
5. International Prestige
   A. Demonstrated commitment to development
   B. Demonstrated commitment to conservation
   C. Relations with neighboring countries.

A next step was to arrange individual objectives under these five major headings. These results are also shown in Table 2.1. The environmental impacts category includes three primary objectives, concerned with species, biodiversity and human experience. The economic impacts category includes separate objectives for direct and indirect effects for five geographic regions: the local area (defined as that region within a 25 kilometer radius of the Maliau Basin), the Kalabakan region (i.e., the region near Tawau), the Kinabatangan basin, the state of Sabah, and the nation of Malaysia. Social impacts include the five objectives that address health, culture, education, crime, and standard of living, with separate categories for the local area, the Kinabatangan basin, the Kalabakan region, and for Sabah. Political impacts cover public opinion and political stability. International prestige, the final major objective, is concerned with the extent to which actions taken within the Maliau Basin affect relations with neighboring countries or demonstrate a commitment to either development or conservation.

In one sense this task is relatively easy to do in that it only requires a reorganization of the objectives elicited earlier. In another sense, however, the results of the reorganization are powerful because they provide a visible, yet transparent, structure for the seemingly chaotic diversity of concerns. Telling the group on the first morning that everything considered to be important should be included in the analysis of project alternatives might have appeared to some workshops participants to be an impossible task. Showing the group on the next afternoon that all of their fundamental concerns could be grouped under only five intuitively appealing headings provided both a strong sense of shared progress and a reassurance that it should be possible to include these concerns in the EIA's analysis of alternatives.

Objectives listed by groups that were not considered fundamental were included on the list of means objectives, shown in Table 2.2. By the end of the second day, therefore, participants were able to see that each of the objectives mentioned by any participant in the small group sessions, as well as several new objectives generated in the course of the group discussion, were accounted for either as part of the fundamental objectives (Table 2.1) or as one of the means objectives (Table 2.2).

Prioritizing Objectives

Priorities were established by asking workshop participants to rank various sets of objectives in terms of their importance to the EIA. This was useful to appraise in more depth the commonality of objectives, to uncover potential hidden objectives, and to guide efforts to gather information about alternatives for the EIA. Any such ranking exercise requires that the range of possible consequences for each objective be made explicit. The ranking then indicates the relative importance of changing an objective from its least desirable consequence to its most desirable consequence.

To establish ranges for the objectives, workshop participants were asked to think about the differences in achieving objectives that might arise when considering the choice between maintaining the status quo and developing the coal mine. The importance of an objective should increase as the range of achievements increases. In the ranking that followed, participants were asked to rank the importance of differences in ranges on the various objectives.

Each of the participants was asked to rank each of the five major objectives in Table 2.1 in terms of its relative importance, with a score of 1 denoting the most important objective and a score of 5 denoting the least important. These results, in aggregated form, are shown in Table 2.3. The five major objectives are listed from top to bottom in the order of their average rankings, as shown in Column 1. The range of individual rankings is shown in Column 2. Obtaining information about the environmental impacts of alternatives was considered the highest priority, with a mean score of 1.7; international prestige was ranked lowest, with a mean score of 4.6.

It is important to recognize that rankings, and particularly averaged rankings, cannot be interpreted directly as indicating the importance of different objectives (von Winterfeldt and Edwards 1986). For example, the 2.2 average rank of economic impacts does not indicate that it is slightly more than twice as important as international prestige, with an average rank of 4.6. It simply indicates that, given the respective ranges of possible consequences, economic impacts are judged more important than international prestige by most participants. Value tradeoffs between the different objectives cannot be made without developing scales to indicate levels of the consequences and the ranges of the consequences used to measure the objectives. Thus, although a small difference in economic impacts is likely to be more significant to project selection than is a small difference in international prestige, a very large change in international prestige probably would be considered more significant than

Table 2.2. Means Objectives for the EIA*

---

water quality (environment, health)
undiscovered species (part of species, biodiversity)
endangered species (value of species)
ecological integrity (best level of biodiversity)
greater access (environmental, social)
waste products (environmental, social)
promote native rights (cultural, political)
illegal hunting (environmental)
hydrology (water quality)
water catchment (water quality)
fisheries (environmental, social)
aesthetic value (flora, social)
waste disposal (water quality)
uniqueness of species (value of species)
protection of indigenous Murut culture (social)
gene banks (follows from biodiversity)
new drugs (follows from biodiversity)
forest fires (environmental)
implications for timber (economic impacts)
BHP past record (information for assessment)
cost of health care (indirect economic)
life support (e.g., agriculture) lost (social)
diversification of economic base (economic)
rehabilitation costs (indirect economics)
illegal immigrants (health, crime)
new settlements (social)
impacts over time (relevant to all objectives)
foreign control of resources (political)
land degradation (environmental, social)
economic diversity (economic impact)
human resources development and training (social, indirect economic)
social and cultural opportunities (standard of living)
proper use of resources (value issue)
conservation (environment)
taxes (direct economics)
multiplier effects (indirect economics)
industrialization of region (indirect economics, social)
spills, discharges (water quality)
transmission of disease (health)
flood implications (social, environmental)
displaced people (local social)
nature of information withheld by BHP (information for assessment)
implications for Kalimantan. Indonesia (relations with neighboring countries)
implications for timber, oil industry (indirect economics)
discovery of other minerals or hydroelectric potential (indirect economics)
resource rents and royalties to the Sabah government (economic)
taxes to the Malaysian government (economic, political)
compensation to people requiring resettlement (social, economic)

---

* The fundamental objectives mainly affected by the means objectives are listed in parentheses.

Table 2.3. Information Priorities for the EIA Process

	Average rankings of major objectives categories	Range of individual ranks for major objectives	Aggregate rankings within major objectives categories	Aggregate rankings of selected objectives
1. ENVIRONMENTAL IMPACTS	1.7	1–3		
A. Species			1	1
a. flora				
b. fauna				
B. Biodiversity			2	3
C. Human experience			3	
a. scenic beauty				
b. wilderness				
c. noise				
2. ECONOMIC IMPACTS (direct/indirect)	2.2	1–5		
A. Local (within 25 kms)			2	5
B. Kalabakan Region			3	
C. Kinabatangan Basin			4	
D. Sabah			1	2
E. Malaysia			5	
3. SOCIAL IMPACTS (Local area: Kalabakan Region; Kinabatangan Basin; Sabah)	2.6	2–4		
A. Health			2	6
B. Culture			4	
C. Education			3	
D. Crime			5	
E. Standard of living			1	4
4. POLITICAL IMPACTS	3.9	2–5		
A. Public opinion			1	8
B. Political stability			2	
5. INTERNATIONAL PRESTIGE	4.6	1.4–5		
A. Demonstrated commitment to development			2	
B. Demonstrated commitment to conservation			1	7
C. Relations with neighbouring countries			3	

would a small change in economic impacts. That is why it is helpful to be able to elicit from stakeholders information about the scale and range appropriate for the measurement of each objective. Unfortunately, time constraints placed on the Sabah workshop precluded the collection of this additional information.

The workshop participants also were asked to set priorities within each of the five major objective categories. The aggregate results are shown in Column 3 of Table 2.3. For example, the aggregate ranking, measured by the average ranking of the objective, for environmental impacts was species, biodiversity, and human experience, in that order.

Partially as a check on the consistency of responses participants were asked to rank several objectives across the major objective categories. Eight objectives were selected, the two ranked highest within each of the three most important objective categories (environmental, economic, and social impacts) and the highest ranked objective within the other two objective categories. These aggregate ranking results are shown as the eight entries in Column 4 of Table 2.3; environmental effects on designated plant and animal species was considered the most important objective, and economic impacts on Sabah were ranked second, followed by the effects on biodiversity and the social impacts of changes in the standard of living. The objective ranked first within each category was always ranked above the corresponding second-ranked objective. Also, as consistency would suggest, the two environmental objectives as a pair were ranked higher than the two economic objectives, which were higher than the social objectives.

DEVELOPING ALTERNATIVES

Creating New Project Alternatives

Much of the final day of the workshop was devoted to the discussion of project alternatives. Workshop discussions up to this point generally had considered only two alternatives: maintaining the status quo and operating the coal mine according to the most likely scenario outlined by BHP in its initial presentation. This focus on two contrasting alternatives, framed as 'preserve' vs. 'develop', is typical of many societal debates involving choices between environmental and economic objectives (e.g., spotted owls vs. timber jobs, or ocean habitat vs. offshore drilling). The problem is that neither perspective provides an accurate depiction of reality: preservation rarely requires locking an area away and resource development rarely requires the destruction of a site's natural amenities. Thus, the preserve/develop polarity creates a false picture of single-objective orientations and ignores the multiple mitigation and compensation options that can be developed to address stakeholder concerns as part of value-based alternatives.

The early workshop discussions in Sabah indicated that many participants, as well as those responsible for carrying out the planned environmental impact assessment, held just this sort of fundamental, preserve/develop misconception. Because of the very limited availability of information about both the Maliau Basin and BHP's development plans, many participants falsely believed that (a) the status quo alternative (i.e., denying a mining license) would mean the environment would forever be preserved in its present state, whereas others believed that (b) granting a mining license would lead to complete destruction of the natural environment of the Maliau Basin.

To develop realistic policy alternatives using the objectives expressed by the workshop participants, we began with the status quo and asked participants how it would measure up in terms of their fundamental objectives. The apparent trivial response, which by now we believed to be completely erroneous, was that the status quo would be great on environmental impacts but contribute nothing to economics. Interestingly enough, by asking participants to think about the consequences of 'status quo' actions in terms of objectives, no one gave this response. Instead, those who had visited the area mentioned evidence of possible poaching of game species currently underway within the Maliau Basin. In addition, the Sabah Foundation, holders of the forestry concession in the region, noted that legal logging would reach the outside rim of the

Maliau Basin in the next few years. This would greatly increase accessibility to the Basin and, based on experience from other areas of Sabah, strongly suggested that slash and burn agriculture and illegal logging soon could begin within the Basin itself. It became clear rather quickly that the status quo alternative would not protect the environment of the Maliau Basin. A different alternative would be required.

The 'protected status' alternatives was defined in terms of the desired impacts on the environmental objectives. It was created to pursue policies to maintain the environmental quality of the Maliau Basin as it now is. This implied many things. The Basin would receive legal protection from detrimental acts and enforcement provisions for that protection. No minerals or resources of any type would be extracted from the Basin; access would be severely limited for scientific purposes only.

The original interest in mining the coal in the Maliau Basin was related to the desire to gain economic benefits. These potential benefits were spelled out by the economic objectives. The other objectives, especially the environmental objectives, indicate how one might design the mining alternative to avoid or mitigate potential impacts. For example, underground mining has less environmental impact than open-pit mining, and this was put forth as the suggested plan. There was also talk of limiting any mining development to less than 25% of the Basin and to only consider underground mining options with aboveground entry from outside the Basin. Different rail developments also could differentially affect the achievement of all of the objectives. One possible mining alternative was therefore proposed, although the workshop participants agreed that if mining becomes a clear contender or the preferred alternative, then various mining options should be specified and evaluated in terms of the objectives.

Since the motivation for any development of the Maliau Basin is economic benefits, we asked participants if there were any other developments other than mining that could provide such benefits. Tourism was prominently raised. The ensuing discussion indicated that the range of tourism alternatives was large. To understand the implications that mattered in terms of the participants' objectives, we needed to define alternatives by what tourists would do, where they would be permitted to go, and how many there would be. Several tourism alternatives were discussed at length, including both low-intensity uses of the area (e.g., backpacking along trails following helicopter access) and several high-intensity uses (e.g., development of luxury hotel facilities with opportunities for viewing wildlife at a central location). For example, one tourism alternative described by workshop participants from the Sabah Tourism Department could result in 5,000 visitors to the Basin each year, with overnight facilities provided at the site but with access restricted to 1–2% of the total land area. As with the mining alternatives, we needed to choose a generic tourism alternative for the EIA that should be refined if the tourism alternative proves to be a real contender.

Our next task was to encourage workshop participants to examine potential pairings of alternatives, perhaps with modifications, to try to obtain the best consequences (in terms of the Table 2.1 objectives). We discussed the feasibility of any combination of mining and protected status that might get most of the economic benefits of mining and most of the environmental benefits of protection. This led to what we defined as the mining and conservation alternative. Using analogous reasoning, a mining and tourism alternative was created. We also considered a tourism and conservation alternative, but realized that this was similar to the tourism alternative because of the access of the tourists was severely limited.

To this stage, the creation of alternatives had largely focused on the environmental and economic objectives. Now we turned to the social, political, and international prestige objectives. It became clear that there were many ways to define the generic alternatives (outlined above) that would affect each of the other objectives. For instance, with either mining or tourism alternatives, one could instigate programs to enhance local health using some funds from the development. Regarding political impacts, the process of how one chooses an alternative and who is involved often has a larger impact than what alternative is eventually chosen. The process can be done poorly or well with each development alternative.

Workshop participants devoted particular attention to the issue of time, because the evolution of these alternatives over the next 5, 25, or even 100 years was considered to be of great concern to Sabahans as well as other Malaysians. The implications of timing were viewed as quite different across the various alternatives; for example, it would be possible to establish a protected status for the Basin for 25 years and then switch to another alternative, such as tourism or limited mining development, whereas choice of the mining alternative probably would rule out the future selection of a protected zone. This dynamic aspect of the alternatives was noted as critical but also difficult to discuss due to the relative lack of information regarding questions such as the ecological uniqueness of the site within Southeast Asia or the anticipated range of future coal prices.

The Suggested Project Alternatives

The six alternatives developed by the workshop participants are shown in Table 2.4. Due to budget constraints, this was about the maximum number of alternatives that could be addressed in the preliminary EIA. Thus the alternatives are somewhat generic, with fine-tuning left until after the preliminary evaluation is completed and until more and better information is available.

The status quo alternative, originally considered as a no-action option that would maintain current conditions essentially as they are now, was substantially redefined by participants because of information presented to the group. The status quo was now viewed not as a policy for maintaining the Maliau Basin in its pristine state but as one that would result in its incremental degradation over time.

The mining alternative originally was considered according to BHP's plan to start mining in the area at low withdrawal rates (e.g., 1 million tons/year), using underground mining technologies. However, questions addressed to BHP officials during the workshop provided evidence that a significant expansion of mining operations, to perhaps 5 million tons of coal per year, could occur after several successful years of operation. An expansion of this magnitude would require construction of a rail spur from the Basin to a new port near the town of Tawau, a distance of about 100 miles. The subsequent discussion in the workshop addressed several related concerns, including the worry expressed by many participants that the coal and rail development ultimately could expand to include multiple sites across south-central Sabah. Other participants questioned whether sufficient information was in hand to make an accurate assessment of the mineral reserves existing within the Maliau Basin and worried about future financial obligations of the Sabah government if the mine were to be unsuccessful. On the other hand, evidence from another area of Sabah suggested that

Table 2.4. Maliau Basin Alternatives

1. Status Quo
   —maintain concession status under the Sabah Foundation
   —no legal protection for resources within Maliau Basin
   —oil and gas exploration can proceed
   —controls on spread of agriculture into Basin
   —minor illegal hunting and timber cutting to continue
2. Mining Development
   —primarily (90%) underground mines
   —two or three years to start-up
   —initial production at 1 million tons per year (mta)
   —rail line becomes viable at production of 3 mta
   —maximum production of 5 (mta)
   —limited development of satellite mines
   —minerals development restricted to 25% of Basin surface
   —road construction in eastern side of Basin and services area
   —hiring preference to Sabahans
3. Protected Status
   —legal protection for Maliau Basin region
   —maintain pristine natural environment
   —enforcement of protected status if necessary
   —no timber taken from within Basin
   —limited reconnaissance permitted for scientific study
   —establish resource management controls in vicinity of Basin
   —discuss financial assistance with international agencies
4. Tourism
   —promote Basin as international tourist destination
   —construct lodge or other overnight facilities in Basin
   —construct road for visitor access
   —anticipate 5,000 visitors each year
   —restrict visitor usage to 1–2% of total Basin area
5. Mining and Conservation
   —mine development follows mining development alternative in the 25% mining area
   —protected status follows protected status alternative in 75% of Basin
   —exclude mining in majority (75%) of Basin
   —evaluate impacts of mining exploration
   —monitor impacts on pristine character of Basin due to mining
6. Mining and Tourism
   —mine development follows mining development alternative in the 25% mining area
   —tourism development follows tourism alternative in 75% of Basin
   —exclude mining in majority (75%) of Basin
   —evaluate impacts of mining exploration
   —monitor impacts on pristine character of Basin due to mining

development of the mine could have a beneficial impact on the local environment. The reason for this surprising result is that a major private company, given secure ownership of a land area, might be more effective at discouraging destructive agriculture and illegal logging practices than would the government.

A third alternative use considered for the Basin was to designate it as a protected area. This could be done in recognition of the pristine condition and poor level of current information about the environmental resources of the Maliau Basin, thus effectively buying time and keeping options open until more became known about the ecology of the area. Alternatively, protection could be pursued as a means for preserving the Basin for scientific study, related to its unusual speciation or to the potential discovery of new products based on resident flora and fauna. The protection alternative in contrast to the status quo option, was viewed by workshop participants as a strategy that would require consistent action (e.g., deploying armed guards) and vigilance on the part of state or national officials.

A fourth alternative created by participants was to develop the Maliau Basin as a tourist site. Access was to be severely limited to less than 2% of the Basin with a single lodge for overnight guests.

The discussions also addressed the long-run viability of two shared-use alternatives, in which the mine would operate in conjunction with either tourism or conservation. These joint-use alternatives (mining/tourism and mining/conservation) excluded all mining activities from 75% of the Basin area. Some participants initially expressed the viewpoint that operation of a coal mine within the Maliau Basin was at odds with the concepts of conserving the area or developing it as a tourist destination. Following discussion of the information provided above, most participants felt that so long as the operator extracted coal from only part of the Basin, development of the mine might increase the likelihood that the natural environment of the area would be preserved because BHP could help to pay for guards and other protection designed to minimize unwanted intrusions into the area. This possibility was counterintuitive to some workshop participants and represents the type of insight that is possible when multiple stakeholder values, rather than single-objective alternatives, guide the creation of project or policy options.

Putting alternatives together with stakeholder values yields a matrix, shown as Figure 2.2, that characterizes the decision faced by Sabah officials and therefore provides direction to the EIA. The rows of this matrix are the six project alternatives, listed in Table 2.4, developed by workshop participants. The columns of the matrix are the objectives, listed in Table 2.1, that participants considered to be important for the evaluation of alternatives as part of the EIA and, ultimately, required for the government of Sabah to make sound decisions about the use of the Maliau Basin.

Subsequent analyses must then address two important issues. The first is a factual issue that involves gathering information to fill in the cells of the matrix. This would describe each alternative in terms of each consequence with respect to each objective. The second is a value issue that involves evaluating the relative importance of the various consequences and combining them to develop an indication of the overall desirability of each alternative.

Information for Understanding the Alternatives

The workshop's focus on creating policy alternatives based on stakeholder values highlighted several important issues that could substantially influence the long-term implications of any resource use decision. One such fundamental issue relates to the understanding of the dynamic nature of the status quo alternative; in the case of Sabah, this point appeared in the substantial disagreement among workshop participants regarding the future of the Maliau Basin if current land-use status is maintained. Some participants stated that the combined effects of logging in adjacent areas (e.g., to the Basin rim) and illegal hunting would result in significant degradation of the Basin's pristine status. Other participants believed that the remote location of the area and the

Fundamental objectives

	Environmental impact			Economic impact					Social impacts					Political impacts		International prestige		
	Species	Biodiversity	Human experience	Local	Kalabakan	Kinabatangan	Sabah	Malaysia	Health	Culture	Education	Crime	Standard of living	Public opinion	Political stability	Commitment to development	Commitment to conservation	Relations with neighbours
Status quo																		
Mining																		
Protecting nature																		
Tourism																		
Mining and conservation																		
Mining and tourism																		

Figure 2.2. Information Needs for the Decision Process

absence of a settled local population would serve effectively to preserve the current resources. We note that this disagreement is about facts and not about values. In other words, the disagreement concerns what the future Basin may be like if a given alternative is chosen rather than what different individuals would like the Basin to be.

Another fundamental issue is the effect of any selected alternative on international perceptions of Sabah and, in turn, Malaysia. For example, the development of mineral resources within the Basin could result in protests from environmental groups that might adversely affect sales of timber from the forests of Sabah or Sarawak. However, limited development of mineral resources combined with the announcement of strong protection status for the Basin's resources could be viewed as a net gain by environmentalists.

Control over the pace of economic development also was noted as a key issue deserving of additional study. Some participants stated that, if BHP is granted a license to mine, then the extent and timing of future coal development largely would be controlled by the company. Others believed that the Malaysia Department of Mines would be able to maintain strict control over exploration and development in the region. The issue was considered important because of uncertainty regarding the size of the inferred in-site resource and because a likely mineral-development option is not a single mine but rather multiple mines, perhaps located in different regions of the Basin and linked by road or rail access.

Ultimately, the concerns expressed by workshop participants are related to alternative futures that influence not just the Maliau Basin but all of Sabah and, perhaps, also affect Malaysia and Southern Asia. If south-central Sabah is preserved as a pristine environment, then Sabah is likely to retain its reputation as a natural area of great beauty and mystery. If the south-central portions of Sabah are instead viewed as a catalyst for economic development, beginning with the mining of coal but linked to development of a rail line, improvements in the port of Tawau, or the creation of an industrial base involving the manufacture of cement or steel, then the character and reputation of Sabah may change.

Questions regarding the future image of Sabah emphasize the point that decisions about resource development options within the Maliau Basin cannot be viewed in isolation. The substantial decline in state revenues from exports of tropical timber, the world-wide concern of environmentalists for preservation of tropical ecosystems, and the shared jurisdiction between the state and national governments over resource use options will all have an effect on the implications of resource development choices within the Maliau Basin. Not all these issues can be discussed in detail as part of the preliminary EIA. However, it is important that the EIA recognize the diverse and fundamental nature of the concerns expressed by workshop participants and provide information based on these stakeholder values that will assist the government to make a wise and defensible decision in the long-term interests of its people.

CONCLUSION

The approach described in this paper attempts to open up the policy planning process considerably by involving representatives of all the key interested parties. In a practical sense, this requires including representatives of all major groups in the identification of objectives and alternatives. This helps to ensure that the values of a broad range of stakeholders will be reflected in the decision-making process and, furthermore, provides a constructive mechanism for individuals with potentially different viewpoints to participate in resolving a problem that they care about. The process of eliciting information about objectives and alternatives thus establishes a basis for future communication, dialogue, and negotiation among these groups.

The primary substantive output of the workshop in Sabah was the identification of objectives and the creation of alternatives that were based on the expressed stakeholder values. Although participants in the workshop reacted with surprise to several of the newly defined project alternatives, their creation followed in a straightforward and transparent manner from the elicitation and open discussion of stakeholder objectives.

Equally important as a product of the workshop was the clear, constructive communication that began among participants and their involvement in an open process for resource-use decision making. All parties invited to the workshop participated as equals in the sense that each of the groups, and each of the individuals, had the opportunity to contribute to the identification and definition of objectives and alternatives. This information, reflecting the concerns and values of the principal stakeholders, formed the basis of a discussion and a dialogue among participants that resulted in the sharing and clarification of information considered to be important to the decision. Establishing these channels of information flow will assist in completion of further studies and should serve as an aid to improved communication and negotiation among the stakeholder groups.

ACKNOWLEDGEMENTS

Without the cooperation and contributions of the Sabah workshop participants, this work would not have occurred. In addition, we thank the Sabah State government, who sponsored the project, and the ARA Consulting Group, Inc. The development and documentation of procedures used in the workshop were supported in part by National Science Foundation grant SES-9022952 and EPA Office of Exploratory Research grant R81-9832-010 to Decision Research for Gregory and by National Science Foundation grant SES-8919502 to the University of Southern California for Keeney. Any opinions, findings, and conclusions or recommendations expressed in this paper are those of the authors and do not necessarily reflect the views of the National Science Foundation or the Environmental Protection Agency.

REFERENCES

Brown, C. A., 'The Central Arizona Water Control Study: A Case for Multiobjective Planning and Public Involvement,' *Water Resources Bulletin*, 20 (1984), 331–337.

Gregory, R., R. Keeney, and D. von Winterfeldt, 'Adapting the Environmental Impact Statement Process to Inform Decision Makers,' *J. Policy Analysis and Management*, 11 (1992), 58–75.

Jungermann, H., I. von Ulardt, and L. Hausmann, 'The Role of the Good for Generating Actions,' in P. Humphreys, O. Svenson, and A. Vari (Eds.), *Analyzing and Aiding Decision Processes*, North-Holland, Amsterdam, 1983.

Keeney, R., 'Structuring Objectives for Problems of Public Interest,' *Oper. Res.*, 36 (1988), 369–405.

Keeney, R., *Value-Focused Thinking*, Harvard University Press, Cambridge, MA, 1992.

Keeney, R., D. von Winterfeldt, and T. Eppel, 'Eliciting Public Values for Complex Policy Decisions,' *Management Sci.*, 36 (1990), 1011–1030.

Keller, L. R., and J. L. Ho, 'Decision Problem Structuring: Generating Options,' *IEEE Transactions of Systems, Man, and Cybernetics*, 18 (1988), 715–728.

Marsh, C., *Expedition to Maliau Basin, Sabah*, (Report No. M45 126/88), prepared for the Yayasan Sabah Forestry Division, 1989.

Peters, C., A. Gentry, and R. Mendelsohn, 'Valuation of an Amazon Rain Forest,' *Nature*, 339 (1989), 655–656.

Pitz, G. F., N. T. Sachs, and T. Heerboth, 'Procedures for Eliciting Choices in the Analysis of Individual Decisions,' *Organizational Behavior and Human Performance*, 26 (1980), 396–408.

Raiffa, H., *The Art and Science of Negotiation*, Harvard University Press, Cambridge, MA, 1982.

Smith, N., J. Williams, and D. Plucknett, 'Conserving the Tropical Cornucopia,' *Environment*, 33 (1991), 7–32.

von Winterfeldt, D., and W. Edwards, *Decision Analysis and Behavioral Research*, Cambridge, NY, 1986.

Wathern, P., *Environmental Impact Assessment: Theory and Practice*. Unwin Hyman, London, 1988.

Chapter 3

Future Visioning: A Case Study of a Scenario-based Approach

Frances A. O'Brien and Maureen Meadows
Warwick Business School, University of Warwick, Coventry

INTRODUCTION

The primary purpose of this chapter is to document a scenario-based visioning methodology which has been applied in the public arena. The methodology was used to actively promote and mobilise the participation of a large body of people in thinking about the long term future of a British city. The chapter begins with a definition of visioning, a discussion of the role and importance of a vision, and a summary of the issues central to a visioning project. The concept of a visioning scenario is introduced as a powerful tool in a successful visioning process. A methodology for conducting a visioning project using scenarios is then described, and illustrated with a case study. Some examples of other visioning projects in a range of organisational contexts are summarised. The chapter concludes by addressing the issue of how visioning projects support strategy development, and the role of scenarios within a visioning process.

WHAT IS A VISION?

A vision is a carefully formulated and clearly articulated statement of intentions that defines a destination or future state of affairs that an individual or group finds desirable,[1] 'group' meaning a body of people such as a community, congregation or company.[2] Attributes of a vision include: ideality (the pursuit of excellence), uniqueness (pride in being different), imagery (vivid pictures of the future) and future orientation.[3,4] A vision does not fluctuate from year to year,[5] it endures beyond the lifetimes of an organisation's products, services and personnel.[6] Lipton[7] argues that the vision statements of highly effective organisations communicate three principle themes: the *mission* or purpose of the organisation, the *strategy* for achieving the mission and the elements of the organisational *culture* that seem necessary to achieve the mission and support the strategy.

A vision is something which is created.[8] Some visions are created deliberately, through controlled conscious thought; others emerge through a less conscious learning process. Some visions appear suddenly, while others build up gradually over time in an incremental process.[9] This chapter will discuss the participative development of a vision involving a group of stakeholders, rather than the ideas of a single visionary leader.

WHY BOTHER WITH VISION?

A vision underpins and promotes change.[10] It is a necessary precondition for strategic planning, and provides the key criteria against which all strategic options should be evaluated.[11,12] A vision sets the agenda for the organisation, and gives it direction and purpose.[13] Walker[14] asserts that effective action-agendas usually *follow* the creation of the vision, not vice-versa; this point is discussed further later. A vision helps the organisation to focus on and enhance key determinants of performance.[15–17] Some studies[18] provide evidence that visionary companies are more successful over the long term. A company which builds a unique and distinctive vision is capable of enduring changes in leadership as well as market conditions; Collins & Porras[19] even suggest that a continual stream of great products and services from visionary companies stems from their being outstanding organisations (for example in their organisational design, structure and processes), not the other way around.

VISIONING PROJECTS: KEY ISSUES

Numerous methodologies exist for conducting visioning projects. Whilst these methodologies differ in the sequence and detail of the steps they advocate, there are a number of fundamental and inter-related features which they have in common, and which are summarised below.

Motivation for Change

A common motivation for engaging in a visioning process is an awareness of dissatisfaction with the way things currently are, or the direction in which things are heading.[20,21] For example, a driving force behind the Peruvian twenty-first century study was a general sense of dissatisfaction with the country's social and economic problems.[22] Another example is when a company's management is convinced that the status quo is totally unacceptable,[23] perhaps due to new competitor activities.

Participation

The visioning process may be initiated by introspection or interaction. Some notable organisations have developed from the basic vision of one individual, for example Walt Disney.[24] However, it is argued by many authors[25–28] that all those who share an interest in the actions of an organisation, i.e. its stakeholders, should be represented in the participants of a process to create a future vision of that organisation. Wide participation brings a diversity of values and viewpoints to the process, and this encourages the development of robust visions. Poor management of participation can lead to the failure of a vision, although broad collaborative efforts can get bogged down by competing agendas and preferences.[29] Thus a balance needs to be achieved. Ziegler[30] also notes that participation should be by invitation, since forced participation is likely to detract from any commitment to the process itself and from any resulting strategy or action plans, perhaps resulting in false visions. If participation is voluntary, care must be taken to ensure that a well-balanced range of inputs is maintained.

Focus on Values

Values or viewpoints surrounding issues of concern exist at different levels: personal, organisational and societal.[31] These different value systems serve to frame the desirability of potential changes to the current state of affairs. Given that different stakeholders themselves may hold different values on a particular issue, and that the visioning process seeks to create a shared vision, the articulation of the different values, perspectives and viewpoints is an important part of a visioning process. For example, Stewart[32] and Kouzes and Posner[33] explicitly incorporate an identification of stakeholder values within their visioning methods.

Communication

In any process that seeks to support groups of people in reaching an agreed standpoint, communication in the form of listening, understanding and dialogue is essential.[34] Effective communication is especially important when the process seeks to bring about change that is likely to have a direct impact on the lives of individuals.

Vision vs. Present State

Connecting a vision to an assessment of the present state of an organisation serves two purposes. The first is to provide an anchor point from which the future state of the organisation must emerge, thus providing a starting point for the development of plans.[35] A vision may fail if people have difficulty identifying with a rosy picture of the future that seems to ignore problems with the current state of affairs. Inayatullah[36] describes a method of 'backcasting' the future from the present, and Ziegler[37] uses the construction of a 'futures history'; both methods are used to identify a path towards the vision. The second purpose is to allow the vision to be contrasted with and tested against the current system in terms of desirability and plausibility.

Commitment to Action

No visioning process should end with the generation of the visions themselves. As Stewart[38] notes, a visioning process that separates vision from action (via communication of the vision down the organisation) is not only hierarchical but also disempowering. Thus participants involved in a visioning process should be encouraged to accept what the visioning process generates and to commit to act from it.[39] In some methods, action planning is an integral part of the visioning process.[40]

INFORMED CHOICE: VISIONING SCENARIOS

Since a common motivation for a visioning project is a sense of dissatisfaction with the current situation, potential changes are likely to be the focus of debate. Different stakeholder groups tend to hold differing views of these potential perspectives, in order to promote dialogue and communication. The vehicle for issue framing proposed in this paper is that of the visioning scenario, which shares features in common with the more usual application of scenario planning to support strategy development.

Scenario planning is a well-established method in the strategic planning field for capturing and assessing the impact of uncertainties in an organisation's external environment over some future time period. Whilst the precepts and processes of scenario planning are not directly relevant here (but are discussed elsewhere[41,42]), some of their features are pertinent to the use of visioning scenarios. Strategic planning scenarios are typically developed in sets, where each scenario describes the behaviour of a collection of key uncertain factors. Since the future is uncertain and may develop along a number of paths, a set of distinct scenarios is used to capture the range of possible future developments in key uncertainties. To use Ducot and Lubben's[43] scenario classification, descriptive and exploratory scenarios are the most commonly used in the assessment of future uncertainties concerning an organisation's external environment. Such scenarios are typically objective, or factually based.

Visioning scenarios, in contrast to strategic planning scenarios, are focused on the internal environment of an organisation and on issues over which the organisation has control. They are exploratory, and also normative, meaning subjective or values-laden, since they are intended to address the deep concerns of participating stakeholders. In a visioning process, visioning scenarios should be produced from the initial concerns of stakeholders in such a way that each one represents a contrasting and strongly held viewpoint or perspective on the issues under consideration. These visioning scenarios serve to act as a transitional object.[44] The intention of their use is not necessarily that a particular vision be chosen, but rather that they act as a vehicle to promote debate and facilitate the consensual selection of themes and actions central to the final vision. In other words, they are used to inform participants of potential future states, and to draw attention to possible trade-offs that might exist between the different, often difficult, choices; it may be that elements from separate visioning scenarios together contribute to the final vision once dialogue and debate have taken place.

An organisation using a visioning scenario based approach for public discourse is Public Voice International who developed the Choices approach described below. The Choices approach to visioning projects was designed intentionally for wide participation on issues of general public concern. It has been previously applied in the 'Choices for Britain'[45,46] project which was piloted with approximately 3,000 British students aged between 14 and 18 years.

The Choices approach addresses each of the general visioning process issues described earlier in this chapter, and in addition incorporates visioning scenarios as discussed above to encourage initial public debate of concerns regarding future issues.

THE CHOICES APPROACH

The Choices approach involves six phases.

Phase 1: Project Definition

First, what drives the need for change should be identified in general terms. A small project team should be set up, and key figures invited to join a steering group to champion and drive the project. Participants should represent a broad range of stakeholders, including groups with power and influence to give credibility to the project.

Phase 2: Issue Exploration

The concerns of representative stakeholders should be identified in more depth. Such a process can be achieved using facilitated focus groups, which again should be formed by invitation and which should seek to represent the diversity of different stakeholder opinions.

Phase 3: Preparing Discussion Materials

From an in-depth exploration of the issues of concern, the project team should prepare a set of materials which will be issued as the basis of discussions about the future by a wider set of participants. These materials should contain:

- A brief history of the organisation, and a summary of the current key issues and concerns, representing different stakeholder perspectives.
- An overview of the project process, with timescales.
- A set of visioning scenarios, each describing a future nature or state of the organisation from a contrasting perspective.

Each visioning scenario should be accompanied by supporting questions to promote dialogue about the pros and cons of that scenario, and the trade-offs involved in its realisation. Materials might also include an invitation to participants to build their own visioning scenario different from or consisting of elements of those scenarios presented to them.

Phase 4: Dialogue and Idea Generation

The materials used need to be widely disseminated, and participation encouraged from as wide an audience as is possible and feasible to manage. Groups of stakeholders should discuss the issues raised by the materials presented. The aim of this phase is for groups to identify ideas for action which will move the organisation towards the vision. The ideas generated should be consolidated under broad headings where possible.

Phase 5: Producing a Vision

Using the consolidated ideas for action, participation should again be sought to discuss the potential ideas, and write a clearly articulated, action-oriented vision statement or series of statements relating to the groups of actions. The generation of ideas for action precedes the development of a vision to ensure that this is a 'bottom-up' process with wide involvement in planning and action, rather than one where a small group of individuals create a vision to be implemented.

Phase 6: Planning for Action

Stakeholders and participants should be invited to commit to implementing specific action components of the vision. A detailed plan of how actions will be implemented should be established.

The following case study illustrates these six phases.

CASE STUDY: CHOICES FOR BRISTOL

Phase 1: Project Definition

Bristol is a major UK city which is geographically fragmented into a number of distinct 'village' areas, with poor public transport leaving some less advantaged districts isolated. The city is also culturally fragmented, with some areas of high unemployment throughout what is known as the Bristol Crescent. The main starting point for the Choices for Bristol project was an awareness in the city of some serious public problems, such as crime, the lack of an integrated transport system, and the need for a stronger civic centre with public spaces.

In 1994, a group of individuals familiar with previous Choices projects in other geographic regions[47] and cities (such as Chattanooga and New Haven in the USA) began to work on the idea of a Choices project in Bristol. One of the key ideas behind a Choices project is to get as many people as possible to generate a wide range of ideas for improving a city, over the short and long term. A time horizon of ten years was used to give focus to the exercise, although any vision developed should endure beyond this timespan. A small project team, including volunteers, was formed. The team felt that they would have to overcome a culture of powerlessness across private, public and voluntary sectors, in order to achieve change.

Between the end of 1994 and Autumn 1995, the team invited a number of local figures to join a steering group for the project. The steering group was intended to reflect the different interest groups, and the bodies with power and/or influence, across the city. It included around twenty representatives of the city council, the local TEC (Western Training and Enterprise Council), the health authority, the Chamber of Commerce, the TUC, the local media, and others from the public, private and voluntary sectors.

During 1994 and 1995, a series of one-to-one meetings were held between the project team and the key people mentioned above (and these meetings have continued, to varying degrees, throughout the project). It was critical to establish the credibility of the project at an early stage with these decision-makers. A well-chosen steering group would then give the project legitimacy with the public and with other interested parties. The project team sought to convey to everyone involved the message that the project should not be about consultation, but participation. They were concerned that the public would become disillusioned with a consultation exercise that did not appear to lead to any actions being taken. Decision-makers were also wary of raising public expectations too high. The team believed that projects that ask the public 'What do you want?' tend to fail; the question should be 'What are *we* going to *do*?'

In late 1995/early 1996, the project team developed a fund-raising proposal, and worked to raise money for the project from a number of sources across sectors. The project would clearly have to run on a very modest budget, and fund-raising remained a vital activity throughout the project, with lack of funds hampering progress.

Phase 2: Issue Exploration

By early 1996, eight focus groups had been held, to discover what the main issues about the future of the city were in local people's thinking. Participating groups (such as schools and churches) were hand-picked to create a balance of participants, young and old, employed and unemployed, some with disabilities, and so on. Facilitators helped these groups think about the future of Bristol, to prioritise the issues that arose, and to generate likely solutions.

Focus group participants discussed core public concerns (such as transport and crime), expressed feelings of disempowerment and disillusionment with the political process, and a desire for real action and change. The facilitators felt that these conversations pointed to a particular fragmentation facing Bristol: a three-way gap between local business, local government, and local citizens. This proposition was discussed and tested before incorporation into the subsequent phases of the project.

Phase 3: Preparing Discussion Materials

This three-way fragmentation outlined above was the basis of the three Choices or viewpoints written by the project team, to provide a starting point for a set of discussion materials. These three pictures of possible alternative ways of achieving change to influence the future of Bristol pointed to the fundamental tensions that were found to exist in the city (see Table 3.1). Early drafts were checked by a large number (and broad range) of people across the city.

The materials contained:

- An overview of the project process.
- An assessment of the current state of affairs to provide an anchor point for change. (This included some facts about Bristol today, and issues facing the city.)
- A set of alternative futures in the form of three visioning scenarios (see Table 3.1).
- A series of questions (see Table 3.2) which could form the basis for conversations about the future of Bristol.

Phase 4: Public Dialogue and Idea Generation

In March 1996, the materials were printed and promoted by the local daily paper, the *Bristol Evening Post*. 90,000 copies were distributed as an insert to the paper, which gave the project front page coverage under the slogan 'Your City, Your Choice'.

Table 3.1. The Three 'Choices for Bristol'

Viewpoint 1: The City Council should play a greater role

Bristol City Council should play a greater role in making Bristol a better place. The Council and its staff have years of experience which they could put to more use.

Unlike businesses and voluntary groups, Bristol City Council is required to listen to us and act on our behalf. If we think our councillors are not doing their job well enough, we can vote them out at the next election.

Now that Bristol City Council has taken on the services that were run by the former Avon County Council, the City Council should run better than ever.

Viewpoint 2: Bristol Businesses should play a greater role

Bristol businesses should play a greater role in making Bristol a better place. Our shops and companies care about their community. They know that their business depends on Bristol being a safe, clean and attractive city.

Because they are independent, businesses can decide to take action quickly if they want. The more they get involved in the community, the more likely it is that they will thrive whilst helping to solve local problems at the same time.

Viewpoint 3: The people should play a greater role

The people of Bristol should play a greater role in making Bristol a better place. People know their own communities better than anyone else, and therefore can act more effectively to improve them.

Unlike government or business led solutions, which can be expensive, hundreds of volunteers can accomplish a lot at a little cost. Besides, many of Bristol's problems are ones that money or experts alone cannot solve. They can only be solved by neighbours working together.

Another 7,000 copies were distributed by the project team to encourage targeted groups to participate.

It estimated that at least 400 groups got together across the city, using the materials as their starting point. They represented a very broad range of citizens, for example people with learning difficulties, Girl Guides, and the Union of Catholic Mothers, and met without facilitation provided by the project. The project team conducted outreach work, to raise awareness of the project and encourage participation. A 'roadshow' was also held at 24 locations across the city, to support idea

Table 3.2. Questions for discussion about the future of Bristol

For each viewpoint	What do we value about our community?	What do we want for our future?
Do you agree or disagree?	What do you most like about living in Bristol, and why?	How will my way of life be different?
Should this happen, even if . . .? (highlighting trade-offs)		How will my neighbourhood be different?
	What do you most like about your neighbourhood, and why?	
Why doesn't this happen at the moment?		How will Bristol be different?
	Where in your neighbourhood and the city would you take friends visiting Bristol, and why?	

generation. Over 2,000 ideas for action were sent in to the project team, demonstrating the broad access achieved.

Phase 5: Producing a Vision

The ideas generated were organised under six headings: Acting together, People, Places, Play, Work, and Transport. In December 1996, over 300 adults and young people attended public meetings, known as Vision Bristol Events, at the City Council House. Individuals chose one of the six categories listed, and joined groups to discuss the category of their choice. With professional facilitators acting in a voluntary capacity, the groups reflected on the ideas generated for improving the city, and set goals for Bristol's future. They worked on six statements that described the Bristol they were aiming for over the next ten years (see Table 3.3), and recommended actions.

Table 3.3. Six Statements that make up the 'Vision Bristol'

Within ten years we want to be able to say this about Bristol:

Acting together
'Everyone in Bristol is proud to live in a city that values all its citizens and welcomes their participation at every level of the city's life. Bristolians are proud of the city's illustrious past and that it is a leader in social and environmental excellence. Bristol is a city of people from many cultures, each of which is celebrated and encouraged to work together to create solutions and strategies for building a better future for all.'

People
'Bristol is a city that values all its citizens, from the youngest to the oldest, and celebrates its rich diversity of cultures. It is a city that encourages care and tolerance together with equality of opportunity in education, health and housing. Bristol recognises that each person has great potential and is working to enable everyone to take an active part in the decisions affecting our community.'

Places
'We live in a clean, healthy, safe and prosperous city where resources are used wisely and distributed fairly. Residents are consulted and work together to create a beneficial, sustainable and enjoyable environment for all its current and future citizens.'

Play
'Bristol supports an enjoyable and healthy quality of life for all its citizens. It encourages active participation in a wide range of easy to use, affordable recreational activities in neighbourhoods as well as at major civic sites. Bristol continues to foster the widest range of arts and music for the benefit of the city and the region.'

Work
'Bristol is a city which attracts and maintains healthy economic activity. Our wealth is fairly shared amongst a highly motivated, well trained workforce and population. It is a city where people's quality of life comes before commercial considerations yet where all sectors work together to provide flexible, rewarding and secure work for all.'

Transport
'Bristol is a city that prioritises environmentally friendly means of transport by actively encouraging people to use public transport and bicycles rather than private vehicles. Bristol's public transport network integrates all forms of transport in an efficient, affordable, reliable system which is easy for everyone to use and answerable to the people who use it.'

Phase 6: Planning for Action

The final output from the roadshow and ideas generation, including all ideas for action, were published in a booklet entitled 'Your Ideal Bristol? Let's make it happen!', in February 1997. This was distributed widely throughout the city, to all contributors, participants, decision-makers and other interested parties. Within this booklet, the ideas generated were further categorised under sub-headings within the six main categories. The headings and sub-headings are shown in Table 3.4.

The next phase (from March 1997) is beginning to put the ideas generated into action. Groups and individuals, helped by the Choices for Bristol team, are expressing their interest in implementing particular actions. Meetings and events are being held to form facilitated Action Groups. A deal-making model is being considered, where individuals declare what they will do (how much of their own time they will invest, for example), and what in return they expect from people in positions of power.

Table 3.4. Headings and Sub-headings for Actions Generated

Acting together	People	Places	Play	Work	Transport
• Citizen involvement/ public information	• Accessibility	• City centre	• Culture and art	• Community regeneration	• Pollution
• Civic price	• Community and social facilities	• Development and planning	• Leisure/events	• Business and the community	• Private transport
• Crime/safety	• Diversity/ equality	• Environment	• Parks and open spaces	• New ways to work	• Public transport
• Regional and European Bristol	• Education	• Shopping	• Sport	• Young workers	• Traffic management
• Leadership	• Health	• Tourism			
• Long term vision	• Heritage and museums	• Waterways			
• Neighbourhoods and communities	• Libraries				
• City economy	• Housing and homelessness				
	• Youth				

REFLECTIONS ON THE CASE STUDY

This case study illustrates the main phases in the Choices methodology, and demonstrates some of its key features. The method was used to build a vision for the future of a major city. A wide range of stakeholders were actively involved in setting strategy and goals for their city, with the aim of encouraging widespread ownership and 'buy-in' to the new strategy.

The Choices for Bristol project has a very broad agenda—the future of a major city. This can be a major strength, as almost every idea generated by participants is bound to be relevant. It is perhaps also the key weakness, as it is difficult to follow through on all of the big issues raised (crime, transport, and so on). A widespread commitment to action from a large number of participants is therefore a vital output of the process, not just an action list. The project has sought to create a 'can-do' spirit in the city, and to act as a catalyst, an intermediary between citizens and decision-makers, and a vehicle for turning talk into action. There are no existing benchmarks for success, but in order to achieve change, other things are needed, such as resources, and possibly capacity building (such as training in new skills) for groups and individuals.

Part of the vehicle for the visioning exercise is multiple scenarios or viewpoints concerning the future. No consensus has been achieved so far on one particular vision for the future of Bristol. The visioning scenarios in this instance identify three different groups within the city (the City Council, local businesses and the people of Bristol) and their possible roles in improving the city (see Table 3.1). It is hoped that bridges have been built between individuals and groups with different value positions. Presenting the public with a number of alternative choices around the future of their city gives a strong message about the openness of the strategy formulation process, and encourages them to create their own vision. This is a major benefit of a scenario-based method. The generation of ideas for action precedes the development of a vision in this case, to ensure that this is a 'bottom-up' project where vision and action are highly integrated through a process of wide involvement, rather than one where a small group of individuals create a vision to be implemented.

VISIONING STUDIES IN A RANGE OF ORGANISATIONAL CONTEXTS

The case study presented above is set in the public arena, addressing issues of wide general concern. It is our proposal that visioning methods are of value in a broad range of different organisational contexts. Some of the issues that have been addressed by visioning projects include: personal development for the individual person;[48] corporate development for both private[49] and public[50] organisations; and urban and socio-economic planning for larger communities, countries[51] and world regions[52]. Three examples of other visioning studies are therefore outlined below, and contrasted with the Choices for Bristol case study. The examples show that while numerous methodologies exist for conducting visioning projects, they differ mainly in the sequence and detail of the steps that they advocate.

An example of visioning at the corporate level is given by Stewart,[53] who describes a Toronto manufacturing company concerned with the need to improve safety performance. The visioning process involved a cross-section of company employees representing hierarchical, functional and geographic dimensions of the organisation. The interests of wider stakeholders were taken into account by the visioning team through a process of role-playing the concerns and responses of other interested parties. Having identified a team, Stewart's process moved on to an assessment of the environment within which the organisation operated. From this a number of key topics were identified which together form the foundations of the vision. These topics were: corporate safety performance, characteristics of management, characteristics of employees, production facilities, safety programmes and systems, off-the-job safety and customers, shareholders and community. Each topic was assessed in more depth and from the perspective of different stakeholders. Once established, the vision (all injuries can be prevented) was contrasted with the current state of affairs (accidents were inevitable and accepted as part of working life). This contrasting process serves to provide a base from which to develop strategy and action plans. The next step in Stewart's process is to support the vision with organisational and personal values since he states that an inspiring vision will not become a reality if it conflicts with the values of the organisation. In this case, an articulated value was that 'people learn best by doing'. Thus, an example of a directly actionable principle to emerge from the visioning process was 'management will create systems to involve all employees in meaningful *doing* activities in safety'.

In contrast to the Toronto case above, the following two examples illustrate the use of multiple vision scenarios within a visioning process.

A number of visioning projects using scenarios in the area of public discourse have been run by the Public Agenda Foundation, a US based organisation founded in 1975 by former Secretary of State Cyrus Vance and public opinion analyst Daniel Yankelovich. Yankelovich[54] notes that public discourse is values-laden and tends to take a broad, long term view, in contrast with expert discourse which tends to be factual, narrowly focused and short term. On complex issues such as health care or foreign policy, public opinion typically goes through seven stages from a dawning awareness of the issue in question, via a greater sense of urgency and resistance to facing difficult trade-offs, ending in a readiness to make responsible judgements which accept the pros and cons of choices. The use of a visioning process in the public arena is a means of accelerating these stages which might otherwise take several years, particularly where large complex issues are concerned.

In 1988, the Public Agenda Foundation and the Center for Foreign Policy Development at Brown University in the USA ran a project in four US cities called 'The Public, The Soviets and Nuclear Arms'.[55] The project's purpose was to bring the public, experts and political leaders together in a process of working through to judgement about the USA's long term goals and relations with the Soviet Union. This was done by contrasting four alternative future vision scenarios for the year 2010. Each vision scenario illustrated a different way in which the relations between the two countries might develop. The scenarios were called: 'The US gains the upper hand', 'Eliminate the nuclear threat; compete otherwise', 'Co-operative problem solving' and 'Defend only North America'. The first phase of the project involved the research and design of discussion materials, where the costs and risks of each scenario were emphasised. In the second phase, public attitudes were evaluated using Citizen Choice Campaigns co-sponsored by local newspapers and television stations; the public expressed their preferences on a ballot paper. The third phase involved dissemination of results both during and after the 1988 Presidential campaign.

An example of visioning using scenarios for a world region (South East Asia) is given by Inayatullah.[56] A workshop was organised by the Malaysian Institute for Policy Research and the World Futures Studies Federation. The purpose of the workshop was to generate alternative visions for South East Asia and to develop consensus on preferred visions. Also, the workshop was seen as the beginning of a wider process of thinking about the future of this world region. Participants included leading Malaysian corporate leaders, scientists, government officials and academics. The workshop used keynote speakers interspersed with practical workshops to achieve its purpose. The issues which emerged covered the environment, social practices and structures, political and economic issues at local, regional and global levels as well as culture and traditions, notably Islam. Participants were individually interviewed by workshop leaders about how they saw a day in their life 30–50 years hence. From these interviews, four visioning scenarios were posited as ideal types and used as the basis of further discussion by smaller groups. Each group considered a scenario with the aim of backcasting the future from the present, i.e. describing a possible path from the present to the future. Group visions along with backcasts were presented to the whole group for further discussion. Resulting from this workshop were a number of recommendations, including broader participation in such a process and further research into specific issues.

In the above examples, the organisational settings were different, but the approaches used shared many similar features and were often based on common principles.

One common characteristic is broad participation in the visioning exercise. The Toronto case is of particular interest because of its approach to the issue of participation. A cross-section of employees were involved, but the views of some stakeholders were incorporated via role-playing rather than direct participation. In the South East Asia case, an exercise with limited participation was used to promote futures thinking which would lead to wider participation on broader issues at a later date. The use of a public survey and ballot to promote participation is a distinguishing feature of the US case. The US case is perhaps the most similar to the Choices for Bristol case in that it also sought direct participation from as many stakeholders as possible.

Another common characteristic is a concern for the different values held by various stakeholders. A distinguishing feature of the South East Asia case was the sensitivity to the culture and traditions of Islam when generating future visions for the region. In the US case, four visioning scenarios were used to represent the distinct perspectives of different stakeholder groups; the development and use of discussion materials also bears similarities to the Choices for Bristol case. The Toronto case, on the other hand, does not explicitly report the use of multiple visioning scenarios as a feature of its method; it does however explicitly support the vision with an articulation of organisational and personal values.

Connecting the vision to the present state is inextricably linked to generating a commitment to action in all of the cases, with the possible exception of the US case. Both of the Toronto and South East Asia cases explicitly link the vision generated to the present state of affairs. Backcasting is a particular feature of the latter case, where a path to the future is described via a series of actions that need to take place. In the Toronto case, a process of contrasting the vision with the present is used to provide a base from which to develop strategy and action plans. In contrast, the Choices for Bristol case, and the Choices methodology in general, adopts a bottom-up approach to generating ideas for action before creating a vision. This process is also designed to encourage commitment to action. In the US case, the results of the visioning exercise were used to persuade politicians and other decision makers to take action.

CONCLUSIONS

This chapter began with a definition of a vision and its role in an organisation. The key features of a visioning project were summarised with emphasis given to the use of vision scenarios. A scenario based approach to visioning was presented, and illustrated with a case study. Examples of other visioning studies were given, to illustrate that visioning has application beyond the public arena.

The creation of a vision that can be clearly articulated is an important foundation for strategy development since any plans implemented are designed to move the organisation towards the vision. The chapter demonstrates that visioning can be a participative approach to strategy development, since a wide range of stakeholders are actively involved in the process of setting goals and developing strategic ideas. Broad participation also encourages a widespread commitment to the action plans generated.

Scenario visions frame possible different states from contrasting, possibly conflicting, value positions and facilitate a process of rich dialogue. They give legitimacy to the values of all participants and, within a visioning process, they encourage individuals to share understanding and meaning via reflection and communication. They also allow the current state of affairs to be contrasted against a number of possible future states, reinforcing the fact that there are a number of options open to participants. Scenario visions facilitate informed choice since they make explicit the breadth of options available, and the consequences of choosing a particular option.

In conclusion, a robust vision is a vital part of the foundations of a good strategy. Visioning processes are advocated here as a useful tool in the portfolio of methods available to support strategy development. In particular, scenario based visioning methods are recommended, as the wide participation and rich dialogue involved are likely to increase widespread understanding of the complex issues concerned, and build a broader commitment to action.

ACKNOWLEDGEMENTS

The authors would like to thank Candida Weston, Karl Berger and Matthew Pike for their help in writing the Choices for Bristol case study. Comments or questions regarding Choices for Bristol should be addressed to Candida Weston, telephone (0117) 9087003, email 101632.56@compuserve.com.

REFERENCES

1. B. Nanus (1996), 'Leading the vision team', *The Futurist*, May–June 1996, pp. 21–23.
2. J. M. Kouzes & B. Z. Posner (1996), 'Envisioning your future: Imaging ideal scenarios', *The Futurist*, May–June 1996, pp. 14–19.
3. Ibid.
4. M. Lipton (1996), 'Demystifying the development of an organizational vision', *Sloan Management Review*, Summer 1996, pp. 83–92.
5. Ibid.
6. J. C. Collins & J. I. Porras (1995), 'Building a visionary company', *California Management Review*, Vol. 37, No. 2, pp. 80–100.
7. Lipton, op. cit.
8. J. Parikh & F. Neubauer (1993), 'Corporate visioning', *International Review of Strategic Management*, Vol. 4, pp. 105–116.
9. F. Westley & H. Mintzberg (1989), 'Visionary leadership and strategic management', *Strategic Management Journal*, Vol. 10, pp. 17–32.
10. P. Walker (1996), *Creating community visions*, The Local Government Management Board, London.
11. Nanus, op. cit.
12. P. Hadridge (1995), 'Tomorrow's World', *Health Service Journal*, 5th January 1995, pp. 18–20.
13. Kouzes & Posner, op. cit.

14. Walker, op. cit.
15. V. Pryce & N. B. Griffin (1996), 'They have a dream', *The Banker*, April 1996, pp. 78–79.
16. Lipton, op. cit.
17. Nanus, op. cit.
18. *Wall Street Journal*, 22nd September 1994.
19. Collins & Porras, op. cit.
20. Walker, op. cit.
21. W. Ziegler (1991), 'Envisioning the future', *Futures*, June 1991, pp. 516–527.
22. G. H. Garland (1990), 'Peru in the 21st Century: Challenges and Possibilities', *Futures*, May 1990, pp. 375–395.
23. J. P. Kotter (1995), 'Leading Change: Why Transformation Efforts Fail', *Harvard Business Review*, March–April 1995, pp. 59–67.
24. Collins & Porras, op. cit.
25. R. L. Ackoff (1993), 'Idealized design: Creative corporate visioning', *OMEGA* Vol. 21, No. 4.
26. Walker, op. cit.
27. Ziegler, op. cit.
28. J. M. Stewart (1993), 'Future state visioning', *Long Range Planning*, Vol. 26, No. 6, pp. 89–98.
29. Collins & Porras, op. cit.
30. Ziegler, op. cit.
31. Ibid.
32. Stewart, op. cit.
33. Kouzes & Posner, op. cit.
34. Ziegler, op. cit.
35. Lipton, op. cit.
36. S. Inayatullah (1995), 'Future visions for S.E. Asia: Some early warning signals', *Futures*, Vol. 27, No. 6, pp. 681–688.
37. Ziegler, op. cit.
38. Stewart, op. cit.
39. Ziegler, op. cit.
40. Walker, op. cit.
41. K. van der Heijden (1996), *Scenarios—The Art of Strategic Conversation*, John Wiley & Sons.
42. D. W. Bunn & A. A. Salo (1993), 'Forecasting with Scenarios', *European Journal of Operational Research*, 68 (3), pp. 291–303.
43. C. Ducot & G. J. Lubben (1980), 'A typology for scenarios', *Futures*, February 1980, pp. 51–57.
44. A. P. de Geus (1988), 'Planning as learning', *Harvard Business Review*, March/April 1988, pp. 70–74.
45. Public Voice International (1994), 'Choices for Britain: Avon Pilot Evaluation', Bristol, Public Voice International.
46. M. Meadows & F. A. O'Brien (1996), 'Scenarios for future visioning', Warwick Business School Working Paper No. 232.
47. A. J. Hahn, J. C. Greene & C. Waterman (1994), 'Educating about Public Issues: Lessons from Eleven Innovative Public Policy Education Projects', Cornell University.
48. Ziegler, op. cit.
49. Stewart, op. cit.
50. Hadridge, op. cit.
51. Garland, op. cit.
52. Inayatullah, op. cit.
53. Stewart, op. cit.
54. D. Yankelovich (1992), 'How Public Opinion Really Works, *Fortune*, 126 (7), October 5th 1992, pp. 102–108.

55. Public Agenda Foundation (1988), 'Public Summit '88: Baltimore, Nashville, San Antonio, Seattle – It's Your Future', Center for Foreign Policy Development, Brown University, USA.
56. Inayatullah, op. cit.

Chapter 4

The Balanced Scorecard—Measures that Drive Performance

Robert S. Kaplan
Harvard Business School

David P. Norton
Nolan, Norton & Company, Inc., Massachusetts

What you measure is what you get. Senior executives understand that their organization's measurement system strongly affects the behavior of managers and employees. Executives also understand that traditional financial accounting measures like return-on-investment and earnings-per-share can give misleading signals for continuous improvements and innovation—activities today's competitive environment demands. The traditional financial performance measures worked well for the industrial era, but they are out of step with the skills and competencies companies are trying to master today.

As managers and academic researchers have tried to remedy the inadequacies of current performance measurement systems, some have focused on making financial measures more relevant. Others have said, 'Forget the financial measures. Improve operational measures like cycle time and defect rates; the financial results will follow.' But managers should not have to choose between financial and operational measures. In observing and working with many companies, we have found that senior executives do not rely on one set of measures to the exclusion of the other. They realize that no single measure can provide a clear performance target or focus attention on the critical areas of the business. Managers want a balanced presentation of both financial and operational measures. During a year-long research project with 12 companies at the leading edge of performance measurement, we devised a 'balanced scorecard'—a set of measures that gives top managers a fast but comprehensive view of the business. The balanced scorecard includes financial measures that tell the results of actions already taken. And it complements the financial measures with operational measures on customer satisfaction, internal processes, and the organization's innovation and improvement activities—operational measures that are the drivers of future financial performance.

Think of the balanced scorecard as the dials and indicators in an airplane cockpit. For the complex task of navigating and flying an airplane, pilots need detailed information about many aspects of the flight. They need information on fuel, air speed, altitude, bearing, destination, and other indicators that summarize the current and predicted environment. Reliance on one instrument can be fatal. Similarly, the complexity of managing an organization today requires that managers be able to view performance in several areas simultaneously.

The balanced scorecard allows managers to look at the business from four important perspectives. (See Figure 4.1.) It provides answers to four basic questions:

- How do customers see us? (customer perspective)
- What must we excel at? (internal perspective)
- Can we continue to improve and create value? (innovation and learning perspective)
- How do we look to shareholders? (financial perspective)

While giving senior managers information from four different perspectives, the balanced scorecard minimizes information overload by limiting the number of measures used. Companies rarely suffer from having too few measures. More commonly,

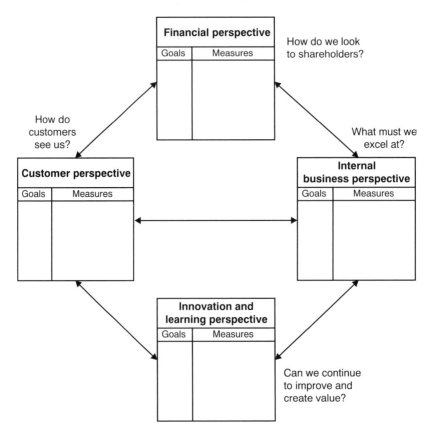

Figure 4.1. The Balanced Scorecard Links Performance Measures

---

Other measures for the customer's perspective

A computer manufacturer wanted to be the competitive leader in customer satisfaction, so it measured competitive rankings. The company got the rankings through an outside organization hired to talk directly with customers. The company also wanted to do a better job of solving customers' problems by creating more partnerships with other suppliers. It measured the percentage of revenue from third-party relationships.

The customers of a producer of very expensive medical equipment demanded high reliability. The company developed two customer-based metrics for its operations: equipment up-time percentage and mean-time response to a service call.

A semiconductor company asked each major customer to rank the company against comparable suppliers on efforts to improve quality, delivery time and price performance. When the manufacturers discovered that it ranked in the middle, managers made improvements that moved the company to the top of customers' rankings.

Figure 4.2. Other Measures for the Customer's Perspective

they keep adding new measures whenever an employee or a consultant makes a worthwhile suggestion. One manager described the proliferation of new measures at his company as its 'kill another tree program'. The balanced scorecard forces managers to focus on the handful of measures that are most critical.

Several companies have already adopted the balanced scorecard. Their early experiences using the scorecard have demonstrated that it meets several managerial needs. First, the scorecard brings together, in a single management report, many of the seemingly disparate elements of a company's competitive agenda: becoming customer oriented, shortening response time, improving quality, emphasizing teamwork, reducing new product launch times, and managing for the long term.

Second, the scorecard guards against suboptimization. By forcing senior managers to consider all the important operational measures together, the balanced scorecard lets them see whether improvement in one area may have been achieved at the expense of another. Even the best objective can be achieved badly. Companies can reduce time to market, for example, in two very different ways: by improving the management of new product introductions or by releasing only products that are incrementally different from existing products. Spending on setups can be cut either by reducing setup times or by increasing batch sizes. Similarly, production output and first-pass yields can rise, but the increases may be due to a shift in the product mix to more standard, easy-to-produce but lower-margin products.

Other measures for the internal business perspective

One company recognized that the success of its TQM program depended on all its employees internalizing and acting on the program's messages. The company performed a monthly survey of 600 randomly selected employees to determine if they were aware of TQM, had changed their behaviour because of it, believed the outcome was favourable, or had become missionaries to others.

Hewlett-Packard uses a metric called breakeven time (BET) to measure the effectiveness of its product development cycle. BET measures the time required for all the accumulated expenses in the product and process development cycle (including equipment acquisition) to be recovered by the product's contribution margin (the selling price less manufacturing, delivery and selling expenses).

A major office products manufacturer, wanting to respond rapidly to changes in the marketplace, set out to reduce cycle time by 50%. Lower levels of the organization aimed to radically cut the times required to process customer orders, order and receive materials from suppliers, move materials and products between plants, produce and assemble products, and deliver products to customers.

Figure 4.3. Other Measures for the Internal Business Perspective

We will illustrate how companies can create their own balanced scorecard with the experiences of one semiconductor company—let's call it 'Electronic Circuits Inc'. ECI saw the scorecard as a way to clarify, simplify, and then operationalize the vision at the top of the organization. The ECI scorecard was designed to focus the attention of its top executives on a short list of critical indicators of current and future performance.

CUSTOMER PERSPECTIVE: HOW DO CUSTOMERS SEE US?

Many companies today have a corporate mission that focuses on the customer. 'To be number one in delivering value to customers' is a typical mission statement. How a company is performing from its customers' perspective has become, therefore, a priority for top management. The balanced scorecard demands that managers translate their general mission statement on customer service into special measures that reflect the factors that really matter to customers.

Customers' concerns tend to fall into four categories: time, quality, performance and service cost. Lead time measures the time required for the company to meet its customers' needs. For existing products, lead time can be measured from the time the company receives an order to the time it actually delivers the product or service to the customer. For new products, lead time represents the time to market, or how long it takes to bring a new product from the product definition stage to the start of shipments. Quality measures the defect level of incoming products as perceived and measured by the customer. Quality could also measure on-time delivery, the accuracy of the company's delivery forecasts.

The combination of performance and service measures how the company's products or services contribute to creating value for its customers.

To put the balanced scorecard to work, companies should articulate goals for time, quality, and performance and service and then translate these goals into specific measures. Senior managers at ECI, for example, established general goals for customer performance: get standard products to market sooner, improve customers' time to market, become customers' supplier of choice through partnerships with them, and develop innovative products tailored to customer needs. The managers translated these general goals into four specific goals and identified an appropriate measure for each. (See the Figure 4.4, 'ECI's Balanced Scorecard'.)

To track the specific goal of providing a continuous stream of attractive solutions, ECI measured the percent of sales from new products and the percent sales from proprietary products. That information was available internally. But certain other measures forced the company to get data from outside. To assess whether the company was achieving its goals of providing reliable, responsive supply, ECI turned to its customers. When it found that each customer defined 'reliable, responsive supply' differently ECI created a database of the factors as defined by each of its major customers. The shift to external measures of performance with customers led ECI to redefine 'on time' so it matched customers' expectations. Some customers defined 'on-time' as any shipment that arrived within five days of scheduled delivery; others used a nine-day window. ECI itself had been using a seven-day window, which meant that the company was not satisfying some of its customers and overachieving at others. ECI also asked its top ten customers to rank the company as a supplier overall.

Depending on customers' evaluations to define some of a company's performance measures forces that company to view its performance through customers' eyes. Some companies hire third parties to perform anonymous customer surveys, resulting in a customer-driven report card. The J.D. Powers quality survey, for example, has become the standard of performance for the automobile industry, while the Department of Transportation's measurement of on-time arrivals and lost baggage provides external standards for airlines. Benchmarking procedures are yet another technique companies use to compare their performance against competitors' best practice. Many companies have introduced 'best of breed' comparison programs: the company looks to one industry to find, say, the best distribution system, to another industry for the lowest cost payroll process, and then forms a composite of those best practices to set objectives for its own performance.

In addition to measures of time, quality, and performance and service, companies must remain sensitive to the cost of their products. But customers see price as only one component of the cost they incur when dealing with their suppliers. Other supplier-driven costs range from ordering, scheduling delivery, and paying for the materials; to receiving, inspecting, handling, and storing the materials; to the scrap, rework, and obsolescence caused by the materials; and schedule disruptions (expediting and value of lost output) from incorrect deliveries. An excellent supplier may charge a higher

Financial perspective	
Goals	Measures
Survive	Cash flow
Succeed	Quarterly sales growth and operating income by division
Prosper	Increased market share and ROE

Customer perspective	
Goals	Measures
New products	Percent of sales from new products
	Percent of sales from proprietary products
Responsive supply	On-time delivery (defined by customer)
Preferred supplier	Share of key accounts' purchases
	Ranking by key accounts
Customer partnership	Number of cooperative engineering efforts

Internal business perspective	
Goals	Measures
Technology capability	Manufacturing geometry vs. competition
Manufacturing excellence	Cycle time Unit cost Yield
Design productivity	Silicon efficiency Engineering efficiency
New product introduction	Actual introduction schedule vs. plan

Innovation and learning perspective	
Goals	Measures
Technology leadership	Time to develop next generation
Manufacturing learning	Process time to maturity
Product focus	Percent of products that equal 80% sales
Time to market	New product introduction vs. competition

Figure 4.4. ECI's Balanced Business Scorecard

unit price for products than other vendors but nonetheless be a lower cost supplier because it can deliver defect-free products in exactly the right quantities at exactly the right time directly to the production process and can minimize, through electronic data interchange, the administrative hassles of ordering, invoicing, and paying for materials.

INTERNAL BUSINESS PERSPECTIVE: WHAT MUST WE EXCEL AT?

Customer-based measures are important, but they must be translated into measures of what the company must do internally to meet its customers' expectations. After all, excellent customer performance derives from processes, decisions, and actions occurring throughout an organization. Managers need to focus on those critical internal operations that enable them to satisfy customer needs. The second part of the balanced scorecard gives managers that internal perspective.

The internal measures for the balanced scorecard should stem from the business processes that have the greatest impact on customer satisfaction—factors that affect cycle time, quality, employee skills, and productivity, for example. Companies should also attempt to identify and measure their company's core competencies, the critical technologies needed to ensure continued market leadership. Companies should decide what processes and competencies they must excel at and specify measures for each.

Managers at ECI determined that submicron technology capability was critical to its market position. They also decided that they had to focus on manufacturing excellence, design productivity, and new product introduction. The company developed operational measures for each of these four internal business goals.

To achieve goals on cycle time, quality, productivity, and cost, managers must devise measures that are influenced by employees' actions. Since much of the action takes place at the department and workstation levels, managers need to decompose overall cycle time, quality, product, and cost measures to local levels. That way, the measures link top management's judgment about key internal processes and competencies to the actions taken by individuals that affect overall corporate objectives. This linkage ensures that employees at lower levels in the organization have clear targets for actions, decisions, and improvement activities that will contribute to the company's overall mission.

Information systems play an invaluable role in helping managers disaggregate the summary measures. When an unexpected signal appears on the balanced scorecard, executives can query their information system to find the source of the trouble. If the aggregate measure for on-time delivery is poor, for example, executives with a good information system can quickly look behind the aggregate measure until they can identify late deliveries, day by day, by a particular plant to an individual customer.

If the information system is unresponsive, however, it can be the Achilles' heel of performance measurement. Managers at ECI are currently limited by the absence of such an operational information system. Their greatest concern is that the scorecard information is not timely; reports are generally a week behind the company's routine management meetings, and the measures have yet to be linked to measures for managers and employees at lower levels of the organization. The company is in the process of developing a more responsive information system to eliminate this constraint.

INNOVATION AND LEARNING PERSPECTIVE: CAN WE CONTINUE TO IMPROVE AND CREATE VALUE?

The customer-based and internal business process measures on the balanced scorecard identify the parameters that the company considers most important for competitive success. But the targets for process keep changing. Intense global competition requires that companies make continual improvements to their *existing* products and processes and have the ability to introduce entirely new products with expanded capabilities.

A company's ability to innovate, improve, and learn ties directly to the company's value. That is, only through the ability to launch new products, create more value for customers, and improve operating efficiencies continually can a company penetrate new markets and increase revenues and margins—in short, grow and thereby increase shareholder value.

ECI's innovation measures focus on the company's ability to develop and introduce standard products rapidly, products that the company expects will form the bulk of its future sales. Its manufacturing improvement measure focuses on new products; the goal is to achieve stability in the manufacturing of new products rather than to improve manufacturing of existing products. Like many other companies, ECI uses the percent of sales from new products as one of its innovation and improvement measures. If sales from new products is trending downward, managers can explore whether problems have arisen in new product design or new product introduction.

In addition to measures on product and process innovation, some companies overlay specific improvement goals for their existing processes. For example, Analog Devices, a Massachusetts-based manufacturer of specialized semiconductors, expects managers to improve their customer and internal business process performance continuously. The company estimates specific rates of improvement for on-time delivery, cycle time, defect rate, and yield.

Other companies, like Milliken & Co., require that managers make improvements within a specific time period. Milliken did not want its 'associates' (Milliken's word for employees) to rest on their laurels after winning the Baldrige Award. Chairman and CEO Roger Milliken asked each plant to implement a 'ten-four' improvement program: measures of process defects, missed deliveries, and scrap were to be reduced by a factor of ten over the next four years. These targets emphasize the role for continuous improvement in customer satisfaction and internal business processes.

FINANCIAL PERSPECTIVE: HOW DO WE LOOK TO SHAREHOLDERS?

Financial performance measures indicate whether the company's strategy, implementation, and execution are contributing to bottom-line improvement. Typical financial goals have to do with profitability, growth, and shareholder value. ECI started its financial goals simply: to survive, to succeed, and to prosper. Survival was measured by cash flow, success by quarterly sales growth and operating income by division, and prosperity by increased market share by segment and return on equity.

But given today's business environment, should senior managers even look at the business from a financial perspective? Should they pay attention to short-term financial measures like quarterly sales and operating income? Many have criticized financial measures because of their well-documented inadequacies, their backward-looking focus, and their inability to reflect contemporary value-creating actions. Shareholder value analysis (SVA), which forecasts future cash flows and discounts them back to a rough estimate of current value, is an attempt to make financial analysis more forward looking. But SVA still is based on cash flow rather than on the activities and processes that drive cash flow.

Some critics go much further in their indictment of financial measures. They argue that the terms of competition have changed and that traditional financial measures do not improve customer satisfaction, quality, cycle time, and employee motivation. In their view, financial performance is the result of operational actions, and financial success should be the logical consequence of doing the fundamentals well. In other words, companies should stop navigating by financial measures. By making fundamental improvements in their operations, the financial numbers will take care of themselves, the argument goes.

Assertions that financial measures are unnecessary are incorrect for at least two reasons. A well-designed financial control system can actually enhance rather than inhibit an organization's total quality management program. (See Figure 4.5.) More important, however, the alleged linkage between improved operating performance and financial success is actually quite tenuous and uncertain. Let us demonstrate rather than argue this point.

Over the three-year period between 1987 and 1990, an NYSE electronics company made an order-of-magnitude improvement in quality and on-time delivery performance. Outgoing defect rate dropped from 500 parts per million to 50, on-time delivery improved from 70% to 96%, and yield jumped from 26% to 51%. Did these breakthrough improvements in quality, productivity, and customer service provide substantial benefits to the company? Unfortunately not. During the same three-year period, the company's financial results showed little improvement, and its stock price plummeted to one-third of its July 1987 value. The considerable improvements in manufacturing capabilities had not been translated into increased profitability. Slow releases of new products and a failure to expand marketing to new and perhaps more demanding customers prevented the company from realizing the benefits of its manufacturing achievements. The operational achievements were real, but the company had failed to capitalize on them.

The disparity between improved operational performance and disappointing financial measures creates frustration for senior executives. This frustration is often vented at nameless Wall Street analysts who allegedly cannot see past quarterly blips in financial performance to the underlying long-term values these executives sincerely

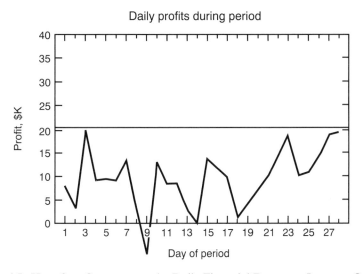

Figure 4.5. How One Company used a Daily Financial Report to Improve Quality

believe they are creating in their organizations. But the hard truth is that if improved performance fails to be reflected in the bottom line, executives should reexamine the basic assumptions of their strategy and mission. Not all long-term strategies are profitable strategies.

Measures of customer satisfaction, internal business performance, and innovation and improvement are derived from the company's particular view of the world and its perspective on key success factors. But that view is not necessarily correct. Even an excellent set of balanced scorecard measures does not guarantee a winning strategy. The balanced scorecard can only translate a company's strategy into specific measurable objectives. A failure to convert improved operational performance, as measured in the scorecard, into improved financial performance should send executives back to their drawing boards to rethink the company's strategy or its implementation plans.

As one example, disappointing financial measures sometimes occur because companies don't follow up their operational improvements with another round of actions. Quality and cycle-time improvements can create excess capacity. Managers should be prepared to either put the excess capacity to work or else get rid of it. The excess capacity must be either used by boosting revenues or eliminated by reducing expenses if operational improvements are to be brought down to the bottom line.

As companies improve their quality and response time, they eliminate the need to build, inspect, and rework out-of-conformance products or to reschedule and expedite delayed orders. Eliminating these tasks means that some of the people who perform them are no longer needed. Companies are understandably reluctant to lay off employees, especially since the employees may have been the source of the ideas that produced the highest quality and reduced cycle time. Layoffs are a poor reward for past improvement and can damage the morale of remaining workers, curtailing further improvement. But companies will not realize all the financial benefits of their improvements until their employees and facilities are working to capacity—or the companies confront the pain of downsizing to eliminate the expenses of the newly created excess capacity.

If executives fully understood the consequences of their quality and cycle-time improvement programs, they might be more aggressive about using the newly created capacity. To capitalize on this self-created new capacity, however, companies must expand sales to existing customers, market existing products to entirely new customers (who are now accessible because of the improved quality and delivery performance), and increase the flow of new products to the market. These actions can generate added revenues with only modest increases in operating expenses. If marketing and sales, and R&D do not generate the increased volume, the operating improvements will stand as excess capacity, redundancy, and untapped capabilities. Periodic financial statements remind executives that improved quality, response time, productivity, or new products benefit the company only when they are translated into improved sales and market share, reduced operating expenses, or higher asset turnover.

Ideally, companies should specify how improvements in quality, cycle time, quoted lead times, delivery, and new product introduction will lead to higher market share, operating margins, and asset turnover or to reduced operating expenses. The challenge is to learn how to make such explicit linkage between operations and finance. Exploring the complex dynamics will likely require simulation and cost modeling.

MEASURES THAT MOVE COMPANIES FORWARD

As companies have applied the balanced scorecard, we have begun to recognize that the scorecard represents a fundamental change in the underlying assumptions about performance measurement. As the controllers and finance vice presidents involved in the research project took the concept back to their organizations, the project participants found that they could not implement the balanced scorecard without the involvement of the senior managers who have the most complete picture of the company's vision and priorities. This was revealing because most existing performance measurement systems have been designed and overseen by financial experts. Rarely do controllers need to have senior managers so heavily involved.

Probably because traditional measurement systems have sprung from the finance function, the systems have a control bias. That is, traditional performance measurement systems specify the particular actions they want employees to take and then measure to see whether the employees have in fact taken those actions. In that way, the systems try to control behavior. Such measurement systems fit with the engineering mentality of the Industrial Age.

The balanced scorecard, on the other hand, is well suited to the kind of organization many companies are trying to become. The scorecard puts strategy and vision, not control, at the centre. It establishes goals but assumes that people will adopt whatever behaviors and take whatever actions are necessary to arrive at those goals. The measures are designed to pull poeple towards the overall vision. Senior managers may know what the end results should be, but they cannot tell employees exactly how to achieve that result, if only because the conditions in which employees operate are constantly changing.

This new approach to performance measurement is consistent with the initiatives under way in many companies: cross-functional integration, customer-supplier partnerships, global scale, continuous improvement, and team rather than individual accountability. By combining the financial, customer, internal process and innovation, and organizational learning perspectives, the balanced scorecard helps managers understand, at least implicitly, many interrelationships. This understanding can help managers transcend traditional notions about functional barriers and ultimately lead to improved decision making and problem solving. The balanced scorecard keeps companies looking—and moving—forward instead of backward.

Part III

Strategy Formulation

Chapter 5

Daimler-Benz's Move towards the Next Century with the TOWS Matrix

Heinz Weihrich
University of San Francisco, CA, USA

The automobile industry is one of the most interesting business sectors in the global environment for analysis. The traditional small Japanese cars are now supplemented by Japanese luxury models, such as Lexus and Infinity, to compete with European cars made by BMW and Mercedes. The Japanese Toyota and Nissan companies not only are targeting luxury car markets in the USA, but also in Europe. Fearing that a 'Fortress Europe' may evolve from the European Community Programme 1992 (in short EC 1992), the Japanese strategy is to establish themselves in the European market by setting up manufacturing plants, especially in England where the former Japanese-friendly Thatcher government encouraged such investments.[1] One interesting question is how European carmakers will respond to the Japanese threat.

The purpose of this article is to analyse Daimler-Benz, renowned for its Mercedes-Benz luxury cars, by using the TOWS Matrix for developing strategies that systematically integrate the threats (T) and opportunities (O) in the external environment with the internal weaknesses (W) and especially strengths (S) of the firm. Daimler-Benz has been selected because its Mercedes cars are known worldwide for engineering excellence. Yet, this firm will face fierce competition from Japanese carmakers. In addition, this traditional car company has been undergoing dramatic changes, venturing into non-defence and defence electronic gear, consumer goods and aerospace. However, these businesses will be mentioned only briefly. This article will introduce a strategic planning model and the TOWS Matrix for the analysis of critical issues faced by Daimler.

STRATEGY FORMULATION

Conceptually, strategy formulation is simple: just analyse the current and expected future environment, determine the direction of the firm, and develop the means for achieving the end. In reality, however, this is a very complex process, especially when

Reprinted with permission from *European Business Review*, Vol. 95 No. 1 © 1993 MCB University Press.

applied to a company as diversified as Daimler-Benz. The strategy formulation process model, shown in Figure 5.1, will aid this analysis and provide the framework for the discussion. Thus, the typical steps in strategic planning are as follows:

(1) Identifying the various organizational inputs, such as people, capital, managerial skills, technical skills, and the goal inputs of stakeholders such as stockholders, employees, suppliers, community, government and, of course, customers.
(2) Preparing the enterprise profile.
(3) Clarifying the orientation of managers, especially top managers.
(4) Determining the purpose and major objectives of the enterprise.
(5) Identifying the present and future external environment. This requires an analysis of the enterprise's threats and opportunities.
(6) Preparing a resource audit with the focus on the firm's internal weaknesses and strengths.
(7) Developing alternative strategies, tactics and other actions.
(8) Evaluating the various strategies and making strategic choices.
(9) Testing the strategy at various stages for consistency.
(10) Preparing contingency plans.
(11) Although not directly a part of the formulation of the strategy, the preparation of medium- and short-range plans as well as the provisions for strategy implementation and control must also be considered and are shown by broken lines in Figure 5.1.

Strategic Planning Inputs

Strategic planning, to be effective, must carefully consider the inputs into the system. These inputs include people, capital, managerial as well as technical knowledge and skills. In addition, various groups of people make demands on the enterprise. Unfortunately, many of the goals of these claimants (also called 'stakeholders') are

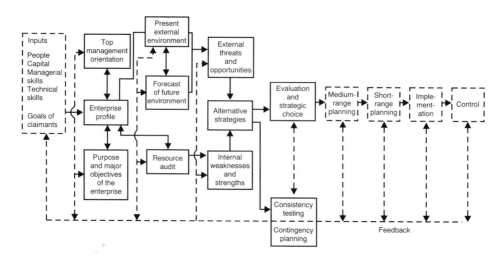

Figure 5.1. Strategic Planning Process

incongruent with each other, and it is the manager's task to integrate these divergent needs and goals. *Employees*, for example, want higher pay, more benefits and job security. Employees' rights, especially in Germany, are to a great extent laid down by laws and regulations. *Consumers* demand safe and reliable products. Car safety has been of paramount importance at Mercedes. *Suppliers*, another group of claimants, want assurance that their products and services will be purchased. For efficient car production, the availability of nearby suppliers is crucial. This makes close cooperation with suppliers easier and keeps transport costs low. *Stockholders* want a high return on their investment with a minimum of risks. In Germany, banks play major roles in directing companies. The Deutsche Bank, which owns 28 per cent of Daimler stocks[3], encourages strategies which result in the long-term success of the company. Thus, Daimler's management is under less pressure from stockholders to show short-term results than managers of US companies.

Federal, state and local *governments* depend on taxes paid by the enterprise. Naturally, organizations are also required to comply with the laws of the governments. Unlike in the USA, German businesses work closely with state and federal governments in an effort to facilitate the achievement of joint objectives. The federal government, for example, played an important role in the merger of Daimler with the state-owned Messerschmitt-Boelkow-Blohm (MBB). Such close relationships between business and government would be frowned upon in the USA.

The community demands that enterprises be 'good citizens' by providing jobs. For example, a car company in southern Germany was prevented from closing its plant because of the negative social impact on the community. Thus, particularly, German employers must take the needs and demands of the citizens into account in their decision making. Other claimants to the enterprise may even include competitors who have a legitimate claim for 'fair play' in the market-place. It is clear, then, that many of these claims are incongruent with each other, and it is management's role to integrate the objectives of these stakeholders.

The Enterprise Profile, Top Management Orientation and the Purpose of Daimler

The enterprise profile is usually the starting-point for determining the current position of the company and where it should go. The firm's history generally reveals what kind of company it is. The values and orientation of top management give the firm direction and determine the basic purpose of the enterprise.

The Enterprise Profile

Determining the enterprise profile requires the company to address some fundamental questions such as:

- What *is* our business?
- Who are our customers?
- What do our customers want?
- What *should* our business be?

The answers to these and similar questions provide information about the basic nature of the company, its products and services, and its geographic domain. In the past, Daimler was known primarily for Mercedes-Benz luxury cars, buses and trucks. But the company profile has been changing. For one, Mercedes has expanded its model range to include smaller cars. Much more drastic has been the diversification into consumer goods, electronics and aerospace. In 1989, Daimler was divided into three operating groups: cars and trucks are in the Mercedes-Benz unit; electronics not related to defence and consumer goods are in the AEG unit; and defence electronics and military aerospace are in the DA (Deutsche Aerospace) group. The common threads integrating the business units are high technology and the development and creative application of new materials.

While it was relatively easy to identify the primary customers for luxury cars, the task is much more complex with the creation of the three operating units. Marketing consumer goods and dealing with the Government in defence contracts requires very different approaches to market penetration because the wants and needs of these divergent customer groups are designed to work in a fairly autonomous manner, at one point the very divergent organizational cultures and management systems need to be integrated—a difficult task indeed.

Top Management Orientation and the Values of Edzard Reuter

The enterprise profile is shaped by people, especially top managers. Their *orientation* is important for formulating the strategy. They set the organizational climate, and they determine the direction of the firm. Consequently, their values, their preferences, and their attitudes towards risks have to be carefully examined for their implications on the strategy.

In 1987, the engineering-driven company selected a non-engineer, Edzard Reuter, as its CEO. He studied mathematics, physics and law. In the middle 1950s, he took the law examination at the Berlin Free University. For the next ten years or so, he held different managerial positions in a variety of business enterprises. In 1964 he joined Daimler in the finance area and later became responsible for corporate planning. As a member of the Board, he was responsible for planning and organization development. In 1987 he was elected as Chairman of the Board of Daimler-Benz.

Reuter's vision is to instill entrepreneurial spirit into the conservative organization culture and to make Daimler a high-tech company. His vision and its resulting strategy evolved over time as documented in articles and his speeches.[4] Already in 1980, he realized the importance of micro-electronics for automobiles as described in the newspaper *Die Welt*. In 1981, he drew attention to the importance of information technology as an integrating factor in the global infrastructure. In 1984, Reuter, at a conference in Cambridge, pointed out the dangers of global competition and urged Europeans to unite into an integrated market, a vision which seems to have come to fruition with the EC 1992 programme.

Purpose and mission of Daimler

The mission and the purpose of an organization are the end points towards which the activities of the enterprise are directed. In the past, it was relatively easy to identify

Daimler's purpose when the company's aim was to produce cars which were 'engineered like no other car in the world'. Now, with the three operating divisions being in different kinds of businesses, this task is much more difficult. Automobiles will remain Daimler's focus; producing and distributing high-quality luxury cars is still the main purpose. However, with the acquisition of the aerospace group Messerschmitt-Boelkow-Blohm GmbH, Daimler became one of the leading defence contractors.[5] While this purchase seemed a wise strategic move at that time, the recent developments in Eastern Europe and the thawing between East and West, suggest that these once profitable defence contracts may be curtailed.

Edzard Reuter's vision of Daimler is to be 'an integrated transportation company, in vehicles, railroads and aircraft'.[6] He wants Daimler to be a global company, yet remain flexible to cope with the dynamic changes. Through the entrance into new fields, the company aims to get access to new information technologies, new materials, and systems knowledge. Although the top priority will remain to build the best automobiles in the world, by the end of the decade the company will also play an important role in aerospace, electronics and factory automation.

STRATEGY FORMULATION AND THE TOWS MATRIX

Most large business firms now prepare strategic plans. At the centre of strategy formulation is the identification of the strengths, weaknesses, opportunities and threats (SWOT). This examination has been traditionally referred to as SWOT analysis. However, this analysis does not show the distinct relationship between the external and internal factors. Therefore, the TOWS Matrix was developed and tested before it was introduced in an article.[7] Since its publication, this tool has been used in different countries and in a variety of situations and levels.[8] The discussion that follows will elaborate on the analysis of the external factors and their integration with the company's resources as they relate to the automobile sector.

The External Environment: Threats and Opportunities

The present and future external environment must be assessed in terms of threats and opportunities. This evaluation focuses on economic, social, political, legal, demographic and geographic factors. In addition, the environment needs to be scanned for technological developments, products and services. The market and the competitive situation must receive special attention. The TOWS Matrix, shown in Figure 5.2, illustrates selected critical external factors for Mercedes-Benz.

External Threats

Daimler faces several threats. The easing of tensions between East and West reduces the need for military hardware. Thus, Daimler's defence unit may fall on hard times in the 1990s. But the focus here will be on the automobile sector.

In Europe, and indeed around the world, the German BMW firm is Daimler's major competitor. While in the past, BMW's strength was in smaller cars, the Series 5 and 7 cars compete directly with Mercedes's middle- and upper-class luxury cars. The recent

	Internal strengths	Internal weaknesses

Strategies
Tactics
Actions
	1. Cash position
	2. Luxury car image
	3. New car models
	4. Location close to
	  suppliers
	5. Engineering and
	  technology
		1. High costs
		2. Venturing into unrelated
		  businesses
		3. Organizational diversity
		4. Reliance on past
		  successes and
		  bureaucracy
		5. Long cycle for new
		  model development
		6. Relatively weak position
		  in Japan

External opportunities	S–O strategy	W–O strategy

1. Demand for luxury cars
2. Eastern Europe, especially
  East Germany
3. Prosperity through EC
  1992
4. Electronics technology
	1. Develop new models
	  (using high-tech) and
	  charge premium prices
	2. Use financial resources
	  to acquire other
	  companies or increase
	  production capacity
		1. Reduce costs through
		  automation and flexible
		  manufacturing
		2. Manufacture parts in
		  Eastern Europe
		3. Reorganization:
		  Daimler–Benz
		  management holding
		  companies

External threats	S–T strategy	W–T strategy

1. Decrease in defence
  needs because of easing
  of East–West tensions
2. BMW, Volvo, Jaguar,
  Lexus, Infinity in Europe
3. BMW in Japan
4. Diesel emissions
5. Renault/Volvo cooperation
6. Political instability in South
  Africa
	1. Transform defence
	  sector to consumer
	  sector
	2. Develop new models
	  to compete especially
	  in Europe
		1. Retrench in South Africa
		2. Form strategic alliance with
		  Mitsubishi to penetrate the
		  Japanese market

Figure 5.2. TOWS Analysis for Daimler Benz–Mercedes–Benz Car Division 1990

agreement of co-operation between the French Renault and Swedish Volvo car-makers reduces their development costs and makes their cars more competitive with Mercedes in the European market.[9] Moreover, Volvo plans a joint project with Mitsubishi for making cars in a plant 70 miles from Amsterdam, Holland.[10] American manufacturers have a strategy of their own. In order to gain access to the Mercedes/ BMW dominated luxury market, Ford acquired the British Jaguar Company. Similarly, General Motors formed a strategic alliance with Swedish Saab-Scania.

An even greater threat to Mercedes are the recently introduced Japanese luxury cars Lexus and Infinity by Toyota and Nissan respectively.[11] Comparisons showed the Japanese cars are up-to-par with those by BMW and Mercedes. BMW, the traditional rival, is not only a threat to Mercedes in the European market, but also in Japan where the appetite for European luxury cars has increased. Daimler is engaged in a co-operative agreement with the Japanese Mitsubishi company. The ties between the two companies go beyond their interests in cars; they extend to electronics and aerospace. For example, the aim is to produce jointly a 75-seat aircraft.[12] Collaboration in the defence sector, however, has been ruled out. The combination of these two giant companies make the competition shudder.

Another threat to carmakers in general and to Mercedes in particular, are laws and regulations governing emission requirements. Diesel engines, Mercedes's traditional strengths, have come under attack by environmentalists for their polluting effects. Moreover, car buyers' preferences have been shifting from the sluggish diesel-powered vehicles to faster accelerating gasoline engines. The external threats, however, are counterbalanced by opportunities.

External Opportunities

The robust economies in the Pacific Rim countries have increased the demand for luxury cars. Moreover, certain European countries (such as Spain) will profit greatly from the EC 1992 programme, thus providing good sales opportunities for Mercedes. While there is a great demand for automobiles in Eastern Europe, the initial demand is likely to be for low-priced cars because of the shortage of hard currency. In the future, however, as the economies improve, the demand for luxury cars is likely to increase.

In Eastern Europe, especially in the former East Germany, there are opportunities for acquiring supplier companies. Daimler, with its strong financial position, has good opportunities for purchasing those companies. However, the concern is that the company's quality image may suffer by producing cars (and perhaps even car parts) in the Eastern part of Germany which in the past produced the Wartburg and Trabant, cars of very low quality.

Increasingly, electronic components are used in cars for fuel injection, brakes, and a variety of other applications. In the future, developments in the electronics and information technologies will become even more important in automobiles and are shown in Figure 5.2 as opportunities.

Internal Factors: Weaknesses and Strengths

The organization's internal environment must be evaluated in terms of its weaknesses and strengths in research and development, production, operations, procurement, marketing, products and services. Other internal factors important for formulating a strategy include the assessment of human resources, financial resources and other factors, such as the company image, the organization structure and climate, the planning and control systems, and the relations with customers. Selected internal factors are listed in Figure 5.2.

Internal Weaknesses

One of the weaknesses of Mercedes is the high cost structure. In Germany, the factory hourly wage is $21.00 compared with $17.50 in Japan and $16.90 in the USA.[13] Germans, work 38 hours per week, Japanese 42 hours, and the Americans work 40 hours. West Germans also have many more holidays than any other industrialized country except for Italy. Germany has 30 holidays, Japan 11; the USA has 12. Although these figures are for the countries and not the automotive industry, they give, nevertheless, an important insight into why automobile production costs are so high for Mercedes.

The size of Daimler and its bureaucratic structure is also a potential weakness; and so is the venturing into non-automotive businesses. Past successes of Daimler can make an organization self-satisfied. The long time it takes to develop a new car model may be an indication of this kind of complacency.

Internal Strengths

With $12 billion available and the strong backing of the Deutsche Bank, Germany's biggest bank, the company is in a strong financial position. Moreover, the high-priced SL roadster has a backlog of orders of several years. Critical in the product line is the new S-Class model which is expected to sell for over $70,000 in the USA; some models are even priced over $100,000. Another Mercedes strength is the company's location near its suppliers. The geographic proximity of internationally competitive suppliers— such as Bosch in Stuttgart—facilitates the close co-operation with them and shortens the transporting time for parts, thus reducing the costs.[14] Because the new car models use electronics for many car functions, Mercedes will benefit from the high-technology strengths of the acquired companies.

Developing Alternatives and Making Strategic Choices

Based on the analysis of the external and internal environments, strategic alternatives are then developed. As shown in the TOWS Matrix (see Figure 5.2), four rather distinct strategies are available:

(1) The SO strategy, or maxi-maxi strategy, aims at maximising both strengths and opportunities.
(2) The ST, or maxi-mini, strategy maximizes the strengths and minimizes the external threats.
(3) The WO, or mini-maxi strategy, is designed to minimize the weaknesses, and to take advantage of opportunities. In general, this is a developmental strategy, which means the company takes steps to transform weaknesses into strengths.
(4) The WT strategy aims at minimizing both weaknesses and threats. This, of course, is the least favourable position for a company. The external threats and opportunities and internal weaknesses and strengths lead to a number of alternative strategies as shown in Figure 5.2.

One *SO strategy* is for Daimler-Benz to develop new models. The company already has several new ones, using its engineering strengths and its technology capabilities. Because of the luxury car image, the company can charge premium prices for satisfying the demand for luxury cars. As consumers become more wealthy, they trade up to more expensive models. Furthermore, the expected prosperity of Europeans through the EC 1992 programme, also increases the demand for luxury models for which Daimler is known. The rapid developments in the electronics field can be engineered into the new models for fuel efficiency (e.g. electronic fuel injection) and safety (e.g.

sophisticated anti-lock brakes). These developments are facilitated by the proximity of well-known suppliers such as Bosch.

The social policies of the Federal Government of Germany encourage investments in companies located in the former East Germany. Daimler certainly has the resources to acquire such companies. Thus the firm would achieve social objectives while at the same time it may gain some cost advantages. Since the distances between these suppliers and the Mercedes plants are greater, the investments may be in factories producing low-tech components using known technologies which do not require frequent interactions with the centralized R&D department. This way, the company could increase the production capacity and reduce the backlog orders for some of its cars.

The *ST strategy* builds on the company's strengths to cope with external threats. One of the threats for Daimler is the decline in the demand for military products. Thus, the company may use its engineering strengths to transform the defence know-how into consumer products or non-military aerospace projects. The company already has certain strengths in these areas through its acquired AEG unit and the Deutsche Aerospace (DA) group. But this strategy would require shifting more resources from the military to the non-defence sectors.

DAIMLER'S BUREAUCRATIC STRUCTURE AND COMPLACENCY MAY BE OVERCOME

The new-model strategy mentioned above in the discussion of the SO strategy also helps in dealing with the competitive threats in the automotive sector in Europe. Specifically, Daimler can maintain its competitive edge over BMW, Volvo, Saab and Jaguar through innovative products. Moroever, the rapid model development will gain in importance when competing with the Japanese entries of Lexus and Infinity into the European market. Those Japanese competitors are known for their short product development cycle and consequently will pose a major future threat for Daimler.

The *WO strategy* aims at transforming the company's weaknesses into strengths to take advantage of opportunities. The high cost structure, partly due to high labour costs, may be alleviated to some extent through investments in automation and flexible manufacturing. Moreover, costs may also be reduced by manufacturing some parts or car components in Eastern Europe. As seen in the SO strategy quadrant in Figure 5.2, Daimler has the resources to purchase suppliers, with special acquisition opportunities in the former East Germany.

Daimler's bureaucratic structure and its complacency caused by past successes may be overcome, in part, through its reorganization. The three operating units, co-ordinated by the Daimler-Benz Holding Company, now can be held accountable for their performance. This, in turn, should result in greater responsiveness to the needs of their customers. Moreover, centralized R&D should result in cost reductions.

The *WT strategy* aims at minimizing internal weaknesses and external threats. Daimler could retrench in or withdraw from South Africa which is characterized by political uncertainty. Moreover, Mercedes can overcome its relative weaknesses in the Japanese car market through its co-operative agreement with Mitsubishi. Thus, the two companies could join forces through service contracts which could provide that Mitsubishi establishes dealerships and service organizations for marketing and servicing Mercedes cars in Japan. In this way, Mercedes could not only become competitive with Japanese luxury cars, but also with its German arch-rival BMW in the Japanese market. Through this co-operative agreement, Mitsubishi, in turn, would gain access not only to the European car market, but also to the European Airbus consortium in which Daimler has a stake in excess of 33 per cent.

From these illustrations it is clear that Daimler can pursue a combination of strategies based on the strengths and weaknesses of the company to take advantage of opportunities and to cope with external threats.

Evaluation and Choice of Strategies

After the development of various strategies, they have to be carefully evaluated before a choice is made. Strategic decisions must be considered in light of the risks involved. Venturing into the defence sector involved some risks for Daimler since this business was outside the automotive field which the company knew best. In hindsight, with the dissolution of the Eastern bloc, it is clear that the risk of entering this industry was greater than was anticipated. It is true that some of the technologies of the acquired aerospace group may have applications for automobiles, but it remains to be seen whether the benefits will outweigh the disadvantages.

Another critical element in choosing a strategy is *timing*. Even the best product may fail if it is introduced at an inappropriate time. Moreover, the reaction of competitors must be taken into consideration. Mercedes takes a long time, in fact too long, for the introduction of new automobile models. Japanese firms, such as Toyota and Nissan, have a much shorter product development cycle. To stay competitive, Daimler has no choice but shorten the model development cycle. Clearly, competitors often force a company to adopt a certain strategy. The Japanese may do just that. This heightened alert of competitive threats may give Daimler the impetus to reinvigorate its organization culture.

Consistency Testing and Preparation of Contingency Plans

The last key aspects of the strategic planning process, shown in Figure 5.1, are the testing for consistency and the preparation for contingency plans. Some observers question Daimler's wisdom of venturing outside the traditional automotive business through the acquisitions of the defence companies and the AEG appliance firm. Also, the cooperation between Daimler and Mitsubishi may be hindered by the difference in organization cultures. The orderly German bureaucratic organization structure appears to be inconsistent with the group-oriented managerial approach of the Japanese.

It is not at all clear that Daimler prepared contingency plans in the event of the deterioration of the Eastern bloc and the unification of Germany. Yet, almost no German company included the 1989/90 developments in Eastern Europe in their strategies either.

SUMMARY AND CONCLUSIONS

As Daimler-Benz moves towards the twenty-first century, it will have to make some strategic choices. Its mission has changed from being an automotive company to an integrated transporting company, defence contractor, and consumer appliances manufacturer. The focus of this article was on the Mercedes-Benz unit which now faces fierce competition from Japanese carmakers in the luxury market. The TOWS Matrix, an analytical tool for identifying Daimler's strengths and weaknesses and the relationships to external opportunities and threats, was used to develop four distinct strategies, the SO, ST, WO and WT strategies. These choices must be made in the light of risks and in congruence with the vision of the CEO, Edzard Reuter. Daimler-Benz must prepare now for the competitive global car market.

NOTES AND REFERENCES

1. Tully, S. 'Now Japan's Autos Push into Europe', *Fortune*, 29 January 1990, pp. 96–106.
2. Adapted from Weihrich, H., *Management Excellence*, McGraw-Hill, New York, NY, 1985, p. 32.
3. Templeman, J., 'Daimler's Drive to Become a High-Tech Speedster', *Business Week*, 12 February 1990, pp. 55–8.
4. The author appreciates receiving information from Edzard Reuter. See also his book *Vom Geist der Wirtschaft — Europa zwischen Technokraten and Mythokraten*, Deutsche Verlags-Anstalt GmbH, Stuttgart, 1986.
5. Aeppel, T. and Roth, T., 'Thaw in Cold War Stymies Daimler-Benz', *The Wall Street Journal*, 3 April 1990.
6. Casey, W. E. and Roth, T., 'Chairman Sees Daimler-Benz on Right Track', *The Wall Street Journal*, 11 May 1990.
7. Weihrich, H., 'The TOWS Matrix—A Tool for Situational Analysis', *Long Range Planning*, Vol. 15, No. 2, 1982, pp. 54–66.
8. For example, the TOWS Matrix has been used as a conceptual framework on the micro level for developing a career strategy and on the macro level for industry analysis.
9. Browning, E. S., 'Renault, Volvo Agree to Enter into Alliance', *Wall Street Journal*, 26 February 1990; Kapstein, J., Toy, S. and Rossant, J., 'Why Renault Feels Safer Buckling Up with Volvo', *Business Week*, 12 March 1990, pp. 53–4.
10. Kapstein, J. and Toy, S., 'Mitsubishi is Taking a Back Road into Europe', *Business Week*, 19 November 1990, p. 64.
11. Taylor, A. III, 'Her Come Japan's New Luxury Cars', *Fortune*, 14 August 1989, pp. 62–6.
12. 'Daimler-Benz, Mitsubishi Group Discuss Expanding Business Ties beyond Autos', *Wall Street Journal*, 7 March 1990.
13. Reichlin, I. and Schares, G. E., 'What's Haunting West German Unions: East Germans', *Business Week*, 21 May 1960, p. 60.
14. For a discussion of the importance of related and supporting industries see Porter, M. E., *The Competitive Advantage of Nations*, The Free Press, New York, NY, 1990, Chapter 3.

Chapter 6

Towards a Dynamic Theory of Strategy

Michael E. Porter
Graduate School of Business Administration, Harvard University, Boston, Massachusetts, USA

INTRODUCTION

The reason why firms succeed or fail is perhaps the central question in strategy. It has preoccupied the strategy field since its inception four decades ago. The causes of firm success or failure encompass all the other questions that have been raised in this collection of essays. It is inextricably bound up in questions such as why firms differ, how they behave, how they choose strategies, and how they are managed. While much of the work in the field has been implicitly domestic, it has become increasingly apparent that any search for the causes of firm success must confront the reality of international competition, and the striking differences in the performance of firms in a given industry based on different nations.

Yet, the question of why firms succeed or fail raises a still broader question. Any effort to understand success must rest on an underlying theory of the firm and an associated theory of strategy. While there has been considerable progress in developing frameworks that explain differing competitive success at any given point in time, our understanding of the dynamic processes by which firms perceive and ultimately attain superior market positions is far less developed. Worse yet, some recent research has tended to fragment or dichotomize the important parts of the problem rather than integrate them, as I will discuss later.

My purpose in this essay is to sketch the outlines of a dynamic theory of strategy. Drawing on recent research, some parts of the outline can be filled in. Many unanswered questions remain, however, and I will try to highlight some of the most important of them.

As a starting point for building a dynamic theory of strategy, we must step back from specific hypotheses or models and look broadly at the literature in both strategy and economics. I will begin by describing the traditional rationale for company success that emerged in the early literature on strategy. This reflected an orientation of the strategy field that has differed in important respects from that which has characterized most research in economics, arguably the discipline with the most obvious connection

Reprinted from *Strategic Management Journal*, Volume 12, pp. 95–117, Winter Special Issue, Copyright © 1991, John Wiley & Sons.

to strategy. The strategy field's traditional answer to why firms succeed or fail was also based on a set of largely implicit, but crucial assumptions about the nature of firms and the environment in which they operate.

Although these assumptions grew out of a deep understanding of practice, they raise profound challenges for a theory of strategy. I will outline some of the most important challenges and the trade-offs they raise in both theory and empirical testing. Taking these challenges as a starting point, I will then describe my own answers to the causes of superior firm performance at a given point in time, which can be framed as a chain of causality. This problem, which I term 'the cross-sectional problem', is logically prior to a consideration of dynamics and better understood. A body of theory which links firm characteristics to market outcomes must provide the foundation for any fully dynamic theory of strategy. Otherwise, dynamic processes that result in superior performance cannot be discriminated from those that create market positions or company skills that are worthless.

I will then move to the dynamic process by which positions are created, which I term 'the longitudinal problem'. To understand the dynamics of strategy, we must move further back in the causality chain. I will explore three recent streams of research that begin to address it: game theoretic models, models of commitment under uncertainty, and the so-called resource-based view of the firm. While illuminating important characteristics of the dynamic processes by which advantage is created and sustained, however, this research still falls short of exposing the true origins of advantage, and I will discuss the reasons why. One important category of these origins, that has emerged from my recent work, is the nature of the 'local' environment in which the firm is based. We observe striking concentrations of successful firms in a particular industry in particular locations, which suggests that something about these locations is fundamental to creating and sustaining advantage. I will summarize some of my findings about these issues. Many questions remain unanswered in our search for a dynamic theory of strategy, however, and this essay will conclude with some challenges for future research.

Determinants of Firm Success: The Early Answers

Any discussion of the determinants of firm success must begin with a clear definition of what success means. For purposes of this essay, I will assume that firm success is manifested in attaining a competitive position or series of competitive positions that lead to superior and sustainable financial performance. Competitive position is measured, in this context, relative to the world's best rivals. Financial success derived from government intervention or from the closing of markets is excluded. A successful firm may 'spend' some of the fruits of its competitive position on meeting social objectives or enjoying slack. Why a firm might do this, however, is treated as a separate question.

To explain firm success, the early literature on strategy defined three essential conditions.[1] The first is that a company develop and implement an internally consistent set of goals and functional policies that collectively defined its position in the market. Strategy is seen as a way of integrating the activities of the diverse functional departments within a firm, including marketing, production, research and development, procurement, finance, and the like. An explicit and mutually reinforcing set of

---

[1] See Learned et al. (1965). See also Andrews (1971).

goals and functional policies is needed to counter the centrifugal forces that lead functional departments in separate directions. Strategy, in modern language, is a solution to the agency problem that arises because senior management cannot participate in or monitor all decisions and directly ensure the consistency of the myriad of individual actions and choices that make up a firm's ongoing activities.[2] If an overarching strategy is well understood throughout the organization, many actions are obviously ruled out and individuals can devise their own ways to contribute to the strategy that management would be hard pressed to replicate.

The second condition for success is that this internally consistent set of goals and policies aligns the firm's strengths and weaknesses with the external (industry) opportunities and threats. Strategy is the act of aligning a company and its environment. That environment, as well as the firm's own capabilities, are subject to change. Thus, the task of strategy is to maintain a dynamic, not a static balance.

The third condition for success is that a firm's strategy be centrally concerned with the creation and exploitation of its so-called 'distinctive competences'.[3] These are the unique strengths a firm possesses, which are seen as central to competitive success. The recent interest in the notion of firm resources or competences is interesting in light of this heritage.[4] I will return to this stream of work later.

The early strategy literature contained only broad principles governing firm success. It is instructive to understand why these authors, coming as they did from a heritage that stressed the administrative point of view and the study of in-depth cases, chose to approach the question in this way. There were two principal reasons. The first was that their orientation, and that of many in the strategy field, was to inform business practice. A theory that sought to explain part of a phenomenon, but which left out important elements that precluded the offering of credible guidance for individual companies, was seen as inadequate to the task.

A second reason for the early formulation was the recognition, indeed the preoccupation, with the fact that competition was complex and highly situation-specific. The early scholars in the strategy field, especially those at Harvard, recognized that firms were composed of numerous functions and subfunctions, and that many diverse aspects of a firm and its environment could be important to success in particular cases. Indeed, it was the act of achieving consistency of action in the many parts of the firm that was seen as crucial to competitive success. Scholars such as Andrews saw each company as unique, with its own history, personality, capabilities, and set of current policies. Every industry was also unique, with its own circumstances and critical success factors. Finally, every period of time was seen as unique, because both companies and their environment were in a state of constant change. Yet firms were seen as possessing considerable ability to build on their strengths and overcome their weaknesses, latitude in influencing or altering their environment, and the ability to influence change over time, not merely respond to it. Indeed, the recognition that industry structure and other exogenous conditions affect performance and constrain choices had to await further work.

---

[2] In the absence of a strategy, the narrow motivations and logistics of each functional area will guide behavior.

[3] This notion is due originally to Selznick (1957).

[4] See, for example, Wernerfelt (1984) and Prahalad and Hamel (1990).

The Challenges for a Theory of Strategy

The view of the world that guided the early efforts to formulate a theory of strategy raises profound challenges for research. The complexity, situation specificity, and changing nature of the firm and its environment strains conventional approaches to theory building and hypothesis testing. Indeed, the early research offered no theory for examining the firm and its competitive environment at all; instead strategy formulation took place through applying the broad principles of consistency and fit to individual case studies.

Four principal issues emerge from the nature of actual economic competition as one contemplates a theory of strategy:

Approach to theory building

First, there is a fundamental question about the approach to theory building that will most advance both knowledge and practice. The broad alternatives are represented in Figure 6.1.

On the one hand, one might approach the task of developing a theory of strategy by creating a wide range of situation-specific but rigorous (read mathematical) models of limited complexity. Each model abstracts the complexity of competition to isolate a few key variables whose interactions are examined in depth. The normative significance of each model depends on the fit between its assumptions and reality. No one model embodies or even approaches embodying all the variables of interest, and hence the applicability of any model's findings are almost inevitably restricted to a small subgroup of firms or industries whose characteristics fit the model's assumptions.

This approach to theory building has been characteristic of economics in the last few decades.[5] It has spawned a wide array of interesting models in both industrial organization and trade theory. These models provide clear conclusions, but it is well known that they are highly sensitive to the assumption underlying them and to the concept of equilibrium that is employed. Another problem with this approach is that it is hard to integrate the many models into a general framework for approaching any situation, or even to make the findings of the various models consistent. While few economists would assert that this body of research in and of itself provides detailed advice for companies, these models, at their best, provide insights into complex situations that are hard to understand without them, which can inform the analysis of a particular company's situation.

Given the goal of informing practice, the style of research in the strategy field, including my own, has involved a very different approach.[6] To make progress, it was necessary to go beyond the broad principles in the early work and provide more structured and precise tools for understanding a firm's competitive environment and

Figure 6.1. Approaches to Theory Building

---

[5] Interestingly, the earlier work in industrial economics, in the Mason/Bain tradition, was much closer to strategy research in its effort to capture complexity.
[6] See examples such as Porter (1985) and Ghemawat (1991).

its relative position. Instead of models, however, the approach was to build frameworks. A framework, such as the competitive forces approach to analyzing industry structure, encompasses many variables and seeks to capture much of the complexity of actual competition. Frameworks identify the relevant variables and the questions which the user must answer in order to develop conclusions tailored to a particular industry and company. In this sense, they can be seen as almost expert systems. The theory embodied in frameworks is contained in the choice of included variables, the way variables are organized, the interactions among the variables, and the way in which the alternative patterns of variables and company choices affect outcomes.

In frameworks, the equilibrium concept is imprecise. My own frameworks embody the notion of optimization, but no equilibrium in the normal sense of the word. Instead there is a continually evolving environment in which a perpetual competitive interaction between rivals takes place. In addition, all the interactions among the many variables in the frameworks cannot be rigorously drawn.[7] The frameworks, however, seek to help the analyst to think through the problem better by understanding the firm and its environment and defining and selecting among the strategic alternatives available, no matter what the industry and starting position.

These two approaches to theory building are not mutually exclusive. Indeed, they should create a constructive tension with each other. Models are particularly valuable in ensuring logical consistency and exploring the subtle interactions involving a limited number of variables. Models should challenge the variables included in frameworks and assertions about their link to outcomes. Frameworks, in turn, should challenge models by highlighting omitted variables, the diversity of competitive situations, the range of actual strategy choices, and the extent to which important parameters are not fixed but continually in flux. The need to inform practice has demanded that strategy researchers such as myself pursue the building of frameworks rather than restrict research only to theories that can be formally modelled. As long as the building of frameworks is based on in-depth empirical research, it has the potential not only to inform practice but to push the development of more rigorous theory.

Chain of Causality

A second fundamental issue in creating a theory of strategy is where to focus the chain of causality. A stylized example will illustrate. We might observe a successful firm and find that its profitability is due to a low relative cost position compared to its rivals. But the firm's cost position is an outcome and not a cause. The question becomes: Why was the firm able to attain this cost position? Some typical answers might be that it is reaping economies of scale, or has moved aggressively down the learning curve. But again, the question becomes why? Some possible answers might include entering the industry early, or the firm's ability to organize itself particularly well for cost reduction. Once again, however, the question becomes why? And we could continue moving along such a chain of causality even further.

Another way of framing the same set of issues is as the problem of drawing the boundary between exogenous and endogenous variables. Should the environment be

---

[7] Frameworks can also be challenged because their complexity makes it difficult to falsify arguments. Yet ascribing this property to models is also problematic if they omit important variables.

taken as given or not? Is the firm's scale an outcome or a cause? And so on. The literature in both strategy and economics addresses many different points in this chain of causality. Indeed, many differences are less conflicts than theory positioned at different points in the chain, as we will see later.

Any theory of strategy must grapple with how far back in the chain of causality to go. The answer may well be different for different purposes. A theory that aims very early in the chain may be intractable or lack operationality. Also, aspects of the firm that are variable in the long run may be fixed or sticky in the short run. Conversely, a theory oriented later in the chain may be overly limiting and miss important possibilities.

Time Horizon

A third challenge for theory is the time period over which to measure and understand competitive success. Should we be building theories for explaining success over two or three years, over decades, or over centuries? Clearly, the likelihood of significant environmental change will differ, as will the exogenous and endogenous variables. A theory that aims at explaining success over 50 years will focus on very different variables, almost inevitably more internal ones, than a theory that addresses success over one or two decades. This is because industry and competitive conditions are likely to be wholly different over a half century, placing greater emphasis on a firm's ability to transform itself. Time period relates closely to position in the chain of causality. Over long periods, theories aimed earlier in the chain would seem more appropriate.

Empirical Testing

A final important issue is how to test theories of strategy empirically. Empirical testing is vital both for frameworks and models. Testing of models is difficult given the need to match their assumptions. Given the myriad of relevant variables in frameworks and the complex interactions among them over time, rigorous statistical testing of frameworks is also difficult, to say the least. In my own research, I pursued cross-sectional econometric studies in the 1970s but ultimately gave up as the complexity of the frameworks I was developing ran ahead of the available cross-sectional data. I was forced to turn to large numbers of in-depth case studies to identify significant variables, explore the relationships among them, and cope with industry and firm specificity in strategy choices.

The need for more and better empirical testing will be a chronic issue in dealing with this subject. Academic journals have traditionally not accepted or encouraged the deep examination of case studies, but the nature of strategy requires it. The greater use of case studies in both books and articles will be necessary for real progress at this stage in the field's development.

TOWARDS A THEORY OF STRATEGY

To explain the competitive success of firms, we need a theory of strategy which links environmental circumstances and firm behavior to market outcomes. My own research would suggest a chain of causality for doing so, outlined in Figure 6.2.

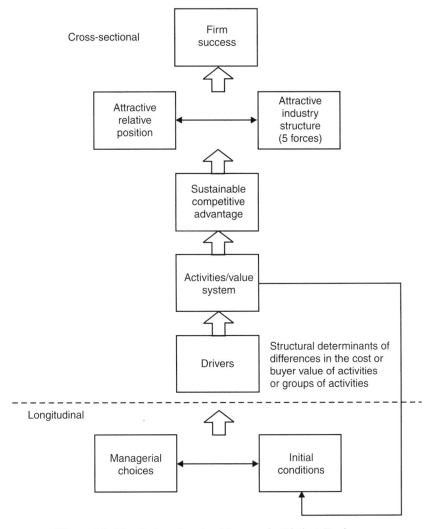

Figure 6.2. The Determinants of Success in Distinct Businesses

The basic unit of analysis in a theory of strategy must ultimately be a strategically distinct business or industry. While firms can redeploy or share resources, activities, and skills across different businesses, the competitive value of such actions can only be measured in terms of some set of rivals delivering a discrete product or service to some set of buyers. Meaningful approaches to corporate-level strategy for diversified firms must grow out of a deep understanding of how companies prosper in individual businesses, and the role of the corporate office and other sister business units in the process.

At the broadest level, firm success is a function of two areas: the attractiveness of the industry in which the firm competes and its relative position in that industry. Firm profitability can be decomposed into an industry effect and a positioning effect. Some firm successes come almost wholly from the industry in which they compete; most of their rivals are successful, too! The distinction between industry structure and relative position is important because, among other things, the firm can choose strategies that will improve one while harming the other. Firms' actions, by triggering imitation, can positively or negatively influence the structure of an industry without leading to competitive advantage. Ideally, however, a firm's actions trigger responses by rivals which improve industry structure but simultaneously allow the firm to gain competitive advantage because rivals' ability to imitate the chosen mode of competition is incomplete.

Industry Structure

I have presented a framework for diagnosing industry structure, built around five competitive forces that erode long-term industry average profitability (see Figure 6.3). This framework has been explored, contributed to, and tested by many others. The industry structure framework can be applied at the level of the industry, the strategic group (or group of firms with similar strategies) or even the individual firm. Its ultimate function is to explain the *sustainability* of profits against bargaining and against direct and indirect competition. Profit differences *vis-à-vis* direct rivals, though, depend on positioning.

Industry structure is partly exogenous, and partly subject to influence by firm actions. Hence structure and firm position ultimately interrelate, which makes separating them a simplification though a useful one for analytical purposes. The firm's scope for influencing industry structure, and ways of modeling it, are a fruitful area for research. My focus here, however, is on relative position because this is where many of the most interesting questions for a dynamic theory of strategy lie.

Relative Position

Holding industry structure constant, a successful firm is one with an attractive relative position. An attractive position is, of course, an outcome and not a cause. The question becomes why, or how did the attractive position arise? The answer must be that the firm possesses a sustainable competitive advantage *vis-à-vis* its rivals. To

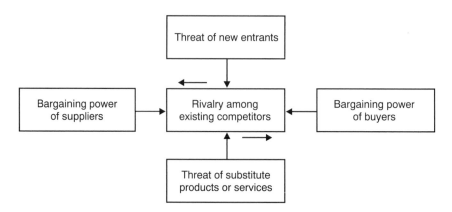

Figure 6.3. Five Forces: Summary of Key Drivers

understand competitive advantage, however, we must decompose it. Competitive advantages can be divided into two basic types: lower cost than rivals, or the ability to differentiate and command a premium price that exceeds the extra cost of doing so. Any superior performing firm has achieved one type of advantage, the other, or both. To say it another way, superior profitability can only logically arise from commanding a higher price than rivals or enjoying lower costs (including, at a lower level in the causality chain, asset costs).[8]

Competitive advantage cannot be examined independently of competitive scope. Scope encompasses a number of dimensions, including the array of product and buyer segments served, the geographic locations in which the firm competes, its degree of vertical integration, and the extent of related businesses in which the firm has a coordinated strategy. Competitive advantage is attained within some scope, and the choice of scope is a central one in strategy. Scope choices can also influence industry structure.

These principles make it clear that the essence of strategy is choice. There is no one way to position within an industry, but many positions involving different choices of the type of advantage sought and the scope of the advantage. Several positions can be attractive in absolute terms, and a variety of positions may be relatively the most attractive depending on the firm's starting position. Choice is essential, however, because there are logical inconsistencies in pursuing several types of advantage or different scopes simultaneously. Also, the firm must stake out a distinct position from its rivals. Imitation almost ensures a lack of competitive advantage and hence mediocre performance.

Activities

If an attractive relative position results from possessing competitive advantage within some scope, the question once again becomes why does that happen? In order to address it, we must decompose cost, differentiation, and scope. This requires a theory which provides an elemental look at what firms do. My own approach to such a theory, and to the sources of competitive advantage, centers around *activities* (Porter, 1985). A firm is a collection of discrete, but interrelated economic activities such as products being assembled, salespeople making sales visits, and orders being processed. A firm's strategy defines its configuration of activities and how they interrelate. Competitive advantage results from a firm's ability to perform the required activities at a collectively lower cost than rivals, or perform some activities in unique ways that create buyer value and hence allow the firm to command a premium price. The required mix and configuration of activities, in turn, is altered by competitive scope.

The basic unit of competitive advantage, then, is the discrete activity. The economics of performing discrete activities determines a firm's relative cost, not attributes of the firm as a whole. Similarly, it is discrete activities that create buyer value and hence differentiation.

The activities in a firm can be schematically arrayed in what I term the value chain and the value system (see Figure 6.4). The term 'value' refers to customer value, from which the potential profit ultimately derives. A firm's strategy is manifested in the way

---

[8] A firm that can command higher volume at a given price takes its superior profitability in the form of lower cost provided costs are scale sensitive.

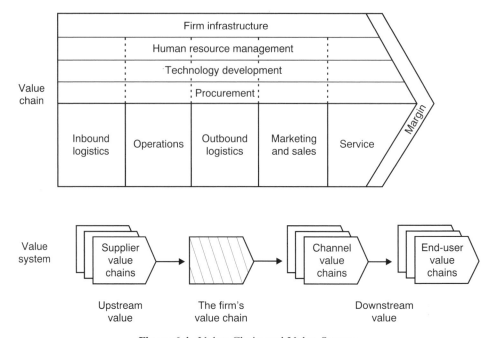

Figure 6.4. Value Chain and Value System

in which it configures and links the many activities in its value chain relative to competitors. The value chain distinguishes centrally between activities that directly produce, market, and deliver the product and those that create or source inputs or factors (including planning and management) required to do so. Support activities, then, are integral to the process by which assets internal to the firm are acquired and accumulated.

Discrete activities are part of an interdependent system in which the cost or effectiveness of one activity can be affected by the way others are performed. I term these 'linkages'. The cost of after-sale service, for example, is influenced by how product design, inspection, and installation are performed. Such linkages can extend outside the firm to encompass the activities of suppliers, channels, and buyers. The concept of linkages begins to operationalize the notion of internal consistency.

Activities involve human resources, purchased inputs, and a 'technology' for performing them, broadly defined to include organizational routines. Activities also use and create information.[9] Performing an activity requires tangible and intangible assets that are *internal* to the firm, such as physical and often financial assets (e.g. working capital) as well as intangible assets embodied in human resources and technology. Performing an activity, or a group of linked activities, also creates assets in the form of skills, organizational routines, and knowledge. While the tangible assets normally depreciate, the intangible assets involved in performing activities can cumulate over time (provided the environment remains relatively stable). These become an important part of corporate balance sheets, as many writers have stressed.[10]

---

[9] See Porter and Millar (1985).
[10] See, for example, Itami (1987) and Baldwin and Clark (1991).

Performing activities can also create assets *external* to the firm. Some are tangible assets such as contracts. Most, however, are intangible assets such as brand images, relationships, and networks. These external assets then feed back to influence the cost or effectiveness of performing activities on an ongoing basis. A strong brand reputation because of cumulative past advertising, for example, can lower the cost of current advertising or make a given rate of spending more effective. Without reinvestment, however, both the external and internal intangible assets attached to activities or groups of activities depreciate. Maintaining or enhancing these assets demands reinvestment through performing activities. Both the external and internal assets are not valuable in and of themselves, however, but because they fit industry structure and a particular strategy. Activities performed poorly, or inconsistently with buyer needs, can create liabilities not assets. At the same time, technological and other industry changes can nullify assets or turn them into liabilities.

The value chain provides a template for understanding cost position, because activities are the elemental unit of cost behavior.[11] The move to activity-based costing is a manifestation of this perspective.[12] The value chain also provides a means to systematically understand the sources of buyer value and hence differentiation. Buyer value is created when a firm lowers its buyer's costs or enhances its buyer's performance. This, in turn, is the result of the ways a firm's product as well as its other activities affect the value chain of the buyer. Firms must not only create value, but 'signal' that they will do so, through their sales forces and other activities. Households and individual consumers have value chains, just as do industrial or institutional buyers. By understanding how households perform activities related to a product (e.g. procurement, storage, use, disposal, etc.), the sources of differentiation can be better understood. Finally, the value chain provides a tool for analyzing the added costs that differentiating may require. Only differentiation that results in a price premium exceeding the extra costs of delivering it results in superior performance.

Drivers

If competitive advantage grows out of discrete activities, however, we once again confront the question, 'why?' Why are some firms able to perform particular activities at lower cost or in ways that create superior value than others? My answer to this question is the concept of *drivers*. These are structural determinants of differences among competitors in the cost or buyer of activities or group of activities. The most important drivers of competitive advantage in an activity include its scale, cumulative learning in the activity, linkages between the activity and others, the ability to share the activity with other business units, the pattern of capacity utilization in the activity over the relevant cycle, the activity's location, the timing of investment choices in the activity, the extent of vertical integration in performing the activity, institutional factors affecting how the activity is performed such as government regulation, and the firm's policy choices about how to configure the activity independent of other drivers. The same set of drivers determines both relative cost and differentiation. The mix and significance of individual drivers varies by activity, by firm, and by industry.

---

[11] See Porter (1985, Chapter 3).
[12] See Johnson and Kaplan (1987), Cooper and Kaplan (1988, 1991).

Moving to the level of drivers also sheds light on the important question of sustainability. The sustainability of competitive advantage *vis-à-vis* rivals depends on the number of competitive advantages in the value chain and, especially, the particular drivers underlying each one. The durability of an advantage based on learning, for example, depends on the ability to keep the learning proprietary, while the sustainability of advantages due to timing of factor positions depends on factor market imperfections.

Drivers constitute the underlying sources of competitive advantage, and make competitive advantage operational. For example, brand reputation is a typical competitive advantage identified by managers. But brand reputation may be a source of cost advantage (less need for marketing) in some cases and a source of differentiation (and a premium price) in others. The substantive implications are very different depending on which it is. Yet, brand reputation is an outcome, not a cause. The real question is how and why brand reputation is an advantage. To understand this, one must move to the level of drivers. For example, timing may have allowed the firm to begin advertising early and hence to develop a reputation uncluttered by the competing claims of rivals. The reputation from cumulative advertising then allows the firm to spend less on current advertising or to spend at a comparable rate to rivals but command a premium price. Alternatively, greater current company sales volume may lead to efficiencies in advertising that allow the firm to enjoy a superior reputation while spending at a rate comparable to its rivals. Only by moving to the level of underlying drivers can the true sources of competitive advantage be identified. Tying advantage to specific activities/drivers is necessary to operationalize the notion in practice.

The value chain also provides the basic architecture for analyzing international strategy and diversification, both fundamentally questions of competitive scope. The central issue in international strategy involves the spread of activities to other countries (configuration) and the integration of dispersed activities (coordination) (Porter, 1986). In corporate-level strategy for diversified firms, the central issue is how firms can share activities across businesses, or share proprietary skills in how to perform particular activities though the value chains of business units are distinct (Porter, 1987).

THE ORIGINS OF COMPETITIVE ADVANTAGE

This set of frameworks aims to build a careful link between the underlying choices a firm makes in terms of its industry, positioning, and configuration of activities and market outcomes. The proper choices depend on a firm's existing position, which can be evaluated systematically via its value chain and drivers. The best strategy also depends on the capabilities and likely behavior of rivals, which can also be assessed through their value chains and drivers. Finally, strategy depends on a sophisticated understanding of industry structure.

Firms inherit positions that constrain and shape their choices, but do not determine them. They have considerable latitude in reconfiguring the value chain with which they compete, expanding or contracting their competitive scope, and influencing important dimensions of their industry environment. Strategy is not a race to occupy one desirable position, but a more texture problem in which many positions can be chosen or created. Success requires the choice of a relatively attractive position given industry structure, the firm's circumstances and the position of competitors. It also requires bringing all the firm's activities into consistency with the chosen position.

While these frameworks have pushed a considerable distance backward along the chain of causality, the focus thus far has been on what might be termed *the cross-sectional* problem. What makes some industries, and some positions within them, more attractive than others? What makes particular competitors advantaged or disadvantaged? What specific activities and drivers underlie the superior positions?

But in answering these questions, we again confront the question of causality. Why were particular firms able to get into the advantaged positions and sustain/or fail to sustain them? This is what might be termed the longitudinal problem, which requires crossing the dotted line on Figure 6.2.[13]

The frameworks for addressing the cross-sectional problem are agnostic as to the process by which the superior positions were attained, and largely unaffected by it. Whether the strategy was consciously chosen, happenstance, the result of incremental steps, or driven by one major decision does not itself affect the attractiveness of the position independently of the activities and drivers on which it rests. Similarly, the past process by which firms accumulated their strengths and capabilities is not, in and of itself, decisive. The cross-sectional frameworks address the choice of strategy given whatever array of capabilities the firm and its rivals possess at a point in time and can feasibly develop in the future. The effort by some to dichotomize process and substance is simply incorrect.[14] Both are necessary and important to understand.

The cross-sectional problem is also logically prior. Without a rather specific understanding of what underpins a desirable position, it is virtually impossible to deal analytically with the process of getting there. Strategy becomes an aimless process in which luck determines the winners.

Assuming an understanding of the cross-sectional problem, however, the longitudinal problem takes on prime importance. Why do some firms achieve favorable positions *vis-à-vis* the drivers in the value chain? Why do some firms gain scale advantages? Why do some firms move early, or late, whichever leads to advantage? Why do some firms conceive of and implement superior configurations of activities or spot entirely new and desirable competitive positions?

Logically, there are two answers. The first is *initial conditions*. Firms may have pre-existing reputations, skills, and in-place activities as a result of their history. These initial conditions may reside within an individual firm or, as I will discuss later, in the environment in which the firm is based. Initial conditions clearly influence feasible choices as well as constrain them.[15]

The second reason that firms might achieve favorable positions is through pure *managerial choices*, or choices independent of initial conditions, putting aside for the moment the process by which the choices were made. These managerial choices, which are made under uncertainty about the future, define the firm's concept for competing (positioning), its configuration of activities, and the supporting investments

---

[13] I avoid the terms static and dynamic intentionally, because both the cross-sectional and longitudinal problems have both static and dynamic components.

[14] See, for example, Mintzberg (1990).

[15] Initial conditions can also be set at different points in time. See below.

in assets and skills. Pure managerial choices lead to the assembly or creation of the particular skills and resources required to carry out the new strategy.

Numerous case studies illustrate vividly that highly successful firms often arise out of creative acts where there were few initial strengths. Wal-Mart decided to locate in small- and medium-sized towns and configure its logistical system in a particular way because it had a better idea, not because of any compelling pre-existing strengths. If anything, its choices were shaped more by what it did not possess than what it did. The same could be said about Federal Express, Apple Computer, Crown Cork and Seal, and many other companies. American Airlines developed its MIS systems almost by accident. Its frequent flyer program was partly a function of the existence of its MIS system, but other airlines had these as well. American's management was simply more creative.

Many strategies clearly reflect some combination of initial conditions and creative choice. The balance between the influence of initial conditions and acts of pure managerial choice varies by company and industry. Yet there may well be a tendency, for a variety of reasons to be discussed later, to overstate the role of initial conditions.

Lying behind all initial conditions internal to the firm were earlier managerial choices. The skills and market position a firm has built today are the result of past choices about how to configure activities and what skills to create or acquire. Some of these choices, as Ghemawat's (1991) work among others had emphasized, involve hard-to-reverse commitments down certain paths (path dependency). Earlier choices, which have led to the current pool of internal skills and assets, are a reflection of the external environment surrounding the firm at the time. The earlier one pushes back in the chain of causality, the more it seems that successive managerial choices and initial conditions *external* to the firm govern outcomes.

The importance of managerial choice is also highlighted by the cross-sectional problem. Whatever configuration of activities and skills a firm has inherited may or may not be competitively valuable. Simply having pools of skills, knowledge, or other resources is not in and of itself a guarantee of success. They must be the right ones. If managers can understand their competitive environment and the sources of competitive advantages, they can better search creatively for favorable positions that are different from competitors', assemble the needed skills and assets, configure the value chain appropriately, and put in place supportive organizational routines and a culture which reinforces the required internal behavior. The most successful firms are notable in employing imagination to define a *new* position, or find *new* value in whatever starting position they have.

Towards a Dynamic Theory

How, then, do we make progress towards a truly dynamic theory of strategy? Scholars, in both strategy, organizational behavior, and economics, sensing this as the frontier question, have made some headway. There are three promising lines of enquiry that have been explored in recent years. Each addresses important questions, though focusing on a somewhat different aspect of the problem.

Game Theoretical Models

The first line of inquiry is the proliferation of game theoretic models of competitive interaction, referred to earlier, which seek to understand the equilibrium consequences of patterns of choices by competitors over a variety of strategic variables such as capacity and R&D. Since this literature is reviewed elsewhere in this volume,[16] the treatment here can be brief. The central concern of these models is to understand the conditions that lead to mutually consistent equilibria and the nature of these equilibria. Each model is restricted to one or a few variables, and the environment (technology, products, preferences, etc.) is assumed fixed except for the variables examined. Given this structure, timing plays a central role in determining outcomes. With a frame of reference in which these assumptions are plausible, Shapiro (1989) terms this literature a theory of business strategy.

These models have helped us understand better the logical consequences of choices over some important strategy variables. In particular, these models highlight the importance of information and beliefs about competitive reaction and the conditions required for a set of internally consistent choices among rivals.

Yet, this line of work stops short of a dynamic theory of strategy. By concentrating sequentially on small numbers of variables, the models fail to capture the simultaneous choices over many variables that characterize most industries. The models force a homogeneity of strategies. Yet it is the trade-offs and interactions involved in configuring the entire set of activities in the value chain that define distinct competitive positions. Finally, the models hold fixed many variables that we know are changing. Ironically, these models explore the dynamics of a largely static world. (The papers by Saloner, Camerer and Postrel raise additional useful questions.)

Commitment and Uncertainty

Another body of work is beginning to emerge on the problem of making irreversible commitments under uncertainty. Ghemawat's recent book (1991) is a notable example. The notion here is that strategy is manifested in a relatively few investment decisions that are hard to reverse, and which tend to define choices in other areas of the firm. These commitments must be made under uncertainty. Ghemawat highlights the importance of such choices, and argues that they should consume much of the attention in strategy analyses. He posits that analysis of such decisions must begin with cross-sectional frameworks. In choosing among feasible positions, however, Ghemawat stresses the need to carefully examine their sustainability and the influence of uncertainty in choosing among them. He brings a broader perspective to bear on sustainability than is present in the game theory models.

Related to Ghemawat's research is work that seeks to define ways of understanding the uncertainties a firm faces, and the alternative ways it can be addressed in strategy choices. The scenario technique for organizing and bounding uncertainty has received much attention.[17] More recently, taxonomies have begun to emerge which attempt to categorize the ways in which firms can respond to uncertainty.[18] In addition, Teisberg (1991b) begins to explore the biases and heuristics in decision-making in complex and uncertain circumstances that distort strategy choices, drawing on work in behavioral decision analysis and cognitive psychology.

---

[16] Editor's Note: See the articles by Garth Saloner, Colin Camerer, and Steven Postrel.
[17] See Wack (1985a,b) and Schwartz (1991).
[18] See Wernerfelt and Karnani (1987), Porter (1985, Chapter 13), Teisberg (1991a), and Collis (1991a).

This emerging stream of work emphasizes the lumpiness of strategy choices and the importance of uncertainty in making them. It sheds important light on how to approach discrete investment decisions from a rich strategic perspective. This comes at the price, however, of a focus on large, discrete, sequential investments rather than the simultaneous set of choices throughout the value chain that define a firm's competitive position. Like the game theoretic models, the environment is taken as relatively stable (though uncertain) so that commitments have long-lived consequences and the possibilities for reconfiguring the value chain are limited. This approach tends to stress the value of flexibility in dealing with change rather than the capacity to rapidly improve and innovate to nullify or overcome it. By focusing on discrete choices, the discretion a firm has to shape its environment, respond to environmental changes, or define entirely new positions is implicitly limited or not operationalized by most treatments.[19]

The Resource-based View

A third body of research in search of the origins of competitive advantage is the so-called resource-based view of the firm.[20] Closely related to the resource-based view is the notion of 'core competences' and treatments that stress intangible assets. Since this literature is more prominent and more extensive than that on commitment/uncertainty, it deserves a more detailed treatment.

Of the three literatures, the resource-based view is the most introspective and centred on the firm itself. The argument is that the origins of competitive advantage are valuable resources (or competences) that firms possess, which are often tangible assets such as skills, reputation, and the like. These resources are seen as relatively immobile, and as strengths to be nurtured and which should guide the choice of strategy. The implicit focus of much of this literature is on the underpinnings of successful diversification. It is, of course, essential when diversifying to understand a firm's distinctive strengths (remember Andrews).

The resource-based view has been proposed as an alternative theory of strategy.[21] What is really unique about a firm, so the argument goes, is its bundle of resources. It is factor market impediments, then, rather than product market circumstances that define success. The role of internal resources is an important insight for economic modelers, though less novel a notion for strategy researchers.

The promise of the resource view for the strategy field is the effort to address the longitudinal problem, or the conditions that allow firms to achieve and sustain favorable competitive positions over time. As with the other literatures, however,

---

[19] Teisberg's (1991a) essay, by making the influencing of industry structure a way of dealing with uncertainty, is an exception.

[20] Conversations with Cynthia Montgomery have stimulated and informed my interest in this literature. Perhaps the pioneer of this school is Penrose (1963). An early paper was Wernerfelt (1984). For other references, see the bibliographies in Peteraf (1990) and Collis (1991b). Recent papers include Barney (1991) and Grant (1991).

[21] Some writers in the resource school draw stylized comparisons with industrial organization (IO) based theories that confuse rather than clarify. For example, Peteraf's survey (1990) asserts that IO-based models focus only on the heterogeneity of markets while denying the heterogeneity of firms and the existence of differential competitive positions, to be based only on monopoly rents, to lead only to strategies of collusion, and to be restricted to formulating strategy at the business unit level. This view is puzzling unless one is talking about the IO-based models of the 1970s, before research aimed at bridging IO and firm strategy began.

more work remains to be done. At its worst, the resource-based view is circular. Successful firms are successful because they have unique resources. They should nurture these resources to be successful.[22] But what is a unique resource? What makes it valuable? Why was a firm able to create or acquire it? Why does the original owner or current holder of the resource not bid the value away? What allows a resource to retain its value in the future? There is once again a chain of causality, that this literature is just beginning to unravel.

Some authors have begun to deal with these questions by seeking to specify the conditions under which resources are valuable. Valuable resources are those that are superior in use, hard to imitate, difficult to substitute for, and more valuable within the firm than outside. Yet valuable resources, in order to yield profits to the firm, have been acquired for less than their intrinsic value due to imperfections in input markets, which Barney (1986) argues are usually due to informational asymmetries (read better managerial choices) or luck.

Yet, the resource-based view cannot be an alternative theory of strategy. It cannot be separated from the cross-sectional determinants of competitive advantage or, for that matter, from the conception of a firm as a collection of activities. Stress on resources must complement, not substitute for, stress on market positions.[23]

Resources are not valuable in and of themselves, but because they allow firms to perform activities that create advantages in particular markets. Resources are only meaningful in the context of performing certain activities to achieve certain competitive advantages. The competitive value of resources can be enhanced or eliminated by changes in technology, competitor behavior, or buyer needs which an inward focus on resources will overlook. More reliable Japanese products, for example, degraded the value of Xerox's copier service organization. The immobility of resources, then, is as likely to be a risk as a source of strength. For every firm with resources that convey advantage, there will be another (and perhaps many others) whose bundle resources impeded change or proved to be a liability in light of environmental changes.

Competitive advantage derives from more than just resources. Scale, sharing across activities, an optimal degree of integration, and other drivers have independent influences unless 'resources' are defined so broadly as to strain credibility. It is the collective advantage gained from all sources that determines relative performance.

The conditions which make a resource valuable bear a strong resemblance to industry structure. Bargaining power of suppliers refers to input markets, substitutability to the threat of substitution, and imitability to barriers to entry/mobility. The bargaining power of buyers, and the dissipation of resource rents through rivalry via price cutting or competition from alternative resource bundles, represent additional threats to the profitability of firms.

The connection between resources and activities is even more fundamental, however, because resources represent an inherently intermediate position in the chain of causality. Resources arise either from performing activities over time, acquiring them from outside, or some combination of the two. Both reflect prior managerial

---

[22] In this respect, the paper by Prahalad and Hamel (1990) is perhaps the most inward looking and the most troubling.

[23] Collis's (1991b) recent paper concludes on this point, which emerges from his detailed case study of ball bearings.

choices. Performing an activity or group of linked activities over time creates internal skills and routines which accumulate. It also can create external assets. A firm's reputation, for example, is a function of the history of its marketing and customer service activities among other things. Both internal and external assets depreciate, however, unless they are reinvigorated through continuing to perform activities. The rate of depreciation appears to vary widely across different types of assets, and can be rapid. Firms, then, have accumulated differing resources because of differing strategies and configuration of activities. Resources and activities are, in a sense, duals of each other.[24]

Resources, then, are intermediate between activities and advantage. An explicit link between resources and activities, along with the clear distinction between internal and external resources that was drawn earlier, is necessary to carefully define a resource in the first place. Some firm attributes termed 'resources' are activities—such as sales forces or R&D organizations. A second and more appropriate category of resources is skills, organizational routines, or other assets attached to particular activities or groups of interrelated activities.

The concept of activity drivers allows more precision in defining how resources were created. Some skills and routines emerge because of learning over time. This learning is a reflection of past strategy choices which have defined how activities are configured. Other resources were obtained through well-timed factor purchases (timing). Still others are the result of the ability to share across units. In turn, the resource view adds an important dimension to the concepts of activities and drivers. Underlying the ability to link activities or share them across business units, for example, are organizational skills and routines that represent important assets.

A final category of resources is external assets such as reputation and relationships.[25] These are normally created through performing activities over time. Recognizing these assets, and their link to the ongoing cost or differentiation of activities, is another valuable contribution of the resource view. The existence of such assets is implicit in the concept of drivers but not well developed.

All this still leaves unanswered the question, however, of the origins of competitive advantage. Why can valuable resources be created and sustained? Interestingly, the requirement of imperfect factor markets points strongly in the direction of managerial choice, and goes against the primacy of prior resources (initial conditions) in determining competitive advantage.

Resources whose value is obvious are bid up in value. Hence the presence of resources/activities within the firm that are rent-yielding is likely to reflect past managerial choices to assemble resources in unique ways, combine particular resources in a consistent way with many others, pursue new undiscovered market positions, or create resources internally. This allows resources to be acquired cheaply and avoids the bargaining away of their value to employees. Few resources begin as inherently scarce. Their scarcity is created through choice. Current managerial choices, in turn,

---

[24] Since the great preponderance of resources are created either by past activities or managerial choices to assemble outside resources in new activity configurations, my own view is that activities are logically prior. Yet it is clear that causality becomes blurred as accumulated resources affect the cost or uniqueness of activities.

[25] Defining a market position as a resource is inappropriate, because it confuses the longitudinal problem with the cross-sectional problem and obscures the mechanism by which advantage is created.

allow the innovative assembly of new resources and the rendering obsolete of prior ones.

The resource-based view will have the greatest significance in environments where change is incremental, the number of strategic variables and combinations is limited, so that a few scarce resources can govern outcomes, and the time period is short to intermediate term so that managerial choices can replicate or offset resource stocks. The greatest value of the resource view will be in assessing opportunities for diversification, provided the resource and activity views are integrated.[26] A resource-based view of diversification that defines resources broadly, however, runs the risk of justifying the sort of unrelated diversification that was so disastrous in the 1970s and 1980s.

THE ORIGINS OF THE ORIGINS

We are left still short of a dynamic theory of strategy, though we are beginning to learn about the subprocesses involved. In order to understand why firms choose and successfully implement the right strategies, and why their internal activities and assets are what they are, at least four important issues must be addressed.

First, a theory must deal simultaneously with both the firm itself as well as the industry and broader environment in which it operates. The environment both constrains and influences outcomes, which the more introspective resource view neglects. Second, a theory must allow centrally for exogenous change, in areas such as buyer needs, technology, and input markets. If there is little exogenous change, the choice of strategy can be viewed as a once-and-for-all game and the initial stock of (properly defined) resources can be crucial. In a world where exogenous change is rapid or relatively continuous, however, the analytical problem becomes far more complicated. The value of past resources is continually depreciated or even rendered negative. The choice of strategy is a series of ever-changing games in which the position in one game can influence, but does not determine, the position in the next one. Case after case illustrates that the leaders in one generation of products often fail to lead in the next.

Third, a theory must provide latitude to the firm not only to choose among well-defined options but to create new ones. The firm cannot be seen only as optimizing within tight constraints, but as having the ability to shift the constraints through creative strategy choices, other innovative activity, and the assembly of skills and other needed capabilities. There are alternative strategies open. The extent to which the environment shapes initial conditions and choice, in contrast to idiosyncratic, creative decision-making process within the firm, is a fundamental question.

A final issue that cuts across the others is the role of historical accident or chance. There is a growing belief that historical accidents influence competitive outcomes. Some of what economists term historical accidents may simply be good strategy choices, or reflect so far unmeasured aspects of the environment. There are often reasons why firms are 'lucky', as I will stress below. Be that as it may, the extent of randomness in competition, and the role of true luck, has an important influence on how one develops a theory of strategy.

---

[26] See Montgomery and Wernerfelt (1988) and Montgomery and Hariharan (1991).

Origins Within the Firm

How then, do we explain good strategic choices and the ability to carry them out? One view is that since the number of variables is substantial and environmental change is continuous and unpredictable, the problem is not selecting good strategies but creating a flexible organization that learns and is able to continually redefine its strategy. The resource view, taken to an unhealthy extreme, is sometimes argued as encompassing this position. The critical resources are the capacity for learning and adaptation.

The problem with this notion is its collision with empirical reality. Most successful organizations improve but do not change strategy very often.[27] They gain advantage from new insights into competition and from consistent refinement of their ability to implement a stable overall strategy (e.g. differentiation) though its details are continually evolving and improving.

Another view of the origins of advantage is that it lies in the ability to make good strategy choices and implement them. While this can happen by chance, the odds are elevated by better information and careful analysis. Once a choice is made, the successful organization is one that can bring all its activities into consistency with the strategy and rapidly accumulate the necessary activities and resources. New choices are made as the environment changes or as accumulating activities and resources open up new options. But, it must be said, a prominent role for choice and capacity for implementation still begs the question of why some firms are better at it than others.

The Environment as the Origin of Advantage

Instead of solely within the firm, the true origin of competitive advantage may be the proximate or local environment in which a firm is based. The proximate environment will define many of the input (factor) markets the firm has to draw on, the information that guides strategic choices, and the incentives and pressures on firms to both innovate and accumulate skills or resources over time. Competitive advantage, then, may reside as much in the environment as in an individual firm. The environment shapes how activities are configured, which resources can be assembled uniquely, and what commitments can be made successfully.

This richer view of the role of the environment has emerged from my study of the causes of international competitive success in a large sample of industries in 10 leading trading nations. This line of work emerged from a puzzle. After having written about global strategy, and the ability of firms to transcend national markets, I observed that competitive advantage in particular industries was often strongly concentrated in one or two countries, often with several if not many successful home-based competitors. These local rivals pursue different strategies and push each other to innovate and improve much more rapidly than foreign rivals, which allows them to penetrate and prosper in foreign markets. The concentration of successful competitors was particularly pronounced if one examined strategically distinct industry segments rather than broad aggregates, and if one excludes cases where firms were not truly successful but merely surviving or sheltered by government intervention. While the focus of the research was on the role of the national environment, it was also clear that successful

---

[27] See Porter (1990) and Ghemawat (1991).

firms were also geographically concentrated *within* nations. The same theoretical framework can be used to help explain the concentration of success in nations, regions within nations, or even cities. It also seems possible to extend it to help explain why one particular firm outperforms others.

The starting point for the theory is that environmental change is relentless and firms, through innovation, have considerable latitude in both influencing their environment and responding to it. Firms create and sustain competitive advantage because of the capacity to continuously improve, innovate, and upgrade their competitive advantages over time. Upgrading is the process of shifting advantages throughout the value chain to more sophisticated types, and employing higher levels of skill and technology. Successful firms are those that improve and innovate in ways that are valued not only at home but elsewhere. Competitive success is enhanced by moving early in each product or process generation, provided that movement is along a path that reflects evolving technology and buyer needs, and that early movers subsequently upgrade their positions rather than rest on them. In this view, firms have considerable discretion in relaxing external and internal constraints.

These imperatives of competitive advantage, however, collide with the organizational tendencies of firms. Firms value stability, and change is difficult and unsettling. Strong external or environmental influences are often essential in overcoming these tendencies.

Environmental Determinants of Innovation and Upgrading

Four broad attributes of the proximate environment of a firm have the greatest influence on its ability to innovate and upgrade, illustrated in Figure 6.5. These attributes, which I collectively term the diamond, shape the information firms have available to perceive opportunities, the pool of inputs, skills and knowledge they can draw on, the goals that condition investment, and the pressures on firms to act. The environment is important in providing the initial insight that underpins competitive advantage, the

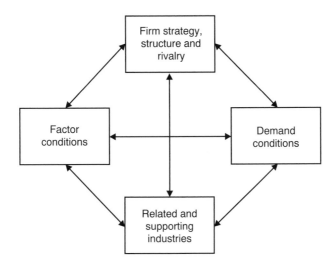

Figure 6.5. Determinants of National Competitive Advantage

inputs needed to act on it, and to accumulate knowledge and skills over time, and the forces needed to keep progressing.

The most important factors of production are highly specialized factors tailored to the needs of particular industries. Generalized factor pools are either readily available or easy to source through global networks. Specialized local factor pools support the most rapid accumulation of skill and the greatest rate of innovation. Generic technology is readily sourced from distant suppliers, but transfer of know-how benefits from proximity. Specialized factors are almost always created through private and social investments. The presence of unique institutional mechanisms for creating them in particular industries is an important determinant of competitive success. Selective disadvantages in the more basic factors (e.g. unskilled labor, natural resources) are, paradoxically, often a source of advantage. They break dependence on factor costs and trigger innovation and upgrading.

Home demand is important more for its character than its size. Home demand plays a disproportionate role in influencing the perception of buyer needs and the capacity of firms to improve products and services over time. Sophisticated and/or especially demanding home customers often stimulate competitive success, as do home market needs that anticipate those elsewhere.

Competitive advantage is also strongly influenced by the presence of home-based suppliers and related industries in those products, components, machines, or services that are specialized and/or integral to the process of innovation in the industry. Inputs themselves are mobile, but there are local externalities for the process of innovation in interactions between the firm and local input suppliers. Home-based suppliers and related industries provide advantages in terms of information, signalling, access to new technologies, and market pressures. In many industries, the scarce technology is know-how, which can be difficult to transfer without cultural and physical proximity. Companies with home-based suppliers have the opportunity to influence their suppliers' technical efforts, help establish specifications to fit particular needs, serve for test sites for R&D work, and maintain senior management contact. All of these accelerate the pace of innovation.

The final determinant of advantage is firm strategy, structure, and rivalry, or the context for competition in a region or nation. The national and local environments have a strong influence on management practices, forms of organization and the goals set by individuals and companies. The presence of local rivalry also has a profound influence on the rate of improvement, innovation, and ultimate success in an industry. Local rivals provide a greater stimulus to upgrading than foreign rivals. Proximity speeds information flow and improves incentives to compete. The presence of domestic competitors negates basic factor advantages and forces firms to develop higher order and more sustainable advantages. Actual rivalry provides a greater stimulus than potential rivalry. Intense local rivalry may hold down profits in the home market but spurs advantages that allow attractive profits (contingent on overall industry structure) in global markets.

Local rivalry also feeds back to improve other parts of the diamond. It overcomes monopsony-based impediments to the development of specialized suppliers, stimulates greater investments in specialized factors such as university programs and specialized infrastructure, helps to upgrade local demand, and so on.

There is a role for true chance events and historical accidents in the process by which competitive advantage is created, an issue which I raised earlier. However, historical accidents are less common than upon first impression. What appear to be accidents are really events driven by conditions in the diamond. Also, the role of accidents cannot be seen independently of more stable aspects of the local or national environment. True accidents rarely result in competitive industries unless other favorable conditions in the diamond are present. Similarly, accidents that simultaneously occur in different locations result in a competitive firm in that location with the most favorable diamond.

There are many cases where a company founded in one location, through an act of pure entrepreneurship, relocated its operations to another location or even to another country because that new location offered a better setting in which to nurture or reap the rewards of that innovation. The pilgrimage of aspiring actors and actresses to Hollywood is simply one example of how ideas and talent flow to the environment in which they can command the highest returns. The ability to command the highest returns depends on the simultaneous presence of unusual local demand, related industries, active rivals bidding, and other aspects of the diamond.

A final influence on the environment for competitive advantage is government. The role of government policy is best understood by looking at how it influences the diamond. Government at all levels can improve or impede national advantage through its investments in factor creation, through its influence on the goals of individuals and firms, through its role as a buyer or influencer of buyer needs, through its competition policies, and through its role in related and supporting industries, among other ways. Government plays an important part in shaping the pressures, incentives, and capabilities of the nation's firms.

Government's proper role is as a catalyst and challenger. It is to encourage, or even push, companies to raise their aspirations and move to higher levels of competitive performance, even though this process may be unpleasant and difficult. Government plays a role that is inherently partial, and that succeeds only when working in tandem with favorable underlying conditions in the diamond. Government policies that succeed are those that create an environment in which companies can gain competitive advantage rather than those that involve government directly in the process. (It is an indirect, rather than direct, role.)

The Diamond as a Dynamic System

These aspects of the local environment constitute a dynamic system. This character of the environment bears centrally on the firm processes that give rise to advantage. The effect of one determinant depends on the state of others. The presence of sophisticated and demanding buyers, for example, will not result in advanced products or production processes unless the quality of human resources enables firms to respond to buyer needs. There must also be a climate that supports sustained investment to fund the development of these products and processes. Similarly, having selective disadvantages in basic factors (e.g. higher labor, energy, or raw material costs) will not spur innovation and upgrading unless there is an environment of vigorous competition among firms to trigger innovation in people, products, and processes. It is this contingent relationship that explains why, for example, a selective factor disadvantage stimulates innovation in one country while hastening decline in another.

The parts of the diamond are also mutually reinforcing. The development of specialized supporting industries, for example, tends to increase the supply of specialized factors. Vigorous domestic rivalry stimulates the development of unique pools of specialized factors. This is particularly likely if the rivals are all located in one city or region. The University of California at Davis, for example, has become the world's leading center for wine-making research, working closely with the California wine industry. Active local rivalry also upgrades home demand through educating buyers and providing choice, and promotes the formation of related and supported industries. Japan's world-leading group of semi-conductor producers, for example, has spawned world-leading Japanese semiconductor equipment manufacturers.[28]

The effects can work in all directions, and causality can become blurred over time. Sometimes world-class suppliers become new entrants in the industry they have been supplying. Or highly sophisticated buyers may enter a supplier industry, particularly when they have relevant skills and view the upstream industry as strategic. In the case of the Japanese robotics industry, for example, Matsushita and Kawasaki originally designed robots for internal use before selling them to others.

The diamond also bears centrally on a nation's ability to *attract* factors of production, rather than merely serve as a location for them. This represents a final form of mutual reinforcement. Mobile factors, particularly ideas and highly skilled individuals, are becoming increasingly important to international competitiveness. Mobile factors tend to be drawn to the location where they can achieve the greatest productivity, because that is where they can obtain the highest returns. The theory outlined above, because it focuses on the determinants of productivity, also explains the attraction of mobile factors. The same features that make a nation an attractive home base also help it attract mobile factors.

The national and local environment for competing in a particular industry itself evolves in a dynamic process. The environment is created over time through the mutual reinforcement of the determinants. It begins with an inheritance drawn from other industries and history, and exists amid a set of local institutions, values, and attitudes. The mutual reinforcement of the determinants, which reflect in part the actions of firms themselves, build up the environment over time. As this process proceeds, causality becomes blurred.

In industries with modest levels of skill and technology, firms can gain advantage solely on the basis of factor advantages such as cheap labor or abundant raw materials. Such advantages are notoriously unstable, however, in a world of globalization, technological change, and rapid substitution. Competitive advantage in more sophisticated industries and industry segments, on the other hand, rarely results from strength in a single determinant. Sustained success in these industries and segments usually requires the interaction of favorable conditions in several of the determinants and at least parity in the others. This is because advantages in various parts of the diamond are self-reinforcing.

It is thus the juxtaposition of advantages throughout the diamond in one location that leads to competitive success, far more than the presence of any single advantage

---

[28] The mutual reinforcement of the determinants suggests a particularly important role for local rivalry, healthy new business formation, and the responsiveness of local institutions to signals from industry. Local rivalry stimulates improvements in all the other determinants. New business formation, whether through start-up or internal development, is a *sine qua non* of developing related and supporting industries as well as healthy rivalry. Competitive advantage also depends on the capacity of the local education system, infrastructure providers, and government institutions to respond to the specialized needs of particular industries. Institutional responsiveness allows the proper types of skills, resources, and infrastructure to be created.

no matter how compelling. The firm's home base, which consists of that group of activities most centrally involved in the process of innovation and learning, must be located in the same place to allow the internal coordination and contact with the local environment that is necessary for rapid progress. The ability of a firm to progress rapidly and appropriately by integrating research and production spread widely among several locations, combining machines sourced from many disparate distant suppliers, and so on is limited. The firm that concentrates its core activities at a favorable home base, while competing nationally and globally, will normally progress more rapidly. Activities outside the home base are focused on sourcing low-cost basic factors and securing market access.

These same arguments explain why we observe *clusters* of competitive industries in one location. Clusters involve supplier industries, customer industries, and related industries that are all competitive. Such clusters are characteristic of every advanced economy—American entertainment, German chemicals, Japanese electronics, Danish foods. Clusters grow and transform themselves through spinoffs and diversification of firms into upstream, downstream, and related industries and activities. The fields where several clusters overlap are often fertile grounds for new business formation. In Japan, for example, the interstices between electronics and new materials are spawning new competitive strengths in fields as diverse as robotics and displays.

Another implication of this theory is the importance of geographic concentration of successful firms and clusters within particular cities or regions. National clusters are often themselves geographically concentrated. Geographic concentration elevates and magnifies the interaction of the four determinants, improves information flow and signaling, makes innovation-enhancing interactions with customers and specialized suppliers less costly, and provides a check on opportunistic behavior, among other benefits.[29]

Firms lose competitive advantage either because of emerging weaknesses in their local environment or due to rigidities or other internal problems that external circumstances cannot overcome.[30] For example, a major shift in technology may require an entirely new set of specialized suppliers that are not present, or local demand characteristics may evolve in ways that distract from instead of foreshadow international needs. However, firms sometimes fail not because their environment is unfavorable but because of organizational or managerial rigidities that block improvement and change. The environment can provide important pressures to advance, but firms differ in their responsiveness to them.

Environmental Influences on the Dynamics of Strategy

The environment, via the diamond, affects both a firm's initial conditions and its managerial choices. The diamond, through its influence on information and incentives, shapes the content of strategies. It influences the ability of firms to carry out particular types of strategies, hence limiting choice. Choices that may look accidental or internally driven are often partly or wholly derived from the local diamond. Over time, through its stress on markets for difficult-to-trade inputs, the state of the diamond conditions the rate of accumulation of resources. It also sets the pressures on firms to

---

[29] For a detailed treatment and empirical tests, see Enright (1990). See, also, Krugman (1991).
[30] I discuss these issues more fully elsewhere. See Porter (1990).

improve and upgrade. The diamond, then, begins to address a dynamic theory of strategy early in the chain of causality.

Yet firms retain a central role. Firms must understand and exploit their local environment in order to achieve competitive advantage. There are often sharp differences in the performance of firms based in the same region or nation. These differences are partly a function of managerial choices, differential rates of resource accumulation, or chance. The differences also appear, however, to be partly a function of the subenvironment of each particular firm—its particular early customers, supplier relationships, factor market access, etc.

An important role for the local environment in competitive success does not eliminate the role of strategy nor the need for competitive analysis. Industry structure, positioning, activities, resources, and commitments remain important. Rather, the diamond highlights new issues for strategy that are normally ignored, such as the importance of developing and nurturing home-based suppliers, the importance of local specialized factor markets, and the balance between home-based activities and those dispersed to other locations as part of a national or global strategy.

The local environment creates potential for competitive success, but firms must sense and respond to it. Firms also have a considerable ability to influence their environment in ways that reinforce or detract from their capacity to accumulate skills and resources and to innovate—there is a feedback loop between firm actions and the local diamond. Many if not most firms, even in favorable environments, do *not* achieve competitive advantage. Firms based in an unattractive environment, however, face profound challenges in achieving competitive success. More and more firms are relocating their home bases accordingly.

Issues for Further Research

Recent research has begun to shed some light on the chain of causality that constitutes a dynamic theory of strategy, but many unanswered questions remain. I would highlight four that deserve special attention. First, we need to better understand the balance between environmental determinism and company/leader choice in shaping competitive outcomes. What is emerging is the beginnings of a more sophisticated way of understanding how the environment surrounding a firm influences both firm choices and outcomes, and of the internal processes of choice and of skill and asset (resource) accumulation that underpin competitive advantage. It is clear that company actions still matter, and that firms in a given environment achieve widely different levels of success. Can we, by looking across different firms in a given nation or city, isolate unique subenvironments that explain these differing levels of performance? Or, can we identify patterns of commitments to activities and resource accumulation that characterize superior performers?

Second, we need to better understand the degree of stickiness or inertia in competitive positions once a firm stops progressing, or, to put it another way, the durability of early mover advantages? How important is a burst of innovation vs. the capacity to improve and innovate continuously? How important are pure rents from scarce factors vs. advantage resulting from innovation or which raise the value of factors? My research suggests that the latter is characteristic of successful firms who have sustained their competitive positions, but much more investigation is necessary.

Third, we need to know how necessary or helpful it is to push even further back in the chain of causality. I have argued that resources are an intermediate step in the chain, from which we can learn. Yet an important theoretical issue is where in the chain of causality to best cut into the problem. An example will illustrate that even a focus on the local environment of the firm does not go to the ultimate origin of advantage. The presence of a specialized skill in a region or nation is often the result of skill pools inherited from other industries as well as human resources trained at pre-existing institutions. These institutions, however, often draw to some extent on the general education system which itself is affected by social values and history. Just how far back to the ultimate source does one need to go to best examine these questions? I chose in my own research to model the phenomenon at the level of the diamond, while highlighting that each of its components is the result of history and other local conditions. The appropriateness of this choice is a subject for research. It should be said that understanding the ultimate origins of advantage may not always be necessary for thinking about how to improve future advantage.

Finally, there is the important challenge of crafting empirical research to make further progress in understanding these questions. Some argue that models that exceed a certain level of complexity can never be tested. Yet it is clear that there are many aspects of both firms and their environment which determine competitive success. How can we collect and analyze data to help us discriminate among explanations and weigh the various factors? I concluded in my most recent research that detailed longitudinal case studies, covering long periods of time, were necessary to study these phenomena. Moreover, these case studies had to encompass a large number and wide range of industries and national contexts in order to develop confidence about the appropriate variables and their influence on outcomes. This style of research nudges strategy research, and indeed industrial economics, into the world of the historian. It also involves enormous fixed costs. I am convinced that more research of this type will be needed to address the dynamics of strategy. It also raises the question of whether there are other approaches to empirical testing to address these issues, or whether we must wait until theories have been much better developed before we can highlight the relatively few variables which can be measured and rigorously examined statistically.

ACKNOWLEDGEMENTS

I am grateful to Pankaj Ghemawat, Cynthia Montgomery, and others in the Competition and Strategy group at Harvard for a long series of discussions that have immensely benefited my thinking about these issues, and to Jay Barney, Richard Rumelt, and Garth Saloner for their insights while visiting. David Collis, Cynthia Montgomery, Richard Rumelt, Elizabeth Teisberg and Dan Schendel provided helpful comments on this manuscript.

REFERENCES

Andrews, K. R. *The Concept of Corporate Strategy*, Dow Jones-Irwin, Homewood, IL, 1971.

Baldwin, C. Y. and K. B. Clark. 'Capabilities and capital investment: New perspectives on capital budgeting', Harvard Business School Working Paper #92–004, Rev. 7/15/1991.

Barney, J. B. 'Strategic factor markets: Expectations, luck and business strategy', *Management Science*, **32**, October 1986, pp. 1231–1241.

Barney, J. B. 'Firm resources and sustained competitive advantage. *Journal of Management*, **17**(1), 1991, pp. 99–120.

Collis, D. J. 'The strategic management of uncertainty', Harvard Business School Working Paper #89–019, Rev. 3/1991a.

Collis, D. J. 'A resource-based analysis of global competition: The case of the bearings industry', *Strategic Management Journal*, Special Issue, Summer 1991b, pp. 49–68.

Cooper, R. and R. S. Kaplan. 'Measure costs right: Make the right decisions', *Harvard Business Review*, September–October 1988, pp. 96–103.

Cooper, R. and R. S. Kaplan. *The Design of Cost Management Systems*, Prentice Hall, Englewood Cliffs, NJ, 1991.

Enright, M. J. 'Geographic concentration and industrial organization', unpublished doctoral dissertation, Business Economics Program, Harvard University, 1990.

Ghemawat, P. *Commitment: The Dynamic of Strategy*. Free Press, New York, 1991.

Grant, R. M. 'The resource-based theory of competitive advantage: Implications for strategy formulations', *California Management Review*, Spring 1991, pp. 119–135.

Itami, H. (with T. W. Roehl). *Mobilizing Invisible Assets*, Harvard University Press, Cambridge, MA and London, England, 1987.

Johnson, H. T. and R. S. Kaplan. *Relevance Lost: The Rise and Fall of Management Accounting*, Harvard Business School Press, Boston, MA, 1987.

Krugman, P. R. *Geography and Trade*, MIT Press, Cambridge, MA, 1991.

Learned, E. P., C. R. Christensen, K. R. Andrews and W. D. Guth. *Business Policy Text and Cases*, Richard D. Irwin, Homewood, IL, 1965.

Mintzberg, H. 'The Design School: Reconsidering the basic premises of strategic management', *Strategic Management Journal*, **11**(3), March–April 1990, pp. 171–195.

Montgomery, C. A. and B. Wernerfelt. 'Diversification, Ricardian Rents, and Tobin's *q*', *Rand Journal of Economics*, **19**(4), Winter 1988, pp. 623–632.

Montgomery, C. A. and S. Hariharan. 'Diversified expansion by large established firms', *Journal of Economic Behavior and Organizations*, **15**, 1991, pp. 71–89.

Penrose, E. T. *The Theory of the Growth of the Firm*, Blackwell, Oxford, 1963.

Peteraf, M. A. 'The resource-based model: An emerging paradigm for strategic management', Discussion Paper 90–29, J. L. Kellogg Graduate School of Management, Northwestern University, August 1990.

Porter, M. E. *Competitive Strategy: Techniques for Analyzing Industries and Competitors*, Free Press, New York, 1980.

Porter, M. E. *Competitive Advantage: Creating and Sustaining Superior Performance*, Free Press, New York, 1985.

Porter, M. E. 'From competitive advantage to corporate strategy', *Harvard Business Review*, May–June, 1987, pp. 43–59.

Porter, M. E. *The Competitive Advantage of Nations*, Free Press, New York, 1990.

Porter, M. E., (ed.) *Competition in Global Industries*, Harvard Business School Press, Boston, MA, 1986.

Porter, M. E. and V. A. Millar. 'How information gives you competitive advantage', *Harvard Business Review*, July–August 1985, pp. 149–160.

Prahalad, C. K. and G. Hamel. 'The core competence of the corporation', *Harvard Business Review*, May–June 1990, pp. 71–91.

Schwartz, P. *The Art of the Long View*, Doubleday, New York, 1991.

Selznick, P. *Leadership in Administration: A Sociological Interpretation*, Harper & Row, New York, 1957.

Shapiro, C. 'The theory of business strategy', *Rand Journal of Economics*, **20**, Spring 1989, pp. 125–137.

Teisberg, E. O. 'Strategic response to uncertainty', Harvard Business School case, #N9–391–192, Rev. 4/11/1991a.

Teisberg, E. O. 'Why do good managers choose poor strategies?' Harvard Business School Case #N9–391–172, Rev. 3/5/1991b.

Wack, P. 'Scenarios: Uncharted waters ahead', *Harvard Business Review*, September–October 1985a, pp. 73–89.

Wack, P. 'Scenarios: Shooting the rapids', *Harvard Business Review*, November–December 1985b, pp. 139–150.

Wernerfelt, B. 'A resource-based view of the firm', *Strategic Management Journal*, **5**(2), April–June 1984, pp. 171–180.

Wernerfelt, B. and A. Karnani. 'Competitive strategy under uncertainty', *Strategic Management Journal*, **8**(2), 1987.

Chapter 7

Strategic Resources: Traits, Configurations and Paths to Sustainable Competitive Advantage

Janice A. Black and Kimberly B. Boal
College of Business Administration, Texas Tech University, Lubbock, Texas, USA

Positioning the firm for a sustainable competitive advantage by utilizing the firm's strengths to exploit opportunities and neutralize threats while avoiding or fixing weaknesses has long served as the core framework for formulating the firm's strategy (Learned *et al.*, 1965). This 'SWOT' analysis benefited greatly from the insights of industrial organizational economics, especially the work of Porter (1980; 1985). Porter's famous five forces model emphasized analyzing industry structure to assess the rent earning potential of the industry based on entry and exit barriers. While Porter's framework has provided many useful insights to both practitioners and researchers by concentrating on the external 'OT' side of the analysis, it nonetheless suffers from several significant problems.

First, it runs the risk of being tautological, i.e., it posits that firms in attractive industries are successful. They are successful because they are in attractive industries. A second, but more important limitation of this framework is pointed out by Porter (1991) himself. The framework is concerned with the cross-sectional problem and not the longitudinal problem. The cross-sectional problem focuses on what makes some industries, and some positions within them more attractive. It does not address why some firms are able to get into advantageous positions in the first place, and why some firms are able to sustain these positions and others are not. A third limitation stems from the implicit advice it gives to managers for formulating strategy. McWilliams and Smart (1993) point out that it misdirects managers to focus on industry level characteristics, encouraging them to expend resources on influencing the industry's structure even though their firm will not uniquely benefit from the changes, thus allowing competitors to free ride on the firm's expenditures. One could possibly justify this if it could be shown that industry structure was the dominant determinant of firm performance. Recent evidence however, (Rumelt, 1991; Roquebert, Phillips, and Duran, 1993), suggests that, at best, industry structure accounts for 8–15 percent of variance in firm performance. Furthermore, strategies based on market power can be disastrous to the firm.

Reprinted from *Strategic Management Journal*, Volume 15, pp. 131–148, Summer Special Issue, Copyright © 1994, John Wiley & Sons.

For example, Carr (1993) in his analysis of the vehicle components industry found that firms utilizing a market power based strategy significantly underperformed, on multiple performance measures, their competitors who followed a resource-based strategy.

These limitations lead many (e.g., Barney, 1986, 1991; Grant, 1991) to argue that strategy formulation starts properly, not with an assessment of the organization's external environment, but with an assessment of the organization's resources, capabilities, and core competencies. This resource based view (RBV) of the firm approach which emphasizes the internal side of 'SWOT' analysis to strategy formulation is gaining in popularity among strategy theorists Reed and DeFillipi, 1990; Summer *et al.*, 1990; Meyer, 1991; Porter, 1991; Peteraf, 1993; Barney, 1991, 1992). This emerging framework already contributes some promising insight into conditions leading to sustainable competitive advantages (Conner, 1991; Grant, 1991; Peteraf, 1993). RBV theory notes that differences in firm resources will lead to differences in sustainable competitive advantage (SCA).

Porter argues that RBV theory also runs the risk of being tautological, 'Successful firms are successful because they have unique resources. They should nurture these resources to be successful (1991: 108).' Barney (1993) points out that the independent variables of RBV are defined at one level of analysis (the level of resources or bundles of resources) while competitive advantage, not economic rent *per se*, (the dependent variable) is at a different level of analysis (the level of strategies that the firm is pursuing). In essence, the independent variable is at the functional level and the dependent variable is either at the business or corporate level. This eliminates the charge of RBV being tautological.

Bromiley (1993) notes that RBV theory requires some concrete definitions of resources that is less than 'anything that leads to performance.' There is acknowledged difficulty in determining *a priori* what firm resources might lead to a sustainable competitive advantage given the inherent uncertainty of the external environment (Peteraf, 1993; Fiol, 1991). Nonetheless, Bromiley's (1993) call for the operationalization of RBV theory is well taken.

Jay Barney begins to address this issue by identifying the needed characteristics of firm resources and presents this in the VRIO framework (Barney and Griffin, 1992; Barney, 1992). This framework assesses the economic performance implications of resources by evaluating the resources for the characteristics of value, rareness, inimitability and organizational orientation (VRIO).

The value of a resource will be dependent upon the firm's combination of resources and the path that the firm is following. In other words, value is the fit of the resource or factor to strategy combined with the fit of the strategy to the external environment. The rareness of a specific resource depends upon the combination of physical rareness in the factor market and/or the rareness of the perceived value of the resource due to a firm's particular resource combination. Inimitability is the continuation of imperfect factor markets via restricted information, the cost of recreating the specific combination of resources that give a synergistic result, or a combination of the two. Substitutability rests on the continuation of imperfect factor markets, the costs involved in the recreation of specific combination, or the cost of finding a new combination of resources that will enable the firm to compete for the same product market (i.e., a new path with new requirements). Barney's framework combines inimitability and nonsubstitutability into one category by treating nonsubstitutability as a specialized case of inimitability. Finally, the VRIO framework also explicitly considers if the organization is oriented to utilize its strategic resources.

However, the VRIO framework, while implicitly acknowledging the importance of a dynamic view, treats the evaluation of resources from a stand alone viewpoint ignoring how resources are nested in and configured with one another and the nature of relationships between them. Thus while Barney *talks* about bundles of resources, the VRIO framework treats resources as singular distinct items.

Another internal analysis that also reflects this bundling problem is the Capital Asset Pricing Model (CAPM). When CAPM is used to assess an investment decision, it considers a portfolio of investments as a cross-sectional point-in-time issue similar to RBV theory and its bundle of resources. CAPM assessments ignore whether an investment in one project will affect the profitability of other ongoing or potential projects (Oviatt, 1989). Rather than investigating these internal relationships it assumes away these problematic interactions. Furthermore, as Robins notes in his evaluation of the CAPM model, the existence of firm specific capital raises 'serious problems in the use of the CAPM to estimate the risk associated with a capital project.' (1992: 528) He points out that all firms have collateral assets (X-assets) that are firm specific but do not have defined opportunity cost and do not exist in isolation from other tradeable assets. A firm's ability to generate quasi-rents is a function of the interaction between these X-assets and other marketable assets that the firm possesses. Yet, these X-assets (e.g., organizational routines, company policy, culture, etc.) will result in errors in the assessment of risk because of the unknown nature of that interaction. This example not only highlights the bundling problems but also points out the inadequacies of financial statements to accurately display asset value. This latter point is also supported by Hall as he too questions 'the significance of any quantification of shareholder' funds which does not recognize the value of intangible assets' (1992: 135).

Although the use of teams or bundles of resources have been acknowledged in RBV theory (Grant, 1991; Dierickx and Cool, 1989; Fiol, 1991), most researchers do not address the dynamic aspects of bundling resources and their implications to RBV. Thus, while the RBV theory runs the risk of evaluating and categorizing resources without reference to the system in which those resources are embedded, it has not totally ignored interfactor relationships. For example, two such postulated relationships are Teece's (1986) discussion of cospecialized assets, and Amit and Schoemaker's (1993) notion of complementarity relationships affecting the value of a resource. However, these ideas of how resources within a firm interact with things both inside and/or outside the firm to create sustainable competitive advantage need further development.

In this paper we operationalize RBV theory by developing the network of relationships among resources that is necessary for the creation of the characteristic traits identified by RBV theorists that are needed to attain a sustainable competitive advantage. The paper is organized as follows. The first section gives definitions of key RBV terms used in this paper. The second section looks closer at the contribution network theory makes to our understanding of firm resources. The third section clarifies the identification of RBV strategic system resources. The fourth section discusses the potential strategic relationship configurations in detail. The last section presents implications from this expansion of the RBV theory and our conclusions.

DEFINITIONS OF FIRM RESOURCES AND RELATIONSHIPS

Given the relative youth of RBV theory, we explain our usage of the key terms and concepts. By accepting resources as the basic unit of analysis (Grant, 1991) and constraining the resources of interest to strategic resources which are those that are theoretically characterized as valuable, rare, neither imitable and/or substitutable, and which an organization is oriented towards using (Barney, 1986, 1991; Dierickx and Cool, 1989; Summer, *et al.*, 1990), we bound our area of interest.

RESOURCE FACTORS AND CATEGORIES

Several researchers decompose firm resources into combinations of resource 'factors' or 'assets' (Barney, 1986; Dierickx and Cool, 1989; Porter, 1991; Grant, 1991; Mahoney and Pandian, 1992). Since 'assets' implies something that is owned by a firm and factors include either ownership and/or control, we choose to use factors as the elements making up a resource. While specific relationships between the factors that make up a particular resource have remained unexplored, general characteristics have been addressed. Barney (1986) points out that resource factors differ in their 'tradeability'. A tradeable factor is one that can be specifically identified and its monetary value determined via a 'strategic factor market. Tradeable factors' availability and monetary value in the factor markets will reflect the market's awareness of those factors' total rareness (physical and/or particular use). By implication, a nontradeable factor will be firm specific and will not directly have its monetary value determined via that 'strategic factor market'. As an example, Arrow has earlier brought attention to the factor of 'trust' which, if purchased, immediately creates doubts in the mind of the purchaser about what he/she purchased. This is a prime example of something built up over time that is valuable but not tradeable. He emphasizes this point in the following:

> Trust and similar value, loyalty, or truthtelling are examples of what an economist would call 'externalities'. They are goods, they are commodities; they have real practice value; they increase the efficiency of the system, enable you to produce more goods or more of whatever values you hold in high esteem. But they are not commodities, for which trade on the open market is technically possible or even meaningful. (1974: 23).

Dierickx and Cool (1989) suggest that resources should be differentiated as either asset flows or asset stocks. An asset flow is a firm resource that can be obtained or adjusted immediately. An asset stock is a firm resource which cannot be adjusted immediately and which is built up over time from asset flows (Dierickx and Cool, 1989). We name this aspect the 'acquisition process'. Again since a company may utilize both something it directly owns and something that it controls, we choose to use 'factor' in referring to the element that helps to create a resource.

The creation of a 2×2 matrix with the two dimensions of 'tradeability aspects' and 'acquisition process aspects' enables us to look at four factor types as described in Table 7.1. Note that four general factors types are possible: tradeable asset flows, nontradeable asset flows, tradeable asset stocks, and nontradeable asset stocks. It is the bundling of these four types of factors that results in a particular resource. Thus

Table 7.1.

Tradeability Factors	Acquisition Process Factors	
	Stocks	Flows
Tradeable	Tradeable asset stocks	Tradeable asset flows
Nontradeable	Nontradeable asset stocks	Nontradeable asset flows

Note: This table has been constructed and inserted by the editors.

resources can be viewed as a configuration or network of factors. This in turn implies that there will be specific relationships between the factors.

RESOURCE CATEGORIES

Several resource level categorizations recently have been presented in the literature. Barney (1991) groups all firm resources into three categories: physical capital resources (Williamson, 1975), human capital resources (Becker, 1964) and organizational capital resources (Tomer, 1987). Grant (1991) lists six categories of firm resources: financial, physical, human, technological, reputation, and organizational. These categorical schemes appear to miss the key issue in the search for sustainable competitive advantage (SCA). The key issue for firm resources, as regards the creation and maintenance of SCA, is based on the ability of the resource to generate rent. While rent generation's economic root is based on the differential between the expected rent and the actual rent attained by a resource (Barney, 1993) the bulk of the work rests also on implications of scarcity.

Scarcity is related to the ease of identification of the bundle of factors that creates or is the resource. If the bundle is a relatively simple one which can be identified, then the ability to imitate or find substitutes is increased and the opportunity for rent generation is decreased (Grant, 1991) and vice versa. Thus a more useful categorization would be one that focuses on this scarcity issue. Because of the link between scarcity and identification, we chose to categorize resources on the degree to which the factors that make up the resource bundle can be identified. This categorization divides firm resources into two types: contained resources and system resources.

Contained Resources

A contained resource is comprised of an identified *simple network* of resource factors that can be monetarily valued. By 'network', we mean the configuration of factors, as well as, their relationships with each other that results in a particular firm resource. We think that including both factors and their relationships is an important distinction, for the same reason that a list of ingredients from a recipe is not a cake. A cake requires the ingredients plus their relationships among them for a successful result. A simple network is one with relatively few, mostly direct, links among a small number of factors. 'Simple,' thus, implies that the network has definite boundaries. It is possible, then, to identify contained resources and, once identified, to monetarily value them (Barney, 1986; 1989). This supports Barney's contention that both asset stocks and asset flows are tradeable either at the resource level or, barring that, at the factor level. This implies that if a factor is nontradeable, then, the nontradeable factor must have a substitute that is tradeable or alternatively be broken into component parts to allow market value to be imputed to the resource. If the nontradeable factor has no tradeable substitute and can not be broken down into tradeable components then, although the network it is embedded in may appear simple, the nested nontradeable factor implies that the network is complex.

When we compare this categorization to Barney's (1991) three categories, it is evident that since physical and some human resources are 'tradeable' (Barney, 1991; Williamson, 1975), contained resources will typically include them. Given the transparency of the simple network, contained resources are unlikely to directly lead to an SCA.

Two conditions may occur where they might support an SCA. First, the contained resource is disguised either by being overlooked by competitors or by being hidden or kept secret by the firm. In either case, since they are either tradeable or have substitutes that are tradeable, they will be subject to quick erosion once discovered. Second, they might be only one factor of a complex network which as a whole creates the competency that supports SCA. Thus only indirect support is possible in the second case.

System Resources

A system resource is created by a *complex network* of firm resource factors. A complex network is one with many direct and indirect links between a large number of factors which are made up of nested system resources, contained resources and other resource factors. 'Complex' implies that the network doesn't have definite boundaries which will make monetary valuing implausible. Generally speaking, a system resource is socially created. As a social creation, it is endowed with the implied creation and recreation of social constructs. By contrast, a contained resource is more similar to a discrete artifact. Indeed, it is the attributes of social creation that make the identification of the complex network of system resources difficult (Barney, 1992; Fiol, 1991). This implies that the complete set or even a significant number of factors will be neither readily nor easily identifiable. This poses problems in monetarily valuing such resources. This also implies that fewer of the factors will be tradeable and that there are fewer substitutes for factors or for the resource as a whole. When Barney's categories of resources (physical resources, human resources and organizational resources) are again evaluated, it becomes evident that all three categories could be involved in the network of a system resource.

In the case of a system resource, organizations are faced with a resource comprised of a complex network that makes an unknown amount of contribution to a capability that may itself be a member of a network of capabilities which lead to a set of competitive advantages. It is clear, that often, while attempting to replicate themselves through autopoietic processes (Morgan, 1983; Smith, 1983), the initial identification of a strategically important system resource happens only when the resource is unintentionally destroyed. For example, consider Xerox's initial decision not to develop further computer hardware and software technologies that later spawned Apple Computers and Microsoft. These firms were participants in the start of major technological changes in which Xerox had given up their ability to create a competitive advantage. Ultimately, it resulted in a loss of competitive advantage in their chosen industry as well. This inadvertent destruction of the support of sustainable competitive advantage can be likened to an internal Schumpeterian shock. In this instance the external environment didn't change but the internal environment evolved and discarded the wrong genetic (resource) endowment. From our example, we can infer that these internal choices may result in a later external Schumpeterian shock. To begin to address the question of identifying the networks of competencies, the general characteristics of networks need to be integrated with RBV theory.

NETWORK THEORY AND THE RESOURCE-BASED VIEW OF THE FIRM

An organization's unique set of assets is the result of the relationships both within and across the levels of factors, resources, and competencies. This results in two types of networks: local networks (McCallister and Fischer, 1983) and structural networks (Berkowitz, 1982). As applied to RBV theory, a local network is the configuration of relationships within a level of analysis as in among the factors, where it is the entire network that results in a resource. The resource is not merely the listing of its factors but is the interaction configuration among the resource factors. Thus if resource D is composed of factors A, B, and C, its local network consists of all the existing relationships among A, B, and C. For example, one can think simplistically of a unit's performance as a result of the interactions among the capacities of unit members (factor A), the motivations present (factor B), and the unit's physical and capital resources (factor C) (Blumberg and Pringle, 1982).

A structural network is the configuration of relationships between local networks and between a factor of a local network and other networks or factors. Again applying social network theory to RBV theory, this is the configuration of relationships between the focal resource and other resources, as well as, the relationships between other resources and the factors of the focal resource. For example, if one looks at the resource, a unit's performance, as a single entity, it will have links to other resources and yet, individually, its factors (people's skills, attitudes, raw materials, etc.) will simultaneously also have links between resources and/or factors. It is the configuration of both of these sets of links that create the resource's structural network. This structural network will be especially dense for nontradeable factors such as 'trust', given Itami and Roehl's (1987) observation about the simultaneous use of intangible assets.

In summary, a resource's internal factor network is its local network (McCallister and Fischer, 1983), and its relationship outside of its local network is its structural network (Berkowitz, 1982). One might think of the product or resource that is a department's end result as the artifact of the local network and its place in a value chain will reveal the structural network. Notice that a factor of that product's network, the manager of that department, will also individually have links to other networks (the chain of command relationships). Sayles (1993) notes that the widespread tactic of downsizing and eliminating middle managers may have a serious impact on the firm's ability to retain previous competencies. Given that middle managers play a crucial role in integrating and aligning competencies, the competency is destroyed in the letting go of the managers (Sayles, 1993). This happened due to a lack of understanding of the inter-resource relationships that make up the competency and results in further destruction of other competencies due to the structural relationships that were involved.

Since a competency includes system resources as factors, the competency's local network will include all its component resources' local networks (since a resource is definitionally its local network). However, we do not expect a competency's structural network to be just the sum of its resource's structural networks. Just as the resource as a distinct entity has relationships to other resources, we also expect a competency will have relationships with other competencies. For example, consider the case where GM, under Roger Smith, spent 50 billion dollars retooling and still wound up being the high cost producer. We argue that this occurred because plant and equipment are only one resource in the competency (lean manufacturing) that they were striving to attain and the weak link was the relationships needed with other resources, such as management, HRM systems, the supply chain, engineering, etc. (Womack, Jones, and Roos, 1990).

A competency's structural network will include all of the factors' structural networks, as well as the overall competency's external relationships. This hierarchical nesting relationship is believed to exist from the most nested single factor through the overall organization as a unit (Berkowitz, 1982). Figure 7.1 shows a pictorial representation of the hierarchical nestings of factors, resources, and competencies.

Notice the dotted local network relationship lines in the system resource linking all the factors together. Then, in the bottom network presentation, note that the system resource is imbedded in the competency's local network. As implied in Figure 7.1, the local networks and the structural networks are not independent. While this creates problems in understanding causal relationships, it helps us to understand the creation of organizational synergy. It provides further support of the idea of 'emergent powers being created when some objects or individuals are internally related to each other to form a structure' (Tsoukas, 1989).

Given the potential complexity of the creation of firm resources, the RBV framework provides a useful heuristic for discriminating between situations of competitive parity, temporary competitive advantage or sustainable competitive advantage (Barney, 1992). Although RBV literature has evaluated a resource as a discrete unit (Barney, 1992; Amit and Schoemaker, 1993; Grant, 1991), in the following section we show how it also can enable us to look for relationships that are believed to lead to high or very high support of sustainable competitive advantage. In other words, to look for the relationships that are resulting in the desired characteristics.

RBV Implied Strategic Relationships

In looking for strategic relationships, we note from the literature that Schoemaker (1990) suggests that it is necessary to explore how socially complex resource factors and resources magnify or diminish each other, but he doesn't specify what form those relationships may take. In a similar vein, Grant (1991) points out the need for

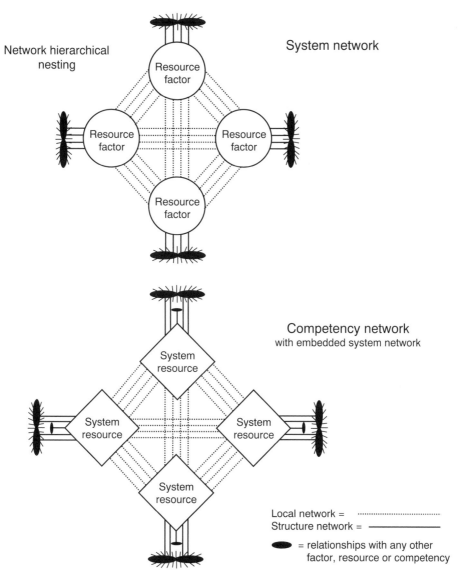

Figure 7.1. Network Hierarchical Nesting

examining intra- and inter-capability resource relationships. Likewise, Conner (1991) has noted a nested condition in regard to asset stocks and flows. Amit and Schoemaker (1993) suggest that these complexities create nestedness problems across organizational level. Robins (1992) argues that it is these firm specific relationships which generate quasi-rents since the tradeable factors (barring market inefficiencies) would have their value bid away.

It has been argued that the needed characteristics of firm resources to generate rents also make it unlikely if not impossible to be able to determine *a priori* the set of resources needed to gain or sustain a competitive advantage (Barney, 1986, 1991;

Peteraf, 1993; Robins, 1992). Certainly, uncertainty in the external environment contributes to this *a priori* determination problem but equally important is the uncertainty in the internal environment due to the relationships between the factors that make up a resource, between resources that make up competencies and between the competencies that are needed to follow a firm's strategy. The nestedness problems may also point to important relationships across the levels, as well as, within them.

We propose that these relationships are implied by the characteristics already identified as needed for SCA. Amit and Schoemaker (1993) expanded upon Barney's VRIO (1992) base characteristics. Valuable was expanded to include the subdimensions of an external link of 'overlap with strategic industry factors, and implied internal fit issue of "complementarity".' Rare was expanded to include scarcity and low tradeability. Inimitable was broken out into inimitability and limited substitutability. Finally Barney's 'O' from 'VRIO', organized to capitalize on the resource, would align with Amit and Schoemaker's appropriability and durability characteristics.

The finer grained characteristics provided by Amit and Schoemaker (1993) do provide a better screening but the dynamic nature involved in the bundling of the factors and resources into competencies remains a mentioned but not integrated feature. Our application of social network theory begins to unravel some of the issues of the dynamics. In our presentation, the choice of a resource to be evaluated is a reflection of the management's belief in the overlap of the resource with the relevant key industry factors (Amit and Schoemaker, 1993). We do not address this external link but turn our attention inwards to the determination of just what it is that causes a resource to exhibit the rest of the needed characteristics. The issues of tradeability, durability and possibly appropriability are reflections of the 2×2 Tradeability and Acquisition Process matrix of factor types. The issues of perceived scarcity and inimitability are reflections of the complexity of the network. While substitutability ramifications may also be a reflection of the complexity of the network, they also may mitigate that complexity and so substitutability stands as a separate relationship. The internal value represented by complementarity, appropriability and possibly durability are the reflections of what we term 'cogency relationships'. These additional dynamic and key relationships are built on Schoemaker (1990), Amit and Schoemaker (1993), and Robins (1992). We suggest that cogency relationships have three forms: compensatory, enhancing, and suppressing/destroying.

A compensatory relationship exists when a change in the level of one resource is offset by a change in the level of another resource. This relationship may be symmetric or asymmetric. Note that here we focus on changes in existing resources and not on replacing the existing resource. Furthermore, compensatory relationships are not equivalent to substitutability relationships. For example, increased effort can make up for differences in ability but it can't substitute for lack of ability.

An enhancing relationship exists when the presence of one factor magnifies the impact of a different factor. Amit and Schoemaker (1993) refer to this as complementarity. We do not think that enhancing relationships require a bilateral dependence as is implied in Amit and Schoemaker's discussion of complementarity. That is, an enhancing relationship may also be unidirectional or asymmetric. Changes in A magnify changes in B but not vice versa. For example, Magic Johnson, a famous US basketball player, was noted for making other players better; other players didn't make him better (some might suppress his ability but not enhance it). Another example arises from

Parthasarthy and Sethi's (1992) analysis of flexible automation use in manufacturing systems. They found that when both scope and speed flexibilities were in place, along with a flexible automation system, then there was a positive significant effect on performance. If there was only the presence of either speed or scope flexibilities with the flexible automation, then there was no significant effect on performance. This illustrates the enhancing relationship between the contained resource (speed and scope flexibilities) and the contained resource (flexible automation system) but not compensatory relationship that result in the positive performance differential.

Likewise, suppressing relationships exist when the presence of one factor diminishes the impact of another. The lack of ability on the part of other players suppressing Magic Johnson's playing was previously acknowledged as a suppressing relationship. Again using Parthasarthy and Sethi (1993), they found that a mechanistic structure had a negative effect on the relationship between flexible automation and performance levels. An extreme case of suppression would be the complete destruction of the resource. An example would be in the clash of cultures in merging companies with the ultimate destruction of the suppressed culture.

The strategic value of cogency relationships is proposed to be dependent upon specific intra- and inter-resource inherited characteristic traits and network and substitutability relationships. This view is consistent with the concept of equifinality in open system theory and supports the concept of multiple paths leading to SCA for firms with heterogeneous resources. In other words, value is the fit of the factor (and its relationships to other factors in the resource network) to strategy combined with the fit of the strategy to the external environment. Indeed, value may not be determined for each resource factor individually but for an entire bundle. For example, if the ways of equally competing include Resources A, B, C, D, E, F, G, H and I but in certain combinations; then Firm 1 may use A + B + C, while Firm 2 may use A + D + E. At the same time, Firm 3 may use G + H + I and Firm 4 may use B + E + F. Therefore, resource A has value for Firms 1 and 2, but not for Firms 3 and 4. The value depends on what other factors are present or controlled by the specific firm in question. This implies that a resource factor as such may not be a substitute but that the entire bundle or configuration of the resource factors may act as a substitute for another and different bundle of resource factors. It is this aspect of configurational use of resource factors that allows firms to pursue similar competitive strategies with different resources. We believe, this also helps to explain why firms following different generic competitive strategies can be equally successful (Conant, Mokwa and Varadarajan, 1990) and why there are no consistent differences in performances between strategic groups (Cool and Schendel, 1988). We present theoretical combinations of factor characteristics (or attributes) and relationships, as well as, potential benefits of these proposed heuristics. Later in this chapter, we develop these relationships more fully (See Figures 7.3–7.6). Before further exploring the relationships among resources, we need to identify the strategic system resource.

IDENTIFICATION OF STRATEGIC SYSTEM RESOURCES

To summarize, a strategic system resource is a socially created complex network comprised of tradeable and nontradeable factor stocks and flows and their relationships with each other. While complexity may be desirable to confound competitors, complexity makes it difficult for firms to create, manage, exploit and nurture their resources. Amit and Schoemaker (1993) highlight the difficulty of making decisions about resource development and deployment in the face of uncertainty and complexity. Although the specifics of a system resource will be dependent upon its context, we develop a conceptual framework to explain the key dimensions and the relationships between them in an effort to enlighten a firm as it copes with this issue and to highlight specifically the implication of a network orientation to the bundling problem noted earlier.

System Resource Local Network Dimensions

In considering the composition of the system resource network, we use the five strategic dimensions presented above. The dimensions are related to basic factor characteristics and their interfactor relationships. Recall that the four basic factor types are derived from the four cell matrix utilizing Tradeability aspects (Barney, 1986) and Acquisition Process aspects (Dierickx and Cool, 1989). The applicable time dynamism issues for this factor are included in the Acquisition Process dimension (Dierickx and Cool, 1989; Grant, 1991; Nelson and Winter, 1982; Porter, 1991). Recall also that the relevant relationships derived from the characteristics needed to support SCA include Network Type (Dierickx and Cool, 1989; Grant, 1991), Substitutability (Barney, 1991, 1992; Grant, 1991), and Cogency (Schoemaker, 1990). The Cogency relationship has three subdimensions: Compensatory, Enhancing and Suppressing relationships. We submit that the relevant relationships can only be considered when a proposed factor has been identified. The specification of these characteristics will enable a firm to determine how much and what type of effort it will take to create and maintain that factor and ultimately the resource and from the resource to the competencies that enable it to achieve its SCA.

Based on the preceding, we now present potential configurations of firm resource factors that we propose are necessary to lead a system resource to high or very high support of competitive advantage. We intend for these paths to be useful heuristics enabling both managers and researchers to address the incredible complexity and uncertainty that the socially created resource inherently has.

POTENTIAL CONFIGURATIONS OF SYSTEM RESOURCE LOCAL NETWORKS

The support of a sustained competitive advantage is proposed to be the result of the specific combinations of the listed key dimensions. Thus strategic resources will have networks with the following configuration attributes. By using the RBV theory as previously presented by Barney (1992), the potential 256 combinations of inferred relationships are reduced to only 22 strategic configurations that theoretically support an SCA. The specific configuration for a particular factor can be identified by tracing a decision line through the proposed strategically necessary relationships. While acknowledging that many of these questions have a range of answers, for the sake of parsimony, these combinations are shown in the form of decision trees (See Figures

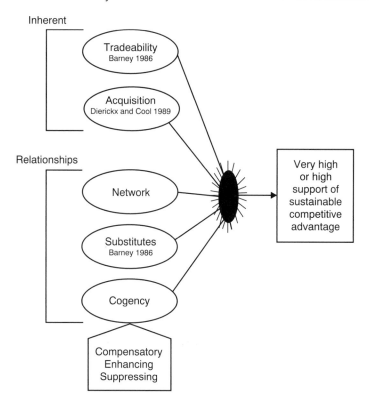

Figure 7.2. Strategic Firm Resource Factor—Inherent Traits and Relationships

7.3–7.6) and are discussed below. To minimize redundancy, the logic for the path choice is presented with the original path presentation. All subsequent presentations of that decision path are based on the original logic.

Tradeable Asset Flow

If a resource factor is a tradeable asset flow, it will only provide support for SCA in the presence of X-assets (Robins, 1992) (recall that an X-asset is the firm specific asset that allows the attainment of a quasi-rent). We propose three configurations that can provide high support. They start with the requirements of the tradeable asset flow being a factor of a system resource that is in a complex network (Node 1, YES) where substitutes for the element are not available (Node 2, NO). These decisions address the issues of rareness and time dependency by creating ambiguity in the factor's role in the firm resource and impacting the amount of time it would take a competitor to imitate it. The firm's path to high support of SCA is attained when the factor has a compensatory cogency relationship only with nontradeable factors (Node 3, NO; and Node 4, YES), because decisions 3 and 4 again diminish the tradeability and flow aspects by allowing it to be offset with a firm specific asset only (Path a). The last two paths (b and c) do not have any compensatory relationships (Nodes 3 and 4, NO) but have either an enhancing (Node 5, YES) or neutral cogency relationship (Nodes 5 and

Resource factor –
Tradeable asset flow

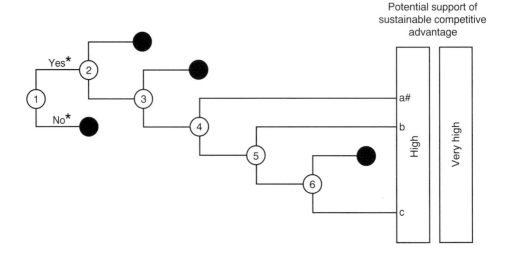

1. Is this factor a member of a complex network?

2. Do substitutes exist for this factor?

3. Is this factor in a compensatory relationship with a tradeable network factor?

4. Is this factor in a compensatory relationship with a nontradeable network factor?

\# Decision Path to probable support of SCA

5. Is this factor in an enhancing relationship with another network factor?

6. Is this factor in a suppressing relationship with another network factor?

● Leads to either competitive parity or competitive disadvantage

* This same pattern is followed for all decision nodes

Figure 7.3. System Resource Local Network Configuration Decision Tree

6, NO) with any other system factor. We present the enhancing cogency relationship as a path since this type of a relationship may increase the particular factor's importance since it may be the only possible factor that can provide that particular enhancing capability.

Nontradeable Asset Flow

A nontradeable asset flow factor can provide high support if it is a member of a system resource with a complex network (Node 1, YES). This context diminishes the problem for SCA from the time dependency aspect of the factor. If it has substitutes (Node 2, YES), but there are no compensatory relationships either with tradeable or nontradeable network factors (Nodes 3 and 4, NO) and there is an enhancing relationship (Node 5, YES; Path d), the factor may still lead to SCA due to the last relationship working to increase its specific importance to the network. Note that this particular configuration may be capable of only temporary high support due to the substitutability relationship, if the substitute also is capable of providing an enhancing relationship.

Resource factor –
Nontradeable asset flow

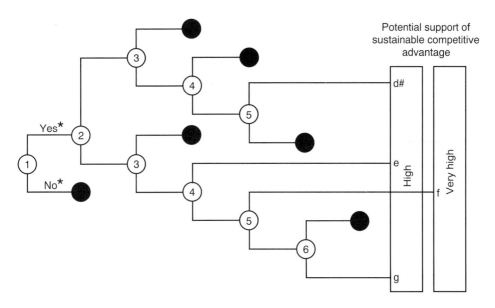

1. Is this factor a member of a complex network?

2. Do substitutes exist for this factor?

3. Is this factor in a compensatory relationship with a tradeable network factor?

4. Is this factor in a compensatory relationship with a nontradeable network factor?

\# Decision Path to probable support of SCA

5. Is this factor in an enhancing relationship with another network factor?

6. Is this factor in a suppressing relationship with another network factor?

● Leads to either competitive parity or competitive disadvantage

* This same pattern is followed for all decision nodes

Figure 7.4. System Resource Local Network Configuration Decision Tree

Additional paths are postulated when this factor has no substitutes (Node 2, NO). Depending upon whether or not this factor has a compensatory relationship with other nontradeable factors, there are three possible paths to SCA. If it does have a compensatory relationship with a nontradeable factor (Node 4, YES), this is sufficient to lead to high support of SCA (Path e). If, however, it does not have any compensatory relationships (Nodes 3 and 4, NO), it can lead to very high support of SCA if it has an enhancing relationship (Node 5, YES; Path f). We believe that if the factor does not have an enhancing relationship it will still support SCA if it also does not have any suppressing relationships (Node 6, NO; Path g). A comparison of Figures 3 and 4 suggests that nontradeable asset flows provide an additional path to SCA and where the paths are similar suggest that in some cases the magnitude of the effects may be greater.

Resource factor –
Tradeable asset stock

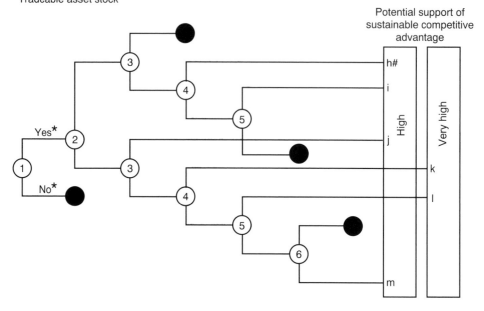

Figure 7.5. System Resource Local Network Configuration Decision Tree

1. Is this factor a member of a complex network?

2. Do substitutes exist for this factor?

3. Is this factor in a compensatory relationship with a tradeable network factor?

4. Is this factor in a compensatory relationship with a nontradeable network factor?

\# Decision Path to probable support of SCA

5. Is this factor in an enhancing relationship with another network factor?

6. Is this factor in a suppressing relationship with another network factor?

● Leads to either competitive parity or competitive disadvantage

* This same pattern is followed for all decision nodes

Tradeable Asset Stock

When the factor under consideration is a tradeable asset stock, it will provide high support when it is a member of a complex network (Node 1, YES). This provides a starting point for assessing the six paths that lead to high support of SCA. We will first discuss the two paths for which substitutes exist (Node 2, YES). If the factor has no compensatory relationships with other treadeable network factors (Node 3, NO) but has a compensatory relationships with other nontradeable factors (Node 4, YES), that is sufficient to provide support of SCA (Path h). If, however, the factor has no compensatory relationships with nontradeable network factors (Node 4, NO), it can still lead to SCA if it has an enhancing relationship with other network factors (Node 5, YES; Path i). While it is possible that due to the availability of a substitute for these two configurations to be imitated or entirely substituted for, the overall effect of the

Resource factor –
Nontradeable asset stock

Potential support of
sustainable competitive
advantage

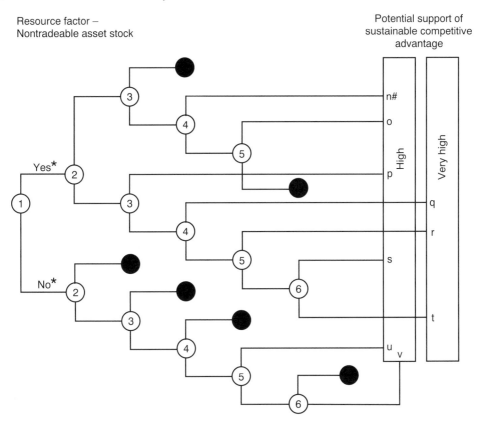

1. Is this factor a member of a complex network?

2. Do substitutes exist for this factor?

3. Is this factor in a compensatory relationship with a tradeable network factor?

4. Is this factor in a compensatory relationship with a nontradeable network factor?

Decision Path to probable support of SCA

5. Is this factor in an enhancing relationship with another network factor?

6. Is this factor in a suppressing relationship with another network factor?

● Leads to either competitive parity or competitive disadvantage

* This same pattern is followed for all decision nodes

Figure 7.6. System Resource Local Network Configuration Decison Tree

enhancing relationship, the time dependency of the stock and the complex network causing ambiguity about the factor's role make it unlikely.

Returning to Node 2, if no substitutes exist (Node 2, NO) and even if this factor has compensatory relationships with other network factors without regard to tradeability (either Nodes 3 or 4, YES), it can still lead to at least high support of SCA (Path j). The compensatory relationship with a nontradeable network factor (Node 4, YES) magnifies the path effects to very high support due to the complex network creating ambiguity about the factor and the offsetting abilities are tied to firm specific, or very rare, factors (Path k).

If no compensatory relationships exist (Node 4, NO), two paths will still lead to SCA. In the first instance, if this factor has an enhancing relationship with another network factor (Node 5, YES), then it will lead to very high support of SCA (Path 1). The more of these enhancing relationships, the stronger the support of SCA. It will still provide support without an enhancing relationship if it does not have a suppressing relationship (Node 6, NO; Path m). This is possible, because given the rest of the factors in that local network, it is not likely that competitors will be able to timely duplicate this resource due to the time constraints in creating this tradeable asset stock and the complex network.

Nontradeable Asset Stock

The strongest supporter for sustained competitive advantage is the nontradeable asset stock. Compared to tradeable asset stocks, nontradeable asset stocks provide the basis for three new paths and the magnification of some path effects. Paths m, o, p, q and r follow the same logic as Paths h, i, j, k, and I explained above with respect to Figure 7.5. Path t suggests that the potential for support of SCA is very high when the asset stock is nontradeable compared to when it is tradeable (Path m, Figure 7.5). This magnifying effect is due to the firm-specific nature of nontradeable asset stock. Below we discuss paths s, u and v.

If a nontradeable asset stock is a complex network member (Node 1, YES) without substitutes (Node 2, NO) despite the fact that there may be no compensatory nor enhancing relationships existing (Nodes 3, 4, and 5, NO), even if there is a suppressing relationship with another network factor (Node 6, YES) providing the suppressing relationship is not resource or competency destroying, high support of SCA (Path s) is still achievable. Note that not all suppressing relationships are harmful to firm resources either because they do not suppress a key success factor or because they suppress a core 'incompetency', i.e., a core competency which hinders the organization's competitiveness. Miller (1990) notes how a firm's focus on its core competencies may ultimately be self-destructive—a process he refers to as the Icarus Paradox.

The last two paths do not require a complex network (Node 1, NO). They do require that no substitutes exist (Node 2, NO) but they do not require compensatory relationships (Nodes 3 and 4, NO). Providing that there is either an enhancing relationship (Node 5, YES) or at least no suppressing relationships (Node 6, NO), they lead to high support of SCA (Paths u and v). Having no substitutes available will increase the importance of the firm specific aspects and time dependency aspects. The lack of compensatory relationships among the factors does not hinder the value and the enhancing relationships increase the firm specific value. The neutral cogency relationship demonstrates that it at least does not detract from value creation.

Configuration Implications

The logic articulated above suggests that while the debate between Barney (1986, 1989) and Dierickx and Cool (1989) may be unimportant in the sense that one can achieve SCA no matter what combination one starts from, it is important in the sense that the number of potential paths available increases as one moves from flows to stocks and tradeable to nontradeable. There are nine unique paths that can at least potentially lead to high support of SCA. When these decision paths are constrained by the resource factor types, the 22 paths just presented occur.

CONCLUSIONS AND IMPLICATIONS

Practitioner Implications

Recall that numerous practitioner problems were noted earlier in this chapter. The problem of inadvertently destroying a strategic resource by divestiture or abandonment (Xerox's example), the problem of choosing incorrectly based on a risk assessment that does not include firm-specific resources (Robin's 1992 argument), the problem of not understanding the relationships among bundled things and their importance to the utilization of those bundles are all problems that practitioners address with each strategic decision they make. This configurational network approach allows practitioners to determine the effort it will take to create and maintain the system asset of interest. By using the six strategic questions, a practitioner should be able, in addition to more fully identifying resources that make up their strategic competencies, to understand the implications of changing one factor of one resource on other apparently unrelated resources.

While the exact set of resource factors, competencies and distinctive competencies will vary from firm to firm and over time, this framework gives practitioners a starting point to more efficiently develop, change and use their resources. It also enables the confirmation of an educated guess about a firm resource and to expand a subset of important factors. As Coff has noted, in many instances a practitioner not only cannot look to a financial statement or analysis for many of the strategic resources of a firm (since these forms explicitly exclude them) but 'must actually IGNORE information from these sources to be successful in the long run' (emphasis in the original, 1993:1). This analysis will provide them with somewhere to look and depending upon their ability to forecast the future, where to invest in system resources.

Research Implications and Conclusions

The configurational aspects of a resource bundle suggest that, while the external environment is important in determining and sustaining rent potential, other elements at either the strategic group or firm level are also important (Rumelt, 1991). Some may argue that rents are not sustained but are earned all at once though they may be extracted over time.[1] We argue that because resources implicitly have different economic life cycles, they are continually bundled, unbundled, and rebundled. This results in rents being sustained rather than earned all at once. This also implies that a firm may be using a portfolio of rents instead of attaining a singular sustainable competitive advantage. The degree to which a firm can keep its currently rent-generating resources from being appropriated by rivals is the degree to which a firm can maintain its competitive position.

---

[1] Our thanks to Jay Barney for pointing this out.

By closely examining the resource-based view of the firm theoretically implied characteristics, necessary relationships (factor type, network membership, substitutability and cogency relationships) among factors can be identified. Following this identification of relationships, factor network configurations that lead to high or very high support of sustainable competitive advantage are proposed. We present a total of 16 projected configurations that should lead to high support and six that lead to very high support of sustainable competitive advantage. These are the configurations of relationships among the factors needed to create a system resource that can support the attaining of a sustainable competitive advantage. In other words, the configuration of factors and relationships allows the creation of a resource that has the needed strategic characteristics of valuable rare, inimitable and organized to utilize.

The specific combination for any firm will be a result of the firm's history (and thus its existing set of firm resource factors), a firm's strategy, and the degree to which the firm's strategy fits the external environment, especially in regard to its competitors. The nesting relationships of factors, resources, competencies and distinctive competencies calls for firm resources comprised of contained resources and system resources.

We specifically see the use of substitution relationships and cogency relationships as the screening for strategic resources. The appropriate combination of substitution, compensatory, enhancing, neutral and suppressing relationships in a system resource makes it possible for all resource factor types to lead to sustainable competitive advantage. If the promise of these configurations holds upon confirmation by field research, then these configurations and their base definitions are an operationalization of resource-based view of the firm theory. In such a case, then the cross-sectional static view of the firm's ability to have a set of resources to attain a sustainable competitive advantage will be clarified as requested by Porter (1991). This would also be a starting point to address the longitudinal processes by which a firm creates and/or maintains such a competitive advantage. With this operationalization, field work and testing of the firm resource-based theory of sustainable competitive advantage on the intrafirm level is attainable.

ACKNOWLEDGEMENTS

An earlier version of this paper was presented at the 34th Annual Meeting of the Western Academy of Management, San Jose, CA. The authors would like to thank Jay Barney, Raphael Amit, anonymous reviewers, participants at the Strategic Management Journal's conference on New Strategy Paradigms, and C. K. Prahalad and Gary Hamel for comments on an earlier version of this paper.

REFERENCES

Amit, R. and P. J. H. Schoemaker (1993). 'Strategic assets and organizational rent', *Strategic Management Journal*, **14**(1), pp. 33–45.

Arrow, K. J. (1974). *The Limits of Organization*. W. W. Norton, New York.

Barney, J. B. (1986). 'Strategic factor markets: Expectations, luck and business strategy', *Management Science*, **32**, pp. 1231–1241.

Barney, J. B. (1989). 'Asset stocks and sustained competitive advantage: A comment', *Management Science*, **35**, pp. 1511–1513.

Barney, J. B. (1991). 'Firm resources and sustained competitive advantage', *Journal of Management*, **17**(1), pp. 99–120.

Barney, J. B. (1992). 'Integrating organizational behavior and strategy formulation research: A resource based view', Working Paper, Texas A&M, College Station, TX.

Barney, J. B. (September 1993). Public communications in Business Policy and Strategy Email Network.

Barney, J. B. and R. W. Griffin (1992). *The Management of Organizations: Strategy, Structure, Behavior*. Houghton Mifflin Company: Boston, MA.

Becker, G. S. (1964). *Human Capital*. Columbia, New York.

Berkowitz, S. D. (1982). *An Introduction to Structural Analysis: The Network Approach to Social Research*. Butterworth and Co., Ltd., Toronto, Canada.

Blumberg, M. and C. D. Pringle (1982). 'The missing opportunity in organizational research: Some implications for a theory of work performance', *Academy of Management Review*, **7**(4), pp. 560–569.

Bromiley, P. (September 1993). Public communications in Business Policy and Strategy Email Network.

Carr, C. (1993). 'Global, national and resource-based strategies: An examination of strategic choice and performance in the vehicle components industry', *Strategic Management Journal*, **14**(7), pp. 551–568.

Coff, R. (September 1993). Public communications in Business Policy and Strategy Email Network.

Cool, K. D. and D. E. Schendel (1988). 'Performance differences among strategic group members'. *Strategic Management Journal*, **9**(3), pp. 207–223.

Conant, J. S., M. P. Mokwa and P. R. Varadarajan (1990). 'Strategic types, distinctive marketing competencies and organizational performance: A multiple measures-based study', *Strategic Management Journal*, **11**(5), pp. 365–383.

Conner, K. (1991). 'Theory of the firm: Firm resources and other economic theories', *Journal of Management*, **17**(1), pp. 121–154.

Dierickx, I. and K. Cool (1989). 'Asset stock accumulation and sustainability of competitive advantage', *Management Science*, **35**, pp. 1504–1511.

Fiol, C. M. (1991). 'Managing culture as a competitive resource: An identity based view of sustainable competitive advantage', *Journal of Management*, **17**, pp. 191–211.

Hall, R. (1992). 'The strategic analysis of intangible resources', *Strategic Management Journal*, **13**(2), pp. 135–144.

Itami, H. and T. W. Roehl (1987). *Mobilizing Invisible Assets*. Harvard University Press, Cambridge, MA.

Grant, R. M. (1991). 'The resource-based theory of competitive advantage'. *California Management Review*, **33**(3), pp. 114–135.

Learned, E. P., C. R. Christensen, K. E. Andrews and W. D. Guth (1965). *Business Policy: Text and Cases*. Irwin, Homewood, IL.

Mahoney, J. T. and J. R. Pandian (1992). 'The resource-based view within the conversation of strategic management', *Strategic Management Journal*, **13**(5), pp. 363–380.

McCallister, L. and C. S. Fischer (1983). 'A procedure for surveying personal networks'. In R. S. Burt and M. J. Minor (eds.), *Applied Network Analysis: A Methodological Introduction*. Sage Publications, Beverly Hills, CA, pp. 75–88.

McWilliams, A. and D. L. Smart (1993). 'Efficiency v. Structure conduct performance: Implications for strategy research & practice, *Journal of Management*, **19**, pp. 63–79.

Meyer, A. D. (1991). 'What is strategy's distinctive competence?', *Journal of Management*, **17**, pp. 821–833.

Miller, D. (1990). *The Icarus Paradox: How Exceptional Companies Bring About Their Own Downfall*. Harper Collins, New York.

Morgan, G. (ed.) (1983). *Beyond Method: Strategies for Social Research*. Sage Publications, Beverly Hills, CA.

Nelson, R. R. and S. Winter (1982). *An Evolutionary Theory of Economic Change*, Harvard University Press, Cambridge, MA.

Oviatt, R. (1989). 'Caveats concerning application of the capital asset pricing model in the strategic management concept'. Proceedings of the Academy of Management, 1989, pp. 37–41.

Parthasarthy, R. and S. P. Sethi (1992). 'The impact of flexible automation on business strategy and organizational structure', *Academy of Management Review*, **17**, pp. 86–111.

Peteraf, M. (1993). 'The cornerstones of competitive advantage: A resource-based view', *Strategic Management Journal*, **14**(3), pp. 179–192.

Porter, M. E. (1980). *Competitive Strategy*. Free Press, New York.

Porter, M. E. (1985). *Competitive Strategy*. Free Press, New York.

Porter, M. E. (1991). 'Towards a dynamic theory of strategy', *Strategic Management Journal*, Summer Special Issue, **12**, pp. 95–117.

Reed, R. and R. J. DeFillippi (1990). 'Causal ambiguity, barriers to imitation, and sustainable competitive advantage', *Academy of Management Review*, **15**(1), pp. 88–102.

Robins, J. A. (1992). 'Organizational considerations in the evaluation of capital assets: Toward a resource-based view of strategic investment by firms', *Organization Science*, **3**(4), pp. 522–536.

Roquebert, J., R. Phillips and C. Duran (August 1993). 'How much does strategic management matter?. Presentation at the National Academy of Management Meeting. Atlanta, GA.

Rumelt, R. P. (1991). 'How much does industry matter?' *Strategic Management Journal*, **12**(3), pp. 167–185.

Sayles, L. R. (1993). 'Doing things right: A new imperative for middle managers', *Organizational Dynamics*, **21**(4), 5–14.

Schoemaker, P. J. H. (1990). 'Strategy, complexity and economic rent', *Management Science*, **36**(10), pp. 1178–1192.

Smircich, L. (1983). 'Studying organizations as cultures'. In G. Morgan (ed.), *Beyond Method: Strategies for Social Research*. Sage Publications, Beverly Hills, CA, pp. 160–172.

Smith, K. K. (1983). 'Social comparison processes and dynamic conservatism in intergroup relations', *Research in Organizational Behavior*, **5**, pp. 199–233.

Summer, C. E., R. A. Bettis, I. H. Duhaime, J. H. Grant, D. C. Hambrick, C. C. Snow and C. P. Zeithaml (1990). '1990 Doctoral education in the field of business policy and strategy', *1990 Yearly Review of Management of the Journal of Management*, **12**, pp. 167–183.

Teece, D. J. (1986). 'Profiting from technological innovation', *Research Policy*, **15**, pp. 285–305.

Tomer, J. F. (1987). *Organizational Capital: The Path to Higher Productivity and Well Being*. Praeger, New York.

Tsoukas, M. (1989). 'The validity of idiographic research explanations', *Academy of Management Review*, **14**(4), pp. 551–561.

Williamson, O. E. (1975). *Markets and Hierarchies*. Free Press, New York.

Womack, J. P., D. T. Jones and D. Roos (1990). *The Machine That Changed the World*. Rawson Associates, New York.

Chapter 8

Designing a Competency-based Human Resources Organization

James T. Kochanski and Donald H. Ruse
Sibson & Company, Raleigh, NC, USA

INTRODUCTION

Organizations today are paying increasing attention to how their Human Resources (HR) function is organized. Meanwhile, HR is under pressure to reduce costs, to improve its services, to increase its impact, and to provide a more satisfying work experience for its own employees, even as the proven ways of organizing the people and the work of the function prove insufficient to meet the new challenges facing HR. Most traditional organizational designs seek to balance several factors, such as functional expertise and customer alignment, which were prominent in the rationale for organizing HR. New organizing factors are emerging, however, as HR seeks performance breakthroughs, with *process* and *competence* emerging as key factors in determining how the HR function is organized. While the process focus rides the wave of interest in TQM and reengineering, a growing number of organizations see *competence* as the key to enduring performance and to making HR most effective. This chapter combines experience from our work with some emerging possibilities to describe a competency-based approach for designing a high performing HR organization.

WHY COMPETENCIES?

The *functional* aspects of HR, such as compensation, benefits, employee relations, staffing, training, and so on, generally have been the most prominent organizing factors for many HR organizations. This can be explained, in part, by a steady focus on HR products such as 401(k) plans, variable pay, and employee assistance programs. In other words, as the number of HR products has increased so has the focus on creating functions to devise, administer, and maintain those products.

The functional focus became institutionalized in HR, to the point that many inside and outside the function with this focus have become HR's Achilles' heel. Here's why:

Reprinted from *Human Resource Management*, Volume 35, No. 1, pp. 19–33, Copyright © 1996, John Wiley & Sons.

The creation or modification of HR products, which has long been the way that HR added value to the organization, has actually become a burden on the core business of the corporation. 'Not another new performance appraisal!' is a common lament among managers already overburdened with change and new initiatives.

HR products are becoming more dynamic with shorter life cycles and increasing interdependencies with other products because of system requirements and client demand for simplicity and connectivity. The hierarchy associated with functions and the tendency to work within ones own 'silo', however, may cause the creation of products by different HR functions that don't work together. For example, the career development and training functions may be promoting the value of cross-functional movement and expatriate assignments at the same time that compensation, relocation, systems, and even benefits functions are driving programs that make lateral moves difficult or even detrimental to employees.

In addition to *function*-driven HR organizations, HR has also organized around its *clients* to mirror the organizations HR supports. For example, if the corporation is organized by business unit, HR may be organized to provide focused support for each business unit. If the corporation is organized by country or territory, then HR is organized by country or territory. This organizing factor, like the product focus, allowed HR to add increased value by providing ease of access to HR professionals; it focused attention on the unique needs of the client unit and created an improved strategic focus on people issues. This approach often helped HR leaders 'get to the table' or get involved in the strategic decision making of the business. In fact, many line executives cannot conceive of not having their own HR executive and staff of HR professionals.

'Client' as organizing factor also has come under pressure as unable to meet the needs of a dynamic, competitive organization. As enterprises increasingly create new units or teams that cross old organizational lines, reengineer, or just reorganize more frequently, HR is constantly trying to realign itself even to the point of confusing the client organization. Further, Chief Executive Officers (CEOS), Research and Development (R&D) heads, sales executives, HR executives, and others who are concerned about the ability to integrate technologies, products, systems, and people across organizational lines are finding the provincial nature of HR groups organized by business unit to be an unwelcome barrier to cross-unit synergy.

As a result of all this, some HR executives have sought to organize HR along *both* function and client lines—to have both corporate functional groups and business unit generalist groups. This approach merely creates the problems of both a functional organization and a client-based organization with the added problem of finding ways to work across functional and client-based groups.

HR executives who are frustrated with the limitations and problems associated with these common ways of organizing have another option—an organizational competence framework.

DEVELOPING AN ORGANIZATIONAL COMPETENCE FRAMEWORK FOR HR

Much has been written concerning core competencies of whole companies and business units. Core competencies alone, however, do not provide enough detail or discrimination to make them useful for making key decisions such as how to organize.

To use competencies to make organization decisions, HR organizations must identify their own core competencies and then further categorize them into tiers of competencies to force prioritization and critical thinking that can ultimately be the key to making organizing decisions (See Figure 8.1). The concept of core competence is helpful but inadequate alone to facilitate logical organization design. Thinking of competencies in several tiers, in addition to core, makes them useful as the central factor in organization design.

The concept of organizational competence is distinct from, but closely related to, the competencies of individual employees in the organization. Unique or large combinations of individual employee competencies can be organizational competencies. For example, if the individual competency of 'business orientation' is demonstrated at high levels by many HR employees it could be considered an organizational competency. Organizational competencies also can include other capabilities such as systems, technologies, or even physical locations or infrastructure.

In addition to tiers of competence, it is helpful to consider different categories of competencies, an idea closely related to the concept of value disciplines (Treacy & Wiersema, 1995). The competencies of HR, and other organizations, can be organized in three fundamentally different categories: (1) Customer Engagement (Blessington & O'Connell, 1995), (2) Invention and Discovery, (3) Making and Delivering. (See Figure 8.2).

Overlaying a modified version of a triangular thinking model (Keidel, 1995) with the three competency categories suggests that there are three circles of focus, or appropriate competency areas, for HR organizations. An analysis of the organization's internal and external needs, both present and future, will drive tier choice for each of the three circles. The area of the triangle located at each point is called the 'white space', which represents an area of over focus or under focus on a competency category. The white space in the middle of the triangle is a tempting area, on which to focus, especially for

Competency tiers	Distinguishing characteristics
Strategic	• Drives competitive advantage • Unique among competitors • Value added to customer • Future-oriented • Dynamic
Core	• Engine of the enterprise–'obvious' • Customer-touching • Enables the strategic
Requisite	• Can't do without • Not unique • Can rely on others
Misfit	• Outside of strategic direction • Of more value elsewhere • Redundant

Figure 8.1. Competency Tiers

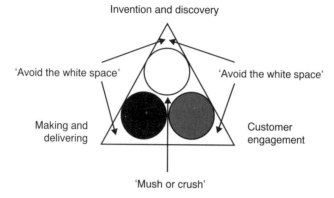

Figure 8.2. Competency Categories

HR organizations that have trouble saying 'no' or that are highly focused on expanding client/generalist ratios in response to cost cutting or downsizing pressures. We call this center area 'mush or crush' because trying to focus on all three competency categories equally can appear like 'mush' to clients and can 'crush' the resources of the organization. Mush and crush are sometimes cloaked in a desire to be good at everything but are rooted in an inability to prioritize and make tough decisions. The remainder of this chapter discusses how two companies approached competency-based HR organization in a way that helped avoid the mush and crush.

A COMPETENCY-BASED TRANSFORMATION

Two multi-national corporations that have redesigned their United States (US) HR organizations sought change so fundamental that merely reshuffling the current boxes on the organization chart was insufficient. Each company sought to prioritize and improve the basic building blocks of its organization and, in that process, examined its organizational competencies. These two organizations' experiences helped us develop an overall competency framework for HR organizations. Although each of the two case study organizations developed its own variation on the competency framework, their similarities illustrate how competencies can be used to make key organizing decisions. In each of the cases, an examination of competencies enabled changes more fundamental than had previously been experienced in the companies.

It is useful to think about transforming an organization's design in terms of the major phases of the redesign process. Although it is easier to be clear in retrospect about the redesign process, the retrospective view of how the transformations of two different organizations both fit into a three-phase process can be useful for planning and guiding future redesign processes. Company A is a leading high technology company, and Company B is a leading chemical manufacturer.

Phase 1: Planning and Discovery

Change that is haphazard, is not based in good information, or is done for the sake of change is a formula for failure. The first phase of competency-based design process includes some fairly standard change management activities plus an increased focus on discovering data that provide the clues to understanding the actual and potential competencies of the organization. Some of the phase one activities are:

- clarifying the need for change,
- developing a plan and approach for change,
- gathering and understanding information about competencies,
- leadership mobilization.

In both case examples, an analysis of the business situation was undertaken to clarify the drivers for HR transformation. For example, in one of the firms, falling product margins drove a need for reduced costs; reduced layers of management in the line organizations drove a need for streamlined processes; and recently deployed wide area networks allowed access by managers to on-line tools and services. This picture of the changing customer environment provided HR leadership with an understanding of the business case for change and provided the foundation from which to plan and focus the transformation process. Based on this analysis, HR leadership accepted the challenge of:

- reducing costs,
- aligning HR with a changing line organization,
- improving service performance through on-line products,
- focusing face to face support for greater strategic impact.

The case for change in both of the case companies was severe and radical enough that a decision was made to use a redesign approach that could lead to change more fundamental than typically used in reorganizations. The strategic and change literature being read by the leaders of both organizations triggered thinking about core competencies as a way of breaking the organization down to redesignable parts, as a way of focusing on the most critical aspects of what HR does, and as a way of potentially shedding aspects of less value.

The identification of competencies came through a combination of methods by which current *and* future HR capabilities were identified and categorized. The most impactful of these methods were those that *discovered* competencies. Less impactful were sessions in which individuals from within the function postulated about what HR's competencies should be. A variety of sources and methods were used during this process, some of which are noted in Figure 8.3.

In company A, the discovery process was fairly public with HR employees sitting face to face with a cross section of line employees who analyzed the value adding aspects of HR in a group setting. The company used a structured facilitation approach to gain customer input. Members of the HR group asked questions only to clarify and confirm their understanding of customer perceptions. This direct dialogue approach provided an opportunity for candid and unfiltered feedback from the line organization which proved invaluable in determining HR's current and future competencies. This straightforward approach allowed HR employees to walk out of the session with a new understanding of what the customer valued, where they were meeting the customers' needs, and where they were not. Both companies also interviewed executives and

Sources	Methods
• Employees	• Interviews
• Customers	• Focus groups
• Suppliers	• Large groups
• Competitors	• Surveys
• Other stakeholders	• Constant dialog
• Artifacts	• Artifact analysis
• Non-customers	

Figure 8.3. Discovering Organizational Competencies

benchmarked external trends to build a picture of the competencies that would be the foundations of their new organizations. (See Figure 8.4.)

The discovery process in each organization revealed competencies in each of the three competency categories—customer engagement, invention and discovery, and making and delivering (although neither company used this typology to organize its competencies). Following are some examples of organizational competencies in each category:

Customer Engagement

- Co-location—the ability of HR employees to reside with their client
- Business Orientation—the ability of HR employees to tie their actions to business needs
- Customer Partnering—the ability of HR employees to act as equal partners with their customers
- Relationships with key customers
- Participation in key decision forums
- Sensing—methods and systems to understand customer needs
- Influence—personal ability to cause a different course of action

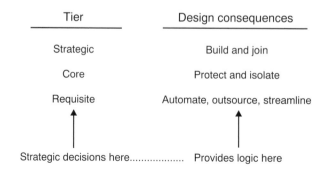

Figure 8.4. Architectural Design Choices

Invention and Discovery

- Environmental scanning mechanisms
- Product creation abilities
- Product testing abilities
- Creative depth and breadth
- External network
- Technical depth in HR specialities
- Methods to encourage synergy between product areas

Making and Delivering

- Efficient service processes
- Customer friendly systems, desktop, kiosk, phone access
- Customer responsiveness (turnaround/cycle time)
- Training design and delivery
- Mass data capture ability, e.g. re-enrollments, salary planning
- Employee communications
- Personal accessibility
- Vendor management

It is worth noting that all of the above examples of competencies are described as strengths. This is a different paradigm than most change initiatives that focus on problem solving or gap analysis. A competencies or capability approach is an inside-out focus (Ulrich & Lake, 1990). Rather than looking at what the organization can't do and trying to transform it into something different, a competencies approach suggests that those strengths that the organization already has, or has the potential for, are the basic building blocks of organization. The advantage of this approach is that the organization can avoid getting into something that it really can't do. In fact, it has the chance to focus on the things it can do uniquely well and dominate its chosen domain. The difficult part begins with phase two and requires strong leadership. In phase two of the organization's strengths are prioritized or 'tiered'. This is when competency is no longer a 'feel good exercise' (Collis & Montgomery, 1995); it is when leadership that is mobilized to make decisions and act on them is critical.

Phase 2: Strategic Architecture

Based on the data and work they had done in phase one, both firms had to make the following decisions about their architecture.

- How to prioritize competencies into strategic, core, or requisite tiers
- How to make design choices and determine the implications of tiering; what are the implications for structure, staffing, roles, and other aspects of design
- How to implement and manage the changes

Prioritizing the Competencies into Tiers

Based on its specific business needs, each organization sought to prioritize its competencies to determine which would be most critical and which would be less critical. Since most of the competencies identified were current strengths, there was almost always someone who thought his/hers was most critical for the future. The outcomes of these deliberations have been categorized according to the strategic, core, and requisite competency tiers in Table 8.1. Both organizations had difficulty avoiding the seduction of the center of the triangle where it is tempting to try to make everything HR does into a core or strategic competency. As service groups to the greater organization, both companies' HR people found it difficult to prioritize competencies knowing that it would require them to tell customers that they would not be able to sustain the same levels of support for capabilities deemed requisite. In Company A, the leader of the organization took a stand and declared that customer engagement was strategic to break the mush or crush stalemate. This was an unpopular decision among some employees, but it was also a key to moving forward.

Making Design Choices

With prioritization becoming more clear through tiering decisions, each organization could begin to make choices about how best to design itself for higher performance. Design choices were made based on competency tiers and provided the basis for re-architecting the respective organizations. The range of choices that are available based on tier selection are illustrated in Figure 8.5 and discussed below.

Table 8.1. Competency Tier Decision

Tier	Company A	Company B
Strategic	Customer Engagement. Customer engagement was determined to be the category of highest value to the customer and the category that would differentiate the future of HR from the past. It was also the category that would differentiate internal HR from external vendors that provide HR services or products.	Customer Engagement. This was determined to be the category of highest value to the customer and the category that would differentiate the future of HR from the past.
Core	Invention and Discovery. This category would be the 'engine of HR' that would enable the organization to realize its strategic objectives in the future. Company A had a long history of being innovative in new product and service development that delighted the customer and made the company into an industry benchmark.	Making and Delivering. This competency was critical to the company achieving its strategic objectives. Analysis of its current capability determined that making and delivering was already a well-developed competency recognized by its customers as being value added and one that needed to be protected in order to realize its desired future state.
Requisite	Making and Delivering. The company recognized that it could not do without this competency, but that the competency was neither unique to the organization nor did it provide a high degree of added value under the current structure.	Invention and Discovery. Never considered a strong capability, the company made this competency into one in which future design choices would be made to reduce costs and to improve customer satisfaction.

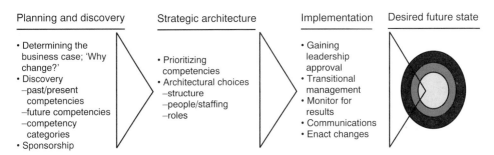

Figure 8.5. Competency-based Design Processes

The strategic tier. Both organizations made architectural choices to grow HR customer engagement competency. Growth occurred both in numbers of professionals and incumbent staff capability. Even though they were downsizing, both companies added to the cadre of people providing strategic face-to-face support for business units and business leaders. Both companies redefined the individual competencies required of the 'business partner' or customer engagement roles emphasizing competencies such as consulting skill, influence, and strategic thinking. These were used to select the persons for the business partner roles as well as for their ongoing development.

The core tier. Company A took actions to maintain and protect its capabilities in the design and development of new products (invention and discovery) which resided in a few key people. To ensure retention of those professionals who possess these competencies and to ensure synergy among them, these resources were centralized into a common unit and location. Even though downsizing was imminent, it was considered critical to protect these core resources and buffer them from the major changes that would take place in the requisite tier.

Company B made a conscious choice to co-locate many of the transaction-based services that historically had been independently delivered at each field site (isolate and protect). This migration to a shared services structure reduced costs by eliminating redundancies. In addition, it realized efficiencies from the development of common systems and processes that were applied across the organization. It also acquired technologies from outside vendors that provided employees with direct access to their benefit data and allowed them to make changes real-time thus reducing cycle time necessary for changes to be reflected in the system. It took action to ensure that customer satisfaction was not impacted due to lack of 'face-to-face' contact by ensuring at least 'voice-to-voice' contact was available by phone. Customer Support teams were put in place to provide employees with easy access to specialists with whom they could discuss topics/issues for which they needed advice and counsel.

The requisite tier. Company A also chose to deploy a shared services approach to services common across business units but considered it requisite rather than core. As a result, the emphasis was on automation and outsourcing to reduce cost. Selected activities were outsourced to third parties, including Consol Omnibus Budget Reconciliation Act (COBRA) administration, 401K administration, and training. Voice-to-voice contact was designed as a back-up to employee self-service phones, and kiosks. Forms boards were put in common areas so employees could get their own forms, and the doors to the service center were locked to prevent walk-ins. New key competencies were identified for requisite areas: vendor management and the ability to shift employees to new delivery methods. HR employees in the requisite areas had to transform from being experts in delivering services themselves to managing vendors and automation and to utilizing methods that encourage employee use of self-service automation and external vendors.

Company B found that its need for creation of new HR products and services (invention and discovery) could be met by purchasing 'off the shelf' from external vendors. It relied on third party vendors to develop training programs, benefit packages, compensation consulting and systems, and HR information systems so that it could channel time and money into developing and maintaining its strategic and core competencies. This approach provided the opportunity to develop existing staff capability in areas such as organization development and design by partnering with external consulting firms who were able to transfer their technologies to the HR professionals now organized around customer engagement. HR leadership realized that one of the quickest ways to becoming a full business partner and key decision maker was to develop capabilities that enable line management to navigate the whitewater associated with operating a business in the 1990s and beyond.

An important observation from the process of organizing by using competency categories is that competency based organizations are fractals—that is, patterns of the larger organization are recreated on a smaller scale in the subunits of the organization (Wheatley, 1992). Within the competency framework, there are similar patterns on the basic triangle that play out at each group level and even to the individual employee. For example, a group set up for the purpose of customer engagement still needs to make or deliver products or services and may invent or discover things. Also, a group that may be considered requisite (such as HR in general) will still have strategic and core elements within it.

Phase 3: Implementation

As a senior HR leader in one of the companies put it, 'Implementing this is like changing the tires on a race car going 200 miles per hour!' Shifting to a competency-based organization while maintaining day to day operations is a challenge. Four key steps compose the implementation approach used by both Company A and Company B.

1. Gain senior leadership approval of the new design. This entailed reviewing the business case for change; detailing the cost and benefits of the change in terms of time, money and productivity; and identifying senior line management sponsorship. It was considered a 'deal breaker' if senior line leadership couldn't support the changes proposed. In both of these companies, there was a greater emphasis on HR support for senior management, but it was important for them to understand how the new HR design would effect the rest of the company.
2. Charter a team to oversee implementation. In company B the implementation steering team had both senior line and HR representatives, in Company A, HR only. One of steering teams chartered implementation sub-teams to be responsible

for making the transition happen in different parts of the organization. It also developed guiding principles or a 'code of conduct' to provide the behavioral and procedural framework for implementation efforts. It also established tracking mechanisms to measure progress against planned cost and schedule.

3. Develop a communications plan that communicates the business case for change and the competencies based rationale for the new design. In one organization that used competencies to redesign the organization, communicating the logic behind the design helped gain employee understanding and commitment. 'Light-bulbs were going on all over the place' said a senior manager. In reorganizations, there never seems to be an end to the questions and details that need to be decided. If the employees don't understand the logic behind and the objectives of the design, the decisions all require senior management attention and communications. Competencies can be the logic framework that helps employees understand.

4. Implement changes ranging from hiring new talent to grow strategic capability, to downsizing in areas of lower priority, to redefining jobs. The defining 'movement' in both companies' implementation was when old jobs were eliminated and new redefined jobs were staffed and started up. For example, field benefit administration jobs were eliminated, and newly defined jobs in service centers were staffed, sometimes with the same people. The companies also launched efforts to develop new capabilities among existing staff through training and on the job development. Vendors were evaluated and contracted to provide products and services chosen to be outsourced or automated.

Spanning all four steps was a feedback process for continuous improvement that collected data to test for desired results so that the companies could decide whether to 'stop, start, and/or continue' with certain activities based on their impact on achieving desired outcomes. Finally, design and implementation modifications were made where needed.

LEARNINGS FROM COMPETENCY-BASED DESIGN

These, and other companies', experiences in redesigning themselves for sustained high performance provide insights into the critical success factors associated with competency-based organization design.

There is clearly a trend toward shared service models in HR organizations for services that are common across business units and geographies. The two case examples show how different approaches to shared services can be driven by analysis of the business case for change and decision making based on an understanding and prioritization of competencies. These companies' experiences are almost certainly more successful than they would have been if they had adopted shared services simply because it is a trend or if the firms had adopted another company's approach to shared services. New organization designs, whether shared services or other organizational forms, can be better designed and better implemented with an analysis of competencies.

There is also a trend toward a greater emphasis on the strategic business partner role of HR. The triangular model of competencies points out that a balance is required between an extreme emphasis on customer engagement and discovery or invention and the making and delivering of products and services. This balance plays out in the interaction among the three competency categories as people and groups within HR work together. There is a danger in calling any area strategic if it leads people in that area to fail to work effectively with other areas. Within the business partner, or customer engagement area, the other two competency categories are also needed. Business partners who only engage, but don't invent, discover, make, or deliver anything, won't be considered a very good partner.

The triangular model should not be used to imply that there will always be three units in a competency-based HR organization. Although several HR organizations, including the two used as cases in this article, have designed three types of units within HR, other combinations are possible and may have more utility in other situations. For example, a two-competency-category organization can be built around those competencies that are applied uniformly across the whole organization, and those that are unique to geographies or business units. In this two unit example the invention and discovery of products is combined in one unit with the making and delivering. A four unit example splits the making and delivering category into those competencies that are applied person to person from those that are delivered through automation, self service, or other non-person-to-person methods.

There can also be more, or fewer, than three tiers of competence. In some newer, growing organizations it may only be necessary to think in terms of two tiers, strategic and core. In these organizations there may not be 'old' competencies to be deemphasized. In older established organizations, a fourth tier called 'misfit' may also be helpful in identifying competencies that were once useful but are now inappropriate. For example, some HR organizations are finding that they had developed skills and procedures to make line managers 'jump through hoops' to get new jobs or job grades approved, and that this competency is not consistent with streamlined processes and managerial accountability.

Competency based design complements process reengineering. Process reengineering alone may be suboptimized without changing the organization. New processes in old organizations may work like old processes. Some companies are not interested in a purely process, or horizontal, organization, yet they need a logic structure for reorganizing that breaks the old paradigms. Additionally, there is an argument for using competencies rather than process as an organizing principle. Despite the amount of effort necessary to reengineer processes properly, a reengineered process has a useful life span that some consider to be less enduring than are core and strategic competencies. Thus competencies may be one of the most enduring factors around which to organize.

SUMMARY

Traditional HR architectures are increasingly taxed by the challenges associated with today's ever evolving business landscape. Architectural designs based on competence provide an alternative to traditional approaches to organizing HR. Competencies can provide the logic for designing an organization that will enable Human Resources to continually add value to its firm.

REFERENCES

Blessington, M., & O'Connell, B. (1995). *Sales reengineering from the outside in: Engaging customers with a new approach to sales, marketing, and service.* New York: McGraw-Hill, Inc.

Collis, D. J., & Montgomery, C. A. (July/August 1995). Competing on Resources: Strategy in the 1990s. *Harvard Business Review.*

Keidel, R. W. (1995). *Seeing organizational patterns.* San Francisco: Berrett-Koehler Publishers.

Treacy, M. & Wiersema, F. (1995). *The discipline of market leaders.* New York: Addison Wesley.

Ulrich, D., & Lake, D. (1990). *Organizational capability: Competing from the inside out.* New York: John Wiley & Sons.

Wheatley, M. J. (1992). *Leadership and the new science: Learning about organization from an orderly universe.* San Francisco: Berrett-Koehler Publishers.

Chapter 9

Forging a Link Between Business Strategy and Business Reengineering

Chris Edwards
Professor of Management Information Systems, Cranfield University School of Management, UK

Joe Peppard
EU Management Fellow, Cranfield University School of Management, UK

For many organisations the crucial issue in the strategy process is that of implementation. This is due in no small way to the distinction which is traditionally made between formulation and implementation and their treatment as sequential activities. The more recent conceptualisation of strategy, captured by the notion of core competencies, is blurring the distinction between formulation and implementation. This emerging 'behavioural perspective' of strategy focuses on the capabilities an organisation needs. Yet it still fails to address fully issues of implementation. In this paper, Chris Edwards and Joe Peppard propose business reengineering as a natural ally of strategy. It is suggested that business reengineering can help bridge the gap between strategy formulation and implementation. In this context, business reengineering is seen as an approach which defines the business architecture enabling the organisation to focus more clearly on customer requirements.

The dominant paradigm in relation to business strategy is of a rational analytical process through which the successful organisation is enabled to adapt intentionally and systematically to its environment, so achieving its predicted objectives. The strategist, either top management or a separate planning department, conceives the strategic options open to the firm when changes occur in the external environment. This focus on formulation contends that strategic analysis and strategy development are the crucial drivers of success.

The top management formulates and middle and junior management implement has become the cornerstone of accepted management wisdom. Yet, research continually shows that the problems occur more with implementation than with formulation. Implementation is about understanding strategic objectives and ensuring

Reprinted with permission from *European Management Journal*, Vol. 12, No. 4, by Edwards, C. and Peppard, J. 'Forging a Link Between Business Strategy and Business Reengineering', 1994, Elsevier Science Ltd, Oxford, England.

that an organisation's operations, human, and technological resources are contributing to the delivery of this strategy. In this regard, it has been argued that strategic thinking has far outdistanced the capabilities organisations have in delivering sophisticated strategies (Bartlett and Ghoshal, 1990). Recent writings have focused on internal strategic drivers and placed strong emphasis on operations excellence as the source of competitive advantage (Kiernan, 1993). This has been mirrored in the strategy literature with the notion of core competencies (Prahalad and Hamel, 1990; Stalk *et al.*, 1992). These can be described as a combination of people, processes and technology blended together to secure competitive advantage. The notion of a process is also the cornerstone of business reengineering (Davenport, 1993; Johansson *et al.*, 1993).

This chapter proposes that business reengineering is the natural ally of strategy, particularly in relation to its implementation, and attempts to understand, develop, and operationalise this link. This is an under-researched area, mainly because it falls between two conventional disciplines one of which is very young and is still inward looking, the other, older but with a distinct external focus. Building upon the comment of Scherr (1993) it is suggested that business processes serve as the means to realise business strategies and are the means to render strategies explicit and precise, facilitating their operationalisation. Without this link, neither business strategy nor business reengineering will achieve the benefits which are sought.

STRATEGY AS DIRECTION SETTING

Business strategy is a key issue for every major organisation. Traditionally, *formal strategic planning* is conducted by establishing a vision and objectives and then a high-level course of action to achieve these objectives. Over the years this focus on planning has been somewhat modified with the term 'strategic management' proposed as an alternative, a result of what was felt was the former's failure. Formal strategic planning would be but one component of a much more complex socio-dynamic process which brings about strategic change (Ansoff *et al.*, 1976). To reach the pinnacle of strategic management, a company must have a sound strategic planning framework, a widespread strategic thinking capability, the right motivational systems and management values, and a good system for negotiation and review (Gluck *et al.*, 1980). Yet this perspective barely addresses the issues of implementation and we shall return to this later.

The traditional focus of strategic planning has been to identify products to sell and markets where they should be sold and the process of strategy formulation has tended to reflect this view. Even Porter's (1980) industry and competitor analysis sought to provide a framework to enable the firm to position itself in the industry in which it competed. This prescriptive view of strategy has been questioned on a number of issues.

The first is the challenge which a number of writers have levelled at the dominant strategic imperative of formulation (Mintzberg and Waters, 1982; Mintzberg and McHugh, 1985). They propose that strategy is emergent (rather than intentional) changing the focus away from planning towards implementation. Descriptive research suggests that a firm's formulated and realised strategy may differ significantly (Mintzberg and Waters, 1982). Indeed, often the strategy is not explicitly devised at the outset, but '[it] grows initially like weeds in a garden' (Mintzberg and McHugh, 1985, p. 194). In his research, Quinn (1978) attempted to document the dynamics of actual strategic change. He concluded that neither the prescriptive nor the descriptive perspectives on strategic change adequately characterise the way the actual strategic process operates. Effective strategies tend to emerge from a series of 'strategic sub-systems', each of which attacks a specific class of strategic issue in a disciplined way, but which are blended incrementally and opportunistically into a cohesive pattern that becomes the company's strategy. Quinn sees this 'logical incrementalism' as a pur-poseful, effective, proactive management technique for improving and integrating both the analytic and behavioural aspect of strategy formulation. This can be con-trasted against the work of Miller and Friesen (1980) who found a significant tendency for periods of organisational history to demonstrate two extremes: periods in which no new strategic initiatives arise, what they termed periods of 'momentum', and periods in which a great number of trends are reversed, which they term periods of 'revolution'.

Second, the logic of a rational view of strategy has been questioned by a number of researchers. In order to address what they see as inadequacies, this research has focused on the psychological, the power, the behavioural relationships, and organisa-tional culture that can determine the strategy of the organisation.

Third, strategic change and its management has surfaced as a crucial area of inter-est. The rational/analytic approach to strategy formulation is based on the premise that the strategist, either top management or a separate planning department, con-ceives of the strategic options open to the organisation when change occurs in the external environment and selects an alternative. With this view, strategic change is consequential with implementation seen as merely problematic.

Fourth, business strategy has also tended to be externally focused. Porter (1980, 1985), probably one of the most influential thinkers on strategy, focuses on industrial dynamics and the sources of competitive advantage. A critical assumption is that competitive advantage is determined by industry dynamics and that organisations must position their products in selected markets to gain advantage, '[A] "war of position" in which companies occupied competitive space like squares on a chess board, build and defend market share in clearly defined products or market segments' (Stalk *et al.*, 1992). Clearly a firm's particular chosen competitive position and the products it sells are important, but only *at any given point in time*. In a rapidly changing competitive environment products quickly become obsolete and static com-petitive positions are rapidly overtaken. This places new demands on organisations to be able to respond consistently to changing markets with new products and ever improving competitiveness. A firm can achieve this ongoing renewal by identifying, developing, and maintaining its critical capabilities (Prahalad and Hamel, 1990; Stalk *et al.*, 1992).

Capabilities are a company's proficiency in combining people, process and technol-ogy which allow it to continually distinguish itself along the dimensions that are important to its customers. For example, in a high-tech industry, the ability to quickly develop new state-of-the-art products with features and performance that deliver value to customers creates an enduring advantage. In a commodity industry, it may be the ability to constantly reduce costs through innovative actions that creates lasting competitive advantage.

Canon, while operating in the camera, copier and printer businesses, have a world leadership in the technology of imaging and micro-electronics and this is where their core competence lies. The core competencies of consulting firm McKinsey are selection, training, and nurturing of its intellectual talent. The biro manufacturer BIC does not have its core competence in manufacturing biros but rather in injection moulding, enabling it to manufacture disposable razors.

Business strategy is therefore composed of both 'market-focused' and 'capabilities-focused' perspectives and, in fact, both are essential. The market-focused elements determine the products and markets where the organisation is presently competing. Capabilities not only support the current strategic thrust but, more importantly, determine future competitiveness. Customers do not buy capabilities *per se*; rather, they buy the results of harnessing the capabilities.

Even this dual pronged attack on strategy formulation does not adequately address the critical issue of implementation. The prescriptions which are developed using a formal approach to strategic planning rest on three underlying assumptions. The first is that managers and employees will act rationally and will cooperate with changes in strategy. The second assumption is that the key problem in strategic change is strategy formulation and that existing systems, procedures and structures should then effectively translate the strategic decisions into action. The third assumption is that strategy formulation and strategy implementation are sequential and independent activities. However, we would suggest that competency-based strategies have a clarity which gives greater direction to implementation. However, even the implementation of competency-based strategies is unclear.

We propose that business reengineering can bridge the gap between strategy formulation and implementation. Through reengineering, a clearer focus is given to the task at hand and identifies the organisational architecture necessary to achieve the formulated strategy.

BUSINESS REENGINEERING

The term business process redesign (BPR) was coined during the MIT's *Management in the 1990s* research programme. This programme was established to examine the profound impact that information technology (IT) is having on organisations of all kinds (Scott Morton, 1991). Researchers such as Davenport, Short and Rockart (Davenport and Short, 1990; Rockart and Short, 1990) identified not only the rule of IT in managing organisational interdependencies but also that IT was being implemented by some organisations in new and innovative ways. Venkatraman (1991) saw BPR as being one level of what he referred to as IT-induced business reconfiguration. These ideas were further popularised by Hammer (1990) who warned against 'paving the cow path' and recommended organisations to actively seek ways of using IT to enable new ways of performing work.

This early conceptualisation of BPR was clearly centred around IT. The key message was that IT systems should be designed around the processes of an organisation rather than localised exploitation as is usually the case. This view is more than just integration but demands a thorough understanding of how work is performed in an organisation. The view was soon extended in relation to the organisation as a whole with the process focus dominating the architecture of an organisation. It is seen as a positive step counteracting the negative impact of functions, hierarchy and command and control type structures.

Business reengineering is focused on developing an organisational architecture linking business strategy and its organisational implementation.

In just a few short years BPR has risen to the top of the agenda of many organisations. Confusingly, the concept has become known by a variety of terms: process innovation, business transformation, business process reengineering, business process transformation and core process redesign. Without wishing to get into a debate, we believe that they all contain two key ingredients: *radical performance improvement* through a focus on *process*. However, we believe that it is useful to make a distinction between business reengineering and business process redesign.

We suggest that business reengineering involves the development of an organisational architecture. It involves identifying and linking the strategy of the business with the required organisation processes to ensure that this strategy is actually delivered. With this perspective, the organisation engages in a fundamental re-thinking and redesign of the business and its underlying processes. This is very much a top-down view driven by senior management. It has close links with the strategy process.

Business process redesign, on the other hand, refers to the redesign of any organisational process. This can include anything from a total supply chain process to a single process within an individual function or department. Some processes can be redesigned with little senior management involvement while others require their active participation. It depends very much on the scale and scope of the initiative. Processes are selected as candidates for redesign either as a result of a business reengineering exercise or chosen in an *ad hoc* manner.

In their process redesign initiative, many organisations merely select a process which they believe is a good candidate for reengineering and begin to redesign it, perhaps following the ESIA principle: Eliminate all non value-adding activities, Simplify the process whenever possible, Integrate, and finally Automate where appropriate. While this perspective has advantage, that the process being redesigned is currently in operation, it is this very advantage which often renders it ineffective in contributing to the bottom line. Many redesign initiatives take place within a single functional area, and while they may exhibit significant performance improvement, they contribute little to the performance of the organisation as a whole. The improvement is measured *relative* to the process or function of which it is part. The oft quoted example of Ford's accounts payable is one such example. While the reduction in staff by 75 per cent may seem impressive, these were relative to the process itself and presumably had little impact on Ford's bottom line.

Following an *ad hoc* selection of processes as candidates for redesign also result in a mismatch between an organisation's strategy and its BPR initiative. The strategy and the BPR initiative may be pulling in different directions or not being mutually supportive. It is no use 'fixing' the wrong thing. Yet, determining these business fundamentals is the realm of business strategy and is not BPR. Take for example the redesign initiative at Mutual Benefit Life Insurance Company (MBL) which is widely quoted as an example of a highly successful business redesign project (Hammer, 1990). MBL cut the time to issue a life insurance policy from 24 days to 4 hours. Yet shortly after redesigning this policy process, MBL filed for Chapter 11 bankruptcy. MBL misread the implications of the depression in US real estate prices and the corresponding impacts on public confidence in its financial position. Streamlining its policy issue processes could not address this problem.

We believe that business reengineering determines the processes which form the 'business architecture' that are central to the long-term success of the organisation. Strategy provides the blueprint of this architecture. Hence business reengineering is the natural ally and supporter of business strategy.

STRATEGIC BUSINESS PROCESSES

Business reengineering is concerned with changing an organization to reflect more what it does (e.g., satisfy customer requirements) rather than what it is (e.g., a manufacturer). Building on the earlier discussion relating to business strategy, we propose that there are two critical types of processes in organisations. These derive from the product and market focused element and the competency element of business strategy.

First, organisations need processes to support their current products and services in the market place. These processes relate directly to an organisation's current basis of competition. These processes, we call *competitive processes*. So, if we are competing on speed to market of new products, the competitive processes would relate to this focus. If providing a prompt turnaround to customer orders, then the competitive processes would be the process that causes this to happen. If we are a low cost producer, our competitive processes will contribute to this stance and hence the processes which we have decided to be of significantly lower cost than our competitors will be our competitive processes. For example, a manufacturer pursuing a low cost strategy could achieve this low cost by very efficient manufacturing or particularly effective and low cost marketing. It is unlikely that a low cost strategy can be pursued by aiming to be significantly lower than the competition in every single area. Choice has to be made and the chosen processes are classified competitive processes. In 'economic-speak' these processes enable the firm to enjoy 'super-normal' profits.

Second, an organisation has what we call *infrastructure processes*. These create the capability to operate effectively in the chosen industry in the future. These processes develop the capability (people, process, technology) that will define tomorrow's competitive strategy. These infrastructure processes can be viewed as providing the 'fertilizer' which nourishes the organisation's future capabilities. Customers and competitors may not recognise these processes or indeed the output of these processes, but they do provide the organisation with the capability for future competitiveness. For example, Motorola believes that in the future, the most crucial competitive weapons will be responsiveness, adaptability, and creativity. To develop these attributes, it is gearing up a new campaign built around lifelong learning (*Business Week*, 1994). It is now putting in place the capability which will provide the necessary training and education and ensure that these are internalised. The processes which put these capabilities in place we call infrastructure processes and are concerned with the future and building the processes, people and technology to yield future competitive advantage.

The Grand Metropolitan (GrandMet) approach to BPR is clearly focused on redesigning and supporting the distinct competencies of the organisation. They use BPR to implement what they call a *competence-based strategy*. They distinguish this from the traditional 'structural strategy' followed by many of their competitors which addresses issues like the composition of the product portfolio, market selection, logistics, acquisitions and divestments. GrandMet claim that such strategic decisions are easily copied by competitors. Their competence-based strategy deals with establishing excellence in the core competencies necessary to operate effectively in its chosen marketplace in the future. For GrandMet, such critical competencies include things such as managing individual brands, product launching, market penetration and manufacturing and operational excellence. They are not readily recognised by competitors as key strengths and they are neither easily nor quickly copied. But it is these competency-based strengths that enable the company to react, adapt and prosper in such a volatile and competitive environment. Such capability was created some while ago by the infrastructure processes.

Look at giant US mass retailer Wal-Mart. On the surface, Wal-Mart is in the business of selling moderately-priced goods to the public. But Wal-Mart took a closer look at its industry value chain and at its own comparative advantages and decided to reframe the competitive challenge. They concluded that the business they were really in was not retailing at all, but communications and transportation logistics. They then focused on redesigning and improving those processes which enabled them to catapult themselves to become the leading retailer in the US (Stalk *et al.*, 1992). The creation of necessary technology, people and processes was created by infrastructure processes some while ago.

On face value, First Direct might seem to be Midland Bank's attempt to get into the home banking market. However, while this is undoubtedly true, on further analysis, it could also be looked upon as developing a capability to be the leader in building telephone relationships. Tele-banking is just one product group which they are currently offering and they have a competitive process associated with the customer interface to support telephone banking. Is it not possible for them to offer other products in such a manner, for example, insurance or holidays? Have they not created an organisation with a clear capability not only in banking, but in doing business over the telephone. The processes that created this capability were the infrastructure processes.

Competitive processes support today's product and market-based strategy. Current capability is encapsulated in competitive processes. Infrastructure processes create the capability for tomorrow's competitive processes and hence support tomorrow's competency-based strategy. Together, we term these two critical types of processes, the *strategic diamond*.

CLASSIFYING BUSINESS PROCESSES: THE PROCESS TRIANGLE

The above analysis begs the question: what about other organisational processes? Observations suggest that organisations also have other processes which are critical for the organisation to function. There may be processes which an organisation must have in place because of government legislation or stewardship such as accounting and filing tax returns. Additionally, mundane tasks such as recruiting secretaries and administrative staff are important, but clearly, in the short term, good secretarial services are not the basis of competition. This suggests that other processes exist and a classification of all these would complete the picture. We propose that in addition to the competitive and infrastructure processes previously discussed, two further process types exist: core processes and underpinning processes.

Core processes are those processes that are valued by the stakeholder and hence must operate satisfactorily but are not presently the chosen basis of competition. They are necessary for the organisation to avoid disadvantage in the market place and may be the minimum entry requirements into the market or perhaps necessary because of government legislation. For example, a vehicle scheduling process is vital to a logistic business but may well not be a chosen basis of competition and hence it is a core process to that organisation. This category should not be confused with the core-process approach of McKinsey & Company (Kaplan and Murdock, 1991) or with Earl and Chan's (1994) similarly titled category. We are using the word stakeholder, rather than merely customer, to include customers, suppliers, employees, shareholders, government, etc. as the focus of core processes. All the processes necessary to satisfy the stakeholders are termed core processes unless they are the chosen bases of competition with customers, in which case they are termed competitive processes.

A combination of competitive and infrastructure processes constitute a 'strategic diamond' supporting business strategy.

Underpinning processes are processes that are undertaken but are not recognised nor valued by stakeholders in the short term. Such processes exist in all organisations and are collections of closely related activities that are grouped together for efficiency and recognised as a process. In reality they are not a 'real' process in the sense that they directly support customers but rather contribute to other categories of processes. A conscious decision is made to treat them as a separate process. One might ask why should management choose to treat them as a process? The answer lies in the benefits of functionalism, namely efficiency and specialisation. In fact, one of the benefits of reengineering is questioning if these underpinning processes should be commonly organised or associated with the customer recognised process that they underpin. We have created this category of process to allow for a management desire to jointly manage similar activities but are not suggesting that this is necessarily the most appropriate way to manage such processes.

For example, in the performance of competitive, infrastructure and core processes, some administrative support is probably necessary. The recruitment of these support staffs may therefore be an element of a number of processes. For efficiency reasons, management may decide to combine this element and manage them as a single process. We term these single shared processes as underpinning processes.

The four types of processes are illustrated in Figure 9.1. We term combination of competitive and infrastructure processes as the *strategic diamond* as they directly support business strategy. Infrastructure processes support the future competency elements of the business strategy and competitive processes support the market and product-based elements of the business strategy.

Various classification schemes have already been proposed by others: operational versus management (Davenport, 1993); customer-facing or otherwise; internal to the business or transcending organisational boundaries. Rockart and Short (1990) suggest that processes relate to developing new products, delivering products to customers

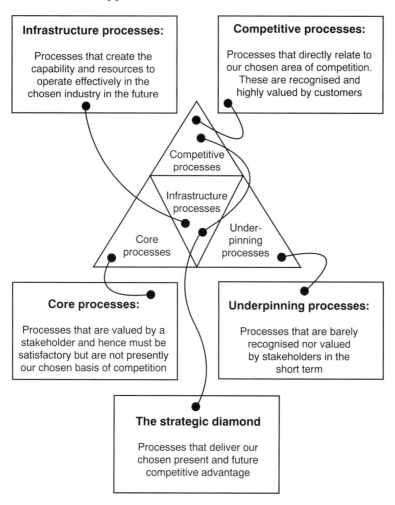

Infrastructure processes:

Processes that create the capability and resources to operate effectively in the chosen industry in the future

Competitive processes:

Processes that directly relate to our chosen area of competition. These are recognised and highly valued by customers

Competitive processes

Infrastructure processes

Core processes

Under-pinning processes

Core processes:

Processes that are valued by a stakeholder and hence must be satisfactory but are not presently our chosen basis of competition

Underpinning processes:

Processes that are barely recognised nor valued by stakeholders in the short term

The strategic diamond

Processes that deliver our chosen present and future competitive advantage

Figure 9.1. Classifying Business Processes: the Process Triangle

and managing customer relationships. Another classification scheme accords with four macro activities that derive from a variant of value chain analysis: product development and launch (which includes concurrent engineering, and corresponds roughly with product-leadership-value discipline), supply chain and operations (corresponding roughly with operational excellence), customer order fulfilment (corresponding to customer intimacy), and management planning and resource allocation (P-E Centre for Management Research, 1993). Earl and Chan (1994) suggests four types of processes: core processes, support processes, business network processes and management processes.

Without wishing to criticise individual schemes, for example, do not all processes have an operational and management element? A more general criticism is that they all focus on what the process does rather than the role processes play in delivering business benefits. While some of these classification schemes may be useful checklists in identifying processes, they give no indication of the importance of these processes to the business or how they should be managed. For example, a business network process which Earl and Chan (1994) describe as extending beyond the boundaries of the organisation into suppliers, customers and allies, could also be a core process using their own definition. Two organisations may have product development and launch processes, but the strategic value of this process to the businesses may differ. Further, these classifications give no indication concerning the management of business processes. It is very possible that different management strategies are appropriate for the same process in different organisations. Finally, they indicate little about the appropriateness of various performance improvement strategies such as continuous improvement or process redesign.

The strength of the process triangle approach primarily resides in its *focusing* qualities. To explain, the triangle can be used as a vehicle for the senior management of a business to discuss and jointly agree which are its most important processes. It helps clarify those processes which are contributing directly to today's bottom line and identifies those that should be contributing to tomorrow's bottom line. Clearly, such processes deserve a great deal of management attention both in redesign and ongoing management. The process reengineering literature talks about quick and big hits. How can redesign produce such benefits without an underlying agreement as to the relative importance of processes?

A further strength of the triangle lies in its ability to suggest *management approaches* that may well be appropriate for each type of process. For example, it would appear to us that underpinning processes are potential candidates for near total outsourcing, as against competitive and infrastructure processes which more sensibly should be managed in-house. This is not to say that some elements of competitive or infrastructure could not be outsourced but it would be folly to outsource the management of such processes as these are the very things that provide our differentiation. Outsourcing is just one example of using the triangle in this way: other management issues are clarified by use of the triangle.

Additionally, using the triangle can assist in reaching a consensus and in communicating to others the importance and contribution of an organisation's various processes. For example, our experience of applying these ideas to a large European automotive importer confirms its capabilities as a communication and discussion vehicle.

MIGRATING PROCESSES THROUGH TIME

This vision of processes presented thus far may appear very static, but to be useful it must take account of the changing contribution of processes through time. There are two major reasons why processes change their status through time. The first is related to a change in our business strategy which will have a consequential effect on the associated processes. The second relates to a change in competitors' actions which may force us to re-evaluate processes which are currently providing advantage. Let us now consider the major movements which may occur around the process triangle.

Infrastructure processes are likely to remain stable over the longer term as capability is not something that will be generated in a short time and a continual changing of direction will be grossly wasteful. Through a process of infusion, the process element output of an infrastructure process, namely capability (people, process and/or technology), becomes a competitive process. These infrastructure processes can be viewed as providing the 'fertilizer' which nourish the organisation's future capabilities.

It must be borne in mind that the organisation does have current capabilities of which the competitive and core processes are an integral part. The renewal of the current capabilities should have been designed into the core and competitive processes at the outset by the infrastructure processes when it was creating them. For example, the output of the management development process is a more skilled workforce and also the ability of that workforce to improve itself. Therefore, the infrastructure processes do support the notion of continuous improvement.

Business reengineering is important for identifying the processes which underly business strategy, and thereby assist in its implementation.

Turning to competitive processes, they may cease to be competitive and become core processes for two reasons. First, other players in the industry create processes that are as efficient, effective and adaptive as those which the organisation is currently using. When this situation arises, there are a number of options open to the firm:

- It may try to redesign the process and achieve greater efficiency, effectiveness or adaptability and hence maintain it as a competitive process.
- The business strategy changes to reflect this new situation and a new competitive process results. In the short term, the process however is still essential to compete in the industry and it must therefore continue to exist to avoid disadvantage and hence it migrates to become a core process.

Second, it may be that despite our lead we do not wish to continue to compete with this process and hence we re-classify it as a core process.

It is also possible for core processes to become competitive processes. For example, one of the products provided by a bank is a cheque account. It can be used to pay bills but also to obtain cash from one's account during banking hours at one's local branch. With the arrival of Automatic Teller Machines (ATMs), the product remained the same but it radically changed the nature of the delivery medium (i.e., the process). Customers could withdraw cash at any of the bank's ATMs at any time of the day. It could have become a competitive process, with the early adopters of this technology carving out an advantage. However, as competitors create similar processes, the advantage begins to evaporate and it then becomes a core process again. Today, banks must have an ATM network if they are going to compete in the retail banking market, yet which bank is gaining advantage from them?

Figure 9.2 illustrates this notion. From this it can be seen that processes migrate through time and it is vital that management recognise such migration and manage accordingly.

SUMMARY AND CONCLUDING REMARKS

One of the critical concerns in the area of business strategy is that of implementation. Researchers have long talked about strategic change and contributed to our understanding of the change process. Yet, useful frameworks are difficult to locate and operationalise.

In this paper we have suggested process reengineering can be used to identify organisational processes. The product and market focused elements of business

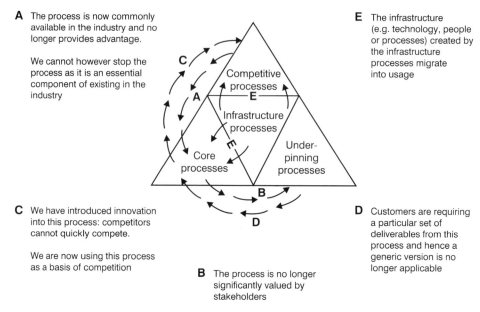

A The process is now commonly available in the industry and no longer provides advantage.

We cannot however stop the process as it is an essential component of existing in the industry

E The infrastructure (e.g. technology, people or processes) created by the infrastructure processes migrate into usage

C We have introduced innovation into this process: competitors cannot quickly compete.

We are now using this process as a basis of competition

B The process is no longer significantly valued by stakeholders

D Customers are requiring a particular set of deliverables from this process and hence a generic version is no longer applicable

Figure 9.2. Migrating Business Processes Through Time

strategy identify which processes the organisation must have in place to satisfy today's customers and hence today's competitiveness. The competency elements of business strategy dictates those processes which must be in place for future competitiveness. This is illustrated in Figure 9.3. It would be useful for organisations to analyse their

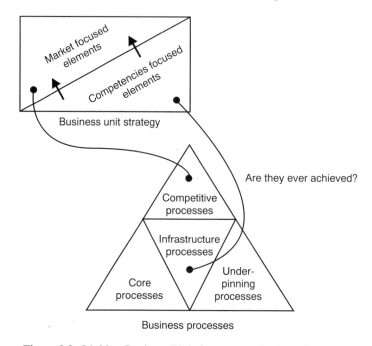

Figure 9.3. Linking Business Unit Strategy to Business Processes

competency and market elements of their business strategy and then identify the associated processes. Our experiences suggest that organisations have strategy without process and processes which do not implement strategy even though they purport to.

In many ways, business reengineering can be considered as business architecture planning and should be recognised as such. This architecture serves as the platform for current and future competitiveness. We believe that this view serves to bridge the gap between strategy formulation and implementation. By identifying the processes which underly the strategy, this gives greater direction to implementation.

This is not to suggest that the problem of strategy implementation is solved. But what it does suggest is that we are one step further down the road. Forging the link between business strategy and business reengineering is but the first step in strategy implementation. Migrating to the new organisation form, undertaking the transition and many other issues all have to be managed. However, recognising that processes underpin strategy implementation is a vital first step.

REFERENCES

Ansoff, H. I., Declerck, R. P. and Hayes, R. (eds.) (1976) *From Strategic Planning to Strategic Management*, Wiley.

Bartlett, C. A. and Ghoshal, S. (1990) Matrix Management: not a Structure, a Frame of Mind. *Harvard Business Review*, July–August, pp. 138–145.

Business Week (1994) Motorola: Training for the Millenium, *Business Week*, March 28th, 1994, pp. 58–60.

Davenport, T. (1993) *Process Innovation: Reengineering Work through Information Technology*. Harvard Business School Press, Boston, Mass.

Davenport, T. H. and Short, U. E. (1990) The New Industrial Engineering: Information Technology and Business Process Redesign. *Sloan Management Review*, Summer, pp. 11–27.

Earl, M., Chan, B. (1994) How New is Business Process Redesign? *European Management Journal*, 12, 1, pp. 20–30.

Gluck, F. W., Kaufman, S. P. and Walleck, A. S. (1980) Strategic Management for Competitive Advantage. *Harvard Business Review*, July–August.

Hamel, G. (1993) The future of Strategy: an Interview with Gary Hamel, by Paul Stonham. *European Management Journal*, 11, 2, pp. 150–157.

Hammer, M. (1990) Reengineering work, don't Automate — Obliterate. *Harvard Business Review*, July–August, pp. 104–112.

Hammer, M. and Champy, J. (1993) *Reengineering the Corporation: A Manifesto for Business Revolution*. Nicholas Brealey Publishing, London.

Johansson, H. J., McHugh, P., Pendleburry, J. and Wheeler, W. A. (1993) *Business Process Reengineering: Break Point Strategies for Market Dominance*, John Wiley.

Kaplan, R. B. and Murdock, L. (1991). Core Process Redesign. *The McKinsey Quarterly*, Autumn, pp. 3–27.

Kiernan, M. (1993) The New Strategic Architecture: Learning to Compete in the Twenty-First Century. *Academy of Management Executive*, 7, 1, pp. 7–21.

Macdonald, K. H. (1991) The Value Process model. In M. S. Scott Morton (ed.), *The Corporation of the 1990s: Information Technology and Organisational Transformation*, Oxford University Press, New York, Appendix D.

Mintzberg, H. (1987) Crafting Strategy. *Harvard Business Review*, July–August, pp. 66–75.

Mintzberg, H. and McHugh, A. (1985) Strategy Formulation in an Adhocracy, *Administration Science Quarterly*, 30, 2, 1985, pp. 160–197.

Mintzberg, H. and Waters, J. A. (1982) Emergent Strategy. *Strategic Management Journal*, 6, 3, pp. 257–272.

Miller, D. and Friesen, P. H. (1980) Momentum and Revolution in Organisational Adaptation, *Academy of Management Journal*, 23, 4, pp. 591–614.

P-E Centre for Management Research (1993), *the Role of IS in Business Process Reengineering*, November.

Porter, M. E. (1980) *Competitive Strategy*. The Free Press, New York.

Porter, M. E. (1985) *Competitive Advantage*. The Free Press, New York.

Prahalad, C. K. and Hamel, G. (1990) The Core Competence of the Corporation. *Harvard Business Review*, May–June, pp. 79–91.

Rockart, J. and Short, J. (1990) IT in the 1990s: Managing Organisational Interdependencies, *Sloan Management Review*, 30, 2, pp. 7–17.

Scherr, A. L. (1993) A New Approach to Business Process. *IBM Systems Journal*, Vol. 32, No. 1, pp. 80–98.

Scott Morton, M. S. (1991) (ed.), *The Corporation of the 1990s: Information Technology and Organisational Transformation*. Oxford University Press, New York.

Stalk, G., Evans, P. and Shulman, L. E. (1992) Competing on Capabilities: the New Rules of Corporate Strategy. *Harvard Business Review*, March–April, pp. 57–69.

Venkatraman, N. (1991) IT-induced Business Reconfiguration. In M. Scott Morton, (ed.), *The Corporation of the 1990s: Information Technology and Organisational Transformation*, Oxford University Press, New York.

Chapter 10

Putting Soft OR Methods to Work: Information Systems Strategy Development at Sainsbury's

Richard J. Ormerod
Warwick University

INTRODUCTION

The purpose of this chapter is to relate practical experience in the use of soft OR, systems thinking and other ideas gained in the course of developing an information systems (IS) strategy for Sainsbury's Supermarkets during 1989. It is written from the perspective of the lead consultant engaged by Sainsbury's for the project, fully committed to the success of the project. Other participants would undoubtedly give a different perspective and the paper does not attempt to represent their views. Nor does the paper attempt a critique of Sainsbury's. The case illustrates how, in this instance, a strategy formulation process combined a number of disparate methods and techniques without adopting exclusively the methodology of any one of them.

The interest of the case lies in the design of the process, the choice of methods used, the mixing of several methods in one project and the experience gained in using them to achieve the desired end result. Although there is evidence that the use of soft OR methods is spreading (see, for instance, Mingers and Taylor[1]), most of the published accounts of use have been by the originators of the methods and their close collaborators: this case is of interest because it was conducted outside the various methodological 'schools', purely for commercial purposes.

Having described the overall approach to IS strategy development adopted and discussed the issue of choosing, mixing and linking methods, the paper describes the Sainsbury's context and outlines the activities and structure of the project. The process design and the facilitation issues are then elaborated. Finally, the lessons learnt are discussed based on the practical experience gained. The paper concerns itself with describing the strategy formulation process itself and the methods used. It does not discuss the strategic issues, nor reveal the emergent strategy which is now being implemented.

APPROACHES TO INFORMATION SYSTEMS STRATEGY DEVELOPMENT

There are many possible approaches to information systems strategy development. Earl[2] suggested that the choice is between 'top-down', 'bottom-up' and 'inside-out'. Ward *et al.*[3] described a range of approaches and how they link with business strategy. Walsham[4] surveyed different ways of viewing the role of information systems in organizations. At the outset of an information systems strategy development exercise for a single business unit, two fundamental choices have to be made, according to Ormerod.[5] The first choice is whether to adopt a conventional or a participative approach. In the conventional approach, the analysis is conducted by specialists who interview and hold meetings with both users and suppliers of IT within an organization. In a participative approach, the users and suppliers carry out the investigation themselves, supported by a process facilitator. This distinction parallels that drawn by Mumford and Henshall[6] in the context of systems design. The second choice is whether to take a data orientated or a decision orientated approach. In the data orientated approach the focus is on the analysis of data flows; the aim is to be comprehensive, resulting in a target architecture and build sequence to guide the development of infrastructure. In the decision orientated approach the method is to identify the most important decisions and to determine how these might be supported by information systems. Both data and decision orientated approaches will result in a list of investment opportunities requiring evaluation against organizational objectives.

The case described in this paper is an example of a participative, decision orientated approach. A participative approach was taken, both because Sainsbury's wanted to develop a new cadre of senior managers to take on the mantle of systems champions, and because it helps gain ownership and commitment to the implementation of the resultant strategy. A key contextual feature was Sainsbury's willingness to commit the necessary resources, particularly senior management time, which has a high opportunity cost. A decision orientated approach was adopted because most of the key operational systems were already in place, supported by a data architecture that was considered by the information technology (IT) managers to be appropriate. More important to the project was to determine how information could be used to support operational and strategic decisions better. With the participative approach, the necessary understanding of how information flows would be useful in making decisions would be available within the project.

CHOOSING, MIXING AND LINKING METHODS

The methodological approach adopted for the project has its roots in the interactive planning paradigm proposed by Ackoff[7,8]. The aim is to design a desirable future and invent ways of bringing it about. Ackoff's 'interactive planning' paradigm, based on the participative, continuity and holistic principles, includes such concepts as formulating the mess, idealized design, technological feasibility and operational viability. Ackoff makes a series of assertions which capture the essence of what was required from this project:

> '. . . there are no experts when it comes to answering the question: what ought a system to be like? Here every stakeholder's opinion is as relevant as any other's.'

> 'Because engaging in such design is fun, participation is not hard to get.'

> '. . . idealized design facilitates the incorporation of the aesthetic values of the stakeholders into its planning.'

> '. . . participation in idealized design tends to generate consensus among the participants.'

> '. . . idealized design mobilizes its participants into a crusade in pursuit of its product.'

> '. . . idealized design releases large amounts of suppressed creativity and focuses it on organizational development.'

> '. . . the idealized design process expands its participants' concept of feasibility.'

These ideas resonate in many of the strategic problem solving methods such as strategic choice[9] and soft systems methodology (SSM).[10]

It was envisaged from the start that a mix of methods would be used within the process decision. At the time of the project there was little in the literature to guide such choice, notable exceptions being the papers by Bennett[11] and Matthews and Bennett.[12] Bennett suggests some useful distinctions and frameworks when considering linking two or more methods. One distinction he draws is between 'theoretical' and 'practical' aspects of each method. He takes 'theory' to include the particular models, formalisms and the background assumptions, stated or unstated. 'Practice' refers to the process of decision-aiding. A second distinction identifies two classes of 'theory'. Methods such as hypergaming are underpinned by 'theories about the structure of the (social) world'. Others, such as cognitive mapping and strategic choice, also contain 'theories of decision processes'. These latter 'theories' can inform 'practice'.

Linkage can be considered between two sets of theories, two sets of practice or between the theory of one method and the practice of another. Further, Bennett distinguishes three types of linkage, which he labels comparison, enrichment and integration. Under 'comparison', methods are compared for theoretical or practical similarities or differences as a precursor to more ambitious forms of linkage. 'It has the direct benefit of clarifying the applicability of the various methods in different circumstances.' 'Enrichment' refers to the improvement of one method by taking on board elements of another, without producing any new overall content. 'Integration' is 're-served for work which while involving elements of existing approaches, also provides something new'. Bennett gives brief examples of 'experiments' involving hypergames, cognitive maps and strategic choice. In one example, cognitive maps are used to enrich a hypergame analysis. In a second, strategic choice is used to pull together the results of hypergame analysis and cognitive mapping conducted in parallel.

Matthews and Bennett describe a case study involving both cognitive mapping and strategic choice. Cognitive mapping was used to support the interviewing stage of the process; strategic choice was used at a group meeting to develop decision packages.

The authors report that 'Translating from the maps into the strategic choice format, while not a mechanical process, had proved fairly easy.'

Since Sainsbury's project was completed a number of other relevant papers have been published, notably in a book edited by Eden and Radford[13]. A section of the book dedicated to mixing methods includes articles by Cropper, Bennett, Bryant and Huxham and Eden. Cropper[14] suggests that the use of methods is constrained by:

- the nature of the problem or task being addressed
- the degree to which a formalism is employed, and
- the personal style of the consultant and the way in which the method is used with clients.

Cropper concludes that a simple contingency theory of choice of method is insufficient as a methodology for group decision support. More specifically, he considers the problems of mixing cognitive maps[15] and hypergame analysis[16].

Bennett[17] considers the combination of conflict analysis (metagames[18], hypergames, etc.), cognitive mapping, and strategic choice. Recognizing an element of happenstance in this choice of methods, Bennett builds the intellectual case for linkage by considering both similarities and differences between them. As to similarities he suggests that all the methods are designed to help small, relatively autonomous groups of people make non-routine choices. His second similarity is that all the methods he considers are designed primarily for a style of working in which consultants work *with* clients, rather than producing analysis *for* them. In terms of differences, Bennett points out that the characteristic nature of 'surprises' produced by each method is different. For instance, the hypergame model may suggest an apparently powerful threat can be evaded whereas cognitive mapping may unearth virtuous and vicious circles. Bennett suggests the choice between, for instance, strategic choice and hypergaming, turns on whether the problem can best be defined in terms of uncertainty or conflict.

Bryant[19] considers mixing cognitive mapping with hypergame analysis. Huxham and Eden[20] consider the use of formal game theory and hypergaming for the analysis of the dynamics of competition. They report on the difficulties they experienced in attempting to use gaming theory within a cognitive mapping process.

Common to all the discussion of choosing, mixing and linking referred to above, is an interest in cognitive mapping and gaming. Ackoff's interactive planning, Checkland's SSM and other possible approaches are not considered. Interactive planning centres on practical aspects, sharing with cognitive mapping and strategic choice the recognition that decision-making practice is a social process. SSM, like hypergame analysis, has at its centre a particular way of conceptualizing the world. However, SSM also includes a process design for practice. Common to all the 'soft' methods considered above is the recognition that there are actors with different points of view, the actors each have their own interpretation of reality, and agreement to act depends on negotiation between the actors. This underlying interpretive philosophy contrasts sharply with the positivist approach assumed in many methods. On the evidence cited, there would appear to be no reason to believe that mixing soft methods within a project leads to insurmountable difficulties.

THE NEED FOR A NEW STRATEGY

Sainsbury's is a leading supermarket chain in the UK with a turnover in the year of the project, 1989, of about £6 billion. A wide range of food and non-food, branded and own label, products are obtained from suppliers. The goods are received into over 20 centralized warehouses which hold stock and prepare daily vehicle loads for the branches. Some 300 branches receive and display the goods and serve customers. A large, out-of-town store will consist of over 30,000 square feet of selling space, a large car park and other facilities which may include a coffee shop and petrol station. Current investment is dominated by a programme of some 20 new stores per annum.

Both inside and outside the company there is widespread recognition that the use of IT has contributed significantly to the successful record of profitable growth. The results can be seen in a direct and measurable way in terms of reduced depot stock and enhanced depot service to the branches. Less measurable, but no less real, has been the ability to manage the increased volume and product range that the systems enable. It is this ability, to reliably handle large volumes of a wide variety of products in a dynamic market environment, that underpins Sainsbury's growth; a growth which Sainsbury's management readily acknowledge would not have been possible without IT.

The foundations for Sainsbury's IT systems were laid in an outline IS strategy in the late 1970s. Against this strategy, a set of computer systems had been progressively developed, providing basic support for the business. Early in 1988, the company concluded that the implementation of the plan, which they believed had successfully put them ahead of the competition, was largely complete; that there was an opportunity to move further ahead; that to do so, a new strategy for the 1990s needed to be devised.

It was decided that the next stage required a formally managed project which came to be referred to as the Corporate Systems Strategy Project. It was envisaged that the project would be progressed by a team of senior managers from the main line departments led by the Data Processing (DP) Department. The team would be required to understand the current business processes, to evaluate the future scope of technology and then to identify user needs and opportunities that would increase profitability, service and competitive advantage and would reduce cost.

It was felt that a one-off exercise such as this would benefit from outside advice and assistance. Proposals were sought from several major consultancies, from which PA Consulting Group were chosen with the author as the lead consultant.

THE CONTEXT

Over the preceding ten years, Sainsbury's had achieved an outstanding financial record of sustained profit growth, year on year. Sainsbury's management believe that clear direction, attention to detail and willingness to innovate had maintained Sainsbury's at the forefront of grocery and food retailing.

Perhaps one of the most surprising things about Sainsbury's, the largest food and grocery retailer in the UK, is the focus it retains. The centre not only determines direction but it is close to the front-line operations and the marketplace. This is possible because the 300 branches are all doing essentially the same thing. The business is comprehensible as a whole: the practical implications of policy changes can be envisaged or seen. Experience is transferable and cumulative: a problem in one branch leads to changes in practice applicable in all; best practice can be captured in standards and procedures. The result is a clarity of purpose emanating from the centre in the form of both direction and standards, supported by a well honed administrative system. A description of Sainsbury's approach to management can be found in Reference 21.

It is part of the company's folklore that attention to detail has been fundamental to success. There have also been a number of upheavals in retailing since the second world war, including the moves to self-service, centralized distribution and out-of-town superstores. However, between these upheavals there have been relatively long periods of stability; during these stable periods protagonists in the marketplace compete on product and service.

Innovation is considered by Sainsbury's to be a key component in the pursuit of the company's objectives of offering the customer quality product, value for money and service, all to high trading and hygiene standards. Notably, Sainsbury's led UK food and grocery retailing in the introduction of high quality own label products, centralized distribution, checkout scanners and debit card facilities. Innovative leadership is not considered by Sainsbury's as an end in itself: they believe that the choice of improvement, the timing of its introduction and getting it to work in the demanding retail environment are all more important attributes.

To achieve the tight, disciplined operation required to handle the variety and volume safely and efficiently, in common with other large food multiples, Sainsbury's have adopted a functional organization, the main three operational functions being the Trading, Retail and Distribution Divisions. Each of these divisions contains an operational hierarchy together with a planning and direction setting capability. There are clear lines of demarcation and established procedures for co-ordination between functions. Operational policies and joint direction are determined centrally by a combination of formal and informal processes. A key role is played by Board sub-committees, many of which meet weekly to respond to market and operational issues as they evolve. Other major divisions include Development (property acquisition, development and construction), Personnel, Finance and Data Processing.

Systems support the ordering–supply–logistic process, the front end of the stores and the buyers. These operational systems, which manage the basic processes of the business, provide data to support the accountability, policy setting and directional activities.

AN OUTLINE OF THE PROJECT

The project commenced in the second week of February 1989. The approach proposed by the consultants was:

> to work closely with Sainsbury's in a learning process, involving a new generation of managers, fostering creativity and mind broadening, producing an IT strategy that fits Sainsbury's, based on a shared understanding to generate commitment at Board Level.

The emphasis on learning, creativity and mind broadening signalled a radical break with traditional IS strategy development exercises. The emphasis on fit is a reminder that before embarking on any course of action the Board needs to reassure itself that Sainsbury's basic trading stance and values remain intact. Thus, a creative approach with a safety net was envisaged. This section of the paper is a formal description of how these high level aspirations were put into effect.

The approach adopted evolved around the participation of different groups in a process of seminars, workshops and project work. The role of each group had to be clearly defined.

The groups

Four groups were distinguished whose composition and roles were as follows.

(1) The Steering Committee consisted of the joint Managing Directors and the Board Member for Distribution and IT, advised by the Director of IT, and the author. The role of the Steering Committee was to monitor progress, provide guidance, explain policy and to exercise judgment on the desirability and feasibility of potential systems. The Steering Committee would provide the bridge to the rest of the Board, reporting on progress and obtaining agreement to the resulting strategy.

(2) The Task Force consisted of 16 senior managers chosen to provide experience of the different aspects of the business. The role of the Task Force was to conduct the study within the guidelines laid down by the Steering Committee, to input their knowledge of the business, to identify those areas of the business where systems might be developed to advantage and to draw up a list of the candidate systems.

(3) The Advisory Group consisted of the senior managers of the DP Department. Their role was to understand the approach taken by the Task Force in order to provide systems support, including the evaluation of the technical feasibility and cost of the suggestions.

(4) The Project Team consisted of the IT Director, the author and two assistants. The role of the Project Team was to guide, stimulate and assist the Task Force, to administer the project and to communicate with the Steering Committee. It was also their task to pull the final strategy together for agreement by the Steering Committee.

The Project Phases

Phase 0. Project initiation

This phase cleared the ground for the strategy development to get underway. The project was to be a major undertaking; participants needed to be chosen and told their roles; the project needed to be made visible within the company; the consultants needed to meet as many of the key actors as possible. Commitment of the participants' time was established in principle. A project plan was drawn up. At the same time the project team familiarized itself with the business and current issues, visiting branches, depots and the head office, and learning area office functions. Some of the visits and meetings served the dual purpose of progressing Phase 1.

Phase 1. Business imperatives

Phase 1 examined the business and its environment in order to identify the business imperatives—those things the business must do if it is to succeed. This involved three activities. First, individual interviews of the Steering Committee Members were conducted from which cognitive maps were drawn up of key aspects of the business. Second, an introductory seminar was held of the Task Force at which strategy, organization and technology concepts were discussed in relation to the company. Third, a two-day workshop of the Task Force was held to explore strategy issues using *inter alia* the cognitive maps developed from the interviews. The results of the workshop were documented and published as a book for all concerned in the project. The key deliverable was a map of the overall business based on the mapping exercises. The map identified areas for further investigation for systems opportunities. This process achieved the 'shaping' of the problem as defined by Friend and Hickling in their strategic choice methodology.[9] As well as cognitive mapping, the methods and models used included conventional SWOT analysis, de Bono's six thinking hats,[22] Porter's five forces and value chain models,[23] Mintzberg's structure in fives model[24] and the seven questions of Burnstine and Soknacki.[25] The models were used to help the participants better understand the company and its competitive environment. For instance, Mintzberg's structure in fives model was used to debate the way the company co-ordinated its activities and the emergent management style. This would inform discussions about systems to support communication, command and control, later in the process. The participants were engaged in a mixture of individual, syndicate and plenary exercises. The tools included six colourful carnival hats.

Phase 2. Future systems

The objective of Phase 2 was to examine in more detail the areas of the business selected in Phase 1, in order to identify candidate systems for investment. Three activities were involved. A one-day workshop was held at which the Task Force, who were by this stage organized in four cross-functional syndicates, learnt to apply soft systems methodology (SSM).[26,27] Each syndicate produced a project plan for a sub-project to apply SSM to their chosen area of investigation. The second activity consisted of the four sub-projects operated independently by the syndicates. Each syndicate investigated the business using the method and models of SSM over a six-week period. Help with applying the method was given if sought. Intermediate workshops were held to discuss progress, problems and overlaps. The third activity was a presentation of the results to the Steering Committee. The main workshop was documented by the Project Team, but documentation of the sub-projects was the responsibility of the syndicates themselves.

During this Phase the Advisory Group, who had been following a similar, but separate, pattern of activities to the Task Force, formed two syndicates to conduct an inquiry using SSM into the DP Division's activities. In addition, the Project Team formed a seventh syndicate to cover an area which it was felt had been neglected at this point. Thus, some 30 people were directly engaged in the analysis.

The Phase was conducted entirely using SSM, following the step-by-step method, using the rich picture, CATWOE, conceptual, real/ideal, desirable/feasible models. No new tools were introduced. Simple project management techniques were used to progress each syndicate.

Phase 3. Evaluation

The approach taken in this phase was based on the comparing and choosing modes of the strategic choice methodology.[9] The costs and benefits of each candidate system were evaluated in terms of the business imperatives. Four activities were involved. A quality check was carried out by the Project Team and the Advisory Group with the Task Force. An evaluation framework was designed by the Project Team in consultation with the Steering Committee. All candidate systems were reviewed by the Steering Committee. Finally, each candidate system was evaluated and given a priority score using the agreed framework; the benefits and costs being estimated by the Task Force and the Advisory Group respectively and the final evaluation determined by the Steering Committee.

During this Phase, the number of participants was widened to include heads of departments and other Board Members where relevant. The main model used was the evaluation framework developed for the project. This involved making quantified estimates of hard and soft costs and benefits, adjusted by factors to reflect the risks and the competitive opportunities. The structure was kept compatible with the decision conferencing software Highview and Equity[28] to allow the option of using the London School of Economics POD facilities, an option which was not, in the event, taken up. During the quality check, use was made of the viable systems model (VSM)[29-32] and a hierarchical functional model of the business to ensure that the communications, control, intelligence and all other processes of the business had been considered. No computerized tools were used.

Phase 4. Strategy

This Phase was conducted by the Project Team and Advisory Group in consultation with the Steering Committee. The objective was to use the prioritized portfolio of candidate systems to produce a strategy, taking account of the current development programme, the technology platform and the operational constraints of the business. Entity analysis was used to identify potential constraints on the build sequence. A sub-project explored some of the technical issues to form the basis of the IT strategy. First cut resource estimates and development and implementation schedules were used to highlight potential difficulties and to provide estimates of phased costs and benefits. The candidates were grouped into 'initiatives' to be carried out by project teams consisting of users and specialists. These initiatives were given development priority to give the new strategy a kick start.

The technical (IT) strategy was progressed by the Advisory Group in workshops. No particular method was used. The issues were debated and then written up by the Project Team. Spreadsheets were used for the resource planning and scheduling.

The Board agreed the strategy. Development and implementation are now in progress. The relationship between an agreed strategy and strategy implementation is, of course, problematic[33] and the links between the two complex.[4] It was agreed at the start that the 'strategy' would be a 'point of departure rather than a blue print'.

However, the purpose of the approach adopted was to provide both a strategic direction and momentum behind that direction.

THE PROCESS DESIGNER'S PERSPECTIVE

Fixed Points

The process design started from a number of points fixed by the client, and the requirement to end up with a strategy and the commitment to implement it. The process was to have at its centre a cadre of selected senior managers, originally expected to be six in number, two from each of the major operational departments. By the time the project had got underway, the number had grown to 16 as a result of requests to be involved from other divisions. This number included a senior member of the DP department. Over the period of intensive activity, Phases 1 and 2, it was agreed by the Board that the Task Force members could spend up to two days a week on the project.

The project was to be overseen by the Steering Committee who were prepared to meet intermittently. They needed to be comfortable with the process and make sure that the company's strategy was correctly understood and supported by the new IS strategy. To allow the DP senior managers to keep abreast and contribute to the project, the Advisory Group was formed. As the project progressed the Advisory Group needed to move centre stage to ensure that the proposals were realistic in technical and cost terms. They also needed to be at one with the strategic direction chosen.

The key decision in determining the group structure was the formation of the Task Force of senior managers who would be at the centre of the participative process. The requirement for the Steering Committee to oversee and the Project Team to facilitate the process needs little explanation but the formation of a separate Advisory Group of the IT professionals is more controversial. The members of the group obviously form a natural interest group who have a stake in the outcome and need to be committed to its success. It could be argued that their expertise should be placed at the centre of process, in the Task Force. This would have risked dominance of the Task Force by a group with a technical rather than business perspective. The compromise was to form the Advisory Group separately with their own agenda of meetings and workshops, and to include one of their number in the Task Force. The predominance of users in the Task Force reflected the company's desire for a user-led strategy.

In developing an IS strategy the subject areas covered are common to most approaches. The structure chosen here is simple and direct. Having started up the project (Phase 0), the business requirements are explored (Phase 1), the systems opportunities are identified (Phase 2) and evaluated (Phase 3), and then the strategy is drawn up (Phase 4). The interest lay in what was going to go on within the phases to make the project a creative and insightful learning experience for the company.

Teams, Learning and Action

Three interrelated ideas played a key role in the design of the project. These were the concept of the learning organization as advocated by Beer,[29] Garrett[34] and others, the action learning approach advocated by Revans[35] and Mumford,[36] and the idea of exceptional performance and superteams as described by Hickman and Silver[37] and Hastings *et al.*[38] These ideas, which seemed consistent with Ackoff's paradigm, contained ways of engendering the creativity, motivation and commitment and would set in motion a process of organizational learning and change.

There were two direct consequences for process design. First, the project would be designed as a learning process. It would start with the ideas and understanding of a few people, the Steering Committee. These ideas and understanding would be widened and deepened by a larger group, the Task Force, who would then 'sell' the ideas to a progressively wider audience, the heads of departments and functional Board members and ultimately the project development teams. Secondly, the Task Force members would be built into 'super-teams' empowered to conduct the heart of the investigation in 'action learning' mode.

Choice of Methods and Models

Two issues should dominate the design of an IS strategy development process. First, the resulting strategy must be driven by the business requirements. Second, the process must develop commitment to, and ownership of, the strategy. Attempts to achieve business driven IS strategies often fall well short of the mark on both accounts. This stems from an over simplistic view of business strategy and how it can be captured and a completely unrealistic expectation that strategies will, in fact, be implemented on their merits. The essence of a business cannot be captured in a few objectives or critical success factors however carefully crafted. The subtleties, implications and interactions need to be understood. As a consequence, the IS strategist must accept that the business is best understood and interpreted by those engaged in running it day to day.

Nor are senior decision makers in very large organizations easily persuaded to act by 'objective' analysis. Their decisions and actions are guided by the understanding they have developed of the nature of the business they are in, the choice of levers that they believe are available to adjust or alter direction, their perception of the views and positions of their colleagues and an implicit model based on experience of how decisions can be turned into action. Any new ideas have to be fitted into their existing framework. Major adjustments to the framework will only come about through a massive assault on their interpretation of reality (such as the major success of a new player) or through new experiences and the opportunity to negotiate and test a new position in non-critical circumstances. Assaults by IS strategists fall well short of being massive and are unlikely to succeed. The way forward is to create the circumstances whereby the decision makers themselves can explore, assess and develop their own understanding.

As a result of the above considerations and the earlier discussion on choosing, mixing and linking methods, guidelines were drawn up in the form of principles which defined the nature of the approach envisaged. These acted as a framework for the process design and choice of methods. The principles were:

- the learning principle: strategy and planning is an organizational learning process;
- the interpretive principle: it is management's task to state and develop their interpretation of the company and its environment;

- the participatory principle: the active participation of management is essential to give commitment and ownership;
- the pluralist principle: diverging interests between groups have to be accommodated;
- the adaptive principle: organizations are complex, open and adaptive systems.

Within the methodology adopted and the action learning approach described above, methods and models were required which would help the participants gain and share insight, explore creative solutions and communicate their proposals to others. The methods that were considered are shown in Figure 10.1. The methodological under-pinnings of cognitive mapping, SSM and strategic choice were felt to be potentially consistent with the five principles and each had a good track record of practical application.[26,39-42] In addition, it was thought that decision conferences could be useful and the VSM and the seven questions could provide insights in a systems context.

In terms of Bennett's linking framework, the three major methods were to be kept theoretically separate, each being used in a different phase of the project (cognitive mapping in Phase 1, SSM in Phase 2 and strategic choice in Phase 3). However, practical linkages exist both in terms of the results feeding through and the groups of participants being common throughout. The use of the other methods can mainly be thought of as enrichment. For instance, the seven questions were used to understand systemic desirability in the SSM analysis better. The relationship between the three main methods and Ackoff's interactive planning is one of mutual enrichment. Conceptual model building in SSM can be seen as Ackoff's idealized planning, creating a vision of the future; cognitive mapping reveals the aesthetic values of the stakeholders, required for Ackoff's idealized design.

	Phase 0	Phase 1	Phase 2	Phase 3	Phase 4
Cognitive mapping	✓	✓	✓	•	•
SSM	✓	✓	✓	•	✓
VSM	✓	✓	✓	•	•
Decision conference	•	✓	✓	✓	•
Strategic choice	✓	✓	✓	✓	•
BIAIT 7 questions	✓	✓	✓	•	•
CSF	✓	✓	•	✓	•
Entity diagrams	✓	•	✓	•	✓
Functional models	✓	✓	✓	•	✓
Porter	✓	✓	✓	•	•

✓ indicates potential for use

Figure 10.1. Potential Methods/Models

Alternative Approaches

There is, of course, a much wider range of choices than those discussed so far. Below the dotted line in Figure 10.1 are the more standard information systems planning (ISP) methods and models, which could be applied, but which are not particularly well suited to the participative project envisaged and which, for technical reasons, were not required for systems architecture purposes. It was considered whether system dynamics[43] could have a role in evaluating the benefits of the proposals but this was not pursued at the time. Discussions had also been held with Flood and Jackson who described possible approaches that they were including within their total systems intervention (TSI) methodology. TSI provides a framework within which methods are placed and which encourages a flexible approach using different methods or combinations of method as appropriate. This has since been published.[44] These discussions introduced the possibility of using the strategic assumption surfacing and testing (SAST) methodology of Mason and Mitroff and critical systems heuristics (CSH) of Ulrich. Surfacing of assumptions was obviously desirable but explicit surfacing of conflicts in the way advocated in CSH was potentially risky and uncertain in its consequences because of the lack of experience with, and available examples of, using the approach.

The list of questions suggested by the approach is sensible and addresses issues that would in any case need to be understood. However, it seemed that considerable methodological development would be required to meet the needs of a consultant entering an unknown managerial culture. The approaches classified by Flood and Jackson as 'pluralist' seemed most suited to the task in hand. This included Ackoff's interactive planning, SSM and cognitive mapping. Some comfort was drawn from the fit between the proposed approach and TSI.

Putting it Together

The methods/models actually used are shown in Figure 10.2, the most important being cognitive mapping, SSM and strategic choice. Cognitive mapping was used to capture the views of senior management. These maps were then turned into prose and used as exercises with the Task Force (and later the Advisory Group) who recreated a version of the same maps. Written down in black and white this sounds bizarre but the process was crucial and effective. The exercises would transfer understanding from the Steering Committee to the Task Force members, build a common understanding of the company's operating and competitive strategy and provide a platform for discussion and development of the ideas further. The maps could then be shaped to focus the next phase. While the use of cognitive mapping to transfer understanding between groups has some parallels with the work of Eden[39] in the publishing industry, the method used departs from that advocated by Eden and his co-workers, extending the practical use of this powerful technique.

SSM would provide the method for the Task Force to conduct its sub-projects: it is easily learnt by non-analysts, sufficiently general to allow creative application and provides models which encourage thinking about essentials. The models also provide a consistent basis for project planning and documentation. SSM was chosen as the key vehicle for 'action learning' by the Task Force. The proposed use of each method is classified in Figure 10.3 using categories suggested by Cropper.[14]

	Phase 0	Phase 1	Phase 2	Phase 3	Phase 4
Cognitive mapping	★	★ ★ ★	★	★	★
SSM	★	★	★ ★ ★	★	★
VSM	★	★	★	★	★
Decision conference	★	★	★	★	★
Strategic choice	★	★	★	★ ★	★
BIAIT 7 questions	★	★	★	★	★
CSF	★	★	★	★	★
Entity diagrams	★	★	★	★	★
Functional models	★	★	★	★	★
Porter	★	★	★	★	★

★ ★ ★ indicates major use   ★ indicates minor use

Figure 10.2. Actual Methods/Models Used

Strategic choice would provide the basis for taking the ideas generated by the SSM analysis and evaluating them according to criteria derived by the Steering Committee in their role as keepers of the company's interests. The main uncertainties to be considered were risks of overrunning on costs and failing to obtain the benefits envisaged.

	Generative metaphor	Conceptual framework	Problem structuring	Preparation for analysis	Formal analysis
Cognitive mapping	●	✓	✓	✓	●
SSM	●	✓	✓	✓	✓
VSM	✓	✓	●	●	●
Decision conference	●	●	✓	✓	●
Strategic choice	●	✓	✓	●	●
BIAIT 7 questions	✓	✓	●	●	●
CSF	●	●	●	●	●
Entity diagrams	●	●	✓	✓	✓
Functional models	●	●	✓	✓	✓
Porter	✓	✓	●	●	●

After Cropper[14]

Figure 10.3. Use of Methods/Models

THE FACILITATOR'S PERSPECTIVE

To achieve the ambitious aims of the project, the facilitator had to orchestrate events, create theatre, choose the props, involve and excite, elicit goals, encourage learning, recognize themes, celebrate success, and smooth the path. It was important from the start to establish the role of facilitator and distinguish it from the roles of expert or doctor, as suggested by Schein.[45] It was also important to establish the confidence of the Steering Committee, who would have to empower the participants to range widely on strategic issues. Above all, the project was to be fun, not for its own sake, but to bring out the best in people in a subject area seen by many as technical, difficult and dull.

A facilitated work group is defined by Phillips and Phillips[46] as a small collection of people who share a goal and perform various tasks, with the help of a facilitator. They distinguish between leading and facilitating a group.

> A leader would typically be concerned with both the 'what' and the 'how'. A facilitator, on the other hand, would refrain from contributing to the content of the group's discussion because involvement in content may interfere with the effective facilitation of the process. The facilitator attends to content, for content and process interact, but active involvement in the content of discussions makes observation of the process difficult.

In this project the role of facilitator was not strictly adhered to, particularly when the group sought contributions to the content. However, the final responsibility for content lay with the participants.

The introductory seminar with the Task Force was a necessary first step and conventional in format. It took place in the windowless bowels of the company's Blackfriars headquarters and had its highlights, but it lacked theatre and excitement. The second major set piece, a two-day seminar had to be different. It was located in an up-market hotel. The stakes were high; the seminar could make or break the project. By the end of the second day, the participants had to be enthusiastic, committed and effective. It could not be assumed that idealized design would automatically engender enthusiasm in the manner envisaged by Ackoff. The process had been designed to this end but it had to be encouraged to happen on the day.

The two-day programme was unusual in the variety it contained. The time was structured with a combination of individual, syndicate and plenary tasks, each involving a mixture of thinking, writing, discussing, drawing pictures and diagrams, reading, describing and listening. These different ways of working were combined to encourage a variety of thought and bring out ideas that any one way on its own would not achieve. The mixing of participants in cross-functional teams was also designed to encourage variety. For some of the time two members of the Steering Committee were invited to attend and participate, to empower the participants to address fundamental questions. Open and creative thinking were to be fostered while the methods were to be used to direct, integrate and record the results.

In the event, the variety of the exercises and the learning involved generated great interest and enthusiasm. Each member of the Task Force was keen to contribute their own understanding of the business and learn from the experience of others. Most important, credibility for the project was built which would provide the essential platform for the following phases.

The next major hurdle was to get the Task Force to master the SSM method that would carry them through their sub-projects. This was essential, as it was the Task Force members who had to conduct the analysis of the business to identify candidate systems. They had to identify the ideal and find opportunities for moving the company towards it. SSM gave them the framework to structure their enquiry and visualize the ideal. The technique was taught by example and participative exercises. The ideas were quickly picked up and the SSM terminology became part of the language of the group.

The realization that progress was now entirely in their hands was initially something of a shock to the Task Force. Up to this point they had been led through the process. From now on, advice and support would be available but the syndicates were encouraged to take the initiative. The facilitator's task was to let go and resist the temptation to interfere. The reward was that the syndicates quickly gathered momentum and applied the SSM approach. In doing this, they enriched the process with ideas of their own: an attitude survey was commissioned, other companies were visited, group discussions of managers and employees were held, and a survey was conducted of a key service indicator in the stores. Senior managers were able to make these things happen in a way that analysts and advisors would have found difficult or impossible. A long and varied list of candidate systems, not all involving IT, was generated and presented.

The evaluation phase needed to be a more controlled part of the process. The results of all the enthusiasm and insight required careful scrutiny if they were to receive the attention and resources of the business. The facilitator's task was much easier at this stage because the project had developed its own style and momentum. Regular workshops were held to maintain the enthusiasm in the, by now, customary place, an area office with excellent training facilities. As the process proceeded and the emphasis moved from creative ideas to business benefit and practicality, the circle of people involved grew. The influence of the project went wider still, affecting debates in other fora. Throughout the project the Task Force held together as a team, crossing normal functional and hierarchical boundaries.

The final phase of putting the strategy together was more analytical in nature and involved more experts. Facilitation still had a role to play but a less significant one.

Throughout the process, diagrams and documentation played vital roles. At each stage everyone had to be reminded of where they had got to, what they had achieved, where they were going and what had to be done next. Diagrams, in particular, played both a practical and symbolic role in summarizing and catching the lessons learnt. The 'books' of the key workshops helped turn ephemeral events into lasting learning experiences that continued to be the subject of discussion.

LESSONS LEARNT

Choosing, Mixing and Linking Methods

Ackoff's interactive planning formed the overarching methodology which informed and enriched the theoretical and practical aspects of the methods used. Many of the theories and principles underlying the different approaches were similar. For instance, both interactive planning and SSM emphasize the importance of recognizing the purposeful nature of human activity systems, and of taking a holistic view of the system. Interactive planning and strategic choice assume that consensus can be reached. Cognitive mapping and strategic choice work with the participants' interpretation of reality and emphasize the importance of participation, as does interactive planning. Setting down guiding principles helped simplify the choice of models and ensured a consistent feel to the process. By locating the three major methods used to carry out the project in three different phases, the methods could be interfaced without the need for a more demanding integration. In Bennett's terms, there were practical but not theoretical links. The three methods each had a process associated with them which could be adjusted to make sense in terms of the overall project.

For strategy development processes, which need to start very wide and end with specific proposals for action, there is a natural flow from cognitive mapping, through SSM to strategic choice. Cognitive mapping and SSM allow wide ranging debates and encourage the recognition of conflicting points of view. Strategic choice provides a mechanism for closing down the debate and reaching decisions. This combination of the three methods used in series, linked by process rather than theory, was found to be effective for IS strategy development. Other methods and models were used to enrich the process. A summary of the relationship between some of the methods used is shown in Figure 10.4. Since the project, a number of books have been published which conveniently cover a number of the methods used.[13,44,47,48] They also provide an easy way into soft and systems approaches for potential designers of mixed process. Coverage of some of the methods included in these books is shown in Figure 10.5; the books do, of course, include other methods.

Interactive Planning

Ackoff's approach articulates the 'what' well but has less in the way of models and techniques to support the 'how'. The approach is built on the premise that there is sufficient commonality of purpose between participants to achieve a consensus view. In so far as conflicting views exist, as they always will, interactive planning encourages their resolution. This is a realistic expectation within the management of many private

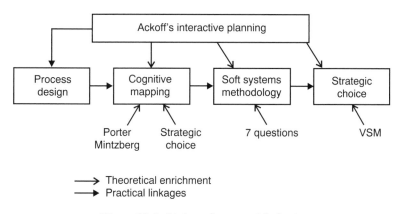

Figure 10.4. Linkage between Methods

	Flood and Jackson	Eden and Radford	Rosenhead	Jackson
Cognitive mapping	●	✓	✓	●
SSM	✓	✓	✓	✓
VSM	✓	●	●	✓
Decision conference	●	✓	●	●
Strategic choice	●	✓	✓	●
Interactive planning	✓	●	●	●
SAST	✓	●	●	✓
Game analysis	●	✓	✓	●
Critical sys. heuristics	✓	●	●	✓
Systems dynamics	✓	●	●	●
Robustness analysis	●	●	✓	●
Reference	44	13	47	48

Figure 10.5. Contents of Books Covering Multiple Approaches

sector organizations but may be more problematic in the more overtly political circumstances of the public sector.

Cognitive Mapping

Cognitive mapping provided powerful insights and stimulated discussion. It is a particularly good method for exploring the interaction between objectives and strategies and competition between companies. By carrying out exercises, participants quickly learnt the conventions and were able to use the technique themselves. Maps derived by the group took on a lasting significance and provided a focus for the ensuing enquiry process. Small maps of limited scope to explore particular issues proved the most effective and memorable. The technique is inherently interesting to participants and immediately engages the group in strategic thinking. Its use signals to the participants that they can explore new ways of looking at things.

Soft Systems Methodology

The syndicate groups of the Task Force used SSM as required, but not without difficulty. Lack of guidance in the methodology as to what 'understanding' the business entailed can be unnerving for an operational manager used to ambiguous procedures. Defining a 'good' transformation often proved difficult and, once chosen, multiple viewpoints usually got left behind. However, it was these very difficulties that prevented the exercise from becoming routine and lacking in challenge for the participants. Four people per group worked well if the personalities were well balanced. An attempt was made in the quality check part of Phase 3 to use a formal systems model to check the conceptual models, as advocated by Checkland. This proved to be too time consuming given the large number of conceptual models generated. The formal systems check was abandoned in favour of a more informal approach. Overall the method proved a robust framework for investigation by non-analysts.

Strategic Choice

In the event, the Steering Committee wanted a far more quantitative analysis of the costs, benefits and risks than is envisaged by the strategic choice method. The method chosen was relatively straightforward but time consuming. It uncovered huge differences in interpretation of what each proposed system would be and how it would change the way the business could be run. In these circumstances, agreeing costs and benefits between participants and board members proved difficult. The debate was necessary at some point but, in other circumstances, a more qualitative assessment, as envisaged by Friend and Hickling, may be preferable.

The Seven Questions

The seven questions are applied to the transactions between an organization with its customers to identify the implied systems requirements. In use the method gave considerable insight into the systemic desirability of suggested improvements thrown up by the SSM enquiry process. The method thus enriched SSM.

The Viable Systems Model

VSM was used in the Phase 3 quality check process to make sure all the elements of the VSM had been covered. It soon became apparent that there was merit in the argument that, as Sainsbury's was evidently viable, all the required functions to achieve viability must be in place if the premise of the VSM model is correct. The process was therefore in danger of turning into a quality check of VSM. Potentially this would have been an interesting exercise but not relevant to the matter in hand. The use of VSM was therefore dropped. This should not be taken to imply anything about the merits of VSM in general.

CONCLUSIONS

This paper describes a major IS strategy project that made use of a mixture of soft OR and systems methods. The project is viewed from several perspectives. While adopting Ackoff's interactive planning paradigm, it was possible to embed a number of methods and models from the soft school. These methods supported the aim of stimulating interest and creativity, helping to generate the commitment to implement the proposed changes.

In this instance, methods and models were mixed in two senses. First, many of the models were simply used to give multiple perspectives. For instance, Porter's models were used to understand better the industry forces, and the Mintzberg's model was used to identify the necessary co-ordination mechanisms in the company. Secondly, where major use was made of cognitive mapping, SSM and strategic choice, each method dominated one phase of the process. They were not formally integrated nor used concurrently. The understanding gained from cognitive mapping was used to shape, inform and stimulate the SSM analysis. Subsequently the results of cognitive mapping were used in the design of the evaluation framework to prioritize the ideas generated by the SSM analysis.

As a result of the experience gained in this project, there is nothing to suggest that cognitive mapping, SSM and strategic choice in particular cannot be used in one strategy development project. Indeed they were found to complement one another. Cognitive mapping allows participants to explore in an unconstrained way their interpretation of the organization's position. SSM encourages continuation of the interpretive and participative approach, recognizing that there are multiple viewpoints. It provides structure and a flexible discipline for analysis and the development of options. Strategic choice provides a participative method of shaping and evaluating the choices in the light of diverging interests. Each approach provides ways of engaging members of organizations in activities which will deepen their understanding of the possibilities and constraints. Thus, each is capable of supporting the desired learning process and no one of the approaches could adequately support all the phases of this project.

Many of the experiences and expressed preferences in this paper find parallels in the published literature, which indicates that, in this field of endeavour, theory and practice are in step. This reflects the action research approach adopted by the originators of the methods and subsequent researchers. A counterbalance is thus provided to the highly theoretical roots of the methods in philosophy, psychology and the social sciences. The project is a testament to the fact that good theory is very practical.

Now that some of the soft methods have become well established, more attention is turning to mixing the methods. Future research interest is likely to concentrate on developing frameworks to guide more formally the use and mixing of approaches in terms of both content (theory) and process (practice). This is already being pursued by a number of researchers, for example, those examining the relationship between SSM and systems development methodologies.[49] If the soft 'technology' is to deliver its full potential in terms of better group problem solving and decision taking, attention will also have to turn to letting go and encouraging the wider use of the methods and models. Widely available computer support could well be the key.

It could be argued that Sainsbury's, with its track record of success in both management and IT and its ability to bring resources to bear, provides a particularly favourable environment for the introduction of the 'participative' approach described in this paper. The author's experience in tailoring the approach for a potentially more hostile environment will be published in a subsequent paper.

ACKNOWLEDGEMENTS

The author would like to acknowledge the contributions of Judith Williams of PA Consulting Group, and Dennis Goulding and Bob Hammersley of Sainsbury's who formed the project team; of Alan Jacobs, IT Director of Sainsbury's, who was the Project Director; and of Angus Clark, Member of Sainsbury's Board, who was the project sponsor and gave permission for the publication of this paper. Credit is also due to the members of the Steering Committee, Task Force and Advisory Group for their wholehearted involvement despite other pressing demands on their time. The author would like to thank Hylton Boothroyd, John Mingers and Jonathan Rosenhead for their comments on an earlier draft of the paper and the referees for their advice.

REFERENCES

1. J. Mingers and S. Taylor (1992) The use of soft systems methodology in practice. *J. Opl. Res. Soc.* **43**, 321–332.
2. M. J. Earl (1989) *Management Strategies for Information Technology.* Prentice-Hall, Englewood Cliffs, New Jersey.
3. J. Ward, P. Griffiths and P. Whitmore (1990) *Strategic Planning for Information Systems.* Wiley, Chichester.
4. G. Walsham (1993) *Interpreting Information Systems in Organizations.* Wiley, Chichester.
5. R. J. Ormerod (1993) On the nature of information systems strategy development. *J. Computing and Infor. Technol.* **1**, 285–294.
6. E. Mumford and D. Henshall (1979) *A Participative Approach to Computer Systems Design.* Associated Business Press, London.
7. R. L. Ackoff (1979) The future of operational research is past. *J. Opl Res. Soc.* **30**, 93–104.
8. R. L. Ackoff (1979) Resurrecting the future of operational research. *J. Opl Res. Soc.* **30**, 189–199.
9. J. K. Friend and A. Hickling (1987) *Planning under Pressure: The Strategic Choice Approach.* Pergamon Press, Oxford.
10. P. B. Checkland (1981) *Systems Thinking, Systems Practice.* Wiley, Chichester.
11. P. G. Bennett (1985) On linking approaches to decision-aiding: issues and prospects. *J. Opl Res. Soc.* **36**, 659–670.
12. L. R. Matthews and P. G. Bennett (1986) The art of course planning: soft OR in action. *J. Opl Res Soc.* **37**, 579–590.
13. C. Eden and J. Radford (1990) *Tackling Strategic Problems: the Role of Group Decision Support.* Sage, London.
14. S. Cropper (1990) Variety, formality and style: choosing amongst decision-support methods. In *Tackling Strategic Problems: the Role of Group Decision Support.* (C. Eden and J. Radford, Eds) pp. 92–98. Sage, London.
15. C. Eden, S. Jones and D. Sims (1983) *Messing About in Problems.* Pergamon Press, Oxford.
16. P. G. Bennett, S. Cropper and C. Huxham (1989) Modelling interactive decisions: the hypergame focus. In *Rational Analysis for a Problematic World.* (J. Rosenhead, Ed.) pp. 293–314. Wiley, Chichester.
17. P. G. Bennett (1990) Mixing methods: combining conflict analysis, SODA and strategic choice. In *Tackling Strategic Problems: the Role of Group Decision Support.* (C. Eden and J. Radford, Eds) pp. 99–109. Sage, London.
18. N. Howard (1989) The manager as politician and general: the metagame approach to analysing cooperation and conflict. In *Rational Analysis for a Problematic World.* (J. Rosenhead, Ed.) pp. 239–261. Wiley, Chichester.
19. J. Bryant (1990) Systems of perceptions: developments in hypermapping. In *Tackling Strategic Problems: the Role of Group Decision Support.* (C. Eden and J. Radford, Eds) pp. 110–119. Sage, London.
20. C. Huxham and C. Eden (1990) Gaming, competitor analysis and strategic management. In *Tackling Strategic Problems: the Role of Group Decision Support.* (C. Eden and J. Radford, Eds) pp. 120–128. Sage, London.
21. D. A. Quarmby (1991) Tackling the challenge of the nineties. *J. Opl Res. Soc.* **42**, 105–112.

22. E. De Bono (1985) *Conflicts: A Better Way to Resolve Them, Six Thinking Hats.* Penguin, London.
23. M. E. Porter (1985) *Competitive Advantage: Creating and Sustaining Superior Advantage.* Free Press, New York.
24. H. Mintzberg (1983) *Structure in Fives: Designing Effective Organisations.* Prentice-Hall, Englewood Cliffs, New Jersey.
25. D. C. Burnstine and D. W. Soknacki (1979) BIAIT—A tool for deciding between doing the right thing and doing the 'thing' right. BIAIT International, Inc, Petersburg, New York.
26. P. Checkland (1985) Achieving 'desirable and feasible' change: an application of soft systems methodology. *J. Opl Res. Soc.* **36**, 821–831.
27. P. Checkland (1985) From optimizing to learning a development of systems thinking for the 1990s. *J. Opl Res. Soc.* **36**, 757–767.
28. L. D. Phillips (1989) Gaining corporate commitment to change. Paper presented at conference, *People Mean Profit in the 90s.* LSE, London.
29. S. Beer (1981) *Brain of the Firm.* Wiley, Chichester.
30. S. Beer (1979) *The Heart of Enterprise.* Wiley, Chichester.
31. S. Beer (1975) *Platform for Change.* Wiley, Chichester.
32. S. Beer (1985) *Diagnosing the System for Organisation.* Wiley, Chichester.
33. H. Mintzberg and J. A. Waters (1985) Of strategies, deliberate and emergent. *Strategic Mgmt J.* **6**, 257–272.
34. R. Garratt (1987) *The Learning Organisation.* Fontana, London.
35. R. Revans (1989) Action learning. Comment in *OR Insight* **2**(1), 22–23.
36. A. Mumford, D. Boddy and C. Margerison (undated) Lecture notes on action learning. The International Management Centre from Buckingham.
37. C. R. Hickman and M. A. Silva (1986) *Creating Excellence: Managing Culture, Strategy & Change in the New Age*, Unwin, London.
38. C. Hastings, P. Bixby and R. Chaudhry-Lawton (1986) *Superteams: a Blueprint for Organisational Success.* Fontana, London.
39. C. Eden and S. Jones (1980) Publish or perish?—a case study. *J. Opl Res. Soc.* **31**, 131–139.
40. C. Eden (1985) Perish the thought! *J. Opl Res. Soc.* **36**, 809–819.
41. C. Eden and C. Huxham (1988) Action-orientated strategic management. *J. Opl Res. Soc.* **39**, 889–899.
42. R. L. Flood and P. Gaisford (1989) Policing vice in the West End: a systemic perspective points to a multi-agency approach. *OR Insight* **2**(3), 10–15.
43. R. G. Coyle (1977) *Management System Dynamics.* Wiley, Chichester.
44. R. L. Flood and M. C. Jackson (1991) *Creative Problem Solving: Total Systems Intervention.* Wiley, Chichester.
45. E. Schein (1990) A general philosophy of helping: process consultation. *Sloan Mgmt Rev.* **57** (Spring), 57–64.
46. L. D. Phillips and M. C. Phillips (1993) Facilitated work groups: theory and practice. *J. Opl Res. Soc.* **44**, 533–550.
47. J. Rosenhead (Ed.) (1989) *Rational Analysis for a Problematic World.* Wiley, Chichester.
48. M. C. Jackson (1991) *Systems Methodologies for the Management Sciences.* Plenum, New York.
49. J. Mingers (1992) SSM and information systems. *Systemist* **14**, 82–89.

Part IV

Modelling Uncertainty

Chapter 11

Scenario Planning: A Tool for Strategic Thinking

Paul J. H. Schoemaker

University of Pennsylvania, USA

Early in this century, it was unclear how airplanes would affect naval warfare. When Brigadier General Billy Mitchell proposed that airplanes might sink battleships by dropping bombs on them, US Secretary of War Newton Baker remarked, 'That idea is so damned nonsensical and impossible that I'm willing to stand on the bridge of a battleship while that nitwit tries to hit it from the air.' Josephus Daniels, Secretary of the Navy, was also incredulous: 'Good God! This man should be writing dime novels.' Even the prestigious *Scientific American* proclaimed in 1910 that 'to affirm that the aeroplane is going to "revolutionize" naval warfare of the future is to be guilty of the wildest exaggeration.'[1]

In hindsight, it is difficult to appreciate why air power's potential was unclear to so many. But can we predict the future any better than these defense leaders did? We are affected by the same biases they were. It was probably as hard for them to evaluate the effect of airplanes in the 1920s as it is for us to assess the impact over the next decades of multimedia, the human genome project, biotechnology, artificial intelligence, organ transplants, superconductivity, space colonization, and myriad other developments. The myopic statements in the sidebar remind us how frequently smart people have made the wrong assumptions about the future with great certainty.

Managers who can expand their imaginations to see a wider range of possible futures will be much better positioned to take advantage of the unexpected opportunities that will come along. And managers today have something those defense leaders did not have—scenario planning. Unfortunately, too few companies use it. If only General Motors in the seventies had explored more fully the consequences of OPEC, the yuppie generation, globalization, environmentalism, and the importance of quality and speed in manufacturing; or IBM and Digital Equipment Corporation in the eighties, the full impact of the personal computer, which prompted the breakdown of the vertically integrated mainframe business and a shift toward distributed computing. Other examples abound: Federal Express's fiascos in Europe, Philips's setback in electronic markets (despite its leading-edge technologies), Disney's union and image problems with its theme park in France, Sony in movies, etc.

Scenario planning is a disciplined method for imagining possible futures that companies have applied to a great range of issues. Royal Dutch/Shell has used scenarios since the early 1970s as part of a process for generating and evaluating its strategic options.[2] Shell has been consistently better in its oil forecasts than other major oil companies, and first saw the overcapacity in the tanker business and Europe's petrochemicals. In the early 1980s, Anglo-American Corporation of South Africa convened an international group of experts to explore South Africa's future through scenarios, which provided a catalyst for profound political reform (as I explain later).[3] Even the Dutch Central Planning Bureau, a leading government agency traditionally wedded to econometrics and time series analyses, issued wide-ranging, twenty-five-year global scenarios.[4] And I have personally developed scenarios with clients to estimate future environmental liability, anticipate health-care cost containment and regulatory control, assess the consequences of deregulation in electric utilities, determine the shifting dimensions of competition in financial services, develop a strategic vision for an R&D division, help Wall Street analysts see future changes in the industries they track, and so forth.

Although scenario planning has been examined by academics and described by practitioners, no previous article has sought to bridge the theory and practice.[5] I try to fill the gap by presenting a systematic methodology, with illustrations drawn from practice, that explains the rationale and process of scenario planning.

A PLANNING TOOL

Suppose you are planning to climb a mountain. Previous planning would provide you a detailed map describing the constant elements of the terrain. Of course, this traditional planning tool is very valuable and, indeed, indispensable in this case. Just as geographical mapping is an honored art and science, so corporate mapping can be very useful. However, it is incomplete. First, it is a distorted representation (i.e., any two-dimensional map distorts the earth's surface). Second, it ignores the variable elements, such as weather, landslides, animals, and other hikers. The most important of these uncertainties is probably the weather, and one option is to gather detailed meteorological data of past seasons, perhaps using computer simulations.

However, scenario planning goes one step further. It simplifies the avalanche of data into a limited number of possible states. Each scenario tells a story of how various elements might interact under certain conditions. When relationships between elements can be formalized, a company can develop quantitative models. It should evaluate each scenario for internal consistency and plausibility; for example, high visibility and heavy snowdrifts are an implausible combination. Although a scenario's boundary might at times be fuzzy, a detailed and realistic narrative can direct your attention to aspects you would otherwise overlook. Thus a vivid snowdrift scenario (with low visibility) may highlight the need for skin protection, goggles, food supplies, radio, shelter, and so on.

Scenario planning differs from other planning methods, such as contingency planning, sensitivity analysis, and computer simulations. First, contingency planning

---

They Believed it

'Heavier-than-air flying machines are impossible.'
Lord Kelvin, British mathematician, physicist, and president of the British Royal Society, c. 1895

'With over fifty foreign cars already on sale here, the Japanese auto industry isn't likely to carve out a big slice of the U.S. market for itself.'
Business Week, 2 August 1968

'A severe depression like that of 1920–1921 is outside the range of probability.'
The Harvard Economic Society, 16 November 1929

'I think there is a world market for about five computers.'
Thomas J. Watson, chairman of IBM, 1943

'There is no reason for any individual to have a computer in their home.'
Ken Olson, president, Digital Equipment Corporation, 1977

'We don't like their sound. Groups of guitars are on the way out.'
Decca Recording Co. executive, turning down the Beatles in 1962

'The phonograph . . . is not of any commercial value.'
Thomas Alva Edison, inventor of the phonograph, c. 1880

'No matter what happens, the U.S. Navy is not going to be caught napping.'
Frank Knox, Secretary of the Navy, 4 December 1941, just before the Japanese attack on Pearl Harbor

'They couldn't hit an elephant at this dist . . .'
General John B. Sedgwick, last words, Battle of Spotsslvania, 1864

Source: C. Cerf and V. Navasky, *The Experts Speak* (New York: Pantheon Books, 1984).

---

examines only one uncertainty, such as 'What if we don't get the patent?' It presents a base case and an exception or contingency. Scenarios explore the joint impact of various uncertainties, which stand side by side as equals.

Second, sensitivity analysis examines the effect of a change in one variable, keeping all other variables constant. Moving one variable at a time makes sense for small changes. For instance, we might ask what will happen to oil demand if the gross national product increases just a fraction of a percent, keeping everything else constant. However, if the change is much larger, other variables (such as interest rates, money supply, and so on) will not stay constant. Scenarios, on the other hand, change several variables at a time without keeping others constant. They try to capture the new states that will develop after major shocks or deviations in key variables.

Third, scenarios are more than just the output of a complex simulation model. Instead they attempt to interpret such output by identifying patterns and clusters among the millions of possible outcomes a computer simulation might generate. They often include elements that were not or cannot be formally modeled, such as new regulations, value shifts, or innovations. Hence, scenarios go beyond objective analyses to include subjective interpretations.

In short, scenario planning attempts to capture the richness and range of possibilities, stimulating decision makers to consider changes they would otherwise ignore. At the same time, it organizes those possibilities into narratives that are easier to grasp and use than great volumes of data. Above all, however, scenarios are aimed at challenging the prevailing mind-set. Hence, scenario planning differs from the three aforementioned techniques in its epistemic level of analysis.

Using Scenarios

How can you use scenarios? In simplified form, people can use the technique to make individual decisions. A function, say, information systems, can also use scenario development to anticipate changes in its role. But perhaps most beneficial is its use in corporatewide strategic planning and vision building. Organizations facing the following conditions will especially benefit from scenario planning:

• Uncertainty is high relative to managers' ability to predict or adjust.
• Too many costly surprises have occurred in the past.
• The company does not perceive or generate new opportunities.
• The quality of strategic thinking is low (i.e., too routinized or bureaucratic).
• The industry has experienced significant change or is about to.
• The company wants a common language and framework, without stifling diversity.
• There are strong differences of opinion, with multiple opinions having merit.
• Your competitors are using scenario planning.

Once it develops strategic scenarios, the executive team might simply disseminate them throughout the organization to stimulate managerial thinking. Or it might use scenarios for evaluating proposals. For example, corporate executives might ask the strategic business units to submit investment proposals that project cash flow in each of several scenarios.[6]

In short, the technique is applicable to virtually any situation in which a decision maker would like to imagine how the future might unfold. In this article, I focus particularly on developing scenarios for strategic planning, but the same basic method applies to other situations of decision making under uncertainty.

CONSTRUCTING SCENARIOS

Scenario planning attempts to compensate for two common errors in decision making—underprediction and overprediction of change. Most people and organizations are guilty of the first error.[7] Although change in all aspects of our lives is accelerating dramatically, we tend to imagine the future without such a rate of change. Think how hard it would have been a hundred years ago to imagine the factors that propelled society into today's brave, new technological world where cars, airplanes, televisions, stereos, computers, ice-makers, and pacemakers are commonplace. Yet a small group of futurists over-predicted, expecting levels of change that failed to materialize, notably in medicine (we are losing the war against cancer), artificial intelligence (robots don't yet outsmart us), and space travel (most of us are still earthbound). Often these forecasters were scientists or entrepreneurs whose general faith in technology, or whose momentary successes in science or business, induced unjustified leaps of faith.[8]

Scenario planning, then, allows us to chart a middle ground between under- and overprediction. It helps expand the range of possibilities we can see, while keeping us from drifting into unbridled science fiction. Scenario planning does this by dividing our knowledge into two areas: (1) things we believe we know something about and (2) elements we consider uncertain or unknowable. The first component casts the past forward, recognizing that our world possesses considerable momentum and continuity. For example, we can safely make assumptions about demographic shifts (such as increases in the average age) and substitution effects of new technologies (e.g., digital recording will replace analog tapes and cassettes). Of course, nothing is ever absolutely certain—not even death and taxes—but to leave everything uncertain will cause paralysis in most organizations. The challenge is to separate aspects you are very confident about (and willing to bet the farm on) from those that are largely uncertain.

Obvious examples of uncertain aspects are future interest rates, oil prices, results of political elections, rates of innovation, and so forth. There are also less obvious examples, such as the probability that certain world-views will reign (e.g., monetarism versus supply-side economics). It is not important to account for all the possible outcomes of each uncertainty; simplifying the possible outcomes is sufficient for scenario planning. For instance, you may want to think in terms of three possible interest rates (high, medium, and low) rather than hundreds of them. The purpose is not to cover all possibilities, but to circumscribe them.

Since scenarios depict possible futures but not specific strategies to deal with them, it makes sense to invite outsiders into the process, such as major customers, key suppliers, regulators, consultants, and academics. Or you can start with trends and scenarios that others have developed (e.g., de Jong and Zalm's four global scenarios, 'global shift', 'European renaissance, 'global crisis', and 'balanced growth').[9] The objective is to see the future broadly in terms of fundamental trends and uncertainties. Line managers develop the basic ideas, while staff people, such as planners, develop the written version later, fill in the gaps, find new data, and so forth. The overall purpose is to build a shared framework for strategic thinking that encourages diversity and sharper perceptions about external changes and opportunities.

Next I describe the process for developing scenarios.

1. Define the Scope

The first step is to set the time frame and scope of analysis (in terms of products, markets, geographic areas, and technologies). Time frame can depend on a number of factors: the rate of technology change, product life cycles, political elections, competitors' planning horizons, and so forth. Once you have determined an appropriate time frame, ask what knowledge would be of greatest value to the organization that far down the road. It is useful to look at the past and think about what you wish you had known then, that you know now.[10] What have been past sources of uncertainty and volatility? Let's say you're developing ten-year scenarios. Look back over the past ten years at the changes that have occurred in your departments, organization, industry, region, country, and even the world. You should anticipate a similar amount of change or even more in the next ten years. Ideally, groups (e.g., the whole management team) will participate in this part of the process. Their unstructured concerns and anxieties are often good starting points for scenario planning.

2. Identify the Major Stakeholders

Who will have an interest in these issues? Who will be affected by them? Who could influence them? Obvious stakeholders include customers, suppliers, competitors, employees, shareholders, government, and so forth. Identify their current roles, interests, and power positions, and ask how they have changed over time and why. For example, in the environmental area, judges, scientists, lawyers, journalists, and regulators are increasingly powerful stakeholders.

3. Identify Basic Trends

What political, economic, societal, technological, legal, and industry trends are sure to affect the issues you identified in step one? For example, a company concerned with the future of environmental issues might identify trends such as increasing environmental regulation, continuing growth of environmental interest groups, scientific advances in molecular biology, and an increasingly liberal judiciary due to a Democratic president. Briefly explain each trend, including how and why it exerts its influence on your organization. It may be helpful to list each trend on a chart or so-called influence diagram to identify its impact on your present strategy as positive, negative, or uncertain. Everyone participating in the process must agree that these trends will continue; any trend on which there is disagreement (within the time frame) belongs in the next step.

4. Identify Key Uncertainties

What events, whose outcomes are uncertain, will significantly affect the issues you are concerned with? Again, consider economic, political, societal, technological, legal, and industry factors. Will the next US president be a Republican or Democrat? Will a particular piece of legislation be passed? Will a new technology be developed? What will consumers value in the future? For each uncertainty, determine possible outcomes (e.g., Republican or Democrat; legislation passed or not passed; technology developed or not developed; whether consumers value service or price). Again, it's best to keep these outcomes simple, with a few possibilities at most.

You may also want to identify relationships among these uncertainties, since not all combinations may occur. For example, if one economic uncertainty is 'level of unemployment' and the other 'level of inflation', then the combination of full employment and zero inflation may be ruled out as implausible. (Later I show how a correlation matrix can help identify such linkages among all pairs of key uncertainties.)

5. Construct Initial Scenario Themes

Once you identify trends and uncertainties, you have the main ingredients for scenario construction. A simple approach is to identify extreme words by putting all positive elements in one and all negatives in another. (Note that positive or negative is defined here relative to the current strategy. What seems to be a negative scenario at first may later prove to be one of innovation and hidden opportunity.) Alternatively, the various strings of possible outcomes (which jointly define a scenario) can be clustered around high versus low continuity, degree of preparedness, turmoil, and so on. Another method for finding some initial themes is to select the top two uncertainties and cross them (as illustrated later in the Anglo-American case). This technique makes the most sense if some uncertainties are clearly more important than others.

6. Check for Consistency and Plausibility

The simple worlds you have just made are not yet full-fledged scenarios, because they probably have internal inconsistencies or lack a compelling story line. There are at least three tests of internal consistency, dealing with the trends, the outcome combinations, and the reactions of major stakeholders. First, are the trends compatible within the chosen time frame? If not, remove the trends that don't fit. Second, do the scenarios combine outcomes of uncertainties that indeed go together? As noted above, full employment and zero inflation do not go together, so eliminate that possible pairing or scenario. Third, are the major stakeholders (e.g., OPEC) placed in positions they do not like and can change? (For example, OPEC may not tolerate low oil prices for very long.) If so, your scenario will evolve into another one. Try to describe this end scenario, which is more stable. The stakeholder test is especially critical when building macroscenarios involving governments, international organizations (e.g., the International Monetary Fund, the World Bank, the United Nations) or strong interest groups like OPEC.[11]

7. Develop Learning Scenarios

From this process of constructing simple scenarios and checking them for consistency, some general themes should emerge. The initial scenarios provide future boundaries, but they may be implausible, inconsistent, or irrelevant. The goal is to identify themes that are strategically relevant and then organize the possible outcomes and trends around them. Although the trends, by definition, appear in all the scenarios, they can be given more or less weight or attention in different scenarios.

For example, a company concerned with its future liability for hazardous waste might construct three scenarios: 'Superfund II,', 'Environmentalists Lose,' and 'Compromise.' The political trends and key uncertainties may get more play in 'Superfund II,' while legal trends and the health of the economy may feature more prominently in the other two scenarios. Naming the scenarios is also important. A scenario is a story; by capturing its essence in a title, you make the story easy to follow and remember. At this stage, you have constructed learning scenarios, which are tools for research and study, rather than for decision making. The titles and themes are focal points around which to develop and test the scenarios.

8. Identify Research Needs

At this point, you may need to do further research to flesh out your understanding of uncertainties and trends. The learning scenarios should help you find your blindspots. For example, do you really understand how a key stakeholder (say, a regulator or judge) will behave in a given scenario? Often, companies know a lot about their own industry but little beyond the fringes, from which the innovations may come. So you may wish to study new technologies that are not yet in the mainstream of your industry but may be someday. Consider the developments in multimedia, where personal computers, telecommunication, entertainment, databases, and television are merging into new products and markets. A company like Apple Computer, traditionally focused on making personal computers, must now master new domains, such as electronic miniaturization (to exploit portability), artificial intelligence (to make PCs smarter), information highways (to connect), and so on.

9. Develop Quantitative Models

After completing additional research, you should reexamine the internal consistencies of the scenarios and assess whether certain interactions should be formalized via a quantitative model. For example, Royal Dutch/Shell has developed a model that keeps oil prices, inflation, GNP growth, taxes, oil inventories, interest rates, and so forth in plausible balances. As managers imagine different outcomes of key uncertainties, they can use formal models to keep from straying into implausible scenarios.[12] The models can also help to quantify the consequences of various scenarios, say, in terms of price behavior, growth rates, market shares, and so on.

10. Evolve toward Decision Scenarios

Finally, in an iterative process, you must converge toward scenarios that you will eventually use to test your strategies and generate new ideas. Retrace steps one through eight to see if the learning scenarios (and any quantitative models from step nine) address the real issues facing your company. Are these the scenarios that you want to give others in the organization to spur their creativity or help them appreciate better the up- and downside risks in various strategies? If yes, you are done. If not, repeat the steps and refocus your scenarios the way an artist judges the balance and focal point in a painting. Half of this judgment is art, half is science.[13]

How can you determine if your final scenarios are any good? The first criterion is relevance. To have impact, your scenarios should connect directly with the mental maps and concerns of the users (e.g., senior executives, middle managers, etc.). Second, the scenarios should be internally consistent (and be perceived as such) to be effective. Third, they should be archetypal. That is, they should describe generically different futures rather than variations on one theme. Fourth, each scenario ideally should describe an equilibrium or a state in which the system might exist for some length of time, as opposed to being highly transient. It does an organization little good to prepare for a possible future that will be quite short-lived. In short, the scenarios should cover a wide range of possibilities and highlight competing perspectives (within and outside the firm), while focusing on interlinkages and the internal logic within each future.

SCENARIO PLANNING AT AN AD AGENCY

The advertising industry has experienced a flurry of takeovers and mergers, which has resulted in giant agency systems like the Interpublic Group, Saatchi and Saatchi, the Omnicom Group, and Dentsu in Japan. A few years ago, I helped Interpublic develop scenarios to assess whether the global agency concept, which Marion Harper pioneered at the agency, was still viable. When interviewing key advertising executives in 1990, I asked them about past changes in the industry (and its causes), current trends, key uncertainties (and their interrelationships), and their overall views of the future.

In the distant past, advertising agencies had been mostly order takers that simply executed ad placement. The traditional price structure of a 15 per cent commission closely reflected the number of calls and paperwork needed for such placements. Improvements in communications technology and the emergence of mass media reduced the agency's placement costs. To justify their higher profit margins, agencies started to add services for clients such as more sophisticated designs, market research, and elaborate pitches for new business. Around 1960, clients began to view the continual addition of services as not worth the implicit price they were paying via the 15 percent commission. Skyrocketing media costs in the 1970s and 1980s for television created excessive commissions for agencies that became increasingly hard to justify with additional, but unnecessary, services. Thus the 12 percent to 15 percent commission structure came under pressure, resulting in reductions in the percentage (to as low as 5 percent to 7 percent) or fee-for-service arrangements.

In the meantime, however, the costs of delivering advertising had started to climb during the 1960s, after many decades of gradual decline. These cost increases reflected the general shift away from broadcasting (in which one message reaches many millions of consumers) to narrowcasting (where many messages reach small, targeted segments). Increasingly fine segmentation, due to reduced costs of identifying and addressing these segments, meant a fragmentation of media. For instance, *Farm Journal* recognizes about 5,000 different segments today, in terms of farming practices, regions, and crops, and it produces a slightly different edition for each. Sophisticated databases, improved software to manage relational databases, and more up-to-date information (e.g., through scanning technology, direct mail response, etc.) is changing marketing into a high-tech, fragmented battlefield where rivals increasingly compete on the basis of speed and integration.[14]

Steps in the Process

As I described earlier, step one involves identifying the relevant issues by studying the past, especially its sources of turmoil and change. Table 11.1 reminds us of the scope and depth of changes in advertising during the past six decades. For this exercise, we decided to consider a seven-year time frame. Changes happen fairly quickly in the fickle world of advertising, so anything beyond seven years is quite uncertain and hard to act on. Planning horizons and budgets rarely extend beyond five years, since most investments (in people, buildings, and equipment) are reversible.

As assets become more specialized (meaning that their salvage is low relative to their costs), it pays to think longer term. For example, Royal Dutch/Shell's scenarios project fifteen years ahead, given the specialized nature of their investments. Ad agencies, in contrast, are more like speedboats than tankers. They are agile and opportunistic; they can hire and fire quickly and continually adapt to their clients. Nonetheless, Interpublic had been paying premiums to acquire agencies in its quest for a global presence. Under CEO Philip H. Geier, Jr., Interpublic assembled McCann-Erickson, Lintas: Worldwide, the Lowe Group, and Ammirati & Puris. In addition, it invested in Interactive Partners and embarked on a joint venture with Time Warner to exploit interactive marketing and entertainment media. In view of this, a time frame extending beyond five (but less than ten) years seemed most appropriate for this exercise.

Table 11.1. Some Past Changes in the US Advertising Industry

1930s
- Radio develops into a mature medium.
- Celebrities' testimony used extensively.
- Social Security supplements the incomes of senior citizens.
- Local breweries flourish (after Prohibition).

1940s
- War unites the country; patriotism flourishes.
- TV blossoms as a new communications medium.
- Population shifts to the suburbs.
- Supermarkets and shopping malls develop.
- Air travel expands greatly.

1950s
- Target markets and focused ads get attention.
- Service and financial institutions grow.
- Color TVs start to replace black and white.
- Psychoanalysis of consumers becomes prevalent.
- Trademark and patent infringement results in heavy litigation.

1960s
- Ads are careful to avoid provincialism and prejudice.
- Negative advertising about competitors emerges.
- Banks start to issue credit cards.
- Computer is a new word and new product.
- Big business expands; agencies follow suit.

1970s
- Segmentation and agency creativity emphasized.
- TV fails to 'kill' radio; broadcasting shifts to narrowcasting.
- Vietnam is stalemated.
- Watergate is revealed.
- Gasoline is in short supply.
- Consumer groups and environmentalists gain power.
- Japanese invade and dominate US markets in electronics and cars.

1980s
- Use of personal computers and servers (replacing mainframes) increases.
- Point-of-sale scanning technology provides real-time market data.
- Money and commodity markets (especially US dollar) are volatile.
- Global mega-agencies form via merger/acquisition.
- Communism crumbles worldwide (with a few exceptions).
- Media are fragmented.
- Brand names decline.

Table 11.2 lists the trends that industry experts, managers, and knowledgeable outsiders identified (step three). The question was whether these trends were mutually consistent within the five- to ten-year time frame and what support existed for each. For example, what was the evidence that food, consumer, and high-tech products are most adaptable to global marketing? Also, why might fee compensation, customary in consulting, legal, and accounting services, be less profitable to advertising agencies than a commission structure, which is common in real estate brokerage, sports promotion, and book writing? By asking such questions, we arrived at the trends in Table 11.2. Such additional analyses are critical to good scenario work, since they challenge

Table 11.2. Perceived Trends in Advertising

T_1	North America, Europe, and the Far East are areas of greatest growth opportunities for global advertising.
T_2	Food, consumer packaged goods, and high-tech products are most adaptable to global marketing.
T_3	Brand names continue to decline in value.
T_4	Agencies will provide increased services in the areas of marketing, research, and public relations.
T_5	Agencies will not provide accounting or financial services.
T_6	Advertising media continue to fragment as integrated marketing increases.
T_7	There will be a further trend toward fee compensation (versus the standard 12 percent to 15 percent commission).
T_8	Interactive marketing (e.g., via the information super-highway) is increasingly important.
T_9	Specialized media buying/planning agencies will expand.
T_{10}	The commoditization of advertising (as a service) will continue.
T_{11}	New alliances will emerge with information companies.

trends in Table 11.2. Such additional analyses are critical to good scenario work, since they challenge and stretch people's thinking. As Will Rogers observed, 'It is not what we don't know that gets us into trouble; it is what we know that ain't so.'

After trend analysis, we needed to identify the critical uncertainties (step four). Part A in Table 11.3 lists seven identified by industry respondents and our own analysis.

Table 11.3. Seven Key Uncertainties in the Ad Industry and Their Correlations

Part A   Uncertainties

U_1 Will the evolution toward a global, borderless civilization continue?

U_2 Can mega-agencies compete with 'boutiques' or Hollywood in creating ads?

U_3 Will advertisers remain very sensitive to potential agency account conflicts?

U_4 Will the trend toward in-house advertising reverse itself by the year 2000?

U_5 Is the fragmentation of media conducive to global, integrated marketing?

U_6 Will agencies supply more than just adds, such as integrated marketing?

U_7 Will the clients' advertising expenses remain fully deductible on tax returns?

Part B   Correlation Matrix

	U_1	U_2	U_3	U_4	U_5	U_6	U_7
U_1	X	+	?	0	+	+	0
U_2	X	X	+	+	+	+	+
U_3	X	X	X	0	?	+	0
U_4	X	X	X	X	+	+	−
U_5	X	X	X	X	X	+	?
U_6	X	X	X	X	X	X	+

X = These entries were already estimated via their mirror image above the diagonal

Again, these presumed uncertainties should be examined further. For example, one uncertainty was whether advertisers would remain sensitive to agency account conflicts (when an agency serves competing clients). Yet agency account conflict appears not to be an issue in Spain or for Dentsu in Japan, which suggests that the assumptions underlying this uncertainty needed to be reconsidered. It was important that each person identify only a few key uncertainties, so we could get to the core issues. Each manager wrote down three questions he or she most wanted to pose to the oracle at Delphi about the company's and industry's future environment.

Next we addressed the interrelationships among the uncertainties. We asked whether a 'yes' answer to, say, U_2 affects the chance of a 'yes' answer for U_3 or another uncertainty (see Part B, Table 3). If the chance of a 'yes' goes up, the correlation between U_2 and U_3 is positive (+); if the chance goes down, the correlation is negative (−), and otherwise it is zero (0) or indeterminate (?). Since mega-agencies can compete better if their clients are less concerned about potential account conflicts, the correlation between U_2 and U_3 is positive. Conversely, the less deductible advertising expenses are, the more likely clients may do it in-house as part of general expenses, resulting in a negative correlation for U_4 and U_7. However, it is not clear how some of the other elements might be correlated (e.g., U_1 and U_3), and sometimes there is no correlation at all (e.g., between U_1 and U_7). More sophisticated procedures for assessing conditional probabilities and cross-impact relationships can, of course, be used, but this simple matrix is a practical way for assessing a scenario's consistency.[15]

We arrived at three possible scenarios for the advertising industry, focusing on the question of global agency viability (see the sidebar). These are just learning scenarios, which require further study and shaping before becoming final decision scenarios. We placed the positive and negative outcomes (from Interpublic's perspective) of the seven uncertainties into different scenarios to obtain the extremes and added a middle-of-the-road scenario. Figure 11.1 profiles each scenario in terms of the weight given to a 'yes' answer for each uncertainty. (Because the correlation matrix in Table 11.3 revealed just one negative correlation, the all-positive or all-negative worlds were internally consistent.) In addition, the trends were an important part of each scenario (but, by definition, are constant across them). What needs more analysis was how the various actors are likely to behave in each scenario. For example, the mega-agencies will not like the 'dinosaur' world, so a critical question is how they might respond if this scenario emerged. The 'Polarization Is "Hot"' scenario combined two outcomes (a 'yes' for U_2 and a clear 'no' for U_3), even though they are presumably positively correlated. Such tension or slight inconsistency should be an impetus for further analysis of the scenarios, perhaps through quantitative modeling.[16]

Implications of the Scenarios

Each scenario poses a different set of strategic challenges and requisite core capabilities. Exploring them turns the initial learning scenarios into final decision scenarios. The globalization scenario, for instance, requires a much stronger emphasis on integrative marketing. First, the account manager has to learn how to sell multiple services at multiple levels within the client organization. Second, the agency's team has to learn how to approach the client's problems from a marketing perspective rather than just an advertising one. These challenges are especially formidable since the world at large

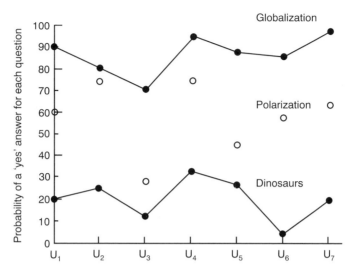

Figure 11.1. Profile of the Advertising Scenarios

is framing advertising agencies as only a place where you can buy bold, creative ads. All other services can be procured elsewhere, including in-house. Yet the global market-place requires integrated marketing solutions that combine advertising with direct mail, channel, and trade management. And such strategies can be devised only if the market itself is thoroughly understood, which requires stronger market research. The key question is who will do it? The client, the ad agency, or other suppliers—market research firms, direct mail specialists, public relations agencies, or marketing consulting firms?

Interpublic is vigorously pursuing the global agency concept, putting its faith in the first scenario. It is upgrading the quality of its local management teams, reducing barriers to cross-agency and cross-country collaboration, building financial muscle, and pursuing global clients. But as its motto ('Think global, act local') indicates, Interpublic is also following the second scenario and is looking for signals that the third might emerge. Each company must decide for itself, once it constructs scenarios, whether to gamble the future on one scenario, stay flexible to exploit multiple scenarios, develop exit routes in case things sour, or hedge the risk through strategic partnering or diversification.

Whichever approach you pursue, developing early indicators for each scenario helps you recognize, before competitors, which way the world is headed. A pharmaceutical company, concerned about the empty industry pipeline for new products, was able to better track the new drug development applications filed with the Food and Drug Administration and foreign regulatory agencies. A major life insurance firm, concerned with the impact of genetic testing, identified indicators that included biotech research on DNA markers and legal rulings with various states involving the use of generic screens in underwriting.

Scenarios can be used to (1) identify early warning signals, (2) assess the robustness of your core competencies, (3) generate better strategic options, and (4) evaluate the risk/return profile of each option in view of the uncertainties. Also, they can help communicate messages within the firm, such as the need for fundamental change and the importance of thinking globally and developing strategic alliances.

Three Scenarios for the Advertising Industry

Total Globalization

The mega-shops dominate the world marketing scene in Europe, China, Japan, Korea, and beyond. The issue of agency account conflicts disappears. Advanced communication technology speeds up the homogenization of the world's cultures as global marketers expand. Attempts to create regional trading blocks fail, and global brand names flourish. Cars, electronic products, packaged foods, clothing, and many other products compete in a global marketplace with global competitors. Although media are fragmented locally, the information highway permits the transmission of targeted messages to increasingly smaller segments (i.e., mass customization).

Agencies provide a broad range of services in view of the external complexities facing clients. As agencies and advertising grow together, they become inextricably linked in terms of profits and information. The world marketing front becomes a battleground of Titans. The profits are enormous, since the barriers to entry are substantial. Fee and performance compensation structures are common, with long-term relationships being the norm. The mega-agencies thrive in part because of their more professional approach to business, with better-trained account executives and office managers. Many mega-agencies invest heavily in managerial training and development, via 'in-house universities', which give them a strong edge.

Polarization Is 'Hot'

Globalization and localization flourish side by side, due to the emergence of strong regional tradeblocks (NAFTA, the European Community, Pacific Blocks, etc.). Negative reactions to the export of US pop culture is on the rise (e.g., Disney's theme park in France). Mega-shops serve global marketers of consumer products, providing a broad range of services and developing close relationships. Global marketers consolidate accounts among a few key agencies. The issue of account conflicts among the high rollers exists in some accounts, in part because of a few well-reported leaks. Compensation structure varies depending on billings and client/agency relationships.

Localized, specialized, or 'boutique' agencies also flourish as the mega-shops cannot maintain profitable relationships with specialized industries, small regional advertisers, or controversial products (e.g., condoms). Specialized support services such as marketing research firms continue to flourish. Some big, disillusioned clients turn increasingly toward nontraditional sources for creative ideas, notably film producers. The mega-agencies are unable to compete for new advertising, and attempts at strategic alliances with Hollywood studios fail due to culture and ego clashes. Also, the increasing fragmentation of media (with more than 500 cable channels, CD-ROMs, radio, print, etc.) favors more specialized players that understand selected niches better. In an attempt to boost their tax revenues, various governments institute percentage caps on the deductible ad expenses.

Mega-Shop Dinosaurs

The mega-shops reign for a short time, just beyond the turn of the century. They are eventually crippled by their sheer size, central ownership, and the bureaucracy that often accompanies such structures. They are slow to adapt to media changes (especially interactive), relying instead on personal relationships through account executives. As a consequence, their flexibility and creativity suffers. Advertising by mega-agency is increasingly seen as a commodity and bought on price. The lumbering mega-shops gradually lose business to the smaller but 'hotter' agencies, especially as clients restructure into networked entities with high personnel turnover. Military conflicts around the world (especially in Eastern Europe and the Middle East) lead to isolationism and nationalism and frustrate any attempts at the creation of truly global markets.

In addition, advertisers in many countries remain highly sensitive to agency account conflicts. Privately held start-ups emerge with revolutionary creative and management styles. Specialized media agencies and cooperatives develop, pooling client resources to profit from media-buying leverage. Creative compensation structures emerge as advertisers demand that agencies be financially accountable and as agencies' competition heats up. On top of this, the Democrats (in their quest to fund social programs) limit the tax deductions associated with advertising. This further undermines firms' investments in brand equity, which together with a poor economy puts an emphasis on value and price discounts. The premiums paid by mega-agencies in the 1970s and 1980s fail to deliver superior returns. The stock prices drop, and several mega-agencies are forced to divest themselves of the premium acquisitions of the 1980s and 1990s.

RULES OF INTERACTION

So far, our scenarios have described futures over which we have limited control, such as the macroeconomic or political environment. The emphasis on 'trends' suggests the importance of static and largely uncontrollable forces in strategy. However, to appreciate how these trends, once combined with the uncertainties, give rise to scenarios, we must understand interactive elements. For example, if the trend in an industry is to compete on price alone, then, at some point, this trend may cease because the companies that are not the low-cost producers will try to shift the competition toward such factors as quality, service, innovation, delivery time, etc. Our earlier emphasis on stakeholder analysis acknowledges that few trends last forever. In this section, I describe how the dynamic interactions in a system, in addition to the more static trend analysis, can be built into scenario planning (see Figure 11.2). While finding all the hidden assumptions and reasoning in managers' mental maps is infeasible, it is worthwhile to find the most important implicit 'rules' that drive key inferences.

The more control the actors can have over a trend, the quicker it may vanish. A company cannot change the demographic trend of an aging population, but an industry can change price competition. When dealing with highly interactive situations (in which stakeholders react to events and each other), you may need to express the scenario elements not just in terms of trends and uncertainties, but also in terms of the rules of interaction. Anglo-American Corporation of South Africa, mentioned earlier, used such explicit rules to guide its scenario work.[17] Its approach, which I broadly summarize next, shows how to use rules along with trends and uncertainties.

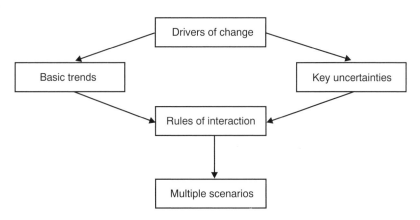

Figure 11.2. Building Blocks for Scenarios

SCENARIO PLANNING AT ANGLO-AMERICAN CORPORATION

In 1984, Anglo began to identify broad global trends. It projected a long-term schism between the Triad (North America, Japan, and Western Europe) and the rest of the world (billions of poor, young people). (The Triad earns just over two-thirds of the world's income, yet accounts for only 15 percent of its total population.) Another presumed trend was that the continent of Africa would remain a 'swamp or pit' for several decades due to poor food production, exploding populations, political turmoil, limited natural resources, and so forth. Hence, Anglo felt that the market for new products and economic growth was in the Triad, not Africa (one of its rules and key inferences). A third global trend Anglo bet on was the emergence of a new technological wave (propelled by advances in microelectronics, telecommunications, bio-technologies, and new material sciences). This wave, it assumed, would bring about fundamental economic change.

Based on these trends and its general beliefs about how the world operated, Anglo postulated the following rules of the game for 'winning nations', which capture the dynamic elements, highlighting how countries can succeed. Anglo's rules emphasized the importance of having (1) a global presence in end markets, (2) a highly educated workforce, (3) access to world capital markets, (4) proprietary, as opposed to licensed, technology, and (5) a sound work ethic. Anglo assumed that countries with these features would do well in global competition, in view of the overall trends, whereas countries without them would do increasingly poorly. However, the pace of this presumed polarization, and therefore the fate of South Africa and Anglo, depended on some key uncertainties whose resolution was yet to be determined.

Hence, the third step in Anglo's process was to identify the key global uncertainties, which at that time (circa 1984) ranged from the US–Soviet arms race to the spread of Islamic fundamentalism (see Table 11.4). It deemed two uncertainties especially critical, namely (1) how the US–Japan trade dilemma would be resolved (i.e., via accommodation or trade conflict), and (2) whether detente or an arms race would prevail between the United States and the former Soviet Union. Of the four possible outcomes implied by these two dichotomies, only one was considered implausible, namely that the United States would embark on both an arms race with the former Soviet Union and a trade war with Japan. The remaining three combinations provided the basic themes for three different global scenarios: 'Industrial Renaissance' (detente and trade accommodation), 'Protracted Transition' (detente and trade war), and 'Imperial Twilight' (arms race and trade accommodation). (See Table 11.4, part B.) To develop a fuller story line for each scenario, Anglo examined the other uncertainties and postulated outcomes that fit the theme. For example, political unrest in the Middle East or an exploding AIDS epidemic fit better within Imperial Twilight than Industrial Renaissance. After completing each cell, using the earlier rules of the game, Anglo then tried to quantify the growth of GNP in different parts of the world under each scenario and predict the economic success of different countries.

In the fourth step, the company examined South Africa's prospects in light of the global scenarios (reflecting the global trends, rules of the game, and key uncertainties). For the political scenarios of South Africa, Anglo presumed the following additional rules: First, whites would not 'unconditionally surrender', due to their military power and the lack of historical precedence. Second, whites could not be militarily victorious, due to escalating violence and foreign pressure. Third, South Africa would be an industrialized nation with great economic potential once its internal problems were resolved. Fourth, South Africa would never fully satisfy the world's political agenda. Fifth, statutory apartheid would end. Research, historical comparisons, and common sense went into drawing up these rules of the political game, which were presented as inescapable realities within which strategic thinking and action had to take place.

Table 11.4. Global Uncertainties for Anglo-American Corporation

Part A   Uncertainties

U_1 Trade conflict between the United States and Japan
U_2 Arms negotiation between the United States and the USSR
U_3 Proliferation of nuclear weapons
U_4 Spread of AIDS
U_5 Rise or fall of Islamic fundamentalism
U_6 Impact of Europe 1992
U_7 Deterioration of ozone layer
U_8 Middle East war (or third world war)

Note: These uncertainties are a subset of those Anglo-American Corporation examined in 1984 as part of its global scenario analysis

Part B   Two Uncertainties Combined

		United States/Japan	
		Trade Accommodation	Trade Conflict
United States/USSR	Arms Race	Imperial Twilight	X
	Detente	Industrial Renaissance	Protracted Transition

Last, Anglo identified key domestic uncertainties, such as 'What will be the future balance of power in South Africa?' 'What will happen to the homelands?' (i.e. areas set aside in South Africa as self-governing states for nonwhites). It then combined these with the trends and rules to develop two domestic scenarios—high road and low road. The high-road scenario required strategic alliances, sharing of power, and democratic welfare (as in Switzerland) in order for South Africa to be a significant actor on the world stage. The low-road scenario was essentially a circle of violence, which would propel South Africa slowly but surely into an economic wasteland. Both scenarios were possible within the rules of the games identified and the uncertainties ahead. Neither one could be guaranteed or forced by any single party. However, their odds could be significantly influenced by future actions.

The Anglo scenarios were not just an intellectual exercise; they were powerful means of shaping the debate and influencing the agenda for political action in South Africa. Anglo apparently recognized, after examining the various scenarios, that its future would be very bleak under the low-road scenario. Consequently, executives decided to share their views and insights (via lectures, a video, and a book) in an effort to embark on the high road. The Anglo scenarios had much impact in South Africa and continue to frame internal debates. The remarkable strides made by then prime minister F. W. de Klerk—freeing Nelson Mandela, phasing out apartheid laws, negotiating with the African National Congress, regaining recognition as an international trading partner, and calling for free elections—are in line with Anglo's high-road scenario and overall hopes for the future. The subsequent election of Mandela as South Africa's first black prime minister further solidifies the high-road scenario, although major challenges remain.

Anglo was successful because the scenarios were intellectually honest, clearly presented, and broad enough to permit a dialogue between opposing power groups. The approach of identifying trends and key uncertainties, and making the rules of interaction explicit, provided a framework for constructive debate. Dynamic, as opposed to static, scenarios help people reason through the multiple pathways an industry or company may traverse in view of the prevailing trends, the presumed rules of the game, the uncertainties that lie ahead, and the stakeholders involved.

Scenario Planning in Your Company

To start scenario planning in your company, you may want to convene a one- or two-day scenario workshop in which the focus is on the outside world, without the complications of internal strategy or competitive issues. If you believe that your industry is not an island unto itself but is shaped by larger political, economic, social, and technological forces, start with the external drivers. Invite from six to twenty bright people to your scenario team, including some from outside the company—suppliers, customers, regulators, board members, analysts, or academics. Then untangle the external issues into underlying trends and uncertainties and repackage them into broad-ranging and fundamentally different scenarios. The recombining of the basic elements (trends, outcomes, rules, and stakeholders) can be done in at least three different ways:

Intuitively

Once all pieces are laid out, you have to find some major themes and story lines around which to organize all the elements.[18]

Heuristically

Select the two most important uncertainties (e.g., by asking members to vote for them individually) and place them in a matrix (see the Anglo-American example in Table 11.4) to get some starting points for the scenarios, and then layer in the other elements.

Statistically

Systematically combine the outcomes of all the key uncertainties into internally consistent strings to provide feasible boundaries, as in the advertising agency example.[19]

DO SCENARIOS WORK?

So far, I have assumed that scenarios (however they are developed) do, in fact, stretch and refocus our thinking. But will they indeed correct, say, our bias toward overconfidence, i.e., the tendency to assume that we know more than we do? And can a manager benefit from scenarios without actively participating in their development? Can, for example, an executive team generate and distribute scenarios to managers and get the same effect as it would if the managers participated in creating the scenarios?

I examined these questions experimentally by contrasting best estimates and confidence ranges before and after scenario construction.[20] (Confidence ranges are the numerical limits on a best estimate to reflect the level of uncertainty.) For instance, a manager might estimate next quarter's sales to be Y units, and be 90 percent certain that the actual level will be between X and Z units. The typical manager is overconfident; the range between X and Z is likely much too narrow.[21] Therefore, if scenario planning works, it should, at a minimum, widen confidence ranges.

The sixty-eight subjects in my study were evening MBA students at the University of Chicago. I asked them to identify several issues relevant to their daytime jobs (e.g., involving product development, competitor behavior, and so on). Then I asked them to provide best estimates as well as subjective confidence ranges of 90 percent and 50 percent. For example, a student might estimate that sales for her company would be 50,000 units per year five years hence. Then she would determine that she was 90 percent sure that the actual sales volume would be between 30,000 and 70,000 and 50 percent sure that it would be between, say, 40,000 and 60,000. Each student also asked a colleague at work who was familiar with the issues for similar estimates.[22]

Several weeks later, each student developed a few scenarios for the initial issues and used them as the basis for a new round of best guesses and confidence ranges (ignoring the first round). As before, each subject requested new estimates from the colleague at work after explaining the specific scenarios. This way I could test whether the scenarios had any systematic effect on the estimates of either the students or their colleagues.

Averaged across all cases, confidence ranges widened about 50 percent. The scenarios affected best guesses less than ranges, although there was considerable variability in both. Because the scenarios had the same impact when developed by the person as when supplied by others, it is clear that not everyone needs to be involved in the scenario development process. However, one benefit of personal involvement is greater intellectual ownership, so senior executives should be intimately involved in the process. Scenarios developed by others may have more surprise or learning value but perhaps lower credibility.[23] But personal involvement may mean that you bias the process or suppress new ideas.

Biases in Scenarios

Although scenarios can free our thinking, they can still be affected by biases. When we are making predictions, we tend to look for confirming evidence and discount disconfirming evidence, and this bias can creep into the scenario development. I asked some MBA students to develop both positive and negative scenarios for the industries in which they expected to be employed after graduation, ranging from banking and management consulting to consumer products and real estate. (I conducted this study in 1985, when none of the students would have imagined that a stock market crash in 1987 would adversely affect jobs on Wall Street and in management consulting for several years after.) I also asked them to score each trend as clearly positive, negative, or indeterminate. On average, each student identified two positive trends in his or her field and only 1.48 negative trends (see Table 11.5). They also weighted the probability of positive outcomes more heavily than negative outcomes.

Table 11.5. Positive versus Negative Elements in Scenarios

	Mean	Standard Deviation	Sample Size	Significance
Number of positive trends identified per subject	2.00	.83	59	.001
Number of negative trends identified per subject	1.48	.94	59	
Number of positive outcomes listed per subject	3.58	.88	59	.16
Number of negative outcomes listed per subject	3.42	.81	59	
Subjective probability of positive outcomes	51%	12	56	.001
Subjective probability of negative outcomes	43%	13	56	
Plausibility of the positive scenario (1–7 scale)	4.7	1.1	57	.18
Plausibility of the negative scenario (1–7 scale)	4.5	1.2	56	

Note: Significance levels in the last column refer to a t-test for differences in means between positive and negative items within each pair (with a z-test for the third pair). Each subject identified about four trends on average (including indeterminate ones in terms of impact) and identified 3.7 uncertainties on average.

People sometimes also presume correlations among the uncertainties that are inconsistent. For example, a person may believe that (1) if inflation is high, employment is high (a positive correlation), (2) if inflation is high, then interest rates will be high (another positive correlation), and (3) if employment is high, then interest rates will be low, reflecting a strong economy (a negative correlation). These three correlations, however, are not internally consistent. If the first two pairs are strongly positive in their correlation, then the third pair must also be, on purely mathematical grounds. When I tested the opinions of my students using such a statistical consistency test, I found that the vast majority held self-contradictory beliefs. Since the perceived correlations drive and constrain the clustering of outcomes in the scenario-building process, such incoherent beliefs need to be adjusted.

Fortunately, however, not all biases in scenario building are disruptive. Indeed, I believe that the method derives its power in part from what Tversky and Kahneman termed the 'conjunction fallacy'.[24] People often deem the conjunction of two events to be more likely than the occurrence of either of these events alone, in clear violation of the elementary laws of probability. To test this, in 1986, I divided seventy-six MBA students into two groups and asked them to assign a subjective probability to one of these two events:

- A. US economic GNP growth will be at least 4 percent per year by 1990.
- B. The United States will have a trade surplus with Japan by the end of 1990.

The average subjective probability for event A was 47 percent; for B, 18 percent. Then I asked the students to judge the probability that both A *and* B would happen and found an average probability of 20 percent.[25] Somehow, they perceived the conjunction of A and B as more plausible than event B alone. One reason may be that the conjunction of A and B provides a causal explanation. A strong economy may be precisely the reason why a trade surplus occurs.

As Kahneman and Tversky put it: 'A scenario is especially satisfying when the path that leads from the initial to the terminal state is not immediately apparent, so that the introduction of intermediate stages actually raises the subjective probability of the target event.'[26] Conjunction fallacies can increase the perceived plausibility of unlikely scenarios, especially if they offer concrete detail and are causally coherent.

CONCLUSION

When contemplating the future, it is useful to consider three classes of knowledge:

1. Things we know we know.
2. Things we know we don't know.
3. Things we don't know we don't know.

Various biases—overconfidence, under- and over-prediction, the tendency to look for confirming evidence—plague all three, but the greatest havoc is caused by the third.[27] Although there are no failproof techniques, focusing attention on two and three can gain much improvement. And this is where scenario planning excels, since it is essentially a study of our collective ignorance. It institutionalizes the hunt for weak signals, such as OPEC's price hikes in 1973 or Gorbachev's political ascent in the early 1980s. The scenario method continually pushes the envelope of possibilities since it views strategic planning as collective learning.[28]

Good scenarios challenge tunnel vision by instilling a deeper appreciation for the myriad factors that shape the future.[29] Scenario planning requires intellectual courage to reveal evidence that does not fit our current conceptual maps, especially when it threatens our very existence. Nonetheless, what may initially seem to be bleak scenarios could, in fact, hold the seeds of new business and unrecognized opportunity. But those opportunities can be perceived only if you actively look for them. Pierre Wack once characterized scenario planning at Royal Dutch/Shell as 'the gentle art of reperceiving'.[30] To him, the test was whether scenario planning would lead to more innovative options. In addition to perceiving richer options, however, we must also have the courage and vision to act on them. As F. Scott Fitzgerald noted, 'The test of a first-rate intelligence is the ability to hold two conflicting ideas in mind at the same time, and still retain the ability to function.'

ACKNOWLEDGEMENTS

I would like to thank J. Edward Russo for his incisive comments; Liz Bromberg, Doug Freiberg, Kevin Holme, Steven Saleh, and Tim Wicks for valuable assistance in researching the advertising case; Gary Billings, Jan Homans, and others within Interpublic for sharing their views on the past and future of advertising; and Allison Green for editorial advice.

REFERENCES

1. C. Cerf and V. Navasky, *The Experts Speak* (New York: Pantheon Books, 1984).
2. P. J. H. Schoemaker and C. A. J. M. van de Heijden, 'Integrating Scenarios into Strategic Planning at Royal Dutch/Shell', *Planning Review* 20 (1992): 41–46.
3. C. Sunter, *The World and South Africa in the 1990s* (Cape Town, South Africa: Human and Rousseau Tafelberg, 1987).
4. A. de Jong and G. Zalm, *Scanning the Future* (The Hague, The Netherlands: Central Planning Bureau, Sdu Publishers, 1992).
5. For an incisive analysis of how the human mind generates explanations and predictions, see: D. Kahneman and A. Tversky, 'The Simulation Heuristic', in D. Kahneman, P. Slovic, and A. Tversky, eds., *Judgment under Uncertainty: Heuristics and Biases* (New York: Cambridge University Press, 1982), pp. 201–210. For additional psychological analyses, see: H. Jungerman, 'Inferential Processes in the Construction of Scenarios', *Journal of Forecasting* 4 (1985): 321–327; and R. M. Dawes, *Rational Choice in an Uncertain World* (New York: Harcourt Brace Jovanovich, 1988). For a forecasting perspective, see: W. R. Huss, 'A Move towards Scenarios', *International Journal of Forecasting* 4 (1988): 377–388. For a conceptual and behavioral perspective, see: P. J. H. Schoemaker, 'Multiple Scenario Development: Its Conceptual and Behavioral Basis', *Strategic Management Journal* 14 (1993): 193–213. For a consultant's approach to scenario planning, see: T. F. Mandel, 'Scenarios and Corporate Strategy: Planning in Uncertain Times' (Menlo Park, California: SRI International, Research Report 669, 1982). For the Royal Dutch/Shell approach, see: P. Wack, 'Scenarios: Uncharted Waters Ahead', *Harvard Business Review*, September–October 1985, pp. 72–89; and P. Schwartz, *The Art of the Long View* (New York: Doubleday, 1991). For scenario planning from an applied perspective, see: *Planning Review*, 20 (1992): 2 and 3. For the Dutch Central Planning Bureau's wide-ranging global scenarios, see: De Jong and Zalm (1992).
6. For connecting scenario planning to project evaluation, using Monte Carlo simulation, see: P. J. H. Schoemaker, 'When and How to Use Scenario Planning: A Heuristic Approach with Illustration', *Journal of Forecasting* 10 (1991): 549–564. For a methodology to link scenarios to competitor analysis, core capabilities, and strategic vision building, see: P. J. H. Schoemaker, 'How to Link Strategic Vision to Core Capabilities', *Sloan Management Review*, Fall 1992, pp. 67–81.
7. See Kahneman and Tversky (1982); and A. Toffler, *The Adaptive Corporation* (New York: McGraw-Hill, 1985). There are several theoretical arguments supporting the hypothesis of underprediction of change from the status quo. First, anchoring on the past or present will likely result in underadjustment away from the present. Second, the availability bias will make it hard to properly weigh new scenarios. Third, overconfidence (with its multiple causes) results in unduly narrow confidence ranges regarding future change. See: J. E. Russo and P. J. H. Schoemaker, 'Managing Overconfidence', *Sloan Management Review*, Winter 1992, pp. 7–18.
8. S. P. Schnaars, *Megamistakes: Forecasting and the Myth of Rapid Technological Change* (New York: Free Press, 1989).
9. De Jong and Zalm (1992).
10. Looking at the past is a two-edged sword. It may unduly anchor us to old trends and realities, or things may seem more predictable in hindsight than they were at the time. However, examining the variability and unpredictability of the past may also help us construct broader scenarios. For example, most companies do not plan for the kind of turmoil that they have witnessed over the past decade. The forces that caused past turmoil (from political to technological) should be studied in order to appreciate better the system's complexity and unpredictability. See: J. Gilovich, 'Seeing the Past in the Present: The Effect of Associations to Familiar Events on Judgments and Decisions', *Journal of Personality and Social Psychology* 40 (1981): 797–808; and B. Fischhoff, 'Hindsight ≠ Foresight: The Effect of Outcome Knowledge on Judgment under Uncertainty', *Journal of Experimental Psychology: Human Perception and Performance* 1 (1975): 288–299.
11. M. Godet, *Scenarios and Strategic Management* (London: Butterworths Scientific, Ltd., 1987).

12. Schoemaker and van der Heijden (1992).
13. For examples of decision scenarios, see: P. Hawken, J. Ogilvy, and P. Schwartz, *Seven Tomorrows* (New York: Bantam Book, 1982).
14. R. C. Blattberg and J. Deighton, 'Interactive Marketing Exploiting the Age of Addressability', *Sloan Management Review*, Fall 1991, pp. 5–14.
15. C. W. Kirkwood and S. M. Pollack, 'Multiple Attribute Scenarios, Bounded Probabilities, and Threats of Nuclear Theft', *Futures*, February 1982, pp. 545–553.
16. Schoemaker (1990).
17. Sunter (1987).
18. For examples of this approach, see: Schwartz (1991).
19. For statistical elaboration and some consistency tests, see: Schoemaker (1991).
20. Schoemaker (1993).
21. Russo and Schoemaker (1992).
22. Schoemaker (1993).
23. Research has shown that generating reasons often improves probability calibration, even if the subjects generate their own reasons. See: A. Koriat, S. Lichtenstein, and B. Fischhoff, 'Reasons for Confidence', *Journal of Experimental Psychology: Human Learning and Memory* 6 (1980): 107–118. However, Schoemaker shows that if subjects are asked to generate reasons for extreme outcomes, their confidence ranges may actually shrink (instead of stretch) because of incredulity about the reasons generated. See: Schoemaker (1993).
24. A. Tversky and D. Kahneman, 'Extensional vs. Intuitive Reasoning: The Conjunction Fallacy in Probability Judgments', *Psychological Review* 90 (1983): 293–315.
25. Schoemaker (1993).
26. Kahneman and Tversky (1982), p. 207.
27. Russo and Schoemaker (1992).
28. A. de Geus, 'Planning As Learning', *Harvard Business Review*, March–April 1988, pp. 70–74; and P. Senge, *The Fifth Discipline* (New York: Doubleday, 1990).
29. J. E. Russo and P. J. H. Schoemaker, *Decision Traps* (New York: Doubleday, 1989).
30. Wack (1985).

Chapter 12

Exploring Competitive Futures Using Cognitive Mapping

Kim Warren
London Business School, London, UK

SCENARIOS FOR STRATEGIC PLANNING

Scenarios are now a fashionable strategy tool. They can equip organizations for unexpected events or enable them to 'design' their future to be as they wish.[1-3] They can help build consensus amongst management teams and hence create alignment with the chosen strategic direction.[4,5] Scenarios have some useful features for assessing policy options:[6]

- They are hypothetical, describing some possible or potential future.
- They are selective, representing just one possible state of some complex, interdependent, dynamic and opaque state of affairs.
- They are bounded, consisting of a limited number of states, events, actions, and consequences.
- They are connected, in that their elements are conditionally or causally related.
- They are assessable, and can be judged with respect to their probability and/or desirability.

Yet scenarios mean different things to different people, and alternative types may be used in various ways, as can be seen from two contrasting definitions of 'scenario':

a hypothetical sequence of events . . . or the purpose of focusing attention on causal processes and decision points[7]

an outline of one conceivable state of affairs, given certain assumptions about the present and the course of events in the intervening period[8]

Reprinted with permission from *Long Range Planning*, Vol. 28, Warren, K. 'Exploring Competitive Futures Using Cognitive Mapping', 1995 Elsevier Science Ltd, Oxford, England.

Scenario types can be distinguished in various ways.[9]

- *Exploratory versus anticipatory.* Exploratory scenarios . . . start with some known or assumed states or events and explore what consequences might then result. Anticipatory scenarios are backward directed, i.e. they start from some assumed final state of affairs and ask for the possible preconditions.
- *Descriptive versus normative.* Descriptive scenarios present potential futures irrespective of their desirability. Normative scenarios, on the other hand, take values and goals explicitly into account.
- *Trend versus peripheral.* A trend scenario extrapolates the normal, surprise-free course of events . . . A peripheral scenario, on the other hand, depicts trend-breaking, surprising or improbable developments.

Management confusion about scenarios is compounded by two common misunderstandings. First, they are thought to be about long-run trends in global social, economic, and political factors, and thus not relevant to the immediate problems of managers. This belief may have arisen from the ground-breaking work in the field by Shell,[1] but it must be understood that the global social, economic, and political environment *is* the relevant operational context for this leading international oil and derivatives company. Managers might find the technique to be useful if they could apply it for themselves to the major uncertainties in their own external environment.

The second misunderstanding concerns the place of the firm itself in the scenario. Scenario techniques were first developed at a time (the 1970s) when planning viewed the external environment as an 'independent variable'—a given with which a firm had to cope. Today's view of strategy is more pro-active, seeking opportunities for the firm to *influence* its environment.[10] On this view, scenario planning is a more usable tool than it has previously seemed. A sound scenario therefore contains some iterative features, allowing the outside world to be affected by the firm's own responses to the emerging future. This might be characterized as a 'linear' versus a 'feedback' view of strategy (see Figure 12.1).

To be useful for discovering strategy options, then, a scenario needs to explore how the future might turn out and how the firm's actions might affect that future. This implies (on the definitions above) an *exploratory, descriptive* and *trend* scenario,[9] though with *normative* and *peripheral* questions being posed. A 'normative' question might be 'How would we *like* the future to turn out?' A 'peripheral' question might be that 'If that's a good description of a possible future, what events could throw it off-course?'

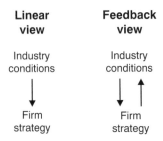

Figure 12.1. Competing Views of Industry Conditions and Firms' Strategy

Methods for building scenarios range from soft processes of discussion amongst managers, through formal forecasting techniques, to sophisticated computer-based modelling.[11–14] Special approaches are available to ensure that scenarios are based on relevant and significant external factors,[15,16] or are robust descriptions of possible future conditions.[17–19] However, one relatively simple technique to help teams build scenarios is cognitive mapping—an approach that makes explicit the views of teams about factors influencing their industry and firm.

COGNITIVE MAPPING

Cognitive mapping starts from the observation that each individual's view of their world is unique. In the managerial context, this means that we each have different views of what factors are important, and different ideas of the consequences of those factors. Members of a management team will therefore have divergent views of how the future may turn out. If opposing views go unrecognized and unresolved, agreement on strategy may be difficult to achieve, but with care this diversity can be used to produce richer and more robust strategic responses for the firm than one based only on a single accepted wisdom.

A cognitive map at its simplest is a network of cause–effect relationships between factors in the situation under debate. Underlying 'causes' may include socio-economic or legislative changes, or competitors' actions. 'Effects' may include expected demand trends or further responses by competitors. A rich cognitive map for a whole team can be produced by first interviewing individuals. The interview typically starts with open questions as to that person's view of important change drivers. Questions then focus on possible consequences, e.g. 'You say that the recent entry of a new rival is a major factor in your industry. What do you think will be the main consequences of this?' Interviewing then moves on to still further consequences, until that train of thought is exhausted. Sometimes an outcome is discovered for which no cause has been identified, in which case explanations can be sought, e.g. 'You state that this competitor is likely to leave the industry. Why do you believe this is likely?'

The next step is to combine these individual views into a composite map of the whole team. Several individuals may identify common driving forces and/or consequences, but the richness of the technique arises from two other features. First, individuals may raise unique issues and consequences not mentioned by others— valuable diversity in the views of the team. Second, individuals may hold opposing views of the outcomes of any causal influence. In this case, further questioning may identify whether the conflict arises from different views of other driving forces or whether there is a fundamental uncertainty to which the team's response needs to be sensitive.

Since each individual map may be quite large, the resulting team map can be very extensive. If the complexity is too great, computer software exists to help manage it and feed it back to the team.

For developing scenarios, the technique's main advantage is that the mental maps produced do not belong to any one person, but incorporate the views of all. This is vital in winning commitment from those on whose actions the organization's future depends, especially if the resulting scenario indicates that radical shifts in strategy may be needed. The composite mental map produced becomes 'a device for facilitating negotiation, synergy, and creativity'.[20] The technique is well-established and widely used by organizations as diverse as British Airways, British Telecom, the Prison Service, and the Health Service.

The technique has few draw-backs. Although consulting many individuals may take more time than delegating scenario-production to a small team, the richness and ownership that results far out-weighs this modest overhead. Like many group-process techniques, cognitive mapping requires good facilitation, in particular avoiding any tendency to 'lead' the interview down particular paths. Questioning and feedback must focus on significant issues, to avoid producing overly detailed pictures that confuse rather than clarify the team's understanding. Finally, questioning must be kept open, to encourage outlying views. Otherwise there is a danger of reinforcing accepted wisdom rather than challenging it. Interviewing a variety of outsiders as well as the team may help avoid this danger.

Cognitive maps may be used to tackle specific current problems,[21] to assess the impact of managers' perceptions of strategy over the very long term,[22] or even to create a firm's entire strategy—from initial assessment of external influences and review of the firm's capabilities, through to the tactical steps needed to implement strategy.[23] The scenarios produced by cognitive mapping must therefore be integrated with the strategy formulation process.[24-26] Commonly proposed processes for using scenarios begin with the main perceived driving forces for future change, move on to a critical development of cause–effect relationships, arriving at a description of future conditions, and leading to policy selection or strategy formulation[27-31]—a process to which cognitive mapping is well-suited.

This article describes scenarios developed for the UK take-home drinks market, and shows how medium-term outcomes could be affected by the strategy options facing one type of firm (specialist off-licence chains). This work was needed to overcome widespread misunderstanding of the market, both by participants and outside commentators, that had created adverse views of the prospects for these firms.

THE UK TAKE-HOME DRINKS MARKET

Rivals in the £6.5bn market fall into two main categories (Table 12.1).

- Major grocery chains (supermarkets), for whom food is the dominant revenue source, now include alcoholic drinks as important ancillary products.
- Specialist off-licence chains (specialists) focus, and depend heavily upon, sales of alcoholic drink, although other products also feature.

The remainder of the market is satisfied by a wide variety of department stores and convenience stores, together with a vast number of independent shops.

Supermarkets' share gain has continued since 1980, and it is widely believed that they will inevitably dominate the market, forcing the specialists into unavoidable extinction. Scenarios were used to explore the driving forces at work in the industry, and hence address three questions.

- How robust is the rationale for this popular view of the market's future?

Table 12.1. Rivals' shares of the UK take-home drinks market

	1989 %	1990 %	1991 %	1992 %	1993 %
Supermarkets					
Sainsbury	7.9	8.5	8.9	9.6	9.8
Tesco	7.9	8.4	8.8	9.2	9.5
Co-op	6.5	6.7	6.9	6.8	6.7
Argyll	6.2	6.5	6.8	6.8	7.1
Asda	4.3	5.5	5.7	5.7	5.5
Kwik Save	n/a	1.0	3.0	3.6	4.6
Gateway	6.1	4.7	4.1	4.1	3.9
Waitrose	1.2	1.2	1.3	1.4	1.6
	40.1	42.5	45.5	47.2	48.7
Marks & Spencer	3.7	3.8	3.8	3.8	3.8
Specialists					
Thresher	6.2	6.2	7.3	9.5	9.6
Victoria Wine	5.8	5.4	5.7	6.2	8.3
Dominic*	5.4	4.6	2.8	–	
Augustus Barnett†	2.8	2.8	2.7	2.6	
Oddbins	1.5	1.6	1.7	1.8	1.9
Unwins	1.5	1.4	1.4	1.4	1.3
Cellar 5	1.2	1.2	1.3	1.7	1.8
Blayneys‡	0.7	0.7	0.7	–	
Majestic	0.5	0.5	0.5	0.5	0.5
	25.6	24.4	24.1	23.7	23.4
Other	30.6	29.3	26.6	25.3	24.1

*Dominic acquired by Thresher in 1991.
†Augustus Barnett acquired by Victoria Wine during 1993.
‡Blayneys subsequently acquired by Cellar 5.
Source: *Verdict*

- What other scenarios for the industry are possible, given the driving forces at work?
- How might specialists act to alter that future?

To answer these questions, a review of the currently accepted scenario and the most likely alternatives was conducted, using cognitive mapping of the views of industry executives.

Market Trends

Total consumption of alcohol in the UK rose modestly during the 1980s, but slipped back with the 1991 recession. However, demand for different product types changed considerably, with beer falling from 60% of alcohol consumed in 1980 to about 54% in 1993, while wine grew from 14% to 21%. The location of drink purchases also shifted over that period, away from pubs and towards shops. Verdict[32] now estimate that shops account for about 25% of alcohol expenditure, making the take-home drinks market a very large retail sector. Even though specialists such as Thresher and Victoria Wine are small subsidiaries of larger brewing firms, they are similar in size to publicly quoted firms in other retail sectors. The market is also relatively stable, having varied little in real terms since 1988, in spite of the retail recession during that period.[33]

Consumers

Consumers are typically well-informed on drinks prices and can switch easily between alternative shops. However, price is only significant if a store is substantially out of line with local rivals. Other factors condition customers' choice of shop, and these buying criteria vary between different consumer groups. Various typologies can be applied to different categories of shopper, but for present purposes a simplified distinction between drinks shoppers favouring large shops and small shops is adequate (Figure 12.2).

All drink shoppers

Price
'Open' layout
No rush
Friendly staff
Special-occasion products
Special offers

Drink shoppers favouring small stores

Traditional style
Knowledgeable staff
Special products
Staff know customers
Extra services
Exclusivity
Convenience of location

Drink shoppers favouring large stores

Modern style
Facilities (toilets, etc.)
Product descriptions
Well known products
Predictable layout
Enclosed environment
Convenience of one-stop shopping

Industry sources

Figure 12.2. Considerations Valued by Buyers of take-home Drinks

Strategies of the Main Categories of Rivals

Supermarkets' gain in market share (Table 12.1) has been driven by increased store numbers, and the building of larger stores. Supermarket chains nearly doubled their selling space over the 1980s from 28 to 48 million square feet, and the space in the largest superstores increased from around 10 million to 27 million square feet. Their greater focus on drink suggests that space devoted to these products has probably risen at a still faster rate. Meanwhile, there have been significant changes in the number of specialist off-licences. After a slight growth in the early 1980s, when independents and small chains exploited healthy market conditions, numbers declined as the more professional chains rationalized their poorer sites.

These factors have a critical implication for the conventional wisdom regarding the market's future. Given the considerable increase in their drinks selling space, supermarkets' gain of take-home drink sales has been only modest, in spite of the closure of many of the stores operated by their specialist rivals. Consequently, specialists have maintained a stable level of sales per store through the recent retail recession (Figure 12.3). The more determined store rationalization of larger chains, which account for about 4600 of these stores, may mean these firms have performed still better.

The strategies of specialist chains have been largely driven by the views of the major brewers who owned them. Some decided that off-licence retailing had a poor future and exited the market (e.g. Grand Met's sale of Dominic and Bass's sale of Augustus Barnett), while others saw opportunities in a rationalizing market to increase their size and profitability through acquisition and growth (e.g. Whitbread's investment in Thresher and Allied's in Victoria Wine). Independent specialists have declined in number, while the remaining place in the market has been taken by a wide range of convenience stores—the highly systematized chains such as 7-Eleven, co-operative groups such as Spar, and many thousands of independently owned outlets.

For supermarkets, alcohol sales are an attractively profitable product line, although recent price competition from low-priced rivals has eroded margins. Competition from supermarkets hit margins for specialists hard during the 1980s. However, some specialists have refocused towards the more attractive parts of the market, improving margins and profitability significantly in recent years.

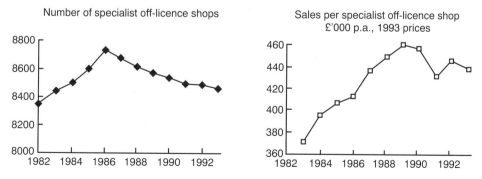

Figure 12.3. Number and Unit Sales of Specialist Off-licences

THE CONVENTIONAL SCENARIO FOR THE FUTURE OF THE TAKE-HOME DRINKS MARKET

The conventional view of the market's future foresees continuing gains by super-markets, not only in sales volume but also in profitability. Specialists, by contrast, are expected to lose volumes, margins, and the meagre profitability they are currently believed to enjoy. Cognitive mapping produces a more detailed picture of this scenario (Figure 12.4). Note that in these maps, an arrow can be read as '. . . may lead to . . .'

This map has the following main features:

- Continuing modest growth in take-home drink expenditure by consumers, against declining expenditure in pubs.
- Continuing pressure on retail prices for take-home alcohol.
- Declining margins for take-home alcohol retailers.
- Supermarket chains and convenience stores continue to gain market share.
- Progressive loss of sales and declining profitability amongst specialists, with the exit of many independents and of major firms.

Whilst this map of conventional wisdom sets out a plausible scenario, cognitive mapping with industry participants uncovered serious inadequacies in the argument—some of the driving forces and their consequences are incomplete or inaccurate, whilst others are missing altogether.

- The potential for more supermarkets is limited—having increased from 300 to 700+ in the last decade, potential locations are increasingly scarce.
- The impact of extended opening hours and Sunday trading is largely complete.

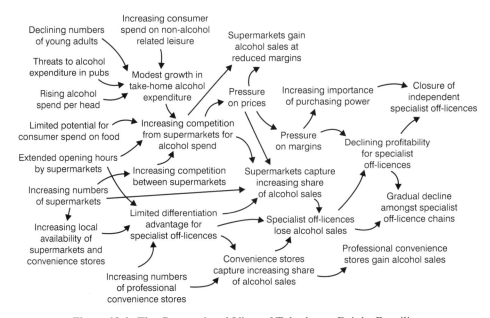

Figure 12.4. The Conventional View of Take-home Drinks Retailing

- Rivalry amongst supermarkets for drink sales is not wholly price-based.
- Most importantly, the participating groups in the market are not uniform, but exhibit sub-groups of their own (Table 12.2).

Furthermore, some specialist off-licence chains may be described as 'focused': having several retail store brand-names designed and located for local consumer markets—i.e. Thresher, Oddbins and Majestic. This contrasts with other specialist chains who have until recently been 'unfocused', offering a single off-licence brand-name. These distinctions have important implications for the industry's future.

Polarization of consumer behaviour

Demographic and social trends reinforce the distinction between routine purchasers of branded alcoholic drink and those wanting quality and service. Moreover, the 'routine' consumer group may be further fragmented by the growth of low-price supermarket chains (Figure 12.5).

This map contains two important features:

- Some outcomes (e.g. 'specialist off-licences with local retail targeting gain sales') are not inherently driven by external forces, but depend on initiatives taken by the retailers themselves.
- The tendency of consumers to be more discerning is reinforced by successful specialists encouraging that need—a critical feedback effect as described in Figure 12.1.

The implications of this new map are considerable:

- Mainstream supermarkets face three attacks on their drink revenues—specialists focused on discerning buyers, low-priced supermarkets taking the most price-sensitive customers, and convenience stores winning impulse purchases.
- The specialists' ability to serve discerning consumers is limited both by the quality and location of existing shops and, except for the focused chains, by a mass-market

Table 12.2. Distinctions between participants in the take-home market

Drink purchasers	Routine customers, interested in one-stop shopping, brand leaders and competitive prices, favouring beer and mass-market wines.	versus	Discriminating consumers of high quality, less common products, needing advice and service, favouring good wines.
Supermarkets	Mainstream superstores, trading on quality, range and added-value products (Tesco, Sainsbury)	versus	Cut-price chains, offering brand-leaders at low prices (Kwik-Save, Aldi).
Convenience stores	Small, individually operated 'corner shops'.	versus	Larger, chain-operated stores (7-Eleven).
Specialist off-licences	Small, individually operated shops or small chains.	versus	Large chains with purchasing power to match the supermarkets.

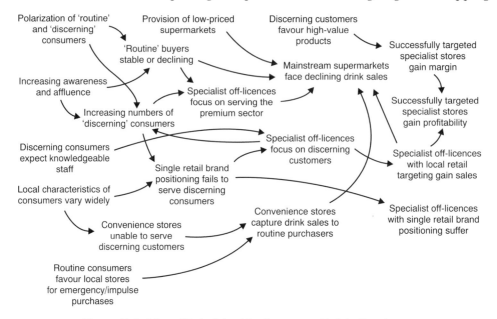

Figure 12.5. Map of Polarizing Needs amongst Drinks Purchasers

positioning ('all things to all men'). Consequently, some further shake-out of specialist off-licence numbers seems likely.

Development plans of retail rivals

The final important driving force is the set of strategic imperatives followed by each class of retailer, summarized in Table 12.3.

Table 12.3

Supermarkets—mainstream
- Continue site expansion to market saturation.
- Resist margin loss from price competition—focus on added-value.
- Appeal via one-stop shopping, cleanliness/brightness, leading brands and clear labelling.
- Margin boosted by buying power.

Supermarkets—price-leaders
- Aggressive site expansion.
- Take revenues via deep discounting on leading brands.
- Margin boosted by buying power.

Convenience stores—chains
- Aggressive site expansion.
- Take revenues via convenience of location and opening times.
- Price premium justified by convenience.
- Margin boosted by buying power.

Convenience stores—individuals
- Take revenues via convenience of location and opening times.
- Price premium justified by convenience.
- Margins threatened by poor buying power.

Specialist off-licences
- Focus brand positioning on local consumer group needs.
- Seek added value and sales via staff with good product knowledge.
- Margin boosted by buying power.
- Rationalize poorly located stores and acquire quality sites.

These strategic thrusts combine to produce the anticipated outcomes for each class of retailer in Figure 12.6.

Figure 12.6. The Impact of Drink Retailers' Strategic Thrusts

Two other strategic initiatives deserve mention. First, supermarkets may consider reverting to High Street sites, but even if this occurs, its impact is unlikely to be significant within five years. Second, the specialists could move towards a 'convenience store' positioning, adding non-drink products to their range. This trend too is in its infancy, and modest in its medium-term impact.

Other factors

Amongst other possible influences, the most important is the easing of customs restrictions due to integration of the European single market. It is estimated that about 10–15% of take home drink currently comes from this source, an effective one-time fall in the size of the UK domestic market.

REVISED CENTRAL SCENARIO—'POLARIZATION LIMITS SUPERMARKETS' SHARE'

Combining the key driving forces results in a new map for the overall development of the sector (Figure 12.7).

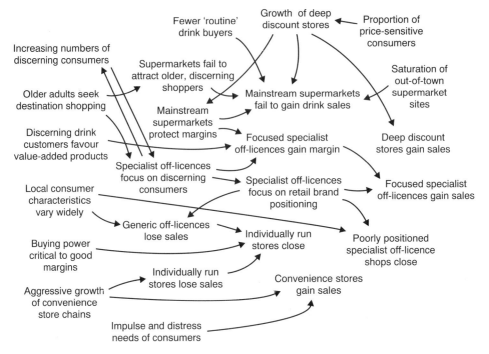

Figure 12.7. Revised Map of Changes in the Take-home Drinks Market

This new map of the industry's evolution implies a scenario that differs from the conventional wisdom on certain critical issues (see Table 12.4).

These implications produce the following outcome for the future of the industry up to 1998:

- Shops' share of total alcohol expenditure rises from 25% to 30%.
- Supermarkets in total, gain market share (Table 12.5), though with swings in market share between them.

Table 12.4

Demand
- Little growth in demand for take-home drink after the loss to personal imports.
- Increasing numbers of discerning consumers switch demand from beer and spirits towards wine and higher value, better margin products.

Store numbers
- Superstores increase at a slower rate than in the 1980s.
- Convenience stores increase in number, whilst 'corner shops' decline.
- Specialist shop numbers decline as poor sites close.

Prospects for firms
- Mainstream supermarkets are squeezed by focused specialists, convenience stores and price-leading supermarkets.
- Convenience stores capture impulse/distress purchases.
- Focused specialists succeed in targeting local markets for discerning consumers. Others fail.

Table 12.5. Central scenario: market shares of retail groups

	1989	1993	1998
Focused specialist chains	13.6	12.0	14
Unfocused specialist chains	12.0	11.4	8
Mainstream Supermarkets	40.1	48.7	52
Other	34.3	27.9	26

- Specialist chains lose stores, and thus market share, but enjoy higher average sales, while gross margins rise. Independent off-licences continue to close.

Although the broad trends in the central scenario and the strategic direction of the rivals are reasonably well-known, the scenario may be untenable since it implies continued poor profitability for the unfocused specialists. Two resolutions are possible:

- Either the unfocused specialists recognize the need to focus, build the capabilities to do so and rationalize their store chains, *and/or*
- One or more unfocused chains decides the task is too great and leaves the market.

Both changes appear to be in progress. Acquiring Augustus Barnett gave over 500 shops and nearly 3 percentage points of market share to Victoria Wine. This group appears to recognize the need to rationalize its now much expanded estate of shops. Oddbins, although one of the focused chains, is a minor part of a larger group (Seagram) with other interests. Its parent could follow Bass in leaving the market. The last member of the group, Unwins, may not have the resources to refocus. A revised scenario therefore needs to recognize that, whatever the specific events, a continued rationalization of poor stores and possible exit of specialist chains is likely, thus further depressing the market share held by the specialists group, but improving sector margins and profitability.

This results in a new scenario—*Shake-out amongst specialists*—in which focused specialists gain further share at the expense of unfocused chains. The number of specialist shops falls faster than in the central scenario, but the rationalization allows average sales per shop to rise (Figure 12.8). The prospects for supermarket and

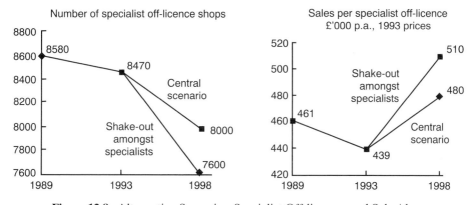

Figure 12.8. Alternative Scenarios: Specialist Off-licences and Sales/shop

convenience store chains are relatively unchanged, but unfocused specialists, both chains and independents, lose out further to supermarkets, convenience stores, and their more focused rivals.

The value of these contrasting scenarios is that they indicate to players in the market what series of future events might unfold and, more importantly, what events and changes they might actively seek to precipitate to create a more prosperous future for themselves. Whilst they are superficially similar to the conventional wisdom with which we started, they differ on critical issues. If certain specialist chains can influence events in the way these scenarios imply, their prospects are good, with the probability of rising sales per store, increasing margins, and healthy profitability.

CONCLUSIONS

The study reported here illustrates important lessons for any attempt to plan a firm's future. First, it shows the danger of accepting generalized assertions about the likely evolution of an industry. A simple acceptance of the conventional wisdom would lead to entirely erroneous strategic decisions by several of the specialist chains. Second, it shows that scenarios must be built with the strategic actions of competitors, and the firm itself, contained within them—no useful scenario can be developed for this sector driven solely by 'external' changes, such as demographics, social factors, or demand for different product-groups. Third, it shows that apparently 'bad' scenarios (here, loss of market share for specialists) can in fact contain promising features (increasing share and profitability for focused specialists). Finally, the example shows the value of just two, quite simple scenarios for informing the strategies of firms within an industry. The focus of this study has been upon the prospects for specialist off-licence chains, for whom its conclusions have important, actionable implications.

The process of developing these scenarios was neither time-consuming nor costly. It needed only some simple data about the recent development of the industry, plus the experience of a small number of industry executives. Nor was the limited availability of accurate data a severe problem. From the shared knowledge base, the mapping of driving forces and outcomes to construct simple, tightly bounded scenarios required only modest effort.

ACKNOWLEDGEMENT

The author acknowledges with gratitude the permission of Verdict and Mintel for the inclusion of data from their reports.

REFERENCES

1. Arie P. de Geus, Planning as Learning, *Harvard Business Review* **66**(2), Mar/Apr, 70–74 (1988).
2. Dale D. McConkey, Planning in a Changing Environment, *Business Horizons* **31**(5), Sept/Oct, 64–72 (1988).
3. Henk A. Becker and Joseph W. M. van Doorn, Scenarios in Organizational Perspective, *Futures* **19**(6), December, 669–677 (1987).

4. Mason Tenaglia and Patrick Noonan, Scenario-Based Strategic Planning: A Process for Building Top Management Consensus, *Planning Review* **20**(2), March/April, 12–19 (1992).
5. Stephen M. Millett, How Scenarios Trigger Strategic Thinking, *Long Range Planning* **21**(5), 61–68 (1988).
6. H. Jungerman and M. Thuring, The use of mental models for generating scenarios, in Wright and Ayton (eds), *Judgemental Forecasting*, Wiley (1987).
7. Kahn, *On Escalation, Metaphor and Scenarios*, Praeger, New York (1965).
8. R. B. Mitchell, J. Tydeman and P. H. Gross, Structuring the future—application of a scenario-generation procedure, *Technological Forecasting and Social Change* **14**, 409–428 (1979).
9. C. Ducot and G. J. Lubben, A typology for scenarios, *Futures* **12**, 51–57 (1980).
10. F. W. Gluck, S. P. Kaufmann and A. S Walleck, Strategic Management for competitive advantage, *Harvard Business Review*, July–August, 154–161 (1980).
11. Rob Bijl, Delphi in a future scenario study on mental health and mental health care, *Futures* **24**(3), April, 232–250 (1992).
12. Jutta Brauers and Martin Weber, A new method of scenario analysis for strategic planning *Journal of Forecasting* **7**(1), Jan/Mar, 31–47 (1988).
13. William R. Huss and Edward J. Honton, Scenario planning—What style should you use?, *Long Range Planning* **20**(4), 21–29 (1987).
14. Michael Hergert, Integration forecasting techniques into corporate financial models, *Business Economics* **22**(3), July, 38–42 (1987).
15. R. M. Narchal, K. Kittappa and P. Bhattacharya, An environmental scanning system for business planning, *Long Range Planning* **20**(6), December, 96–105 (1987).
16. Burt Nanus and Craig Lundberg, In quest of strategic planning, *Cornell Hotel and Restaurant Administration Quarterly* **29**(2), August, 18–23 (1988).
17. Sathiadev Mahesh and Herbert Moskowitz, An information-maximizing interactive procedure for scenario probability elicitation, *Decision Sciences* **21**(3), Summer, 533–550 (1990).
18. Manuel Werner, Planning for uncertain futures: building commitment through scenario planning, *Business Horizons* **33**(3), May/June, 55–58 (1990).
19. Francis Mechner, Present certainty equivalents and weighted scenario valuations, *Journal of Business Venturing* **4**(2), March, 85–92 (1989).
20. C. Eden, Strategic thinking with computers, *Long Range Planning* **23**(6), December, 35–43 (1990).
21. C. Eden, S. Jones and D. Sims, *Messing About in Problems*, Pergamon, Oxford (1983).
22. Liam Fahey and V. K. Narayanan, Linking changes in revealed causal maps and environmental changes: an empirical study, *Journal of Management Studies* **26**(4), July, 361–378 (1989).
23. Colin Eden and Chris Huxham, Action-oriented strategic management, *Journal of the Operational Research Society* **39**(10), October, 889–899 (1988).
24. Paul J. H. Schoemaker and Cornelius A. J. M. van der Heijden, Integrating scenarios into strategic planning at Royal Dutch/Shell, *Planning Review* **20**(3), May/June, 41–46 (1992).
25. Ian Wilson, Teaching decision makers to learn from scenarios: a blueprint for implementation, *Planning Review* **20**(3), May/June, 18–22 (1992).
26. Derrick A. Crandall, Focus on tomorrow, *Association Management* **42**(1), January, 24–28 (1990).
27. Harold S. Becker, Developing and using scenarios—assisting business decisions, *Journal of Business and Industrial Marketing* **4**(1), 61–70 (1989).
28. P. R. Stokke, W. K. Ralston, T. A. Boyce and I. H. Wilson, Scenario planning for Norwegian oil and gas, *Long Range Planning* **23**(2), April, 17–26 (1990).
29. W. Whipple, Evaluating alternative strategies using scenarios, *Long Range Planning* **22**(3), June, 82–86 (1989).
30. Abdul Khakee, Relationship between future studies and planning, *European Journal of Operational Research* (Netherlands) **33**(2), January, 200–211 (1988).

31. Steven P. Schnaars, How to develop and use scenarios, *Long Range Planning* **20**(1), February, 105–114 (1987).
32. Verdict, December 1993, *Off-licences*, London.
33. Mintel, July 1992, *Alcoholic drink retailing in the UK*, London.

_____ Part V

Corporate Modelling

Chapter 13

Cognitive Mapping and Problem Structuring for System Dynamics Model Building

Colin Eden
Strathclyde Business School, Glasgow, UK

This chapter responds to a request by the editor to consider 'the potential and promise of systems thinking.' In writing it, I have taken an idiosyncratic view of systems thinking rather than a formal view. However, although this view would be seen as idiosyncratic by those who identify themselves as systems thinkers, it does adhere to some of the key principles about the nature of systems. My difficulty is that the view of problem solving and strategy making in organizations that drives my approach to organizational intervention is not informed by systems theory but rather by theories of organization, of groups, and of human thinking and action. Many systems thinkers derive their approach to problem solving by treating an organization as a reified entity with properties that translate across many sorts of entities—it is the property of a system that matters rather than the nature of organized humanity.

But the undeniably true flagship statements of systems thinkers do guide my thinking and practice. That 'a system is greater than the sum of its parts,' that 'systems exist in an environment and need to interact with it in order to survive,' that 'there are systems, and wider systems, and subsystems,' that 'systems have needs, that they are adaptive, have inputs and outputs,' and so on, do have practical import.

The big difficulty is getting a management team to agree about the definition of the system they need to address in order to agree on a course of action or way forward. The definition will need to be requisite (Phillips, 1984) so that time is used effectively and the attention of the team can be retained.

This article is about how we decide what the system is that will be modeled. It is about problem-structuring processes that give assurance we have not focused too early on one definition of the system rather than another. It is about understanding and managing the complexity of problem definition. In the end, it is about reducing the risk of finding the right solution to the wrong problem. Thus, it discusses (1) the nature of management decision making; (2) the nature of problem definition; (3) the role of cognition in problem definition; (4) cognitive mapping as a modeling tool for acknowledging the richness from recognizing multiple perspectives, managing this

Reprinted from *Systems Dynamics Review*, Volume 10, Nos. 2–3, pp. 257–276, Copyright © 1994, John Wiley & Sons.

complexity, and identifying feedback loops; and (5) group support system software, which facilitates the negotiation of problem definition with a client group, the analysis of cognitive maps, validating feedback loops, moving from cognitive map to influence 2diagram, and their relation to one another and to a simulation model.

THE NATURE OF MANAGEMENT DECISION MAKING

Building models that will influence the decision making of managers must be related to an understanding of the reality of organizational life. Formal and scientific model-building activity is aimed at helping people tackle real-world problems. It is thus an activity that addresses itself to the choices and actions of persons other than the management science practitioner. Its success is only measured by the extent to which it influences the thinking and action of such persons. Models are client-oriented, not solution-oriented. Model-building practice must therefore involve the dispassionate and objective activities of science combined with the passion of social intercourse in organizations.

In what is now an old, but still relevant, study of management, Mintzberg (1973) identified a number of characteristics inherent in the clients of modeling activity. For our purposes, those that are significant are that managers prefer verbal over numeric information; prefer conversation over reading; prefer to make incremental decisions; are highly mistrustful of others' theories; need to gather information on an anecdotal basis; and prefer to let a decision emerge. Thus, language, negotiation, and incrementalism are the common currency of organizational life and so need to be the basis for the early stages of modeling problem definition. Modeling is about helping managers 'muddle through' better (Lindblom, 1959).

Problem solving in organizations is predominantly a social activity. For example, even if an individual has thought through a problem and decided what to do, there is another part of solving the problem that derives from the need to persuade others to join in implementation. The process of ensuring effective implementation will change not only the nature of the solution but also the nature of the problem—the problem becomes redefined through the discovery of new knowledge about the problem situation. The implication is that the nature of the problem cannot be and is not separable from the practicalities of implementation (Eden, 1987). Crucial to this assertion is the view that effective problem solving, or what is more accurately described by the term 'problem finishing' (Eden, 1987), involves a careful balance between negotiated social order and socially negotiated order.

The expected outcome of problem solving is the creation of order, a sense of direction and commitments about which the problem owner will feel comfortable. Order as the outcome of problem solving suggests that the inherent characteristic of a problem is a perceived lack of order seen by the problem owner. *Negotiated order* recognizes that whatever happens will be the result of the shifting of working relationships, the creation of new routines for transactions between those involved in the implementation of progress toward order. Moving towards order—toward the solution of a problem—depends upon facilitating this negotiation.

Socially negotiated order recognizes that the negotiated order is the consequence of a social negotiation where work on problems involves a negotiation that pays attention to social history and anticipated future relationships between key actors.

On the other hand, *negotiated social order* describes a problem-solving process where the emphasis is not on negotiating order but rather on negotiating social relationships. The difference is one of emphasis, where negotiated social order is likely to lead to 'group-think' (Janis, 1972) and 'the Abilene paradox' (Harvey, 1988) because the group is unable to be straightforward about beliefs and values as they pertain to the problem situation. Instead, the group protects the existing social order—the maintenance of current behavior patterns, ways of relating to one another, current well-rehearsed scripts, current coalitions—not 'rocking the boat' (Vickers, 1983).

If too much emphasis is put on negotiating order without a recognition of the impact on social relationships, then also group-think can be the result, where the logic and rationality driving toward creating order means that the group cannot address the significance the new order has on social relationships, a significance that everyone knows means the solutions will not be implemented or will be sabotaged, or will have ignored the reality of the social history and context for this particular group.

Attaining the correct balance between these two aspects of the needs of groups is the role of professional facilitation of problem management (Bryant, 1989) for a group of managers.

In part, recognizing the need for careful balance between negotiated social order and socially negotiated order also recognizes how crucial organizational politics can be during the problem construction stage.

POWER AND POLITICS

The traditional view of power is relatively unhelpful to the modeler. This view of power relates to the ability to control scarce and critical resources required by others. It is a view that is relevant to an analysis of the client problem situation but not particularly relevant to managing the problem-structuring stage or the overall modeling intervention. The modeler is very rarely powerful in this way and so cannot use coercion as a method of persuading the client that the model is correct. The modeler is more dependent upon psychological and social psychological devices for persuasion. Similarly, the client as individual rarely has enough power to ensure commitment from other critical actors in the organization—the model becomes a vehicle to facilitate negotiation, a dialectical device (Eden, 1992b) or 'transitional object' (de Geus, 1988) for 'the creation of legitimacy for certain ideas, values, and demands—not just action performed as a result of previously acquired legitimacy' (Pettigrew, 1977).

Within modeling practice, and particularly the problem definition stage, there is one overriding consideration—the power to manage meaning, as the ability to 'mobilize bias' (Schattsneider, 1960) and to let agendas define which issues are to be addressed and which not. 'Key concepts for analyzing meaning are symbolism, language, belief, and myth. Language is not just a means of expressing thoughts, categories, and concepts: it is also a vehicle for achieving practical effects' (Pettigrew, 1977). Once again, this description emphasizes the role of language and argument as the currency for organizational problem solving.

It is this more psychological view of power that is most difficult to understand. We are accustomed to Machiavellian views of power and politics where careerism, ambition and sheer bloody-mindedness are the focus of attention. The maneuvering of people along Machiavellian dimensions is relatively easy to identify, but it is in my experience much less common than the politics that result from the wish to define reality (Perrow, 1972). This latter form of politics is the essence of human life; it derives from honest people believing they know what is best for the organization. This belief means that meaning will be managed by the formation of coalitions, by trading support for different versions of reality—socially negotiating order.

A modeler sits in the middle of this with yet another belief about what should be done (for analysis is never neutral or without implied action, however much the intelligent bystander role is sold). It is therefore a matter of practical force that the modeler also must actively seek out coalitions and bargain realities (problem definitions). Within this context of the social construction of reality the role of the problem-structuring phase can be seen as crucial.

It is during these early stages of a modeling project that social forces can shape the definition of the problem in a manner that commits the analyst irrevocably and often unknowingly to a particular structure for the system dynamics simulation model. This point is acknowledged to be important by many system dynamics modelers (Morecroft, 1983; Richardson et al., 1989; Vennix, 1990; Lane, 1992); however the processes involved need to be particularly carefully designed to reflect a clear theoretical perspective on the nature of organizations and groups, let alone the psychology of problem construal. The activity needs to adequately reflect the parameters of political feasibility, coordination and cooperation, meeting productivity, negotiation, and creativity.

Situations that are worth modeling are always complex. Choices have to be made about what to model. These choices only exist if the complexity is acknowledged—you can't choose A from A. With much modeling practice and method it is a real danger that the part of a situation to be modeled is chosen accidentally.

PROBLEM DEFINITION

Complexity of problem definition derives from the differences in interpretation each key actor in a situation gives to the events and to explanations of the influences between events. The first part is about recognizing that personal values play a part in interpretation, and the second part recognizes that individuals bring to bear different experience and wisdom that has created different belief systems (Sims et al., 1981). It is not that one person is right and another wrong; rather it is that the measure of 'truth' is related to context and relevance in problem solving. Context and relevance are related to whom the modeling is for, who is responsible for deciding, and who needs to be committed to act. Thus, context and relevance, and so requisiteness, is determined by issues of political feasibility and negotiating a new social order.

Choosing what to model . . . through ignorance

The most common default choice about problem definition comes from not seeing or hearing about the complexity (see Figure 13.1). Modelers, who often come to the profession from mathematics and the pure sciences, do not take seriously subjectivity and social negotiation but rather seek to discover their own truths about the situation. They do not deliberately seek to discover the richness of multiple perspectives and the associated conflicts in beliefs and values. To do so is inconvenient. These models often

Figure 13.1. Choosing what to Model: Version 1

recognize that asking key actors will reveal different understandings and so, rather than ask them, they will take on the role of definer of the situation or take the view of a single person as somehow representative. This approach to modeling focuses on facts, not on the relations between them and the way in which these relations give meaning to situations. It is complexity reduction by not being aware of the complexity.

Choosing what to model . . . through politics

The alternative common approach to ignoring choice in modeling stems from the politics of defining the truth (see Figure 13.2). The modeler listens predominantly to those persons, or that person, who speaks first or loudest, or who proffers a view from another basis of power such as expertise or authority or the sort of scientific logic that fits the modeler's frame of reference.

These are two simple but common versions of the lack of care in choosing what to model. What this means in practice is that the modeler must keep opening up the problem (Beer, 1966) by attending to the depth and richness of different perspectives on the problem until the emergent patterns (including conflicts) begin to stabilize and there is enough linkage between different perspectives from each of the key actors to obtain a basis for negotiation about problem definition, but enough deep knowledge surfaced for the group to go beyond maintaining social order and toward negotiating order.

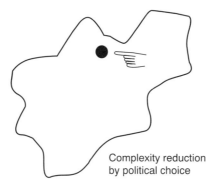

Figure 13.2. Choosing what to Model: Version 2

THE ROLE OF COGNITION IN PROBLEM DEFINITION AND PROBLEM STRUCTURING

In discussing the nature of management decision making, I have suggested that language is a proxy for thinking and at least the currency of problem solving in organizations. If this is so, then a useful (not correct) model for understanding cognition and its relation to language within the context of problem solving is required. One such model is illustrated in Figure 13.3. The separation of perception and construal reflects a view of problem solving that follows Kelly's (1955) theory of personal constructs in supposing that we 'make sense' of our world in order to 'predict and control'. The emphasis on selective perception as 'filtering in' rather than filtering out (the information-processing view) follows Neisser (1976). The distinction between values and beliefs is never easy, either conceptually or practically (Eden et al., 1979). However, the distinction is important, for it forces the need to understand cognition and action in terms of preference and in terms of intervention. Important is the view of beliefs and values as systems, where one value is supported by a network of others and beliefs are not entities but rather an understanding of causality. Without values and beliefs being seen as a system of interconnected causality we cannot conceive of actors intervening to change problematic situations.

Decision making in complex situations is the consequence of construal, situation defining (McHugh, 1968; Ball, 1972; Eden, 1980), and choice (Duncker, 1972; Neisser, 1976); for these reasons alone, information-processing models are not helpful. Defining a problem situation is a positive process of selection guided by a schema rather than a process of massive perception and then rejection (Dearborn and Simon, 1958). Decision making is a consequence of attaching meaning and significance to the events that occur around us—perception filters in data, and construal interprets; thus perception and construal are not the same thing. For problem solving, it is construal that most significantly determines action.

COGNITIVE MAPPING FOR PROBLEM STRUCTURING

Cognitive mapping as a method for problem structuring is, not surprisingly, based upon the preceding view of cognition. It is based upon the theories of Kelly (1955), which focus upon human beings as problem solvers. The theory is not taken to be a correct theory of cognition but rather one that is wholesome (complete, self-reflexive, and practice-related) and absolutely relevant to model building for problem solving.

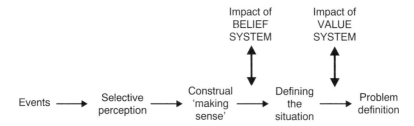

Figure 13.3. Cognition as the Interaction between a Value System and a Belief System

It is therefore in essence a theory that has resulted in a modeling method that seeks to portray the way in which problem owners are making sense of their situation. It aims to set out their explanations for why the situation is as they construe it and why it matters to them. Thus, the cognitive map is a directed graph, much like an influence diagram, that focuses on a qualitative understanding of the situation through the linkages between bipolar constructs. Constructs are chunks of language used to construct an argument or line of argument, where the line of argument is depicted by a string of arrows. Each chunk of what in practice turns out to be about 10–12 words encompasses an implicit or explicit subject, active verb, and object. The meaning of each chunk is not deduced from a semantic analysis but rather from the context of the construct—what it explains (consequences) and what explains it. Thus, the model is about depicting meaning, not semantics.

A cognitive map is designed to help depict the structure of a problem. It is a representation of the way in which a client believes a situation has come about and why it is problematic (impinges values). A cognitive map includes both a description of a problem situation and, by implication or explication, an understanding about what can and cannot be done about a problem. In this way, the map recognizes the problem as something that includes within its definition the practical problems of getting something done—the problem we face is often that of how to get something done.

The system of beliefs captured by a cognitive map gives an indication of why the situation is problematic. The mapping process helps identify the sense of direction ('goals'), or disappointment about current direction ('not-goals'), embedded in statements made about the situation. It does not assume that a problem owner knows what his or her objectives are, or how to proceed toward solution. The problem owner is not expected to describe the problem in any set order or structure; indeed, the presumption on the part of the cognitive mapper is that the problem may exist partly because there is doubt about the relevance of some aspects of the situation, because there may be conflicting goals, and because there are uncomfortable ramifications of possible actions.

A cognitive map is intended to be problem-oriented, and thus constructs in the map are propositional, suggesting a possible option for action (for a guide to cognitive mapping, see Ackermann et al., 1991). As often as possible, a construct includes a contrasting pole to declare the psychological (not necessarily logical) opposite circumstance to the primary pole of the construct. Many of the assertions made by clients about the world do not have obvious reasons for being stated and so are ignored by the consultant as if they were simply background, irrelevancies, or 'red herrings' and therefore a waste of the consultant's time. Alternatively, the modeler sees them as so obvious in their importance that a presumption is made incorrectly about why the statement has been made. Experience in problem structuring using maps suggests that it is often these so-called asides that are crucial to identifying possible actions.

For example, if the client says, 'We're a nice organization to work in,' it sounds like a throwaway line. But if we presume always that every statement is made to give meaning, then the requirement for the mapper is to note the construct and attempt to understand the meaning of the statement in terms of action consequences. Thus, with prompting or energetic listening, it may be followed by the critical and related belief, 'I can't understand why the labor force won't accept the changes'.

While a cognitive map looks, on the face of it, like an influence diagram, it is different in what it seeks to do (Eden, 1988). When used as the basis for problem structuring aimed at building a system dynamics model, it will later be rolled into an influence diagram before the influence diagram becomes a system dynamics flow diagram of rates, levels, and auxiliaries. For problem construction a cognitive map is a model of action-oriented thinking about a situation; it is driven by the need to represent a belief system linked to a value system rather than a system of interacting variables.

Figure 13.4 represents a cognitive map of my thinking as it was set out in the first few paragraphs of the section in this article entitled 'The Nature of Management Decision Making'. In Figure 13.5, the cognitive map has been extended by the constructs in italics, which represent some of the arguments developed in this article as ways of dealing with the issue described in Figure 13.4. In this model—the cognitive map—the ellipses separating two phrases in a construct (node) should be read as *rather than*, thus separating the two contrasting poles. As with influence diagrams, the arrows signify influences or lines of argument leading from means to ends (options to outcomes, beliefs to values), where at the top of the hierarchy are those constructs most closely representing values and at the bottom of the hierarchy are options for influencing the situation.

In practice, cognitive maps for a messy problem will comprise at least 100 constructs for each key actor. Thus, for a typical management team, a merged map, which is the aggregation of all definitions of the situation (including all contradictions and differences in perspective) will contain 600–900 constructs.

The merged map (or what is now more formally a cause map rather than a cognitive map, as it does not represent the cognition of a single person) will very often have a number of feedback loops in it. It is these feedback loops that will be of interest to the system dynamics modeler (see Eden and Jones, 1980 and Eden et al., 1983 for examples of the use of cognitive mapping in relation to system dynamics modeling) and of course to any modeler not concerned with a simulation model but simply having an

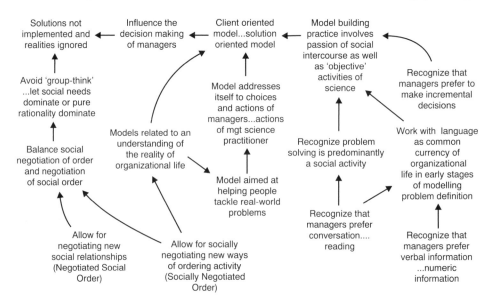

Figure 13.4. A Cognitive Map on the Nature of Decision Making

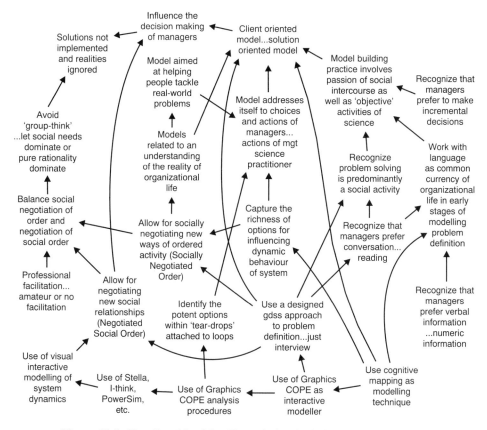

Figure 13.5. The Cognitive Map Extended to Include Potential Options

interest in helping the team understand the nature of the problem. An extension of the cognitive map of Figure 13.4 shows two small loops (see Figure 13.6).

GROUP SUPPORT SYSTEM SOFTWARE—GRAPHICS COPE

Analysis of cognitive maps

Recent research reinforces the view that more efficient decision makers are those who use a reduced processing strategy when faced with complex tasks. Thus, they focus on a small number of crucial elements in a problem. This matches well with research conducted during the 1960s on psychological stress and cognitive strain. This research used information-processing models to consider the relation between information demands and information-processing capacity. In essence, the conclusions are that decision makers exhibit rationality but only within the constraints of their bounded view of the problem—thus the term 'bounded rationality' (March and Simon, 1958). And so, the argument went, decision makers compensate for their limited abilities for processing information by constructing a simplified representation of the problem. If

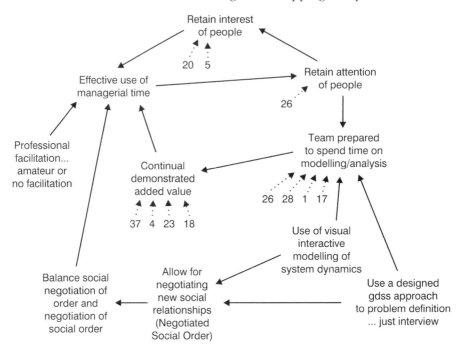

Figure 13.6. Two Loops that relate to the Other Parts of the Model of Figure 16.4

so, then a map of 900 constructs is unhelpful to a management team, but the challenge is to keep the richness and ownership without the overwhelming debilitation arising from too much detail: manage complexity without reducing it. Thus, some form of computer-aided group decision support system is required (Eden, 1992a), preferably a support system that also facilitates more quantitative modeling support should that prove helpful.

For cognitive maps the group decision support system is from computer software known as Graphics COPE.[1] This software is designed to be used with managers in real time (Eden and Ackermann, 1992) so that they can understand interactively the problem as it has been defined by each member and aggregated into a group view, so that they can change it, understand its structure and emergent properties (Eden, 1991; Eden et al., 1992). The discovery of emergent properties includes real-time analysis to discover and display the feedback loops, analysis that enables the problem to be seen from alternative perspectives by focusing on different slices or categories as required, seeing an overview of the problem, and so on. Thus, the software is usually, but not always, facilitator-driven and has the capability of representing a cognitive map graphically in a variety of different display formats at any time the facilitator or group calls for it. It is able to analyze the map on request and make changes to constructs, links, categories, constructs in categories subject to group demands rather than subject to the structure of the software.

A group often spends a whole day in front of a large color computer display during the early stages of problem structuring, and so the displays, editing and analysis routines must be simple to understand and communicate essential characteristics easily. The use of colors, different fonts, and reference sets is important in providing productive support that immediately communicates patterns within the model.

Specifically, the analysis methods embedded in the software enable the identification of central constructs, clustering, hierarchical clustering, identification of potent options, set logic between multiple categories, loop analysis, merging of constructs while retaining all linkages, and collapsing a model onto selected constructs while holding onto all linkage paths. Thus, for system dynamics modeling it is possible to focus attention on only some constructs in the model—those amenable to quantitative judgment and important in constructing a model of the feedback dynamics. Figure 13.7 shows a Graphics COPE screen display of the loop in Figure 13.6 after it has been translated one stage toward an influence diagram by changing constructs to a tighter phraseology and closer to that of variables. The dashed arrows on the screen show that each of the variables relate to 'tear-drops' of options and consequences not an integral part of any loop. As loops are identified and validated, the model becomes focused upon the aggregation of loops only, where the hierarchical maps attached to the loop variables ('tear-drops') can be called up when necessary. Detecting feedback loops within a cognitive map is analytically straightforward using the software. However, it is problematic for other reasons.

When one person is trying to describe a complex situation, he will find it difficult to be complete. In order to cope with complexity, a person needs to fragment his view, an act that can often seem like bounded vision. Thus, each fragment is likely to be coherent within itself but possibly incoherent in relation to other fragments. This risks the modeler's believing that the person is incoherent and not to be trusted, whereas what is required is some help to the person in reflecting upon, elaborating, and exploring the interconnections between the fragments.

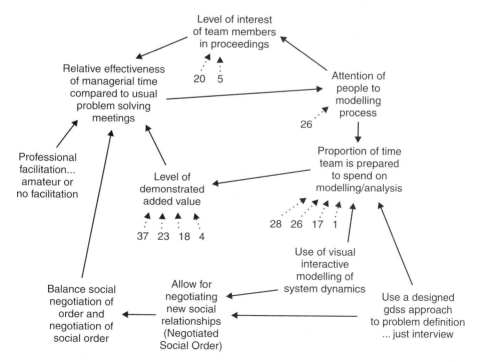

Figure 13.7. A Graphics COPE Screen Display of the First Stage of an Influence Diagram

We expect different members of a group to arrive at different definitions of the situation. It has been suggested that one reason is different value systems. This means that a model for one person would properly have a different emphasis from that which is appropriate for another person. For model building we need to establish who is the client and so establish the values that determine the outcomes (endogenous variables) of interest to the client. So we might expect the core of a model of the economy for right-wing political parties to be built from the 'public sector borrowing requirement' and for left-wing parties built from 'levels of unemployment.' Each model will have some parts that are the same; many parts would be not only different in emphasis but also not there at all. It is tempting to argue that since the model needs to become correct, these perspectives must be reconciled.

Take, for example, the consequences of merging problem definitions of several members of a team about explanations for a situation. Suppose we are interested in feedback loops as the basis for system dynamics modeling. Our analysis of the rich data in the cognitive map suggests the loops shown at the left in Figure 13.8. Here the link between C and D becomes critical. Typically this may mean that: (1) two persons disagree, one arguing that C→D and the other that D→C, and so the linkages may create the loop ABCD or not, depending on which view is to be believed; (2) the two persons may be articulating different explanations but meaning the same and so can reach agreement or not about the loop ABCD; (3) each view may be a summary of more detailed explanation of the influence between C and D, both may be correct, and so the ABCD loop exists and has within it a nested loop, which when elaborated is as shown at the right in Figure 13.8. These alternatives must be explored by the modeler, for the outcome of the exploration can be absolutely critical to the structure of the simulation model and to ownership.

From Cognitive Maps to Influence Diagrams

Following the processes of analysis suggested in preceding sections, a cognitive map with its embedded and validated feedback loops is the basis for choosing those constructs that can be usefully treated as variables in modeling dynamic behavior. The process is relatively simple using the software: selected constructs become the nodes of a collapsed influence map, from which the nodes can be edited into variables. Because the software can collapse onto any subset of constructs within the map, by retaining all the paths that link members of the subset and also temporarily hiding the unwanted constructs, the process of moving from cause map to influence diagram can be tentative and experimental. A collapsed map can be explored and uncollapsed, the subset

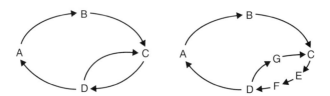

Figure 13.8. Loops that May Result when Merging Cognitive Maps from Individuals Asserting Different Links between C and D

modified, and a new collapsed model explored. In practice, this process cycles between cause map, collapsed cause map, influence diagram, and system dynamics model—each helps the process of verification of the other, and the close relation between each visual interactive model helps with transparency in model building for both client group and modeler. Simple procedures such as retaining the same reference numbers for each of the original constructs, variables within the influence diagram, and state, rate, or auxiliary variables in the simulation model facilitate the use of each model in support of the other.

The importance of treating each model as a visual interactive model, which can be interlaced and so evaluated in relation to another by the client group, should not be underestimated. As experiments with the simulation model suggest possible incoherence, inconsistency, and illogic, then the possibility for exploring the implications for necessary changes in the original cognitive map (as a 'naturalistic' client group definition of the situation can be debated, explored, researched, verified, and so modified with agreement and ownership. It is this role for the Graphics COPE display with the cognitive map and the influence diagram available for view in alternative windows, coupled with the system dynamics model running in another window (for example, PowerSim[2]) that can give powerful group decision support. Although current system dynamics modeling packages offer many visual interactive benefits, the original modeling software (GRIPS) developed at Karlsruhe (Hudetz, 1977) created what was perhaps the first and best visual interactive system dynamics modeling package—in some ways easier to use than current mouse-driven software because of its use of a light pen.

Figure 13.9 shows the process of interaction between the three models, which ensures that the richness and complexity of the situation are faithfully translated into the simulation model and that the issues of validation and coherence apparent from the quantitative modeling are translated back to a debate about the nature of the situation as seen by the problem owners. In this figure, the illustration refers to a forensic system dynamics model that was constructed to form the basis of an analysis of disruption and delay costs and successful litigation on behalf of a Channel Tunnel contractor (Williams et al., 1994).

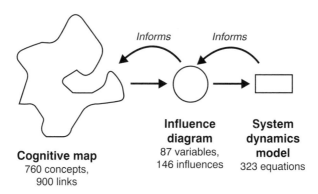

Figure 13.9. An Example of the Relation Between Cognitive Map, Influence Diagram and System Dynamics Model

CONCLUDING REMARKS

As the elaborated cognitive map (Figure 13.4) shows, experience with and theory to support cognitive mapping and associated software (Graphics COPE) can provide a powerful contribution to the practice of problem structuring in organizations and a link to system dynamics simulation modeling. Because of the richness of cognitive maps and the role of interactive group decision support the process of building appropriate and relevant models has become easier. The process of facilitating a negotiation toward increased emotional and cognitive commitment to effective action is also easier. The power of portable group decision support technology has now entered a new age (Eden, 1993). However, notwithstanding this increased potential for management science modeling and its ability to enter more directly the decision-making debate at strategic levels, there is also some evidence, and considerable force of argument, that the role of rational science in organizations is decreasing. The demise of many management science and operational research groups in North Europe is not encouraging.

Nevertheless, even given the force of postmodernism as a way of understanding the world of today, I do not believe that we have seen the death of rational analytic processes for guiding policy making. The organizational and management studies world has not moved away from rational science; rather, it may have found additional (and seductive) approaches to both commenting on, and prescribing, ways in which human endeavor comes together to form the future. Even the current fad for seeing organizations through the metaphor of chaos theory is not, as many seem to suppose, an argument for dismissing a role for rational science and rational analytic methods and frameworks; on the contrary, it is itself rational science commenting on the adequacy, not irrelevance, of rational science. Indeed, I suspect that the rational analytic method will rise again as the 1990s unfold and people become increasingly wary of the politics and art of image management as if image were substance. In no way does this argue against subjectivism or the extent to which rationalism is culture- and value-laden.

Developments discussed here and proposed by many others could be the source of a balance between the power of social theory and the urge people have for the security of policy analysis as a major contributor in resolving their future predicaments. Ideology as the sole basis for policy making has had a good run and is beginning to be seen as the explanation for ill-thought-out and impractical policy in education, health provision, public transport, and so on. As the UK government is forced to recover from a string of policy decisions that were supported by no policy analysis whatsoever (Rosenhead, 1992), the role of the sort of rational analysis that characterizes management science models is likely to become more rather than less significant.

Nevertheless, modeling is at best a negotiated settlement between the logic and analysis sustained by the model and the judgment of the person who will act in relation to the insights provided by the model. It is also the facilitative device that enables negotiation between different members of a team who wish to act. In this sense it is also a learning device, a formalism, which can enable people to change their minds, feel more confident about their views, and develop commitment. However, the model as a learning instrument is secondary; in the end the primary relevance of the model depends upon the political feasibility of the policies considered. This is true whether the model is intended to help exploration about future actions or intended to help with system design, or whether it is forensic modeling that must be validated and calibrated in relation to historical output characteristics.

Thus, in part, this article can be seen as a plea for modeling to be done with a respect for what Hurst (1984) set out as both the 'boxes and bubbles' aspects of decision making, the soft and the hard, the socially negotiated order and the negotiated social order of making things happen in organizations.

NOTES

1. Graphics COPE runs in a Microsoft Windows environment and requires 4 MB of RAM with color VGA display. It was designed at the University of Strathclyde, Scotland, and is available from the university.
2. PowerSim is available from Powersim AS, Nygaten 3, P.O. Box 642, N-5001 Bergen, Norway.

REFERENCES

Ackermann, F., S. A. Cropper, and C. Eden. 1991. Cognitive Mapping for Community Operational Research—A User's Guide. In *Operation Research Tutorial Papers*, ed. A. Munford and T. Bailey. London: Macmillan.

Ball, D. W. 1972. 'Definition of the Situation': Some Theoretical and Methodological Consequences of Taking W. I. Thomas. *Journal for the Theory of Social Behavior* 2: 1.

Beer, S. 1966. *Decision and Control*. Chichester, UK: Wiley.

Bryant, J. 1989. *Problem Management: A Guide for Producers and Players*. Chichester, U.K.: Wiley.

de Geus, A. 1988. Planning as Learning. *Harvard Business Review* (March–April): 70–74.

Dearborn, D. C., and H. A. Simon. 1958. Selective Perception: A Note on the Departmental Identification of Executives. *Sociometry*, 21: 140–144.

Duncker, K. 1972. *On Problem-Solving*. Westport, Conn.: Greenwood.

Eden, C. 1980. Modelling Cognition in Complex Decision Problems. *Journal of Interdisciplinary Modelling and Simulations* 3: 119–144.

Eden, C. 1987. Problem Solving or Problem Finishing? In *New Directions in Management Science*, ed. M. C. Jackson and P. Keys. Gower.

Eden, C. 1988. Cognitive Mapping: A Review. *European Journal of Operational Research* 36: 1–13.

Eden, C. 1991. Working on Problems Using Cognitive Mapping. In *Operations Research in Management*, ed. S. C. Littlechild and M. Shutler. London: Prentice Hall.

Eden, C. 1992a. A Framework for Thinking about Group Decision Support Systems (GDSS). *Group Decision and Negotiation* 1: 199–218.

Eden, C. 1992b. Strategic Management as a Social Process. *Journal of Management Studies* 29: 799–811.

Eden, C. 1993. From the Playpen to the Bombsite: The Changing Nature of Management Science. *Omega* 21: 139–154.

Eden, C., and F. Ackermann. 1992. Strategy Development and Implementation: The Role of a Group Decision Support System. In *Computer Augmented Teamwork*, ed. B. Bostrom, S. Kinney, and R. Watson. New York: Van Nostrand and Reinhold.

Eden, C., F. Ackermann and S. Cropper. 1992. The Analysis of Cause Maps. *Journal of Management Studies* 29: 309–324.

Eden, C., and S. Jones. 1980. Publish or Perish—A Case Study. *Journal of the Operational Research Society*, 31: 131–139.

Eden, C., S. Jones, and D. Sims. 1979. *Thinking in Organizations*. London: Macmillan.

Eden, C., S. Jones, and D. Sims 1983. *Messing About in Problems*. Oxford: Pergamon.

Harvey, J. 1988. The Abilene Paradox: The Management of Agreement. *Organizational Dynamics* (Summer): 17–34.

Hudetz, W. 1977. Construction of Dynamic System Models Using Interactive Computer Graphics. In *Concepts and Tools of Computer Assisted Policy Analysis*. ed. H. Bossell, II, 266–299.

Hurst, D. K. 1984. Of Boxes and Bubbles, and Effective Management. *Harvard Business Review* (May–June): 78–88.

Janis, I. L. 1972. *Victims of Groupthink*. Boston: Houghton Mifflin.

Kelly, G. A. 1955. *The Psychology of Personal Constructs*. New York: Norton.

Lane, D. C. 1992. Modelling as Learning. *European Journal of Operational Research* 59: 64–84.

Lindblom, C. E. 1959. The Science of Muddling Through. *Public Administration Review* 19: 79–88.

March, J. G., and H. A. Simon. 1958. *Organizations*. Chichester, U.K.: Wiley.

McHugh, P. 1968. *Defining the Situation*. New York: Bobbs-Merrill.

Meadows, D. H., D. L. Meadows, J. Randers, and W. W. Behrens III. 1972. *The Limits to Growth*. London: Earth Island.

Mintzberg, H. 1973. *The Nature of Managerial Work*. New York: Harper and Row.

Morecroft, J. 1983. Systems Dynamics: Portraying Bounded Rationality. *Omega* 11: 131–142.

Morecroft, J. 1990. Strategy Support Models. In *Strategic Planning: Models and Analytical Techniques*, ed. R. G. Dyson. Chichester, U.K.: Wiley.

Neisser, U. 1976. *Cognition and Reality*. San Francisco: Freeman.

Perrow, C. 1972. *Complex Organizations*. Glenview, Ill.: Scott, Foresman.

Pettigrew, A. 1977. Strategy Formulation as a Political Process. *International Studies in Management and Organization* 7: 78–87.

Phillips, L. D. 1984. A Theory of Requisite Decision Models. *Acta Psychologica* 56: 29–48.

Richardson, G. P., J. A. M. Vennix, D. F. Anderson, J. Rohrbaugh, and W. A. Wallace. 1989. Eliciting Group Knowledge for Model Building. In *Computer-Based Management of Complex Systems*, ed. P. M. Milling and E. O. K. Zahn, 343–357. Berlin: Springer-Verlag.

Rosenhead, J. 1992. Into the Swamp: The Analysis of Social Issues. *Journal of the Operational Research Society* 43: 293–305.

Schattsneider, E. E. 1960. *The Semi-Sovereign People*. New York: Holt, Rinehart, Winston.

Sims, D., C. Eden, and S. Jones. 1981. Facilitating Problem Definition in Teams. *European Journal of Operational Research* 6: 360–366.

Vennix, J. A. M. 1990. Mental Models and Computer Models: Design and Evaluation of Computer-Based Learning Environment for Policy Making. Ph.D. dissertation, Catholic University of Nijmegen, Netherlands.

Vickers, G. 1983. *The Art of Judgment*. New York: Harper and Row.

Williams, T. W., C. Eden, A. Tait, and F. Ackermann. 1994. Using Cognitive Mapping to Develop a Large Forensic System Dynamics Model. In *Proceedings of the 1994 International System Dynamics Conference*, Stirling, Scotland. Submitted.

Chapter 14

Simulating the Controllability of Feebates

Andrew Ford
Washington State University, USA

System dynamics has been defined as 'that branch of control theory which deals with socioeconomic systems, and that branch of management science which deals with problems of controllability' (Coyle, 1977). This article explains an application of system dynamics to learn about the controllability of a complex socioeconomic system involving motor vehicles in southern California. There are about 8 million vehicles operating in southern California, and planners expect to see about 10 million vehicles in the coming decades. The vehicles' tailpipe emissions contribute to the dangerously high levels of ozone (smog) in southern California. State and local policymakers are discussing policies that would promote the sale of alternative-fuel vehicles that may be powered by electricity, compressed natural gas, or methanol. The policymakers have two worthwhile goals in mind. First, they would like to reduce the tailpipe emissions that contribute to the smog in southern California, and second, to reduce the consumption of gasoline, because the United States is heavily dependent on foreign oil.

California policymakers are studying and implementing a variety of measures, including state mandates, state and federal incentives, and incentives from electric or gas utilities. One of the most interesting proposals is the feebate proposal. A fee would be imposed on the purchase price of a dirty vehicle, and a rebate would be used to lower the purchase price of a clean vehicle. The idea is to finance the rebates on clean vehicles with the fees imposed on dirty vehicles. Feebate proposals are under consideration at both the state and federal levels,[1] and they have been endorsed by some of the nation's most knowledgeable energy analysts. The most resounding endorsement comes from Amory Lovins, Director of Research at the Rocky Mountain Institute. He thinks feebates hold the ultimate promise of replacing prescriptive regulations, and he is particularly impressed by the DRIVE+ proposal from California (Lovins, 1991):

> The feebate concept embodied in DRIVE+ is the single most important energy policy
> initiative now being considered at any level of government anywhere in the United States.

This chapter begins with a description of a system dynamics model designed to simulate the effect of incentives for alternative-fuel vehicles in southern California. I

Reprinted from *Systems Dynamics Review*, Volume 11, No. 1, pp. 3–29, Copyright © 1995, John Wiley & Sons.

provide a brief description of the model sectors and the key feedback loops that tie the sectors together. Additional information is given in separate publications.[2] I explain the simulation results when the model is operated in a step-by-step manner from a special cockpit designed with the MicroWorld Creator.[3] Several explorations are presented to demonstrate one of the principal applications of the model: to learn if a feebate system can be controlled by the state official who would be charged with running the program in a financially prudent manner. I conclude with general findings on the controllability of feebates and plans for further research.

MODEL DESIGN

The model is called AVISS because it provides an Alternative Vehicles Incentives Simulation System. Figure 14.1 portrays the model as a combination of three sectors. The utility sector has been designed around a recent case study of the Southern California Edison (SCE) system. This sector represents the effect of extra electricity loads that would arise if electric vehicles appeared in SCE's service territory. The utility sector is the most detailed sector in the model, accounting for about half the equations. Its most important feature is the ability to simulate the complicated effect of vehicle loads on utility operations. This was achieved (without slowing the execution of the model) by calculating operating costs in a deterministic manner. The deterministic results were calibrated against the results from a more complicated model through a heuristic rotation in the load duration curve (Ford, 1994b).

The vehicle sector represents the decisions by the almost 1 million southern Californians who purchase a new vehicle each year. Their simulated decision making is based

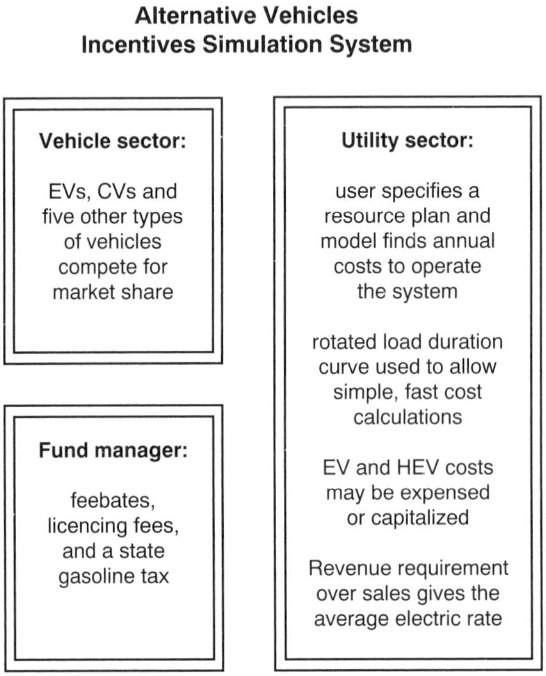

**Alternative Vehicles
Incentives Simulation System**

Vehicle sector:

EVs, CVs and
five other types
of vehicles
compete for
market share

Fund manager:

feebates,
licencing fees,
and a state
gasoline tax

Utility sector:

user specifies a
resource plan and
model finds annual
costs to operate
the system

rotated load duration
curve used to allow
simple, fast cost
calculations

EV and HEV costs
may be expensed
or capitalized

Revenue requirement
over sales gives the
average electric rate

Figure 14.1. Sectors of the Model

on the findings from a recent stated-preference survey (Bunch et al., 1993). Vehicle choice was limited to conventional vehicles (CVs) and electric vehicles (EVs) in an initial version of the model (Ford, 1994a). This article explains the more complicated situation in which southern Californians choose among:

CVs: conventional vehicles fueled by gasoline
EVs: electronic vehicles powered totally by a battery
HEVs: hybrid electric vehicles fueled by a battery and gasoline
CNGs: compressed natural gas vehicles
ALCs: alcohol vehicles (methanol)
FLEXs: flexible-fuel vehicles (gasoline and methanol)
CELLs: vehicles powered by a fuel cell

The vehicle sector uses a multinomial logit function to divide new car sales among the seven categories based on each car's price, fuel cost, emissions, range, and so on. The model keeps track of sales, retirements, and the population of vehicles in use. From the vehicles in operation, one can determine the demand for key fuels (gasoline, electricity, natural gas) and the total tailpipe emissions in the south coast air basin.

The third model sector is the Fund Manager. This is the smallest sector, but its operations are key to learning about the controllability of feebates. This sector simulates the operation of a state fund to encourage the sale of cleaner vehicles. The fund might be built up over time from fees on the sale of CVs or a tax on the sale of gasoline. The fund might then be used to provide rebates to encourage the sale of EVs. Figure 14.2 shows a STELLA[4] flow diagram that highlights selected cash flows

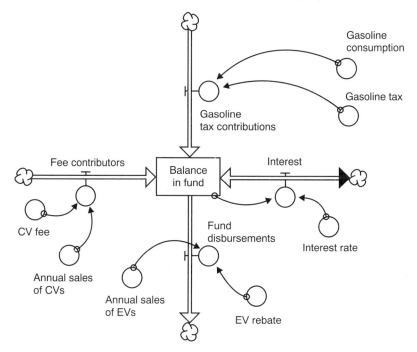

Figure 14.2. Selected Cash Flows in the Fund Manager Sector

into and out of the state fund. The cash flows depend on the size of the fee, the size of the rebate, and the annual sales of CVs and EVs. Since no one can expect state officials to predict sales of EVs in the future, it is unreasonable to expect the state to balance the cash flows into and out of the fund each year. Rather, one should expect that the state would build up a balance in the fund during the initial years of the program, which would then provide the cushion for operating the feebate system past the turn of the century. I assume that the long-run goal of a state feebate program is to promote the sale of cleaner vehicles and bring the balance in the state fund to zero by the end of the program.

The most important feature of AVISS is that all three sectors have been combined into an integrated system where information flows continuously across the sector boundaries. The integrated portrayal of system structure will seem like common practice to readers of the *System Dynamics Review*, but it is important to emphasize that many energy planners are not accustomed to this approach,[5] and there are no other models available to simulate the information feedback in this system.[6]

INFORMATION FEEDBACK

Figure 14.3 shows two feedback loops that link the utility sector and the vehicle sector. Both loops act through the price of electricity to EV owners. If the price were lowered, for example, the EV's fuel cost would be lowered; EVs would gain market share; and there would eventually be more EVs in operation. Working through the inner loop, more EVs in operation would lead to greater electricity sales and a reduction in the average electricity price needed to meet the company's revenue requirement. Working around the outer loop, greater EV loads would lead to higher costs of electricity generation, an increase in the allowed revenues, and an increase in the average price of electricity. Detailed assessment of the SCE system has revealed that the outer loop in Figure 14.3 is slightly stronger than the inner loop.[7] Thus, the overall effect of the

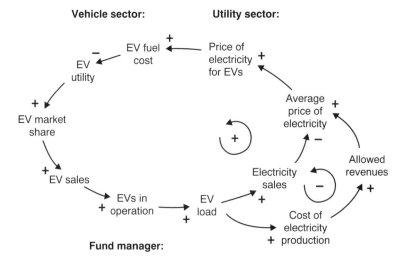

Figure 14.3. Examples of Information Feedback in the System

two loops in Figure 14.3 is to generate positive feedback—more EVs lead to greater electricity sales, lower electricity prices, lower fuel costs, higher market share, and still more EVs in the future. But one should not expect this positive feedback to play a dominating role in the system because consumers typically do not assign great importance to fuel costs when selecting which vehicle to purchase.

Figure 14.4, on the other hand, shows two feedback loops that operate through the vehicles' purchase price. This is a point of greater leverage because consumers have been observed to place great importance on the purchase price in selecting a new vehicle. Both loops in Figure 14.4 involve the size of the EV rebate and the underlying assumption that the fund manager must lower the rebate if the balance in the state fund declines below a prudent level. The inner loop is a negative feedback loop that acts to control the balance remaining in the fund. Should the balance decline below a prudent level, the manager could lower the rebate; fund disbursements would decline, and the balance would increase over time. The outer loop ties the vehicle sector and the fund manager sector together in an integrated system and also acts to generate negative feedback. To see that this is true, imagine that the utility chooses to make a purchase price incentive available to promote the sale of EVs. This incentive would lower the EV price, increase EV market share, increase EV sales, increase disbursements, and lower the balance in the fund. The fund manager, in turn, would be forced to lower the size of the EV rebate to protect the fund. The two loops in Figure 14.4 are much stronger than those in Figure 14.3, and they are likely to dominate the dynamic behavior of a feebate system.

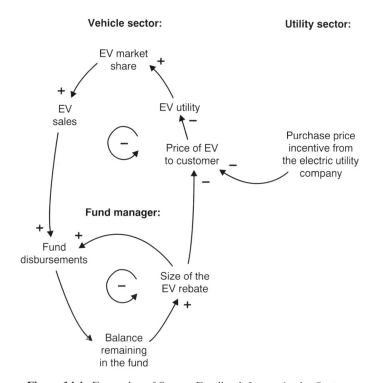

Figure 14.4. Examples of Strong Feedback Loops in the System

MODEL OPERATION

AVISS was originally developed and tested using the Professional DYNAMO Plus software. Then MicroWorld Creator (S**4) was used to allow model users more control over the inputs, to display results in familiar formats, and to take advantage of the analytical lens (Diehl, 1994). Further details on this combination of programs are available from the author (Ford, 1994b).

Figure 14.5 shows one of the MicroWorld cockpits developed for the model. In this view, the cockpit is ready to step through the first three years of a simulation. This first step would take the simulation from 1995 to 1998, the first year when EVs are expected to be sold in great numbers in California. The top panel is reserved for decision variables that may be entered by the model user. A list of Fee/Bate Decisions is partly visible in Figure 14.5. This display shows that the fees on all vehicles have been set to zero. If one were to scroll through the remainder of this decision list, one would see that the rebates for all vehicles had also been set to zero. The middle panel in Figure 14.5 provides a menu of ten reports that can be selected to learn about the simulated system. The vehicle choices report is commonly used to see the vehicles available for sale in the current year and their projected market shares. Figure 14.6 shows this report for 1998 in the initial exploration. It shows that the base price and the purchase price for each type of vehicle are identical, since there are no fees, rebates, or incentives in this exploration. Figure 14.6 also shows the fuel costs, ranges, and horsepowers of the competing vehicles. The final column shows the projected market shares in the personal vehicle market. One important result early in this first exploration is the low market share for conventional vehicles. CVs are projected to gain only 31 percent of the sales in southern California in 1998. Flexible-fuel vehicles are projected to sell almost as well (28 per cent of the market), and vehicles that run on compressed natural gas would be third-best (19 percent of the market). Alcohol vehicles fueled by methanol get 12 percent of the market, and HEVs and EVs get 6 percent and 4 percent of the market, respectively.[8]

The 4 percent EV market share is of special interest in California because state regulators have singled out EVs for promotion. An EV is powered by an electric motor that derives its energy from a battery. It has no tailpipe missions, and it has been designated a zero emission vehicle, or ZEV. California regulators now require vehicle manufacturers to meet production targets for ZEVs, and the EV is the only technology currently designated as satisfying the ZEV requirement. The requirement first takes effect in 1998, when vehicle manufacturers are required to produce 2 percent of total production as ZEVs. Since Figure 14.6 shows that EVs could capture 4 percent of the personal market in this year without incentives, one is encouraged to continue this first exploration without intervening in the system with fees or incentives.

Figure 14.7 summarizes EV market share over a 25-year period if the first exploration is continued to the year 2020 without special policies to promote any of the alternative-fuel vehicles. This figure is of particular interest because there is a vigorous debate in California about the ZEV targets issued by the California Air Resource Board (CARB). The CARB targets call for 2 percent ZEVs in 1998, 5 percent by 2001, and 10 percent by 2003. Figure 14.7 compares EV market share with the CARB targets. EV market share is a weighted combination of the market share in the

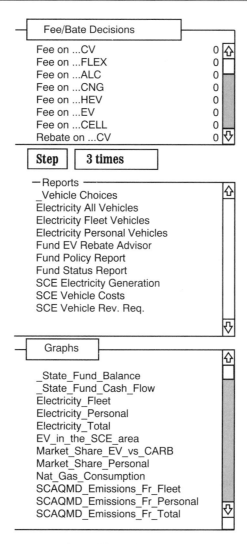

Figure 14.5. The Cockpit

personal vehicle market and the market for fleet vehicles. The personal market is simulated endogenously, but the fleet market uses exogenously specified market share because this market is dominated by state and federal mandates. Figure 14.7 shows that EVs would meet the near-term CARB goals but would fall short of the goals once the target is elevated to 10 percent. EV market share is projected to improve gradually over time because of improvements in battery technology that allow longer range and improved efficiency. According to Figure 14.7, EVs would eventually reach the 10 percent goal, but not until the year 2013, one decade later than the 2003 date set by California regulators.

Figures 14.8, 9, 10 and 11 provide additional information from this initial exploration. Figure 14.8 shows the vehicle choices report from the final year of the exploration. EVs are projected to capture 13 percent of the market, and HEVs are expected

In Year: 1998

	Base price	Purchase price	Fuel cost (cent/mile)	Range (mile)	Horse power	Market share (personal)
CVs	$17 300	$17 300	4.68	450	123	0.31
EVs	$22 000	$22 000	5.91	116	65	0.04
HEVs	$23 000	$23 000	6.84	190	78	0.06
CNGs	$19 300	$19 300	2.66	200	116	0.19
ALCs	$17 800	$17 800	5.28	252	136	0.12
FLEXs	$18 400	$18 400	4.78	445	127	0.28
CELLs	$24 000	$24 000	1.10	111	100	0.00

Note: All $ and cents are in constant 1990$.
      To convert to nominal $, multiply by 1.49

Figure 14.6. Vehicle Choices in 1998

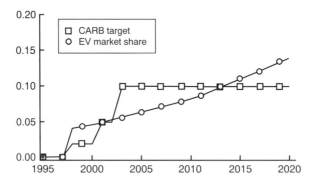

Figure 14.7. EV Market Share Compared to the CARB Requirements

to get 12 percent of the market. CVs get only 18 percent of the market, and CNGs are projected to capture 21 percent, the largest market share at the end of the simulation. Figure 14.9 shows the total vehicle population in southern California. This is a stacked

In Year: 2020

	Base price	Purchase price	Fuel cost (cent/mile)	Range (mile)	Horse power	Market share (personal)
CVs	$19 000	$19 000	5.62	450	110	0.18
EVs	$22 000	$22 000	3.12	200	77	0.13
HEVs	$23 000	$23 000	5.34	300	90	0.12
CNGs	$21 500	$21 500	2.22	225	104	0.21
ALCs	$19 000	$19 000	4.90	450	110	0.16
FLEXs	$19 000	$19 000	5.50	445	113	0.19
CELLs	$24 000	$24 000	3.30	350	100	0.00

Note: All $ and cents are in constant 1990$.
      To convert to nominal $, multiply by 4.48

Figure 14.8. Vehical Choices at the End of the Base Case Exploration

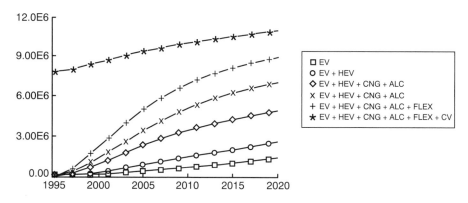

Figure 14.9. Stacked Graph of Vehicles Operating in Southern California

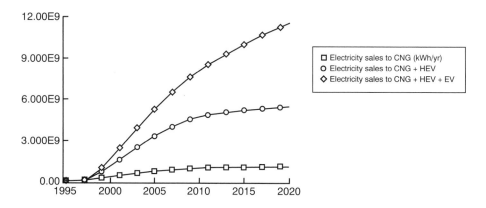

Figure 14.10. Stacked Graph of Electricity Sales to Vehicles Operating in Southern California

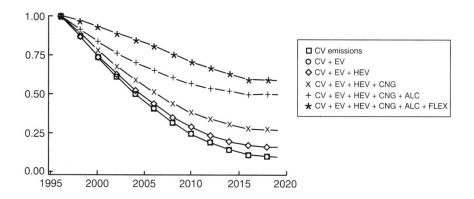

Figure 14.11. Stacked Graph of Tailpipe Emissions Measured Relative to 1995

graph with the first curve showing the number of EVs operating in the region. The second curve is the sum of EVs and HEVs, the third curve adds in the CNGs, and so on. The graph shows the exploration starting with about 8 million CVs in 1995. There would be over 10 million vehicles by the end of the exploration, and all six types of vehicles contribute important slices of the total.

Of special interest to the electric utilities is the electricity load that these vehicles would impose on their system. Figure 14.10 shows the total electricity sold to all vehicles operating in southern California. The bottom slice of this stacked chart is the electricity needed for CNGs. These vehicles are fueled by natural gas, which must be compressed by electric motors for on-board storage. The second curve in Figure 14.10 adds in the demand for electricity by HEVs, and the final curve, the electricity sold to EVs. The total demand exceeds 11 billion kwh/year by the end of the exploration.

Figure 14.11 completes the description of the first exploration by showing the variable that has triggered so much interest in alternative vehicles—tailpipe emissions. This graph is a stacked portrayal of tailpipe emissions with the vertical axis scaled to 1.0, which represents the total emissions of vehicles at the start of the simulation. If nothing were done to improve vehicle emission factors or to promote alternative vehicles, the emissions would continue to grow over the time period because of growth in the population of vehicles. But Figure 14.11 shows the emissions fraction declining over time, reaching 61 percent by the year 2020. CVs are shown to contribute a declining share of the total because of a decline in their numbers and improvements in their emissions performance. Figure 14.11 shows that ALCs (methanol) would contribute the biggest slice of the emissions. Since they have no tailpipe emissions, EVs contribute nothing to Figure 14.11. The decline in total emissions would improve air quality, but larger declines would be needed to satisfy ambient ozone standards. Further information on emissions is given in the Appendix.

This initial exploration suggests that EV sales will fall short of the CARB targets shown in Figure 14.7. Many planners agree with this conclusion, and there is a vigorous debate in California about the appropriate combination of incentives to increase the attractiveness of alternative vehicles in general and EVs in particular.

POLICIES TO PROMOTE ALTERNATIVE VEHICLE SALES

AVISS was originally developed to test the effect of utility incentives on the sale of EVs. The incentives may take the form of lower electricity prices or direct incentives to lower the purchase price of an EV or an HEV. The utility company must decide how it would recover the costs of an incentive program, and AVISS allows the model user to specify the fraction of EV or HEV program costs that is to be recovered immediately or over the life of the vehicle. (These decision variables may be changed from the cockpit, but they are not visible in Figure 14.5 because the SCE decisions list is hidden below the Fee/Bate Decisions list.)

The idea that an electric utility might offer incentives to promote the sale of EVs is not new. It was first proposed by Thomas Edison when he suggested that the electric utilities of his day get into the garage-building business to promote the sale of EVs. The California legislature has given utilities and their regulators the green light to design a package of incentives for both EVs and CNGs. AVISS has been used to simulate the effect of utility incentives when implemented alone or in combination with a state feebate program. The general conclusion is that it would be quite difficult for an electric utility to contribute a major share of an EV purchase price incentive without imposing a penalty on the average ratepayer (Ford, 1994a).

AVISS also allows planners to experiment with changes in annual licensing fees and the state gasoline tax. Planners generally expect these variables to have minimal impact on consumers' vehicle choice because the costs to fuel and license a vehicle do not weigh heavily in consumers' decision making. But these options do provide a relatively stable source of funds that could be used to fund a rebate program. The stability arises from the fact that the fees and tax are imposed on the entire population of vehicles rather than just on new vehicles sold each year. These other funding sources might prove useful if planners learn that a feebate system is difficult to control.

ILLUSTRATIVE EXPLORATION OF A FEEBATE PROPOSAL

I now illustrate the use of the model by stepping through an exploration over a 20-year time period from 1995 to 2015. To keep the illustration simple, I limit the fees to CVs and the rebates to EVs. And to illustrate the use of the model in a learning mode, I try out a feebate program that a first-time user might devise.[9] The purpose of the exploration is to learn if the fund manager can promote the sale of EVs and keep the state from running a serious negative balance. I begin the exploration with two additional goals. First, in the interest of relatively constant signals to the consumer, I select fees and rebates and hold to them for five-year intervals. And second, I strive for a combined fee/rebate that is consistent with my estimate that the environmental benefit from displacing a CV with an EV is roughly $9,000 (Ford, 1992). A typical user will study multiple reports and graphs before committing to the feebates for the next five-year interval. I show some of this information in Figures 14.12–15 and provide the following step-by-step narration of the thinking of a first-time user.

1995–2000, $1,000 CV fee/$8,000 EV rebate (see Figure 14.12): EVs are not available until 1998, so the first three years of this period would see a growth in the state fund provided by the $1,000 fees imposed on the sale of CVs. Payments of $8,000 per EV sold would begin in 1998, and one would expect the combined incentives to elevate EV market share. By the year 2000, EVs are projected to capture 13 percent of the market, well above the 5 percent obtained in the previous exploration (Figure 14.7). Meanwhile, the balance in the state fund is $290 million, so there is still a cushion for the future. CV market share, however, has declined to 24 percent. With this market share, only about two CVs are sold for every EV. With this ratio, we would expect problems with the EV rebate set eight times higher than the CV fee. So it seems appropriate to raise the fee or lower the rebate for the next interval.

2000–2005, $2,000 CV fee/$7,000 EV rebate (see Figure 14.13): A new feebate combination is announced for the second five-year interval, and the model steps through a simulation to 2005. By the end of this interval, EV market share has climbed to 15 percent, well above the 6 percent obtained in the same year of the previous exploration (Figure 14.7). The feebate program is certainly meeting the prime goal of promoting EV sales. Unfortunately, rebate payments have driven the state fund deeply into the red (Figure 14.13 bottom). By the year 2005, the state faces a negative balance of $4 billion. The CV market share in this year is down to 17 percent, only slightly higher than the 15 percent share for

For the year 2000

Balance in state fund ($ million)	290
Cash flow ($ million/year)	
purchase price fees	299
licence fees	0
extra gasoline tax	0
interest earnings	23
disbursements for rebates	1329

Note: All $ are nominal

In Year: 2000

	Base price	Purchase price	Fuel cost (cent/mile)	Range (mile)	Horse power	Market share (personal)
CVs	$17 500	$18 500	4.66	450	121	0.24
EVs	$22 000	$14 000	5.48	120	65	0.13
HEVs	$23 000	$23 000	6.55	200	78	0.07
CNGs	$19 500	$19 500	2.59	200	115	0.19
ALCs	$18 000	$18 000	5.20	253	134	0.11
FLEXs	$18 500	$18 500	4.80	445	125	0.25
CELLs	$24 000	$24 000	1.10	111	100	0.00

Note: All $ and cents are in constant 1990$.
     To convert to nominal $, multiply by 1.65

Figure 14.12. First-timer's Exploration: (*top*) Fund Status Report in 2000, and (*bottom*) Vehicle Choices Report in 2000

EVs. Perhaps we can eliminate the cash flow problem and rebuild the state fund by switching to a £2,000/$2,000 feebate for the next five-year interval.

2005–2010, $2,000 CV fee/$2,000 EV rebate (see Figure 14.14): As one might expect, the lowering of the EV rebate leads to a decline in EV market share during this five-year interval. EVs capture only 10 percent of the market in 2010, a marked decline from the 15 percent at the start of the interval. One might think that this drop in EV market share is to be expected if the state is to rebuild the fund from the negative $4 billion in 2005. Unfortunately, the state fund is approximately $4 billion in the red in 2010 as well (Figure 14.14 middle). The bottom graph of Figure 14.14 shows the cash flows that create the problem. Specifically, annual disbursements for rebates grow quite large, peaking at over $1.5 billion just before 2005. The disbursements then drop below the revenues earned from the fees imposed on CV sales. But the difference between the two cash flows does not allow the state to rebuild the fund. Rather, the difference is only sufficient to pay the annual interest on the $4 billion of debt inherited from the previous time period. By the end of the interval, the state is still $4 billion in the red.

2010–2015, $2,000 CV fee/no EV rebate (see Figure 14.15): The final five years of the exploration show what would happen if we eliminated the EV rebate altogether in an attempt to rebuild the state fund. EVs are projected to capture 10 percent of the market by 2015, approximately the same as their market share in the same year of the previous exploration (Figure 14.7). But the main goal in this final interval is to rebuild the fund, and there would be some success in this direction. By the year 2015, the fund's negative balance would improve to $1.6 billion (Figure 14.15 bottom).

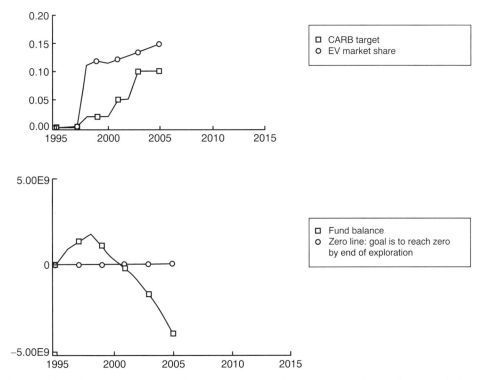

Figure 14.13. First-timer's Exploration: (*top*) EV Market Share to 2005, and (*bottom*) State Fund Balance to 2005

One way to summarize the simulated effects of this first-timer's feebate programme is to review what California would have accomplished by the end of the 20-year time period. The disappointing outcome is that the state would pass on a $1.6 billion debt to the future. But the program would lead to higher EV sales, especially during the years when high rebates were in effect. The feebate exploration concludes with about 1.3 million EVs in southern California versus 0.9 million projected in the initial exploration. So the program would increase the number of EVs by around 400,000. But the $1.6 billion debt burden amounts to roughly $4,000 for every extra EV to appear in southern California. In terms of tailpipe emissions, the feebate program would lead to a small but significant improvement. Total vehicle emissions in the year 2015 would be 60 percent of their current levels (compared to a 61 percent result without a feebate program). The Appendix explains that this small decline is a significant accomplishment for the south coast air basin.

But with a $1.6 billion debt at the end of the exploration, most readers would not judge the feebate program successful. I suspect they would feel that it is possible to improve upon this first-timer's effort. If, for example, the feebates were adjusted more frequently than every five years, the state might avoid slipping into debt shortly after the year 2000. If this were possible, the state could avoid the high interest expenses of the latter part of the exploration. The purpose of AVISS is to allow planners to experiment with alternative proposals to learn what might be accomplished. To illustrate, I present additional explorations in which the fund manager is willing to adjust feebates on a more frequent schedule.

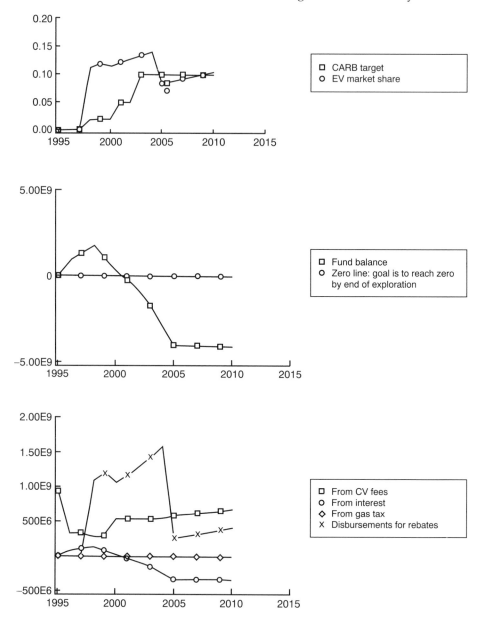

Figure 14.14. First-timer's Exploration: (*top*) EV Market Share to 2010, and (*middle*) State Fund Balance to 2010, and (*bottom*) State Fund Cash Flow to 2010

EXPLORING FEEBATES WITH HELP FROM AN ADVISER

An important reason for the financial problems in the first-timer's exploration was the commitment to a five-year interval over which consumers could rely on a constant set

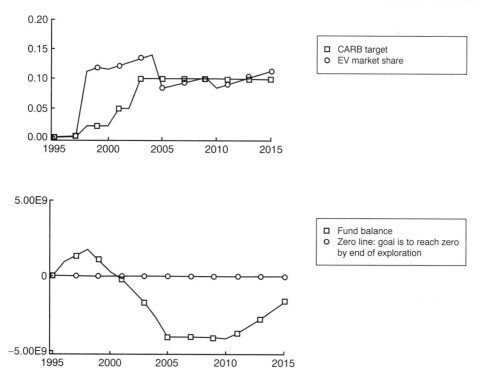

Figure 14.15. First-timer's Exploration: (*top*) EV Market Share, and (*bottom*) State Fund Balance

of fees and rebates. But another problem was the ad hoc nature of the adjustments in rebates as market share changed over time. In the next exploration, I illustrate how a feebate program could be operated without putting the state into the red. The exploration uses the same $1,000/$8,000 feebate during the 1995–2000 interval, but the feebates are adjusted on an annual basis after 2000. Moreover, the adjustments take advantage of the information presented in an adviser's report. An example of this report for the year 2000 is given in Figure 14.16.

The report begins with current market shares—EVs have 13 percent of the market, and CVs have 24 percent. The next entries are average market shares over the past two or three years—EVs at 10 percent, CVs at 31 percent. The adviser also reports current sales, past sales, and a maximum prudent rebate that may be offered for EVs if the CV fee is fixed at its current value. In this example, the fee is set at $1,000. CVs have captured 31 percent of the market over the past few years, and EVs have averaged 10 percent of the market. With about three CVs sold for every EV sold, a prudent approach would be to set the EV rebate at no more than three times the $1,000 fee. Figure 14.16 shows approximately the expected result—the maximum prudent rebate based solely on purchase price fees is $3,289. The adviser informs the user that interest earnings could be used to add $325 to the size of the rebate. The subtotal of $3,614 is a maximum prudent rebate if the state were willing to draw down the fund another $812 could be added to the rebate, making it $4,426.

```
┌─────────────────────────────────────────────────────────────────┐
│                                                                   │
│  For the year 2000                               EVs        CVs   │
│  Current market share, personal sales             13         24   │
│  Market share over past few years                 10         31   │
│  Sales this year in personal market           100 748    181 245  │
│  Sales over past few years                     71 396    234 846  │
│                                                                   │
│  Maximum prudent rebate based solely on                           │
│        purchase price fees                      $3289             │
│        state gas tax                               $0             │
│        annual licence fees                         $0             │
│        interest earnings                         $325             │
│  Sub total                                              $3614     │
│        draw down balance in fund                        $812     │
│  Grand total                                           $4426      │
│                                                                   │
│  Emission factors (0–1) for vehicles sold this year:              │
│        CV         0.81                                            │
│        EV         0.01                                            │
│        HEV        0.37                                            │
│        CNG        0.37                                            │
│        ALC        0.81                                            │
│        FLEX       0.81                                            │
│        CELL       0.01                                            │
│                                                                   │
└─────────────────────────────────────────────────────────────────┘
```

Note: The environmental costs from the tailpipe emissions have
      been estimated at about $9000 for the life of a vehicle with
      a 1.0 emissions factor

Figure 14.16. EV Rebate Adviser Report in 2000

The top graph in Figure 14.17 shows the fees and rebates over the course of the entire exploration. The CV fee is constant at $1,000, and the EV rebate remains constant at $8,000 until about the year 2000. The rebate is cut approximately in half in the next year and is gradually lowered throughout the rest of the exploration. The middle graph in Figure 14.17 shows that this strategy allows the balance in the state fund to gradually approach zero. This 'soft landing' is quite an accomplishment because the feebate program remains in effect throughout the 20-year exploration. The bottom graph of Figure 14.17 shows the cash flows that make this dynamic equilibrium possible. The exploration begins with a high income from CV fees which create the initial cushion in the state fund. But the cash from CV fees declines rapidly when CVs lose market share in the late 1990s. (This loss in market share is due, in part, to the feebate program.) Disbursements for EV rebates exceed $1 billion per year in about the year 2000, far exceeding the cash flow from fees. But disbursements for rebates decline over time as the EV rebate is gradually lowered based on the adviser's maximum prudent rebate report. The system reaches a dynamic equilibrium in about 2005—cash flowing in from CV fees is balanced by cash flowing out for EV rebates. This controlled situation leads to approximately the same tailpipe benefits as in the previous exploration.

It is important to note that the information given in the adviser's report (Figure 14.16) would be readily available to a state official charged with managing a feebate program. The market share and sales information is either current or averaged over the past few years. The adviser's report does not provide a 'crystal ball' estimate of

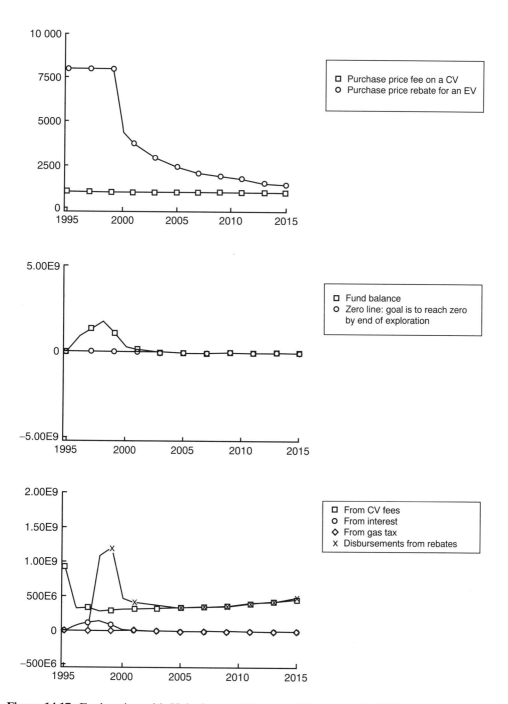

Figure 14.17. Exploration with Help from Adviser: (*top*) Feebates, (*middle*) State Fund Balance, and (*bottom*) State Fund Cash Flow

future EV sales. Rather, it draws from the recent past to provide relevant information that a state official might use in setting a maximum prudent rebate for EVs.

IMPORTANCE OF ANNUAL FEEBATE ADJUSTMENTS

I conclude the simulation analyses with a feebate program with biennial adjustments on the EV rebate. This example is quite similar to the previous example—the CV fee is fixed at $1,000, and the EV rebate is set at $8,000 as long as it does not exceed the maximum prudent rebate specified by the adviser. The simulation proceeds in two-year intervals with the idea that a state official might wish to stick with a rebate for at least two years (in the interest of constant signals to customers). The top graph in Figure 14.18 shows feebates that would result from following this strategy. The pattern is generally similar to that in Figure 14.17, but Figure 14.18 shows that the fund manager would be placed in an awkward situation during the second half of the exploration. Rebates would be raised in one interval, lowered in the next, then raised again. The bottom graph of Figure 14.18 shows the oscillations in cash flow over the

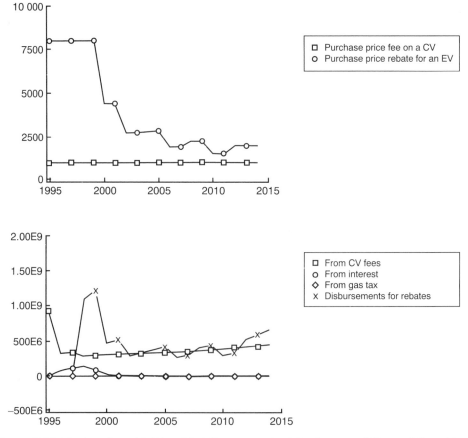

Figure 14.18. Exploration with Biennial Adjustments: (*top*) Feebates, and (*bottom*) State Fund Cash Flow

exploration. The oscillations grow progressively larger over time, indicating that the feebate system cannot be controlled in a stable manner. This exploration suggests that the fund manager be given the latitude to adjust feebates on an annual basis.

SUMMARY AND CONCLUDING DISCUSSION

The market for alternative vehicles will be an exciting business in the coming decades because of the many attractive alternatives to the conventional, gas burning vehicle. California is at the center of the excitement because of its ambitious policies to promote the sale of alternative vehicles (Woodruff, 1994). This article describes the structure and use of a model that has been developed to help California planners learn about the likely effects of incentives through interactive computer simulation. A previous article used the model to focus on the role of the electric utility company (Ford, 1994a); the present article uses the model to examine the controllability of a state feebate program.

The explorations shown here demonstrate that it is possible to control a feebate system using information that is readily available to the fund manager; no 'crystal ball' forecasts of EV sales are required. The explorations focus on a simple CV/EV feebate system in which the CV fee is held constant over time and the EV rebate is set to environmentally appropriate values or to the maximum prudent value based on the cash flows in the fund. The explorations show that the state could promote the sale of EVs while managing the fund in a prudent manner, and that the fund manager should be given the latitude to build a cushion in the early years of the program and to adjust rebates on an annual basis.

My main focus has been on the controllability of feebates, but policymakers will also wish to know if the feebates can result in significant reductions in tailpipe emissions which contribute to smog in southern California. The feebates discussed here are projected to reduce the total emissions in the south coast air basin by a small but significant amount. The Appendix explains the significance of the reduction and how further reductions could be achieved with alternative feebate designs.

Amory Lovins and other experts have praised feebates for their flexibility in a marketplace with rapid changes in technology. Compared to high gasoline taxes or fixed government mandates, feebates reward auto manufacturers for bringing their best offerings to market quickly and consumers for buying them. This article supports the interest in feebates by demonstrating that a feebate system could be controlled in a prudent manner.

Finally, the article demonstrates how system dynamics may be used to help planners experiment with feebate designs. The goal is not to predict future sales of EVs but to learn about the controllability of a feebate system. Arie de Geus, former coordinator of group planning at Shell, explains that planners frequently forget the distinction between learning and predicting in a business with insatiable demands for predictions (de Geus, 1994). The EV business is such a business, and it is important to remember that the figures in this article are not predictions. I do not think any of the modelers or planners in California know enough about vehicle attributes and customer attitudes to predict future EV sales. But we do know enough to predict that a feebate system could be designed to promote EV sales and the system could be controlled in a financially prudent manner.

FURTHER RESEARCH

For simplicity, the feebate strategy explained here concentrates on promoting the sale of EVs with funding from fees on CVs. But feebates are most likely to be implemented in a fuel-neutral form where no particular vehicle deserves special consideration unless it can deliver lower emissions. Our current research looks at fuel-neutral feebates in which the size of any fee or rebate is linked to the vehicles' emissions rather than to the type of fuel consumed. These feebates are more complicated to simulate, but they may turn out to be more stable than the simple CV/EV feebates described here. Improved stability should result when the program is funded from fees on several types of vehicles rather than just on CVs.

Other plans for future research include updating the vehicle sector of AVISS as the state agencies and utility companies complete new surveys on Californians' preferences, and a test of the transferability of AVISS to the situation faced by the San Diego Gas and Electric Company. Finally, I plan to repeat the simple CV/EV controllability analysis with variations in the coefficients in the consumer preference model. These variations will be used to test the controllability of feebates if consumer preferences change over time or if the preferences are different than indicated by the early survey results.

APPENDIX: ELECTRIC VEHICLES, EMISSIONS, AND FEEBATES

An EV produces no emissions at the tailpipe; it is a zero emissions vehicle. But a CV fueled by gasoline releases hydrocarbons (HC), nitrogen dioxides (NOx), carbon monoxide (CO), and other pollutants at the tailpipe. I have estimated that an EV sold in the mid-1990s would eliminate over 100 pounds of HC, over 100 pounds of NOx, and over 1,000 pounds of CO during its operating life. Assigning monetary values to the reduced emissions in the south coast air basins leads to a total value of around $9,000 per EV (Ford, 1992).

But tailpipe emissions are not the whole story. There are power plant emissions associated with an EV, just as there are refinery emissions associated with a CV. The relative importance of these upstream emissions depends heavily on the fuel used in power plants. The utility sector of AVISS shows that about 90 percent of the electric energy to recharge EVs in the SCE area will come from power stations burning natural gas, and about two thirds of these plants will employ new, cleaner-burning technologies. These plants still release some NOx, and the EVs total NOx benefit is reduced by around 10 percent. But the refineries that operate upstream from a CV are not as clean. When counting HC emissions from the CV, the gas stations, and the refinery, the total can easily be twice as high as the tailpipe emissions.

Because of the upstream effects, one should interpret the $9,000 estimate as a lower bound of the monetary value of displacing a CV with an EV. The $9,000 estimate is highly sensitive to the method used to assign monetary value to avoided emissions. Nevertheless, it is worth keeping this value in mind when thinking about the worth of an individual EV because the apparent value of EVs changes dramatically when we turn to a basinwide perspective.

The most difficult air pollution problem in the south coast air basin is ozone (or smog). Ozone is formed by a photochemical reaction involving HC and NOx emissions. The South Coast Air Quality Management District estimates that over 2,000 tons per day of HC and NOx emissions would be released in 1994, and their urban air shed model projected that these emissions would lead to peak ozone concentrations of two to three times the ambient standards. To judge the basinwide benefit of EVs, I considered the extreme example of displacing 1 million CVs by EVs in 1994. Ignoring upstream effects, I estimated that the EVs would reduce HC and NOx emissions by only 1 percent, and the peak ozone concentration would decline by only 0.7 percent (Ford, 1992). This small improvement is not a sign that the EV is unimportant. (After all, the EV is worth at least $9,000.) Rather, the small improvement is a sign of the enormous challenge in bringing southern California's ozone concentrations down to safe levels.

Judging the Significance of Emissions Reductions

Figure 14.11 projects that total HC and NOx emissions from the entire population of vehicles operating in the south coast will decline over time in an exploration without incentives to promote the sale of EVs. This decline is achieved in the face of a growing population of vehicles because of the sale of alternative-fuel vehicles and improvements in the emissions factors for conventional vehicles fueled by gasoline. As a benchmark, I note that Figure 14.11 shows total emissions in 2015 at 61 percent of their current value.

Table 14.1 records total emissions in 2015 from additional simulations selected to help one judge the significance of EVs and feebates. The second entry records the emissions when EVs are simply too expensive to compete in the personal market. The model projects that their previous share would be distributed rather evenly between CVs, HEVs, CNGs, ALCs, and FLEX vehicles, and that total emissions in 2015 would be at 65 percent of current emissions. The next entry shows the 60 percent result found in the Figure 14.15 exploration of a first-timer's feebate program that concluded with a negative balance of $1.6 billion in the state fund. But the fourth entry notes that the same 60 percent result could be achieved when the rebates are adjusted on an annual basis with the help of the adviser (Figure 14.16).

Thus, the emissions impact of the feebate example shown in Figures 14.16 and 17 is to reduce total tailpipe emissions in 2015 from 61 percent to 60 percent. This small reduction arises from the fact that an EV is not simply displacing a CV with current emissions factors as well as several alternative-fuel vehicles. A second reason for the

Table 14.1. Tailpipe emissions from all vehicles in the south coast in 2015 relative to emissions in 1995

61%	Base case example (Figure 14.11); no incentives to promote EV sales
65%	EVs removed from the personal vehicle market but still appear in fleets
60%	First-timer's feebate exploration (Figure 14.15) with $1.6 billion negative balance in 2015
60%	Feebate set to $1,000/$8,000 with annual adjustments with the adviser (Figure 14.17)
58%	Simple $5,000 rebate but no fees; state fund over $30 billion in the red by 2015
59%	Feebate set to $2,000/$7,000 with annual adjustments with the adviser
58%	Feebate set to $3,000/$6,000 with annual adjustments with the adviser

small reduction is the long delay in the turnover of the stock of vehicles in operation.

The fifth entry in Table 14.1 provides a simple example to place the 61 percent to 60 percent reduction in perspective. This example assumes that EVs receive a permanent $5,000 rebate and that the state does not bother with fees or gasoline taxes to finance the rebates. The $5,000 incentive is illustrative of a combination of state, federal, and utility incentives under discussion in California. For simplicity, the $5,000 incentive was simulated as a rebate, and the balance in the state fund was used to keep track of the costs over the 20-year period. Table 14.1 notes that maintaining the $5,000 incentive throughout the exploration would lower emissions to 58 percent by 2015 and leave the state fund with a negative balance exceeding $30 billion. Thus, one may conclude that the feebate proposal shown in Figures 14.16 and 17 can deliver one third of the emissions reduction available from an extremely costly, $5,000 permanent incentive.

The final two entries in Table 14.1 show that it is possible to capture the remaining two thirds of the emissions reduction if one is willing to increase the size of the CV fee. If the fee is raised to $2,000, for example, the initial EV rebate could be lowered to $7,000. The larger CV fee would generate higher cash flow into the state fund, and the $7,000 rebate could be maintained over a longer interval. Table 14.1 notes that emissions would be reduced to 59 percent of their current value. The final entry in the table shows that a $3,000/$6,000 feebate combination could go one step further, achieving the 58 percent value found in the exploration with the permanent $5,000 rebate.

CONCLUSION

Alternative-fuel vehicles, cleaner conventional vehicles, electric vehicles, and feebates can all contribute to reduced emissions of the pollutants that lead to smog in the south coast air basin. This appendix shows that a feebate program targeting EVs can make a small but significant contribution. Total emissions can be reduced from a 61 percent benchmark to 58 percent, 59 percent, or 60 percent depending on the feebate design. But much more needs to be done. South coast air shed modeling indicates that basin-wide emissions must eventually decline to around 25 percent of current values if peak ozone is to meet federal and state standards (Ford, 1992). One way to gain further improvements from feebates is to expand the fees and rebates to apply to all vehicles rather than just to CVs and EVs. The impact of more comprehensive feebate designs is the subject of our current research.

NOTES

1. The State of Maryland enacted (but never implemented) a feebate program with fees for vehicles with low fuel efficiency and rebates for vehicles with high fuel efficiency. A similar program, called DRIVE+, passed the California legislature in 1990 but was vetoed by the governor. A comprehensive discussion of feebates is given by DeCicco et al. (1992).
2. This research has been supported by the California Institute for Energy Efficiency (CIEE). The project began with a detailed assessment of the impact on an electric utility company of large-scale use of electric vehicles in southern California. The initial research results are documented in a lengthy report available from the CIEE (Ford, 1992). The project then turned to the question of incentives and how one might simulate their impact, especially on

the electric utility company. The results are published in *Energy Policy* (Ford, 1994a). And finally, a longer version of this article is available from the author (Ford, 1994b). The views given in all these documents are my own. They do not represent a position taken by the CIEE or by the gas and electric utilities that support the CIEE.

3. The main software used in preparing this article was MicroWorld Creator (S**4), described by Diehl (1994). Further information on S**4 and other software used in this project is given in the working paper available from the author (Ford 1994b).

4. STELLA software was used to draw this diagram, but the model equations were written in Professional DYNAMO Plus (PD+). STELLA is available from High Performance Systems, Inc., 45 Lyme Rd., Hanover, NH 03755, U.S.A., and PD+ from Pugh-Roberts Associates, Inc., 41 Linskey Way, Cambridge, MA 02142, U.S.A.

5. A typical energy planner would work with a series of separate models that would provide detailed treatment of each sector but fail to close the feedback loops linking the sectors. This approach is contrasted with the system dynamics approach by Ford and Bull (1989).

6. System dynamics has been used to examine automobile manufacturers' strategies for investing in greater fuel efficiency (Cooper et al., 1976; Ford, 1982), but these studies are not relevant to the California situation. The most relevant system dynamics effort is currently under way at the AES Corporation, where the vehicle sector of the IDEAS model has been expanded to treat policies to promote alternative vehicles. Information on IDEAS is available from AES (1993), and information on FOSSIL2, the predecessor to IDEAS, has been published by Naill (1992).

7. Readers unfamiliar with the electric utility industry in the United States should remember that the price of electricity is subject to the approval of state commissions, which are simulated to adjust the average electricity price so that the price multiplied by the electricity sales gives the required revenue. When this calculation is conducted with millions of EVs added to the SCE system, one finds that it would be possible for the utility to lower the average electricity price. For example, the appearance of two million EVs in the SCE area would allow the utility to lower the average price by around 3 percent (Ford, 1994a).

8. For simplicity, fuel cell vehicles are eliminated from the simulations shown here. The initial projections of market share for the other six vehicle types should be interpreted as simply an opening example of simulations to learn about the controllability of a feebate system.

9. Utility planners have experimented with the MicroWorld version of AVISS but only in a workshop to get acquainted with the approach. Consequently, the first-timer's strategy is my characterization of an initial exploration.

REFERENCES

AES, 1993. *An Overview of the Ideas Model: A Dynamic Long-Term Policy Simulation Model of the U.S. Energy Supply and Demand.* AES Corporation, 1001 North 19th St., Arlington, VA 22209, U.S.A.

Bunch, D., M Bradley, T. Golob, and R. Kitamura. 1993. A Demand for Clean-Fuel Vehicles in California: A Discrete-Choice State-Preference Pilot Project. *Transportation Research* 27A: 237–253.

Cooper, K., A. L. Pugh III, and J. Lyneis. 1976. A Model of the Automobile Industry Implementation of More Fuel-Efficient Technologies. In *Proceedings of the Summer Computer Simulation Conference.* Simulation Councils, Inc., P.O.B. 2228, La Jolla, CA 92037, U.S.A.

Coyle, G. 1977. *Management System Dynamics.* London: Wiley.

DeCicco, J., H. Geller, and J. Morrill. 1992. *Feebates for Fuel Economy.* Draft report. American Council for an Energy-Efficient Economy, 1001 Connecticut Ave., NW, Washington, DC 20036, U.S.A.

de Geus, A. 1994. Modeling to Predict or to Learn? Foreword. In *Modeling for Learning Organizations*, ed. J. Morecroft and J. Sterman. Portland, Ore.: Productivity Press.

Diehl, E. 1994. Managerial Microworld as Learning Support Tools. In *Modeling for Learning Organizations*, ed. J. Morecroft and J. Sterman. Portland Ore.: Productivity Press.

Ford, A. 1982. Automobile Fuel Efficiency and Government Policy after 1985. *Energy* 7 (9).

Ford, A. 1992. *The Impact of Electric Vehicles on the Southern California Edison System.* Report. California Institute for Energy Efficiency, Lawrence Berkeley Laboratory, 1 Cyclotron Rd., Berkeley, CA 94720, U.S.A.

Ford, A. 1994a. Electric Vehicles and the Electric Utility Company. *Energy Policy* (July).

Ford, A. 1994b. Simulating the Controllability of Feebates. Working paper. Available from the author.

Ford, A., and M. Bull, 1989. Using System Dynamics for Conservation Policy Analysis in the Pacific Northwest. *System Dynamics Review* 5 (1): 1–16.

Lovins, A. 1991. *Supercars: The Coming Light Vehicle Revolution.* Report. Rocky Mountain Institute, 1739 Snowmass Creek Rd., Snowmass, CO 81654-9199, U.S.A.

Naill, R. 1992. A System Dynamics Model for National Energy Policy Planning. *System Dynamics Review* 8 (1): 1–20.

Woodruff, D. 1994. Electric Cars. *Business Week*, May 30.

Part VI

Evaluation and Selection

Chapter 15

The Financial Evaluation of Strategic Investments

Robert G. Dyson
University of Warwick

Robert H. Berry
University of Nottingham

This chapter introduces and discusses a number of financial appraisal methods in the context of the evaluation of strategic investments. Traditional discounting methods which are designed to take account of the time value of money are described, and their link to shareholder value approaches explored. Various approaches to handling the uncertainty of future cash flows are presented, including risk analysis, the capital asset pricing model, and real option pricing. The sources of interdependencies between capital projects and methods of resolving the resultant complications are discussed. Finally the role of financial evaluation in the strategy evaluation process is considered.

INTRODUCTION

It is argued in Chapter 1 that the evaluation of strategic initiatives is concerned with identifying the extent to which the proposed strategy moves the organisation in the direction of its objectives. Those objectives invariably include financial criteria which in the public sector might involve balancing the investment against the contribution to the future financial health of the organisation. In the private sector this balance may be the primary objective and, with appropriate measures, can be characterised as the increase in shareholder value due to the initiative. This chapter is concerned with evaluating that financial balance as a part of the overall evaluation of the strategic initiative. (It is assumed throughout that a strategic initiative will have an associated capital investment, and it will often be referred to as a 'project'. The financial appraisal process will sometimes be referred to as 'capital investment appraisal'.)

The methods and measures involved in current best practice are discussed as are the ideas, methods and measures which seem likely to underpin best practice in the next decade. Best practice here refers to the advice of specialists in many management disciplines. The gap between best practice and actual practice as discovered by the various studies of business behaviour will also be commented on and some explanations for the gap offered. These explanations have implications for attempts to put best practice into action.

Financial appraisal is often presented as an adequate basis for deciding whether or not to undertake a capital investment, and for some levels and classes of expenditure this may be so. However for others, and in particular for major strategic decisions involving capital investments, financial appraisal by no means forms a complete framework for analysis. It clearly fails to deal with non-financial issues such as the extent to which a project contributes to the broader objectives of the organisation. Even some economic factors such as improvements in the firm's competitive position may be difficult to quantify in strictly financial terms, so that measures such as market share and size of product range become relevant to the decision making process.[1] As a consequence of all this, the fact that an investment project is financially acceptable does not necessarily mean that the project should be undertaken.

It is of course possible to argue that the techniques of cost benefit analysis can be brought to bear on the social aspects of an investment, and that conceptually at least, factors such as market share can be translated into cash flow figures. However there are consequences of putting these responses into action which should not be overlooked: the cost–benefit approach involves implicit value judgements which might be better kept explicit, and translation of non-financial measures into cash flows may involve a loss in quality of estimate.[2]

There is another sense in which financial appraisal is not the whole of the story. Before any appraisal, project ideas must have been generated and forecasts produced. After any appraisal a decision must be made, and if that decision is to undertake the project, the project must be implemented, and a series of post completion audits carried out. In this sense appraisal is a part of a larger capital budgeting exercise, and although the non-appraisal aspects of capital budgeting are not dealt with in this paper, this does not imply that they are unimportant.

AN OVERVIEW OF STRATEGIC INVESTMENT APPRAISAL

A capital investment typically involves a current cash outflow which may be relatively certain in amount and a series of rather less certain cash inflows spread over several years. This is not to say that uncertain future cash outflows cannot occur. Indeed the need to be aware of potential problems with standard appraisal approaches when faced with uncertain future outflows will be emphasised later. However, many real life investments (and most text book examples) have an initial outflow of cash followed by a series of anticipated inflows. The end product of a financial appraisal is a meaningful summary measure of this stream of financial costs and benefits. There are two obvious problems involved in developing a summary measure. The first arises from the fact that the cash flows occur at different points in time. Cash available in the current period can often be lent at a positive real rate of interest. Therefore a cash amount available now is worth more than a similar amount available at some point in the future. A summary measure of a series of cash flows must cope with this time dimension, either by discounting, or some other procedure. This chapter discusses summary measures based on discounting, truncation of the cash flow stream, and the simple response of ignoring the problem.

A second problem involved in developing a summary measure stems from the uncertainty inherent in future cash flows and indeed in the future development of the strategic initiative. Approaches to this problem include risk analysis where the uncertainty is described by probability density functions, the use of risk adjusted discount rates as in the capital asset pricing model, and real option pricing.

There are two less obvious problems involved in financial appraisal: what are financial benefits and what problems are involved in measuring them? So far in this paper, financial costs and benefits have been identified with cash flow rather than profit concepts based on accounting, and this will continue to be the case. (Only during the discussion of the accounting rate of return summary measure is there any consideration of accounting profit.) Two simple arguments can be marshalled in support of cash flow. Firstly cash and not accounting profit pays bills, interest and dividends. Secondly accounting profit is designed to provide a measure of performance over an arbitrary slice of the life of a firm or project. In investment appraisal the concern is with the entire economic life of the project. There is no need to worry about apportioning costs to arbitrary accounting periods. The differences between profit and cash flow for investment appraisal purposes will be discussed later in the chapter. It is certainly the case that managers often express concern about the consequences of accepting a project for the appearance of profit and loss accounts. The potential impact on share price seems to be the focus of their concern. However evidence[3] supports the view that it is cash flow to which stock markets respond, not accounting profits.

The secondary subsidiary problem relates to the difficulty of identifying a project's cash flows. Because of interdependencies that can arise between the project being evaluated, other proposed projects and the existing activities of the organisation, it can be difficult to identify the cash flow consequences attributable to a specific project. A variety of sources of interdependencies and their resolution will be discussed in the chapter.

CASH FLOW DATA

It has been argued that it is cash flow rather than accounting profit which is relevant to the financial appraisal process. A probability distribution of cash flow in each period, which allows calculation of expected cash flow per period, is a prerequisite of all performance measures to be discussed later. Except in the simplest cases these expected cash flows are probably best produced by a financial simulation model. Table 15.1 shows the pattern of output which might be generated by such a model. It illustrates the way in which cash flow figures can be derived from accounting numbers.

Row F in the table shows that the investment project under consideration involves a capital spend now of £5,000. Row A shows the consequences of this investment in terms of Net Profit before Tax. Profits are assumed to occur one year after the capital spend, and each year thereafter for a further four years. The problem is that the components which go to make up the profit of a period are not all cash flows in the period in question. For example, turnover includes sales on credit as well as sales for

Table 15.1. Computation of Cash Flows

Period	0	1	2	3	4	5	6
Turnover		16,500	30,300	46,600	51,200	56,400	
Cost of Goods Sold		−12,200	−21,900	−33,000	−35,700	−38,600	
Expenses		−2,000	−2,100	−2,200	−2,300	−2,400	
Net Profit before Tax A		2,300	6,300	11,400	13,200	15,400	
Depreciation B		1,000	1,000	1,000	1,000	1,000	
Change in Stock C	−4,500	−3,000	−2,000			6,000	3,500
Change in Debtors D		−1,400	−1,100	−1,300	−400	2,200	2,000
Change in Creditors E	500	300	300			−600	−500
Investment F	−5,000						
Cash Flow before Tax G	−9,000	−800	4,500	11,100	13,800	24,000	5,000
Tax at 33%			−1,089	−2,409	−4,092	−4,686	−5,412
Allowances at 25%		−1,250	−938	−703	−527	−1,582	
Tax benefit of Alls at 33%			413	309	232	174	522
Tax Cash Flow H			676	−2,100	−3,860	−4,512	−4,890
Cash Flow after Tax I	−9,000	−800	3,823	9,000	9,940	19,488	110

cash. Cost of Goods Sold may include the cost of raw materials not purchased in the period in question but already held as stock. Somewhere in Cost of Goods Sold, or Expenses an accountant will have included a charge for the deterioration of machinery, i.e. depreciation. Depreciation in a given year does not represent a flow of cash from the company. The cash outflow occurred when the machine in question was bought.

The accounting figures need to be adjusted to get to cash flow. Firstly, depreciation must be added back to accounting profit. This is shown in row B. Secondly, the accounting figures must be adjusted for changes in working capital. The fact that an investment in raw materials, work in progress and finished goods is necessary at the start of a project, but is recovered at the end of the project is shown in line C. The credit sales mentioned earlier lead to a build up of money owed to the company—debtors. Allowing the level of debtors to build up is another use of cash consequent on the investment decision. When the debtors pay up cash is released into the company. This use of cash followed by release of cash is shown in row D. Row E shows the mirror image of debtors–creditors. At the start of the project some purchases of raw materials will have been credit purchases; the project is generating purchasing power, and any evaluation should reflect this characteristic. At the end of the project this borrowing by the company must be repaid. As has been said this pattern of cash flow followed by cash outflow is shown in line E. The end result of this adjustments is shown in row G, Cash Flow before Tax.

Tax is a fact of life, and tax cash flows must be deducted before the benefits of the project to the company can be assessed. The details of tax systems vary between national economies. In this example it is assumed that tax is levied at 33%. Further, depreciation is not an allowable deduction from profit for tax purposes. Instead a system of capital allowances is available; 25% of the cost of the investment, calculated on a reducing balance basis, can be deducted from the accounting profit before depreciation to generate taxable profit. This pattern of allowances is a feature of the UK tax system. Row H shows the tax cash outflow. The calculation has two components, the tax charge on the profit figures before the deduction of allowances, and the reduction in the tax charge due to the allowance system.

Two other tax system features are involved in this example. Firstly, it has been assumed that tax is paid with a lag. In the UK tax is paid nine months after the end of a company's accounting year. To generate the tax cash flow pattern in the example it has been assumed that the capital spend occurs three months before the company's accounting year end. Secondly, it has been assumed that at the end of the project all remaining allowances can be taken up. In the UK a project with a life less than five years can be treated in this way. For longer life projects, allowances continue to become available to reduce tax according to the 25% reducing balance pattern. A variety of OECD tax systems are discussed in Berry and Dyson.[4]

The tax end result of these various adjustments to accounting profit is row I, Cash Flow after Tax.

Calculating the tax flow consequences of a project requires more than the adjustment of profit figures. Care must be taken to ensure that incremental cash flow has been calculated. This is the difference between the company's cash flow if the project is undertaken, and the cash flow if it is not. The comparator, the company's cash flow if the project is not undertaken, may not be a continuation of pre-project cash flows. Not undertaking a project may imply a decline in cash flows. Project interactions, discussed later, can also complicate the calculation of incremental cash flow.

Care must also be taken to ensure that inflation has been treated consistently across all cash flow elements. While it is possible to carry out investment appraisals, correctly in constant price terms, it is more usual to estimate cash flows in current price terms.

Finally, care must be taken to include in the cash flow calculation the opportunity cost of already owned assets. Suppose that the project will make use of vacant space in an already owned warehouse. There is not obvious cash flow consequence. However, the vacant space has a value based on the cash flow that could have been earned if it had been put to another use, for example rented out. There is thus another cash cost that must be taken into account in the project's net cash flow, the cash flow foregone by not renting out the vacant space.

SUMMARY MEASURES AND DECISION RULES

A number of measures are available for summarising into a single value the stream of cash flows associated with a capital investment. These include the payback period, the accounting rate of return, the net present value and the internal rate of return.

In what follows C_0 will represent the cash flow at the beginning of the life of the capital project (usually a negative initial investment), and C_i the cash flow in each following year i. It is assumed that C_i occurs at the end of year i. The cash stream representing the project is thus:

$$C_0, C_1 \ldots, C_i, \ldots, C_n,$$

where n is the life of the project in years. The cash flows from C_1 to C_n are usually assumed to be positive at the planning stage (as distinct from the outcome) but this may not be generally true and C_n in particular may be negative if the end of the project involves a tax payment or some kind of cleaning up operation (e.g. levelling and restoring the site after mining).

Payback Period

The simplest summary measure in common use is the payback period. This is the number of years before the project's initial investment is paid back by the project's later cash flows. For the cash stream shown below, the payback period is three years. This is calculated by cumulating project cash flows, after the initial investment, until the cumulative exceeds the initial investment.

Year	0	1	2	3	4	5	6	7
Cash Flow	(10,000)	985	3,739	8,840	9,682	17,096	7,485	(622)
Cumulative Cash Flow		985	4,724	13,564				

Note ( ) indicates a cash outflow.

A decision rule would involve comparing the calculated payback period with some predetermined target period. A calculated figure less than target indicates that the project should be accepted.

There are a number of obvious inadequacies with the payback period. Firstly it does not use all the available information, ignoring as it does the cash flows outside the payback period. Secondly it ignores the issue of time value of money for cash flows within the payback period. (The discounted payback rule is a variant designed to remedy this shortcoming.) Finally there is no indication of how to set the target payback period. Despite these factors, the payback period has its defenders, and surveys indicate that it is in common use in combination with other summary measures. This may be because it is a crude measure of liquidity, and hence useful to firms unwilling to use outside sources of finance. It may also be a reflection of management's perception of the quality of available cash flow data or of the costs of data collection. Finally there is always the possibility that it is a simple approach to dealing with uncertainty by managers who see cash flows arising further in the future as having greater risk.

Accounting Rates of Return (ARR)

This summary measure, alone among those considered in this paper, is based on accounting profit rather than cash flow. There are innumerable variants of the measure, differing only in the way in which the accounting numbers involved are defined. Essentially the measure is a ratio. The numerator is the average profits of the project after depreciation and taxes, while the denominator is the average book value of the investment. The profit figures, and book value of investment corresponding to the cash flow figures used earlier in this section, might be as follows. (Remember there are many possible depreciation patterns.)

Year	0	1	2	3	4	5	6	7
Profit		2,825	5,539	9,140	9,082	10,596	485	(2,112)
Asset	6,000	5,000	4,000	3,000	2,000	1,000	0	0

The project ceases operation after six years (although there are tax consequences in year 7). Average profit over the six years is £6,278; average asset value is £3,000. Therefore accounting rate of return is 209%! A decision rule would be based on some predetermined target value. Calculated ARR greater than target value would indicate that the project should be accepted.

Once again this summary measure suffers from a number of problems, arbitrary target value and arbitrary definition of accounting numbers being the major ones. Finance texts, and more and more firms are tending to ignore this measure.[5,6]

Net Present Value

The fact that £1 received next year is worth less than £1 received now has already been pointed out. If money can be lent at 10%, £1 today will be worth £1.10 next year, assuming no inflation. The link between value today (present value) and value next year (future value) is:

$$\text{PRESENT VALUE } (1 + r) = \text{FUTURE VALUE}$$

where r is the interest rate, an opportunity cost of holding cash. The link between value today and value in N years time is equally simple:

$$\text{PRESENT VALUE } (1 + r)^N = \text{FUTURE VALUE}$$

Discounting makes use of this simple relationship to express future cash flows as present values.

$$\text{PRESENT VALUE} = \text{FUTURE VALUE}/(1 + r)^N$$

This approach allows cash flows arising at different times to be compared.

Net Present Value (NPV) is a cash flow based summary measure produced by a discounting exercise. All the cash flows generated during the project's economic life are discounted back to their present values. These present values are then aggregated. The initial investment is included in the aggregation and is of course already in present value terms. The general formula for the Net Present Value is:

$$\text{NPV} = C_0 + C_1/(1 + r) + C_2/(1 + r)^2 + \ldots + C_n/(1 + r)^n$$

If the interest rate is 10% then the NPV of the cash flow data used earlier in this chapter is:

$$\text{NPV} = -1,000 + 985/1.1 + 3,739/(1.1)^2 + 8,840/(1.1)^3 + \ldots -622/(1.1)^7 = 21,761$$

A decision rule for NPV would be to accept any project with a positive NPV and reject all others. A positive NPV means that the project is yielding higher returns than can be obtained by simply lending at the rate of return r. This interpretation suggests that r is a minimum acceptable rate of return.

The rate of return r is usually known as the discount rate in NPV calculations and its determination is not straightforward. In fact r is usually taken to have three components: a real rate of interest, a component equal to the expected level of inflation and a component to allow for the riskiness of the project. A typical value for r in percentage terms might thus be made up as follows:

$r\%$ = real rate of interest + inflation rate + risk premium
= 1+5+3
= 9% say

The problems posed by inflation and risk in capital investment appraisal, particularly the problem posed by risk, will be considered in later sections. NPV is much favoured by the finance textbooks. It is cash flow based, takes all cash flows into account, and takes into account the time value of money. Furthermore, with an appropriate discount rate, it has an interpretation in terms of impact on share price and can therefore be construed as reflecting shareholder value. According to surveys the use of this and other discounting methods is increasing (Sangster, 1993).

Net Terminal Value

A similar measure to NPV which uses the same discount rate but assesses the value of the project at its termination is the net terminal value (NTV). Using the previous notation we have:

$$NTV = C_0 (1 + r)^n + C_1(1 + r)^{n-1} + \ldots + C_i(1 + r)^{n-i} + \ldots + C_n$$

and hence

$NTV = NPV (1 + r)^n.$

NTV is thus the surplus available at the end of the project after repaying the investment and assuming that money borrowed or surpluses invested during the life of the project both attract an interest rate of r. A decision rule to accept any project with a positive NTV would lead to the same decision as the NPV decision rule.

Internal Rate of Return

The internal rate of return (IRR) is a discounted cash flow method like NPV and is defined as the rate of return that yields a zero NPV. Hence it is the value of r such that:

$$C_0 + C_1/(1 + r) + \ldots + C_i/(1 + r)^i + \ldots + C_n/(1 + r)^n = 0$$

The above equation can be solved by an iterative procedure. The attraction of IRR is that it yields a rate of return measure which can be interpreted as the highest rate of interest at which the company could afford to finance the project. Hence a decision for IRR would involve a target rate of interest to be exceeded by the IRR if the project is to be accepted.

IRR and NPV will generally yield similar results in determining the acceptability of a project, assuming NPV is a smoothly declining function of the discount rate. However, the methods can rank projects differently so that if not all acceptable projects can be undertaken, for example because they are mutually exclusive, the methods can yield a different decision. There is also the problem that a project can have multiple rates of return. For the cash stream evaluated in the NPV section, the corresponding IRR is 48.8%.

Textbook wisdom compares IRR unfavourably with NPV because it can fail to give rankings consistent with NPV. However it remains popular with practitioners. This may be because it reflects corporate objectives such as growth,[7] or because it is a familiar measure which managers feel they understand, or simply because it is a rate of return rather than a lump sum.

Fixed Interest Equivalent Rate of Return (FIE)

The popularity of IRR has led to several reformulations designed to remove perceived problems with the measure while retaining its essential characteristics. FIE is one example. In the calculation of IRR it is assumed that any surplus funds generated by the project can be reinvested at a rate of return equal to the IRR. For a project yielding a high return this may be an optimistic assumption, and as a result the IRR may be an unrealistically high measure. A more realistic assumption would be to assume that surplus funds can be reinvested, and capital raised at the discount rate used in an NPV calculation.

An alternative interest rate measure can be obtained using these assumptions by computing the net terminal value of the project and calculating the interest rate required to yield a similar terminal value if the funds were invested in a fixed interest investment. Using the same example, and a 10% discount rate, we have:

Year	0	1	2	3	4	5	6	7
Cash Flow (£)	(10,000)	985	3,739	8,840	9,682	17,096	7,485	(622)

$$NTV = -10,000\,(1.1)^7 + 985\,(1.1)^6 + \ldots -622 = 42,407$$

Net terminal value of an equivalent fixed interest investment at $r\%$

$$= TV\,(investment) - TV\,(cost\ of\ investment)$$
$$= 10,000\,(1 + r)^7 + 622 - 10,000\,(1.1)^7 - 622.$$

(This assumes the investment to be 10,000 initially and 622 at the end of year 7.)

The rate of interest required for the two terminal values to be equal is obtained by solving:

$$10,000\,(1 + r)^7 - 10,000\,(1.1)^7 = 42,407$$
i.e. $(1 + r) = 1.299$, and

$$r = FIE = 29.9\%.$$

(This compares with an IRR of 48.8%.)

FIE is thus a rate of return measure taking account of the time value of money. In general it will give a lower rate of return than IRR for acceptable projects. Its computation can be done simply and precisely and it has a straightforward interpretation. FIE is a similar measure to IRR* as defined by Weston and Brigham[8] in that it is terminal value based. It has been presented here to stress its interpretative value.

RISK IN FINANCIAL EVALUATION

The approach to financial appraisal introduced in the previous section implicitly assumed that the future cash flows are known with certainty. This is generally an invalid assumption. Future revenues depend on uncertain demand conditions in markets for final products and future costs depend on uncertain activity levels and factor market conditions. A number of approaches to handling this uncertainty exist. They differ in technique but also in whose perception of risk, shareholder or manager is involved. This paper discusses several approaches, taking care to identify the interest group involved in each case. Since risk may mean different things to managers and share holders, the implication is that multiple appraisals may have to be carried out for a project and a trade off between conflicting interests established in companies that are not just shareholder value maximisers.

Risk Analysis: A Management Viewpoint

Risk analysis has a long history, being first proposed by Hertz[9] in this context. It explicitly recognizes uncertainty by assigning probability distributions to factors affecting the various components that are aggregated to make up project cash flow. So for example sales revenue in a given year might be represented by the equation:

$$\text{SALES REVENUE} = \text{SALES} \times \text{PRICE}$$

and both sales and price would be assigned probability distributions. This would of course result in sales revenue having a probability distribution. The same approach would be applied to the various cost elements, tax flows and changes in working capital generated by a project. Hence cash flow in each time period appears with a probability distribution. These cash flow distributions are then combined to give a probability distribution for any summary measure of interest, e.g. NPV or IRR. A flow diagram of the risk analysis process appears in Figure 15.1.

The probabilities of cash flows and summary measures are produced by simulation. This involves selecting a single value from the distribution of each component of the cash stream using random numbers and combining these values through the appropriate computation to produce a value for NPV of whatever summary measures are of interest. This procedure is then repeated many times until distributions for each relevant measure are built up. This procedure is illustrated in Figure 15.2.

The result of the simulation exercise is that management has available a distribution for each summary measure of interest. These are pictures of project risk as well as expected performance. Management can use them in decision making perhaps by calculating probabilities of failing to meet set targets.

The risk analysis process presents few computational problems assuming computing facilities are available. It does, however, present measurement problems. A requirement of the process is an ability to build up a probability distribution of the components of the cash stream. This is likely to involve experts in interrogating management to determine firstly, the plausible range of the value of a component and secondly, a picture of the relative chances of different values occurring. This procedure may be difficult and hence when distributions are obtained their validity is still open to doubt. A further complication arises from the existence of interdependencies between

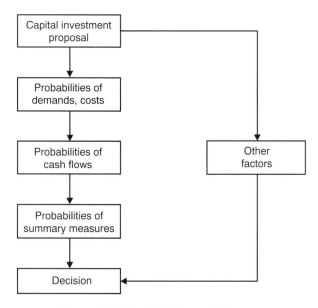

Figure 15.1. The Risk Analysis Process

components and between time periods. For example, price and demand components will be related, with higher prices tending to lead to lower demand. Ideally such relationships should be taken account of in the computer simulation, but the specification of conditional probability distributions considerably complicates the process.

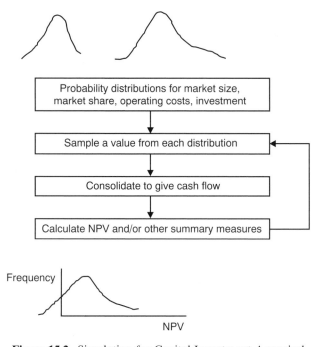

Figure 15.2. Simulation for Capital Investment Appraisal

Hertz and Thomas[10] discuss all these issues. As far as dependency is concerned, they consider that suitable approaches are not yet well developed. Hull[11] also addresses the dependency problem.

The advantage of the approach is that the fullest possible picture of the uncertainty is developed and used in the analysis. The management can assess the financial benefits and risks of the project and apply their judgement, values, and knowledge of non-financial aspects to determine the acceptability of a project.

Risk Adjusted Discount Rates and Certainty Equivalents: Management Viewpoint

In risk analysis, the management attitude to risk enters the analysis after distributions of summary measures have been obtained. This means of course that any discounting involved in the calculation of the distributions should use a risk free discount rate. There is an alternative approach; in fact a linked pair of alternative approaches. One possibility is to represent an uncertain future cash flow by its expected value and discount it at a rate which reflects the riskiness of the cash flow and management's attitude to risk. This approach is called risk adjusted discounting. The present value of an uncertain future cash flow, occurring one period hence, is given by:

$$PV = EV(X)/(1 + k)$$

where EV is the expected value operation and k is the risk adjusted discount rate.

A second possibility is to find a certain cash amount which management views as no more and no less acceptable than the uncertain cash flow X. This new cash amount is called a certainty equivalent. A more precise treatment in the context of a utility function is given shortly. The present value of an uncertain cash flow X occurring one period hence, is then given by:

$$PV = CE(X)/(1 + i)$$

where CE is the certainty equivalent operator and i is the risk free rate.

It is often useful to recognise that:

$$PV = EV(X)/(1 + k) = CE(X)/(1 + i) = (EV(X) - RP)/(1 + i)$$

where RP is a risk premium which changes EV into CE. These approaches are similar to risk analysis in so far as a thorough analysis of the uncertainty of the components of the cash stream is required. These components are then combined to give a cash flow distribution for each future time period. The present value of an uncertain future cash flow is then obtained by applying the risk adjusted discount rate to the expected value of the future cash flow or by discounting the certainty equivalent at the risk free rate. The process will yield an NPV for a project which in general will be lower than the expected value of the NPV obtained via risk analysis, assuming that management is risk averse.

The process can be illustrated analytically by assuming that a future cash flow is normally distributed with known parameters, and assuming a particular utility function for management. Suppose that the uncertain cash flow is assumed to be normally distributed with mean μ and variance σ^2 and that the utility function for a cash amount x can be represented by:

$$U(x) = 1 - \exp(-ax)$$

This form of utility function exhibits constant risk aversion. To determine the appropriate risk adjusted discount rate it is necessary to use the notion of a certainty equivalent (CE) to an uncertain cash amount. The CE is defined as being the certain cash amount that would be equally as acceptable as the uncertain cash amount, given management's attitude to risk. In other words the certain cash amount has utility equal to the expected utility of the uncertain cash amount.

If x is the uncertain cash amount then given the assumptions on the distribution of x and the utility function, it follows that:

Expected utility of $x = \text{EV}\{U(x)\}$
$$= \int \{1 - \exp(-ax)\}\, 1/(\sigma \sqrt{2\pi}) \exp\{-(x - \mu^2)(^2/(2\sigma^2))\}\, dx$$
$$= 1 - \exp(-a\mu + \tfrac{1}{2}\, a^2\sigma^2)$$

where EV stands for expected value.

By definition:

$$U\{CE(x)\} = \text{EV}\{U(x)\}$$

hence:

$$CE(x) = U^{-1}\text{EV}\{U(x)\}$$

If

$U(x) = 1 - \exp(-ax)$, then $U^{-1}(y) = -1/a \times \log(1 - y)$, for any y, and

$$CE(x) = -1/a \times \log\{1- (1 - \exp(-a\mu + \tfrac{1}{2}\, a^2\sigma^2))\}$$
$$= \mu - \tfrac{1}{2}\, a\sigma^2$$

If the cash flow x occurs one year ahead, then as has been said, either $CE(x)$ can be discounted at a risk free rate i, or μ can be discounted at the risk adjusted rate r.

$$CE(x)/(1 + i) = \mu/(1 + r)$$

hence

$$1 + r = \mu(1 + i)/CE(x) = \mu(1 + i)/(\mu - \tfrac{1}{2}a\sigma^2)$$

so that for positive a, implying risk aversion, for this cash flow r will exceed the risk free rate i. However, if the cash flow is an uncertain cash outflow, r will be less than the risk free rate.

Example

Let $\mu = \pounds2{,}000$, $\sigma^2 = 800$, $i = 10\%$ and $a = 0.2$ then:

$1 + r = (2{,}000 \times 1.1)/(2.000 - \tfrac{1}{2} \times 0.2 \times 800) = 1.146$

Hence the risk adjusted discount rate $r = 14.6\%$.

This approach to accommodating risk presents a number of practical difficulties. As in risk analysis, it requires the formulation of probability density functions, but additionally it requires the formulation of a utility function. The latter raises a number of questions, such as whose utility function it is and how a utility function can be formulated. Hertz and Thomas (1983) describe methods of formulating utility functions for individuals and groups of individuals, and the problem of validity has been addressed by Hershey, Kunreuther and Schoemaker.[12] Berry and Dyson[13,14] discuss the treatment of cash outflows, and consider the issue of incrementality as do Lioukas and Moore.[15]

Risk Adjusted Rates and Certainty Equivalents: Shareholders' Viewpoint

An alternative to managerial expected utility maximisation as an objective in capital budgeting is maximising the expected utility of the firm's current shareholders. It might appear that this is an impossible objective, since different shareholders are likely to have different utility functions. However, in well functioning capital markets, maximising the price of current shares is equivalent to maximising current shareholders' expected utility.[16] The basic idea is that by maximising its contribution to shareholders' wealth the firm allows each shareholder to make his/her own utility maximising choice of consumption pattern.

If management is to act in the interests of its shareholders, then it must accept investments that increase share value and reject those that do not. What management would like to be able to do is to find a firm traded on the stock market which is an exact replica of the project it is considering. It can then compare the cost of undertaking the project with the value the stock market places on the project. An excess of market value over cost would indicate that the project should be accepted. If a replica cannot be found, then management must try and discover, and apply, the valuation mechanism which generates share prices.

One view of this mechanism which has achieved widespread popularity is the capital asset pricing model (CAPM), Copeland and Weston (1988). This model identifies a risk adjusted discount rate which can be applied to project cash flows. The process of applying CAPM is described in the next section.

Capital Asset Pricing Model: A Practical Approach

Given that a set of expected cash flows has been developed, the requirement is for a risk adjusted discount rate to apply to them. Given that impact on share price is a consideration, the stock market is an obvious place to look for one. Whatever the nature of the investment project under consideration the aim is to find a stock market investment, a share, of comparable risk, and calculate the required rate of return on this.

CAPM defines the required rate of return as:

$$kj = i + \beta j[EV(R_m{}^*) - i].$$

Here i is once again the risk free rate, $[EV(R_m{}^*) - i]$ is the return the market portfolio (a value weighted portfolio of all shares) earns over and above the risk free rate, and βj, or Beta, is a measure of the share's risk relative to that of the market. In other words, kj is the risk free rate plus a risk premium. The risk adjustment is, however, unusual in that it is based on the covariance between the return on the share and the market portfolio. Covariance is the relevant risk measure because shareholders are seen as capable of holding diversified portfolios of shares. Therefore, relevant risk is non-diversifiable risk, the extent to which returns on a share move in line with the market portfolio.

As has been said, Beta is covariance based, showing the extent to which return on a share moves with the return on a well diversified portfolio. Beta is usually measured as the slope coefficient in a regression of return on a share against return on a very well diversified portfolio, Copeland and Weston (1988). So, if the investment project under consideration involved a foundry operation say, the Beta of a share in an existing foundry operation could be used as a proxy for the project's risk. In fact it might be better to calculate Betas for several such firms and average them. An alternative to carrying out the Beta calculations is of course to use a 'Beta Book' such as the London Business School 'Risk Management Service'.[17]

Having calculated a project risk measure, the next step is to calculate a required rate of return using CAPM. The elements in the CAPM equation are relatively easily available: i can be found in a daily newspaper, as the rate on Treasury Bills. βj can be calculated as described; a long term average of $[EV(R_m{}^*) - i]$ of about 8% after personal tax has been calculated by Dimson and Brealey.[18] If $\beta j = 0.7$, $i = 6\%$ and $[EV(R_m{}^*) - i]$ is 8%, then an investment in the stock market of comparable risk to the investment project under consideration offers an expected return of:

$$kj = 0.06 + (0.7 \times 0.08)$$
$$= 0.116 = 11.6\%$$

Updated estimates of the market risk premium are available.[19]

This discount rate should be applied to cash flow data, such as that included in the discussion of NPV. The investment project under consideration must offer at least this rate of return if it is not to depress the company's share price.

There is one complicating factor still to be taken into account. Calculating project Beta by averaging firm Betas, has allowed financing mix to affect the calculation. Each firm's Beta will reflect the line of business the firm is in and the presence of any debt in the firm's capital structure. Thus firm Betas must be ungeared before they can be used as a proxy for project risk. This is easily done if the simplifying assumption of risk free debt is made (formulae which do not require this assumption are given in Buckley[20] and Schnabel[21]). Then the equation:

$$\beta(\text{business}) = \beta(\text{equity}) \, [\text{equity}/(\text{equity} + \text{debt})] + \beta \, (\text{debt}) \, [\text{debt}/(\text{debt} + \text{equity})]$$

reduces to:

$$\beta \, (\text{business}) = \beta \, (\text{equity}) \, [\text{equity}/(\text{equity} + \text{debt})]$$

It must be remembered in both these equations that equity and debt are in market values. The simple equation form is due to the additivity of covariances. If the 0.7 Beta in the numerical example related to one firm, and that firm had 30% debt in its capital structure, then the business Beta or all equity Beta would be 0.49 and the corresponding required rate of return for the project, p, would be:

$$p = 0.06 + (0.49 \times 0.080)$$
$$= 0.099$$

The traditional finance argument for the use of debt is that interest payments are deductible for corporation tax purposes. It has been suggested that since a project will increase a firm's borrowing capacity, the project should be credited with the tax shield generated by the interest on new debt raised. However, modern finance indicates that the cheapness of debt relative to equity finance may be an illusion. Thus the project's weighted average cost of capital (WACC, the most commonly advocated mechanism for taking into account the cheapness of debt) would simply be:

$$\text{WACC} = kj.\text{equity}/(\text{equity} + \text{debt}) + i \times \text{debt}/(\text{debt} + \text{equity})$$
$$= 0.116 * 0.7 + 0.06 * 0.3$$
$$= 0.099.$$

This is simply the required rate of return on ungeared equity.

There is an alternative method for taking the tax shields on debt into account. This is Myer's Adjusted Present Value method. This is advocated (Brealey and Myers, 1996) on the grounds that it involves fewer unrealistic assumptions than the calculation of a weighted average cost of capital. Since it is a simple way of taking into account other 'special' cash flows, it deserves attention even in the absence of debt based tax shields.

Time State Preference

In the time state preference model (TSP) uncertainty about the future takes the form of not knowing which one of a set of mutually exclusive states of nature will occur.[22] An uncertain cash flow can then be viewed as a set of cash payoffs, each one associated with a particular state of nature. A simple, one period, two state example should make these ideas clear. Tomorrow the economy will be in one of two possible states, 1 = boom or 2 = slump. Boom has probability P(1) and slump probability P(2). An investment of £100 by a firm in plant and machinery now generates a cash flow of £200 tomorrow if a boom occurs, and a cash flow of £40 tomorrow if a slump occurs. This is diagrammed below:

INVESTMENT	STATE	PROBABILITY	CASH
	1	P(1)	200
−100			
	2	P(2)	40

Cash flow uncertainty is then simply a reflection of uncertainty about which future state will occur.

Suppose that in the capital market it is possible to find a pair of securities (a pure security is one which pays £1 in one state and £0 in all others), one of which, S(1), pays off in state 1, while the other, S(2), pays off in state 2. Let the pure security which pays off in state 1 have a current price V(1) and the one which pays off in state 2 a current price V(2). These prices are formed in the market. To mimic the future consequences of the investment opportunity it would be necessary to spend 200V(1) + 40V(2). Therefore if 200V(1) + 40V(2) > 100 the firm has a positive NPV investment which should be taken on. The firm can purchase the future cash flows more cheaply than its shareholders can buy them in the market, and therefore should do so on their behalf.

In the above description of the TSP framework no specific pricing mechanism has been introduced. V(1) and V(2) have been assumed to be known. The pricing mechanism most commonly assumed to operate in well developed capital markets is the capital asset pricing model (CAPM). In certainty equivalent form this is:

$$PV(X^*) = EV(X^*) - \lambda \, cov(X^*, R_m)/(1 + i)$$

where:

X^* is the uncertain future cash flow,
R_m is the uncertain future return on the market portfolio,
PV indicates present value,
EV indicates expectation,
cov indicates covariance, and
i is the risk free rate of interest.

The remaining element in the formula is λ, which is:

$$\lambda = (EV(R_m) - 1)/\sigma^2_m$$

where:

$$\sigma^2_m \text{ is the variance of the market return.}$$

The derivation of this equation from the risk adjusted discount rate form can be found in, among others, Haley and Schall (1979).

The economics of this pricing model are quite straightforward. Present value is given by discounting, at the risk free rate, a certain cash amount equivalent to the uncertain cash flow. The only unusual feature is the nature of the adjustment factor which transforms the expected value $EV(X)$ into a certainty equivalent. This is based on cash flow risk as measured by covariance. As has been said, shareholders are seen as capable of holding diversified portfolios of shares. Therefore relevant risk is non-diversifiable risk, the extent to which the cash flow moves in line with the market portfolio.

Given forecasts about R_m, the return on the market, and i, the risk free rate, CAPM can be used to calculate time state prices $V(1)$ and $V(2)$ and hence can be used to value the firm's investment opportunity. The calculation of covariances is straightforward, as is shown below, because of the simple cash flow pattern offered by a pure security.

INVESTMENT	PROBABILITY	CASH	S(1)	S(2)	R_m	i
	0.6	200	1	0	.2	.1
−100						
	0.4	40	0	1	.05	.1

Preliminary calculations of market parameters gives:

$$\lambda = (EV(R_m) - i)/\sigma^2_m = (0.14 - 0.1)/0.0054 = 0.74$$

Let $V(1)$ be the price of pure security $S(2)$, then by CAPM:

$$V(1) = (0.6 - 7.4 \times 0.6 \times 0.06)/1.1 = 0.303$$

Let $V(2)$ be the price of pure security $S(2)$, then by CAPM:

$$V(2) = (0.4 - 7.4 \times 0.4 \times -0.09)/1.1 = 0.606$$

From TSP:

$$NPV = 200\ V(1) + 40\ V(2) - 100$$
$$= (200 \times 0.303) + (40 \times 0.606) - 100$$
$$= -15.16$$

Hence the firm should not take on the investment.

Arbitrage Pricing Theory

Another pricing model deserves mention in this overview of risk from the point of view of shareholders. This is the arbitrage pricing model, APT, developed by Ross.[23] The argument here is simple. In a world of well functioning capital markets two assets offering the same outcomes should trade at the same prices. Look again at the data used in the CAPM numerical example. The following diagram simply presents once again the assumptions about market returns and risk free rates but this time as cash payoffs.

INVESTMENT	STATE	CASH	$1 + i$	$CASH_m$
	1	200	1.10	1.20
−100				
	2	40	1.10	1.05

The diagram shows that £1 lent at the risk free rate will generate £1.10 one period from now and an investment of £1.00 in the market portfolio will generate, one period from now, £1.20 if state 1 occurs and £1.05 if state 2 occurs. To apply APT to the capital budgeting problem it is necessary to identify a portfolio of lending and investment in the market portfolio that mimics the project's cash flow. This can be done by solving a pair of simultaneous equations.[24]

$$200 = 1.10X + 1.20Y$$
$$40 = 1.10X + 1.05Y$$

The LHS of the equations are simply project cash flows and the RHS of the equations are the cash flows from the lending and portfolio investment decisions. The values $x = -981.82$; $y = 1066.67$ solve the equations. These imply that an investment of £1,066.67 in the market portfolio, and borrowing of £981.82 will mimic the project's uncertain future cash flow. The investment in the market portfolio and the borrowing imply a current cash outflow of (£981.83 − £1,066.67) = £84.84. To acquire the future cash flow by undertaking the project would involve a current cash outflow of £100. This is £15.16 more than is required to acquire a similar future cash flow in the capital market. (NB: Compare this amount with the project NPV as calculated using CAPM.) Therefore the project should not be undertaken.

This section has identified three models which can be used to price future uncertain cash flows. (TSP is essentially a framework into which specific pricing models can be slotted.) CAPM is the most widely recommended in finance texts while APT is a relative newcomer. The shift from the statistical computations of CAPM to the more general, economic style of argument implicit in APT is symptomatic of what is happening in financial theory at the present time.

The simple examples used in this section have made use of discrete distributions and single period cash flows. These restrictions were introduced for convenience only. CAPM and APT can cope with their relaxation.

A Synthesis of Shareholder and Managerial Viewpoints

The managerial attempts to cope with risks that have been examined have been based around the variance of project cash flow. An alternative view would be that it is a project's contribution to the variance of firm's cash flow that is important. But even so, concern is with a total risk measure. However, for a shareholder, relevant risk is based on covariance with the market portfolio. These are different concepts of risk rather than different ways of looking at the same thing. Therefore, as we said earlier, two separate evaluations may be appropriate. There is another possible source of confusion stemming from these two viewpoints. The NPV figure, which is generated using a capital market based valuation mechanism, can be interpreted as a market value. This is not the case if valuation is based on a managerial utility function. Nor is it the case that the expected value of a distribution of NPVs generated by a risk analysis can be interpreted as a market value. Different concepts underpin the NPV title in these situations and this can be a source of confusion.

Real Options

The calculation of an NPV on the basis of incremental cash flow and a CAPM based risk adjusted discount rate has been the core of modern financial management. Nevertheless alternative approaches to investment appraisal have their proponents.

The decision tree approach offers a tool for exploring management's ability to respond to the risk factors which generate cash flow distributions. Management can defer making an investment, expand or contract the scale of operations during a project's life, abandon a project, and design facilities in such a way that they can be truncated so that many adverse cash flows can be avoided. Unfortunately, decision tree analysts have not convincingly dealt with the problem of discounting the resulting cash flow values.

Many analysts have proposed a less financial, more strategic, analysis of investment decisions. Here the emphasis has been on the role of some investments as necessary to allow management the right to undertake other projects in the future. In these circumstances a strategist might regard even a negative NPV project as attractive because of the possibilities it opens up.

This conflict between finance and strategy has led to the dismissal of the finance approach by some analysts, and even in some cases to its identification as a barrier to good decision making. Financial analysts have responded in two ways. Firstly, some have identified the problem as an inappropriate application of the NPV approach. A frequent argument has been that incremental cash flow has not been appropriately identified, because the 'without project base case' has been unduly optimistic. However, a more telling response has been to augment the traditional NPV calculation by recognising that it does not capture the financial value of the options which projects make available.

Alternatives to the NPV approach recognise, however partially, the existence and value of the options which are present. An option is a right, but not an obligation to do something. A 'Call' option is the right to buy an asset on or before a given date (the exercise date) for a price, (the exercise price) agreed now. A 'Put' option is the right to sell an asset on or before a given date for a price agreed now. The phrase 'on or before' identifies the option as an American option. If the option had been exercisable only on a particular date it would have been a European option. Options have value, and there is a well developed market in many economies to allow the buying and selling of options on shares. Because an option involves the right to do nothing, an option cannot have a negative value to its holder.

Real option theory is based on the recognition that the types of managerial flexibility identified by decision theorists and strategists involve the possession of options. Deferring the start of a project involves owning a call option on a project with an exercise price equal to the capital cost of undertaking the project. Abandoning a project can be thought of as exercising a put option with the exercise price equal to any break up value. In a similar vein the strategic approach to investment can involve the creation of options to undertake future projects. The failure of the traditional finance approach is simply a failure to attribute to a project the value of any options associated with the project.

Financial investment appraisal thus becomes a two stage affair. Firstly a base case NPV is calculated using traditional finance methods. Secondly the value of any options associated with the project is added to this base case NPV. There only remains the problem of how to value the options. A qualitative approach of simply recognising the presence of options is a minimalist response to the problem. However, for many companies at the moment this may be all that is achievable, given the novelty of the ideas involved. One approach to valuation involves mimicking the payoff of an option by a portfolio of securities the values of which are already known. This approach is described in detail in the following chapter.

INTERDEPENDENCIES

Capital investment often assumes that a project can be evaluated in isolation from the other activities of the organisation, although it is recognised that the appropriate cash stream for the project is the marginal change in the overall cash stream of the organisation, due to adding the project to the existing activities. In practice isolating the project cash stream may be complicated, due to a variety of reasons, and in general interdependencies will arise between the project, existing activities and other proposed projects and competitors. The cases of interdepency can be due to logistics, capital rationing, manpower rationing, the tax system, correlations between cash flows, competitive reaction and utility. The latter case was referred to in the section on risk adjusted discount rates.

Logistics

Logistics come into play when the capital investment is associated with introducing new capacity into a production/distribution system. For example, if a new production facility were added to an existing system the pattern of supplying the various markets would be perturbed. The resultant change in product flow would need to be evaluated, perhaps using a model of the system, in order to determine the cash stream corresponding to the new facility.

Capital and Manpower Rationing

Capital and manpower rationing can both constrain the number of projects undertaken. The implications for project selection are that simple accept/reject decisions cannot be made on individual project proposals as the total number of projects accepted might require capital or manpower in excess of the amounts available. If this is the case then formal constraints must be added to the appraisal process and as a result a model including the resource pattern of the ongoing activities and all proposed projects may be required. The use of linear programming for capital rationing was proposed by Weingartner[25] and an early application in a practical situation is due to Chambers.[26] These models are typically multi-time-period models with constraints applying in each year. A linear programming approach assumes the divisibility of a project and if this is unrealistic then an integer programming formulation may be necessary. A solution to a linear or integer programming model would give the set of projects which maximises the NPV or NTV subject to the various constraints imposed. An alternative to a (mathematical) programming approach would be to use a financial simulation model which evaluates the financial consequences of accepting any particular selection of projects.

It is often argued that capital rationing constraints are illusory in the sense that capital for good projects is always available through the financial markets. Certainly there is usually no reason why capital constraints should be hard in the sense that they cannot be violated under any circumstances. Mathematical programming models need not be rejected under this assumption, however, and indeed can be an effective tool for exploring the consequences of different levels of availability of capital. This can be particularly useful if additional capital can be obtained at a premium rate of interest.

Manpower constraints can become necessary, due to the limited availability of management and other skills. These are also unlikely to lead to hard constraints and can be accommodated in the same way as capital constraints. If necessary both kinds of constraints could be modelled simultaneously.

The existence of capital or manpower constraints implies that projects can no longer be assessed in isolation. If uncertainty is to be admitted into the assessment, then a risk analysis approach is still feasible as a financial simulation model can be designed to allow a risk analysis. The incorporation of uncertainty into a mathematical programming model leads to the field of stochastic programming, in which the models are generally difficult to solve.

Taxation Induced Interdependencies

Tax systems are always in transition in so far as the system of capital allowances and corporate tax rates is liable to be changed. For example in the UK, prior to April 1984, a capital investment in plant or machinery attracted up to 100% initial allowance which meant that the entire investment could be offset against profits. Lower allowances were available for other investments such as buildings and offices. As a result of the capital allowances, companies were required to pay corporation tax only on the profits that exceeded the capital allowances due. Berry and Dyson[27] showed that this allowance system itself caused interdependencies between ongoing activities and proposed projects, even in the absence of capital rationing constraints. This process is illustrated in the following example. As a result of the erosion of the 100% initial allowance the interdependencies due to the tax system are less strong, but nevertheless still exist (Berry and Dyson, 1997).

Consider a firm with profits from ongoing activities and with two projects being considered for adoption with the cash streams shown in Table 15.2.

Table 15.2. Cash Streams £000's

	Year 1	Year 2	Year 3
Ongoing profits	20	20	20
Project A	(100)	200	110
Project B	(140)		190

If the projects are evaluated independently then for Project A, assuming a 10% discount rate, and ignoring taxation:

$$NPV(A) = -100 + 200/1.1 + 110 1/.1^2$$
$$= 172.7 \text{ and}$$
$$NPV(B) = 17.0$$

Each project, when evaluated independently, has a positive NPV and is therefore acceptable under the usual decision rule.

A project should ideally be evaluated in terms of the marginal benefit contributed by the project and this should include the taxation effects. Assuming a 100% initial allowance, and a 52% corporate tax rate, we can evaluate the NPV of the firm's ongoing activities, and the change in NPV due to each project. The analysis is as follows:

Ongoing activities:

	Year 1	Year 2	Year 3
Firm ongoing activities	20	20	20
Tax at 52%	10.4	10.4	10.4
Net profit	9.6	9.6	9.6

$$NPV(ongoing) = 9.6 + 9.6/1.1 + 9.6/1.1^2 = 28.26.$$

Ongoing plus project A:

	Year 1	Year 2	Year 3
Ongoing profits	20	20	20
Project A	(100)	200	110
Capital allowance used	20	80	
Taxable profit		140	130
Tax at 52%		72.8	67.6
Net cash flow	(80)	147.2	62.4

In the above computations the taxable profits have been calculated after taking account of the capital allowance as follows. The investment of 100 secures a capital allowance of 100, assuming 100% initial allowance. As profits available in year 1 are 20, these can be offset by an equal capital allowance so that no tax is payable in year 1. The remaining capital allowance, 80, not used in year 1 is carried forward to year 2. The taxable profit in year 2 is then the amount by which total profits exceed the allowance carried forward, i.e. $220 - 80 = 140$. The net cash flows are calculated by subtracting the tax payments from the total income.

$$NPV(\text{ongoing} + A) = -80 + 147.2/1.1 + 62.4/1.1^2 = 105.39$$

The net benefit from project A is thus:

$$NPV\ (\text{ongoing} + A) - NPV\ (\text{ongoing}) = 77.13$$

Thus allowing for tax, project A is still worthwhile.

Ongoing plus project B:

	Year 1	Year 2	Year 3
Ongoing profits	20	20	20
Project B	(140)		190
Capital allowance used	20	20	100
Taxable profit			110
Tax at 52%			57.2
Net cash flow	(120)	20	152.8

$$NPV\ (\text{ongoing} + B) = 24.46$$

The net benefit from project B is thus:

$$NPV\ (\text{ongoing} + B) - NPV\ (\text{ongoing}) = 24.46 - 28.26$$
$$= (3.8)$$

Project B makes a negative contribution.

The above evaluation of project B ignored the possibility of project B being undertaken along with project A. It is possible, therefore, to obtain another evaluation of project B, its marginal contribution to the firm plus project A.

	Year 1	Year 2	Year 3
Ongoing profits	20	20	20
Project A	(100)	200	110
Project B	(140)		190
Capital allowance used	20	220	
Taxable profit			320
Tax at 52%			166.4
Net cash flow	(220)	220	153.6

$$NPV\ (\text{ongoing} + A + B) = 106.94$$

Under this assumption the net benefit of project B becomes:

$$NPV\ (\text{ongoing} + A + B) - NPV\ (\text{ongoing} + A) = 1.55$$

Project B thus makes a positive contribution and is worth undertaking (just) provided project A is undertaken.

The above analysis demonstrates the interdependency of proposed projects amongst themselves and with ongoing activities, and demonstrates that individual project evaluation may not be sensible under a tax system incorporating capital allowances (and other features of the UK tax system), in which profits from one project can be offset against investments in another. Berry and Dyson (1997) show how various aspects of the UK tax system can be incorporated into a mathematical programming model for project selection. The tax rules could also be incorporated into a financial simulation model. (It is worth noting that capital allowances taken in subsequent years are not increased in line with inflation so that the benefit is diminished in inflationary times.)

Correlations

Assuming that future cash flows are uncertain, a further source of interdependency can be due to correlations between a project's cash flows and other uncertainties. In the section on the CAPM the importance of the correlation of a project with the market portfolio was stressed. The assumption there is that a diversified shareholder is concerned to reduce his risk and an important aspect of the evaluation of a project is the risk pattern of the project, compared with that of the capital market.

Correlations can also be important if a project appraisal is being carried out taking account of the management preferences and attitude to risk. The concern now is with the correlation of a project's cash stream with the cash streams from ongoing activities and from other proposed projects. It is the existence of such correlations which might cause a project to sell ice cream to be viewed particularly attractively by the manager of a fish and chip shop thinking of diversification as it would reduce the total risk of the operation. These correlations can be incorporated into a financial simulation model for corporate risk analysis, and Berry and Dyson (1984) discuss the modification of risk adjusted discount rates to allow for statistical dependencies. The identification of these dependencies and the measurement of the correlations is by no means straightforward.

Competitive Reaction

A capital investment proposal can often involve an attempted expansion of market share and such a proposal can lead to a strong competitive reaction. This interdependency with competitors can be a major source of uncertainty affecting market size, market share, price and revenue. Risk analysis does not, of course, exclude the competitive dimension, but contemporary business policy teaching and research places competitiveness as the primary issue for many organisations (see Porter[28]).

Adopting this stance, the risk analysis process can be elaborated as shown in Figure 15.3.

As in risk analysis the probabilities of the summary measures are produced by a simulation process, but the simulation of the competitive element becomes an explicit component. Competitive reaction also affects the calculation of risk adjusted discount rates. If the management viewpoint is taken, the effect of competition will be reflected

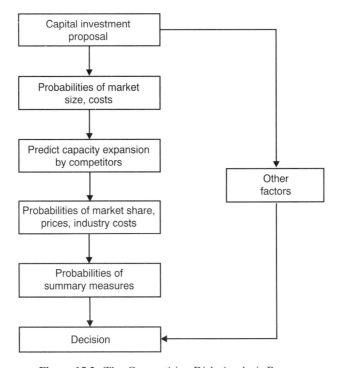

Figure 15.3. The Competitive Risk Analysis Process

in the level of uncertainty of the cash stream and hence in the risk premium. If the shareholder's viewpoint is taken, in a competitive market the additional uncertainty should be reflected in the Beta value and also in the mean level of the return on the project. Again this will lead to a change in the risk premium.

FINANCIAL APPRAISAL AND STRATEGIC EVALUATION

The financial appraisal of a strategic initiative involves representing the initiatives as a cash flow stream and then computing summary measures such as NPV. The uncertainty of the future can be recognised by the use of risk analysis, scenario planning (Chapter 13), the capital asset pricing model or real option theory, with the summary measures manifesting themselves as probability density functions, contrasting collections of measures, or true expected values (in the latter two cases) respectively.

A shareholder value approach would suggest that appropriate financial appraisal is sufficient, and the sole criterion of acceptance of a strategic initiative should be the enhancement of shareholder value. This position can be criticised from two contrasting standpoints however. Firstly even if it is accepted that the shareholders are the only relevant group of stakeholders, it may not be possible to capture all aspects of a strategic initiative in a financial appraisal, so that non-quantifiable factors, or factors that do not readily translate into cash may be considered pertinent to the evaluation and selection process. Secondly a multiple stakeholder perspective would inevitably

Objectives/Performance Measures	Targets	Prediction (Base case)	Gap
Profitability	PT	PP	PT–PP
Employment	ET	EP	ET–EP
Growth	GT	GP	GT–GP
Market share	MT	MP	MT–MP

(PT represents the target profitability and PP the predicted profitability.)

Figure 15.4. Gap Analysis

bring non-financial criteria into play such as employment levels or supplier relation-ships. In either case the strategic initiative needs to be evaluated against a set of multiple objectives of which financial objectives will be important but not exclusive.

A long-standing approach is via gap analysis. This firstly involves specifying a de-sired future position for the organisation in terms of objectives, performance measures and targets; predicting the likely future of the organisation if no new strategic develop-ment takes place (the base case); and evaluating the multi-dimensional gap. This is illustrated in Figure 15.4. A significant predicted gap acts as a trigger in the search for new strategies.

The balanced scorecard approach to performance measurement (Chapter 4) would require the introduction of four classes of objectives/measures corresponding to a financial perspective, a customer perspective, an internal business perspective and an innovation and learning perspective. This is illustrated in Figure 15.5 where each row now represents a set of measures rather than individual ones.

Objectives/Performance Measures	Targets	Prediction	Gap
Financial measures	FT	FP	FT–FP
Customer measures	CT	CP	CT–CP
Internal business measures	IBT	IBP	IBT–IBP
Innovation and learning measures	ILT	ILP	ILT–ILP

Figure 15.5. Gap Analysis and the Balanced Scorecard

To evaluate strategic initiatives gap analysis needs to be extended in two directions. Firstly the impact of any new initiative on the measures must be evaluated and displayed, and secondly uncertainty needs to be taken into account. The latter can be achieved by one of the approaches such as the use of a risk adjusted discount rate already described. However, many companies adopt a scenario approach to uncertainty; this approach would involve evaluating the impact of a new initiative under each scenario. Figure 15.6 illustrates the gap analysis approach to evaluating two initiatives under two scenarios assuming the same measures as in Figure 15.5.

A robust or effective strategy would be one which is predicted to close the gaps under each scenario.

		Scenario A		Scenario B	
	Targets	Prediction	Gap	Prediction	Gap
Initiative 1	FT	FP1A	FT–FP1A	FP1B	FT–FP1B
	CT	CP1A	CT–CP1A	CP1B	CT–CP1B
	IBT	IBP1A	IBT–IBP1A	IBP1B	IBT–IBP1B
	ILT	ILP1A	ILT–ILP1A	ILP1B	ILT–ILP1B
Initiative 2	FT	FP2A	FT–FP2A	FP2B	FT–FP2B
	CT	CP2A	CT–CT2A	CP2B	CT–CP2B
	IBT	IBP2A	IBT–IBP2A	IBP2B	IBT–IBP2B
	ILT	ILP2A	ILT–ILP2A	ILP2B	ILT–ILP2B

(FP1A represents the predictions for the financial measures under scenario A if initiative 1 is undertaken.)

Figure 15.6. Gap Analysis and Strategic Initiative Evaluation

CONCLUSION

This chapter has provided an overview of financial investment appraisal. A variety of approaches which can contribute to the process have been discussed, and the sources of difference between them emphasised. One question remains to be answered: how to put the component parts of an appraisal together in practice?

This chapter takes the view that there is no single procedure which is correct at all times. Current orthodoxy in finance couples a stochastic simulation to generate cash flow distributions and expected values with risk adjusted discount rates based on CAPM. However, for many projects this may be like taking a sledgehammer to crack a nut. For others it may ignore important strategic and social issues, as among other things it assumes that the interest of shareholders is pre-eminent. Risk analysis and scenarios provide an alternative perspective.

In essence this chapter recommends a flexible approach in which multiple summary measures are generated and in which both financial and non-financial issues appear.

To this extent the recommendations of the chapter mirror current practice far more than many, how to do it, tracts. However, this is not simply an easy path to acceptance by management. It is more a reflection of a belief that a gap between the recommendation of experts and management practice should prompt a search for reasons why, rather than a simple statement that management is wrong again!

Theory should certainly inform practice. This paper includes comments on tax induced links between projects, and discounting future cash outflows, among other things, of which practitioners of investment appraisal should be aware. However, it is not impossible that the environment in which they work requires a response other than slavish conformity to theory. Hopefully the theories and approaches of this chapter can support practice in both the short and the longer term.

REFERENCES

1. I. G. Ansoff (1965) *Corporate Strategy*, McGraw-Hill, US.
2. G. J. A. Stern (1976) SOSIPing, or sophistical obfuscation of self-interest and prejudice, *Operational Research Quarterly*, 27, 915–930.
3. G. Biddle and F. Lindahl (1982) Stock price reductions to LIFO adoptions, *Journal of Accounting Research*, Autumn, 548–551.
4. R. H. Berry and R. G. Dyson (1997) Tax induced project interactions, in I. Lapsey and R. Wilson eds. *Explorations in Financial Control*, ITB Press, London.
5. R. Brealey and S. Myers (1996) *Principles of Corporate Finance*, McGraw-Hill, USA.
6. A. Sangster (1993) Capital investment appraisal techniques: a survey of current usage. *Journal of Business Finance and Accounting*, 20, 307–332.
7. R. Dorfman (1981) The meaning of internal rates of return, *Journal of Finance*, 36, 1011–1021.
8. J. F. Weston and E. F. Brigham (1981) *Managerial Finance*, The Dryden Press, Hinsdale, Illinois.
9. D. B. Hertz (1964) Risk analysis in capital investment, *Harvard Business Review* 42, 95–106.
10. D. B. Hertz and H. Thomas (1983) *Risk Analysis and its Applications*, Wiley.
11. J. C. Hull (1980) *The Evaluation of Risk in Business Investment*, Pergamon.
12. J. C. Hershey, H. C. Kunreuther and P. J. H. Schoemaker (1982), Sources of bias in assessment procedures for utility functions, *Management Science*, 28, 936–954.
13. R. H. Berry and R. G. Dyson (1980) On the negative risk premium for risk adjusted discount rates, *Journal of Business Finance and Accounting* 7, 427–436.
14. R. H. Berry and R. G. Dyson (1984) On the negative risk premium for risk adjusted discount rates: reply and extension, *Journal of Business Finance and Accounting*, 11, 257–268.
15. S. K. Lioukas and P. M. Moore (1983) Incremental evaluation of risky choices, *Journal of the Operational Research Society*, 34, 413–418.
16. J. E. Copeland and J. F. Weston (1988) *Financial Theory and Corporate Policy*, Addison-Wesley.
17. E. Dimson and P. Marsh (eds) Risk Measurement Service, *London Business School Quarterly*.
18. E. Dimson and R. A. Brealey (1978) The risk premium on UK equities, *The Investment Analyst*, 38, 14–18.
19. T. Jenkinson (1993) The cost of equity finance: conventional wisdom reconsidered, *Stock Exchange Quarterly* with Quality of Markets Review, Autumn.

20. A. Buckley (1981) Beta geared and ungeared, *Accounting and Business Research*, 42, 121–126.
21. J. A. Schnabel (1983) Beta geared and ungeared: an extension, *Accounting and Business Research* 50, 128–130.
22. C. W. Haley and L. D. Schall (1979) *The Theory of Financial Decisions*, McGraw Hill.
23. S. A. Ross (1976) The arbitrage theory of capital asset pricing, *journal of Economic Theory*, December, 343–362.
24. A. K. Gehr (1981) Risk adjusted capital budgeting using arbitrage, *Financial Management* 10, 14–19.
25. H. M. Weingartner (1963) *Mathematical Programming and the Analysis of Capital Budgeting Problems*, Prentice Hall, Englewood Cliffs, NJ.
26. D. J. Chambers (1967) Programming the allocation of funds subject to restrictions on reported results, *Operational Research Quarterly*, 18, 407–432.
27. R. H. Berry and R. G. Dyson (1979) A mathematical programming approach to taxation induced interdependencies in investment appraisal, *Journal of Business Finance and Accounting* 6, 425–442.
28. M. E. Porter (1980) *Competitive Strategy*, The Free Press.

Chapter 16

Real Options and Interactions with Financial Flexibility

Lenos Trigeorgis

Boston University, Boston, MA

Many academics and practising managers now recognize that the net present value (NPV) rule and other discounted cash flow (DCF) approaches to capital budgeting are inadequate in that they cannot properly capture management's flexibility to adapt and revise later decisions in response to unexpected market developments. Traditional NPV makes implicit assumptions concerning an 'expected scenario' of cash flows and presumes management's passive commitment to a certain 'operating strategy' (e.g., to initiate the project immediately, and operate it continuously at base scale until the end of its prespecified expected useful life).

In the actual marketplace, characterized by change, uncertainty and competitive interactions, however, the realization of cash flows will probably differ from what management expected initially. As new information arrives and uncertainty about market conditions and future cash flows is gradually resolved, management may have valuable flexibility to alter its operating strategy in order to capitalize on favorable future opportunities or mitigate losses. For example, management may be able to defer, expand, contract, abandon, or otherwise alter a project at different stages during its useful operating life.

Management's flexibility to adapt its future actions in response to altered future market conditions expands an investment opportunity's value by improving its upside potential while limiting downside losses relative to management's initial expectations under passive management. The resulting asymmetry caused by managerial adaptability calls for an 'expanded NPV' rule reflecting both value components: the traditional (static or passive) NPV of direct cash flows, and the option value of operating and strategic adaptability. This does not mean that traditional NPV should be

I would like to thank George M. Constantinides, Nalin Kulatilaka, Scott P. Mason, Stewart C. Myers, Martha A. Schary, Han Smit, two anonymous reviewers, and the editor of *Financial Management*, James S. Ang, for useful comments on earlier versions of parts of this work. The usual disclaimer applies.

scrapped, but rather should be seen as a crucial and necessary input to an options-based, expanded NPV analysis, i.e.:

$$\text{Expanded (strategic) NPV} = \frac{\text{static (passive) NPV of expected cash flows}}{\text{+ value of options from active management.}} \quad (1)$$

An options approach to capital budgeting has the potential to conceptualize and even quantify the value of options from active management. This value is manifest as a collection of real (call or put) options embedded in capital investment opportunities, having as an underlying asset the gross project value of expected operating cash flows. Many of these real options occur naturally (e.g., to defer, contract, shut down or abandon), while others may be planned and built-in at some extra cost (e.g., to expand capacity or build growth options, to default when investment is staged sequentially, or to switch between alternative inputs or outputs). Figure 6.1 describes briefly the most common categories of encountered real options, the types of industries they are important in, and lists representative authors that have analyzed them.[1] A more comprehensive review of the real options literature is given in the first section.

This chapter has two main goals. First, it provides a comprehensive overview of the existing real options literature and applications, and presents practical principles for quantifying the value of various real options. Second, it takes a first step towards extending the real options literature to recognize interactions with financial flexibility. The comprehensive literature review traces the evolution of the real options revolution, organized around thematic developments covering the early criticisms, conceptual approaches, foundations and building blocks, risk-neutral valuation and risk adjustment, analytic contributions in valuing different options separately, option interactions, numerical techniques, competition and strategic options, various applications, and future research directions. An example is then used to conceptually discuss the basic nature of the various real options that may be embedded in capital investments. Initially assuming all-equity financing, the paper presents principles useful for valuing both upside-potential operating options, such as to defer an investment or expand production, as well as various downside protection options, such as to abandon for salvage value or switch use (inputs/outputs), and abandon project construction by defaulting on planned, staged future outlays.

Building on the above principles, the chapter subsequently extends the analysis in the presence of financial leverage within a venture capital context and examines the improvement in equityholders' value as a result of additional financial flexibility, noting potential interactions with operating flexibility. The beneficial impact of staging venture capital financing in instalments (thereby creating an option to abandon by the lender, as well as an option to revalue later at potentially better terms by each party), and other issues related to the mix of debt and equity venture capital financing are also explored.

The chapter is organized as follows. Following the comprehensive literature review in Section I, Section II uses an example to motivate discussion of various real options and presents practical principles for valuing several such options. Section III then

---

[1] Parts of Figure 16.1 are adapted from Baldwin and Trigeorgis [8].

Category	Description	Important In	Analyzed by
Option to defer	Management holds a lease on (or an option to buy) valuable land or resource. It can wait (*x* years) to see if output prices justify constructing a building or plant, or developing a field.	All natural resource extraction industries; real estate development; farming; paper products.	Tourinho[98]; Titman[97]; McDonald & Siegel[76]; Paddock, Siegel & Smith[83]; Ingersoll & Ross[44];
Time to build option (staged investment)	Staging investment as a series of outlays creates the option to abandon the enterprise in midstream if new information is unfavorable. Each stage can be viewed as an option on the value of subsequent stages, and valued as a compound option.	All R&D intensive industries, especially pharmaceuticals; long-development capital-intensive projects, e.g., large-scale construction or energy-generating plants; start-up ventures.	Majd & Pindyck[68]; Carr[22]; Trigeorgis[106].
Option to alter operating scale (e.g., to expand; to contract; to shut down and restart)	If market conditions are more favorable than expected, the firm can expand the scale of production or accelerate resource utilization. Conversely, if conditions are *less* favorable than expected, it can reduce the scale of operations. In extreme cases, production may temporarily halt and start up again.	Natural resource industries such as mine operations; facilities planning and construction in cyclical industries; fashion apparel; consumer goods; commercial real estate.	Brennan & Schwartz[19]; McDonald & Siegel[75]; Trigeorgis & Mason[10]; Pindyck[84]
Option to abandon	If market conditions decline severely, management can abandon current operations permanently and realize the resale value of capital equipment and other assets in secondhand markets.	Capital intensive industries, such as airlines and railroads; financial services; new product introductions in uncertain markets.	Myers & Majd[82].
Option to switch (e.g. outputs or inputs)	If prices or demand change, management can change the output mix of the facility ('product' flexibility). Alternatively, the same outputs can be produced using different types of inputs ('process' flexibility).	*Output shifts:* any good sought in small batches or subject to volatile demand, e.g., consumer electronics; toys; specialty paper; machine parts; autos. *Input shifts:* all feedstock-dependent facilities, e.g., oil; electric power, chemicals; crop switching; sourcing.	Margrabe[69]; Kensinger[50]; Kulatilaka[55]; Kulitilaka & Trigeorgis[63].
Growth options	An early investment (e.g., R&D, lease on undeveloped land or oil reserves, strategic acquisition, information network/infrastructure) is a prerequisite or link in a chain of interrelated projects, opening up future growth opportunities (e.g., new generation product or process, oil reserves, access to new market, strengthening of core capabilities). Like inter-project compound options.	All infrastructure-based or strategic industries, especially high-tech, R&D, or industries with multiple product generations or applications (e.g., computers, pharmaceuticals); multinational operations; strategic acquisitions.	Myers[80]; Brealey & Myers[16]; Kester[51,52]; Trigeorgis[100]; Pindyck[84]; Chung & Charoenwong[23].
Multiple interacting options	Real-life projects often involve a 'collection' of various options, both upward-potential enhancing calls and downward-protection put options present in combination. Their combined option value may differ from the sum of separate option values, i.e., they interact. They may also interact with financial flexibility options.	Real-life projects in most industries discussed above.	Brennan & Schwartz[19]; Trigeorgis[106]; Kulatilaka[58]

Figure 16.1. Common Real Options

illustrates how options valuation can be extended to capture interactions with financial flexibility. The last section concludes and discusses some extensions.

1. A REVIEW OF THE REAL OPTIONS LITERATURE

Corporate value creation and competitive position in different markets are critically determined by corporate resource allocation and the evaluation of investment opportunities. The field of capital budgeting remained stagnant for several decades, until recent developments in real options provided the tools and unlocked the possibilities to revolutionize the field. In what follows, I will attempt to describe briefly some stages in the development and evolution of the real options literature, while organizing the presentation around several broad themes. This is not an easy task, and I apologize to those authors and readers who may find my treatment here rather subjective and non-exhaustive.

A. Symptoms, Diagnosis, and Traditional Medicine: Early Critics, the Underinvestment Problem, and Alternative Valuation Paradigms

The real options revolution arose in part as a response to the dissatisfaction of corporate practitioners, strategists, and some academics with traditional capital budgeting techniques. Well before the development of real options, corporate managers and strategists were grappling intuitively with the elusive elements of managerial operating flexibility and strategic interactions. Early critics (e.g., Dean[29], Hayes and Abernathy[35], and Hayes and Garvin[36] recognized that standard discounted cashflow (DCF) criteria often undervalued investment opportunities, leading to myopic decisions, underinvestment and eventual loss of competitive position, because they either ignored or did not properly value important strategic considerations. Decision scientists further maintained that the problem lay in the application of the wrong valuation techniques altogether, proposing instead the use of simulation and decision tree analysis (see Hertz[38] and Magee[67]) to capture the value of future operating flexibility associated with many projects. Proponents (e.g., Hodder and Riggs[41] and Hodder[40]) have argued that the problem arises from misuse of DCF techniques as commonly applied in practice. Myers[81], while confirming that part of the problem results from various misapplications of the underlying theory, acknowledges that traditional DCF methods have inherent limitations when it comes to valuing investments with significant operating or strategic options (e.g., in capturing the sequential interdependence among investments over time), suggesting that option pricing holds the best promise of valuing such investments. Later, Trigeorgis and Mason[110] explain that option valuation can be seen operationally as a special, economically corrected version of decision tree analysis that is better suited in valuing a variety of corporate operating and strategic options, while Teisberg[95] provides a practical comparative discussion of the DCF, decision analysis, and real option valuation paradigms. Baldwin and Clark[5] discuss the importance of organizational capabilities in strategic capital investment, while Baldwin and Trigeorgis[8] propose remedying the underinvestment problem and restoring competitiveness by developing specific adaptive capabilities viewed as an infrastructure for acquiring and managing real options.

B. A New Direction: Conceptual Real Options Approaches

Building on Myers'[80] initial idea of thinking of discretionary investment opportunities as 'growth options', Kester[51] conceptually discusses strategic and competitive aspects of growth opportunities. Other general, conceptual real options frameworks are presented in Mason and Merton[71], Trigeorgis and Mason[110], Trigeorgis[100], Brealey and Myers[16], and Kulatilaka and Marcus[59,60]. Mason and Merton[71], for example, provide a good discussion of many operating as well as financing options, and integrate them in a project financing for a hypothetical, large-scale energy project.

C. Generic Medicine: Foundations and Building Blocks

The quantitative origins of real options, of course, derive from the seminal work of Black and Scholes[13] and Merton[78] in pricing financial options. Cox, Ross, and Rubinstein's[27] binomial approach enabled a more simplified valuation of options in discrete-time. Margrabe[69] values an option to exchange one risky asset for another, while Stulz[94] analyzes options on the maximum (or minimum) of two risky assets and Johnson[45] extends it to several risky assets. These papers have the potential to help analyze the generic options (e.g., abandon for salvage value or switch among alternative inputs or outputs). Geske[31] values a compound option (i.e., an option to acquire another option), which, in principle, may be applied in valuing growth opportunities which become available only if earlier investments are undertaken. Carr[22] combines the above two building blocks to value sequential (compound) exchange options, involving an option to acquire a subsequent option to exchange the underlying asset for another risky alternative. Kulatilaka[55,57] describes an equivalent dynamic programming formulation for the option to switch among operating modes. The above line of work has the potential, in principle, to value investments with a series of investment outlays that can be switched to alternative states of operation, and particularly to eventually help value strategic interproject dependencies.

D. Slightly Different Medicine: Risk-Neutral Valuation and Risk Adjustment

The actual valuation of options in practice has been greatly facilitated by Cox and Ross's[26] recognition that an option can be replicated (or a 'synthetic option' created) from an equivalent portfolio of traded securities. Being independent of risk attitudes or capital market equilibrium considerations, such risk-neutral valuation enables present-value discounting, at the risk-free interest rate, of expected future payoffs (with actual probabilities replaced with risk-neutral ones), a fundamental characteristic of 'arbitrage-free' price systems involving traded securities. Rubinstein[87] further showed that standard option pricing formulas can be alternatively derived under risk aversion, and that the existence of continuous trading opportunities enabling a riskless hedge or risk neutrality are not really necessary. Mason and Merton[71] and Kasanen and Trigeorgis[48] maintain that real options may, in principle, be valued similar to financial options, even though they may not be traded, since in capital budgeting we are interested in determining what the project cash flows would be worth if they were traded in the market, i.e., their contribution to the *market* value of a publicly traded firm. The existence of a traded 'twin security' (or dynamic portfolio) that has the same risk characteristics (i.e., is perfectly correlated) with the nontraded real asset in complete markets is sufficient for real option valuation. More generally, Constantinides[24], Cox, Ingersoll and Ross[28], (lemma[4]), and Harrison and Kreps[34], among others, have suggested that any contingent claim on an asset, traded or not, can be priced in a world with systematic risk by replacing its actual growth rate with a certainty-equivalent rate (by subtracting a risk premium that would be appropriate in market equilibrium), and then behaving as if the world were risk-neutral. This is analogous to discounting certainty-equivalent cash flows at the risk-free rate, rather than actual expected cash flows at a risk-adjusted rate. For traded assets in equilibrium or for those real assets with no systematic risk (e.g., R&D, exploration or drilling for certain precious metals or natural resources), the certainty-equivalent or risk-neutral rate just equals the risk-free interest rate (minus any dividends). However, if the underlying asset is not traded, as may often be the case in capital budgeting associated options, its growth rate may actually fall below the equilibrium total expected return required of an equivalent-risk traded financial security, with the difference or 'rate of return shortfall' necessitating a dividend-like adjustment in option valuation (e.g., see McDonald and Siegel[74,75]. If the underlying asset is traded in futures markets, though, this dividend- (or convenience-yield-) like return shortfall or rate of foregone earnings can be easily derived from the futures prices of contracts with different maturities (see Brennan and Schwartz[19]). In other cases, however, estimating this return shortfall may require use of a market equilibrium model (e.g., see McDonald and Siegel[75]).

E. A Tablet for Each Case: Valuing Each Different Real Option Separately

There came a series of papers which gave a boost to the real options literature by focusing on valuing quantitatively—in many cases, deriving analytic, closed-form solutions—one type after another of a variety of real options, although each option was typically analyzed in isolation. As summarized in Figure 16.1, the option to defer or initiate investment has been examined by McDonald and Siegel[76], by Paddock, Siegel, and Smith[83] in valuing offshore petroleum leases, and by Tourinho[98] in valuing reserves of natural resources. Ingersoll and Ross[44] reconsider the decision to wait in light of the beneficial impact of a potential future interest rate decline on project value. Majd and Pindyck[68] value the option to delay sequential construction for projects that take time to build, or there is a maximum rate at which investment can proceed. Carr[22] and Trigeorgis[106] also deal with valuing sequential or staged (compound) investments. Trigeorgis and Mason[110] and Pindyck[84] examine options to alter (i.e., expand or contract) operating scale or capacity choice. The option to temporarily shut down and restart operations was analyzed by McDonald and Siegel[75] and by Brennan and Schwartz[19]. Myers and Majd[82] analyze the option to permanently abandon a project for its salvage value seen as an American put option. Options to switch use (i.e., outputs or inputs) have been examined, among others, by Margrabe[69], Kensinger[50], Kulatilaka[55], and Kulatilaka and Trigeorgis[63]. Baldwin and Ruback[7] show that future price uncertainty creates a valuable switching option that benefits short-lived projects. Future investment opportunities that are seen as corporate growth options are discussed in Myers[80], Brealey and Myers[16], Kester[51,52], Trigeorgis and Mason[110], Trigeorgis[100], Pindyck[84], and Chung and Charoenwong[23].

F. The Tablets Interact: Multiple Options and Interdependencies

Despite its enormous theoretical contribution, the focus of the earlier literature on valuing individual real options (i.e., one type of option at a time) has nevertheless limited its practical value. Real-life projects are often more complex in that they involve a collection of multiple real options whose values may interact. An early exception is Brennan and Schwartz[19], who determine the combined value of the options to shut down (and restart) a mine, and to abandon it for salvage. They recognize that partial irreversibility resulting from the costs of switching the mine's operating state may create a persistence, inertia or *hysteresis* effect, making it long-term optimal to remain in the same operating state even though short-term consider-ations (i.e., current cash flows) may seem to favor immediate switching. Although hysteresis can be seen as a form of interaction between early and later decisions, Brennan and Schwartz do not explicitly address the interactions among individual option values. Trigeorgis[106] focuses on the nature of real option interactions, pointing out, for example, that the presence of subsequent options can increase the value of the effective underlying asset for earlier options, while exercise of prior real options may alter (e.g., expand or contract) the underlying asset itself, and hence the value of subsequent options on it. Thus, the combined value of a collection of real options may differ from the sum of separate option values. Using a numerical analysis method suitable for valuing complex multi-option investments (Trigeorgis[104]), he presents the valuation of options to defer, abandon, contract or expand investment, and switch use in the context of a generic investment, first with each option in isolation and later in combination. He shows, for example, that the incremental value of an additional option, in the presence of other options, is generally less than its value in isolation and declines as more options are present. More generally, he identifies situations where option interactions can be small or large and negative as well as positive. Kulatilaka[58] subsequently examines the impact of interactions among three such options on their optimal exercise schedules. The recent recognition of real option interdependencies should subsequently enable a smoother transition from a theoretical stage to an application phase.

G. The Bitter Pill: Numerical Techniques

In the more complex real-life option situations, such as those involving multiple inter-acting real option, analytic solutions may not exist and one may not even be always able to write down the partial differential equations describing the underlying stochas-tic processes. The ability to value such complex option situations has been enhanced, however, with various numerical analysis techniques, many of which take advantage of risk-neutral valuation. Generally, there are two types of numerical techniques for option valuation: (*i*) those that approximate the underlying stochastic processes dir-ectly and are generally more intuitive; and (*ii*) those approximating the resulting partial differential equations. The first category includes Monte Carlo simulation used by Boyle[14], and various lattice approaches such as Cox, Ross, and Rubinstein's[27] standard binomial lattice method, and Trigeorgis'[104] log-transformed binomial method; the latter are particularly well-suited to valuing complex projects with mul-tiple embedded real options, a series of investment outlays, dividend-like effects, as well as option interactions. Boyle[15] shows how lattice frameworks can be extended to handle two state variables, while Hull and White[43] suggest a control variate technique to improve computational efficiency when a similar derivative asset with an analytic solution is available. Examples of the second category include numerical integration, and implicit or explicit finite difference schemes used by Brennan[17], Brennan and Schwartz[18], and Majd and Pindyck[68]. Finally, a number of analytic approximations are also available: Geske and Johnson[32] have proposed a compound-option analytic polynomial approximation approach; Barone-Adesi and Whaley[9] have suggested a quadratic approximation, while others have used various problem-specific heuristic approximations. A comprehensive review of such numerical techniques is given in the articles by Geske and Shastri[33] and Trigeorgis[104], as well as in a book by Hull[42].

H. The General Environment: Competition and Strategic Options

An important area that deserves more attention, and where real options have the potential to make a significant difference, is that of competition and strategy. Sustainable competitive advantages resulting from patents, proprietary technologies, ownership of valuable natural resources, managerial capital, reputation or brand name, scale, and market power, empower companies with valuable options to grow through future profitable investments and to more effectively respond to unexpected adversity or opportunities in a changing technological, competitive, or general business environment. A number of economists have addressed several competitive and strategic aspects of capital investment early on. For example, Roberts and Weitzman[86] find that in sequential decision-making, it may be worthwhile to undertake investments with negative NPV when early investment can provide information about future project benefits, especially when their uncertainty is greater. Baldwin[3] finds that optimal sequential investment for firms with market power facing irreversible decisions may require a positive premium over NPV to compensate for the loss in value of future opportunities that results from undertaking an investment. Pindyck[84] analyzes options to choose capacity under product price uncertainty when investment is, again, irreversible. Dixit[30] considers firm entry and exit decisions under uncertainty, showing that in the presence of sunk or switching costs it may not be long-term optimal to reverse a decision even when prices appear attractive in the short-term. Bell[10] combines Dixit's entry and exit decisions with Pindyck's capacity options for the multinational firm under volatile exchange rates. Kogut and Kulatilaka[53] analyze the international plant location option in the presence of mean-reverting exchange rate volatility, while Kulatilaka and Marks[61] examine the strategic bargaining value of flexibility in the firm's negotiations with input suppliers.

From a more explicit real options perspective, a number of authors (e.g., Myers[81], Kester[51,52], Trigeorgis and Mason[110], Trigeorgis[100], Brealey and Myers[16], and Trigeorgis and Kasanen[109] have initially dealt with competitive and strategic options rather conceptually. For example, Kester[51] develops qualitatively various competitive and strategic aspects of inter-project growth options, while Kester[52] proposes a planned sequential, rather than parallel, implementation of a collection of interrelated consumer products when learning results from early product introductions (e.g., about available shelf space needed for similar subsequent products) and when competitive advantage is eroding. Trigeorgis and Kasanen[109] also examine sequential project interdependencies and synergies as part of an ongoing strategic planning and control process. Kasanen[47] also deals with the strategic problem of the interaction between current investments and future opportunities, using the rather novel concept of a spawning matrix structure (capturing the firm's ability to generate investment opportunities *across* projects through feedback effects) to determine an optimal mix of strategic and operating projects.

Trigeorgis[103] uses quantitative option pricing techniques to examine early investment that may preempt anticipated competitive entry, and to value the option to defer investment when impacted by random competitive entry (Trigeorgis[102]). Ang and Dukas[2] incorporate both competitive and asymmetric information, arguing that the time pattern of discounted cash flows also matters due to the possibility of premature project termination as a result of random competitive entry. Further departing from the common assumption of perfect competition, Kulatilaka and Perotti[62] examine how the investment decisions of a firm will influence the production decisions of competitors and the market price when early investment generates a cost advantage. Smit and Ankum[91] combine the real options approach to investment timing with basic principles from game theory and industrial organization to explore various investment timing strategies in follow-up projects based on the reaction of competitors under different market structures. Supplementing options analysis with game theoretic tools capable of incorporating strategic competitive counteractions promises to be an important and challenging direction for future research.

I. Cure for All Kinds of Cases: A Variety of Applications

Besides theoretical developments, real option applications are currently also receiving increased attention. Real options valuation has been applied in a variety of contexts, such as in natural resource investments, land development, leasing, flexible manufacturing, government subsidies and regulation, R&D, new ventures and acquisitions, foreign investment and strategy, and elsewhere.

Early applications naturally arose in the area of *natural resource investments* due to the availability of traded resource or commodity prices, high volatilities and long durations, resulting in higher and better option value estimates. Brennan and Schwartz[19] first utilize the convenience yield derived from futures and spot prices of a commodity to value the options to shut down or abandon a mine. Paddock, Siegel, and Smith[83] value options embedded in undeveloped oil reserves and provide the first empirical evidence that option values are better than actual DCF-based bids in valuing offshore oil leases. Trigeorgis[101] values an actual minerals project considered by a major multinational company involving options to cancel during construction, expand production, and abandon for salvage. Bjerksund and Ekern[11] value a Norwegian oil field with options to defer and abandon. Mørck, Schwartz, and Stangeland[79] value forestry resources under stochastic inventories and prices. Stensland and Tjostheim[93] also discuss some applications of dynamic programming to natural resource exploration. Laughton and Jacoby[65] examine biases in the valuation of real options and long-term decision-making when a mean-reversion price process is more appropriate, as may be the case in certain commodity projects, than the traditional Brownian motion or random walk assumption. They find that ignoring reversion would overestimate long-term uncertainty, but may over- or undervalue associated timing options. On the more applied side, Kemna[49] shares her experiences with Shell in analyzing actual cases involving the timing of developing an offshore oil field, valuing a growth option in a manufacturing venture, and the abandonment decision of a refining production unit, and discusses problem formulation and implementation issues in the process of adapting option theory in practice.

In the area of *land development*, Titman[97], Williams[111], Capozza and Sick[21], and Quigg[85B] show that the value of vacant land should reflect not only its value based on its best immediate use (e.g., from constructing a building now), but also its option value if development is delayed and the land is converted into its best alternative use in the future. It may thus pay to hold land vacant for its option value even in the presence of currently thriving real estate markets. Quigg[85A] reports empirical results indicating that option-based land valuation that incorporates the option to wait to develop land provides better approximations of actual market prices. In a different context, McLaughlin and Taggart[77] view the opportunity cost of using excess capacity as the change in the value of the firm's options caused by diverting capacity to an alternative use. In *leasing*, Copeland and Weston[25], Lee, Martin, and Senchack[66], McConnell and Schallheim[73], and Trigeorgis[105] value various operating options embedded in leasing contracts.

In the area of *flexible manufacturing*, the flexibility provided by flexible manufacturing systems, flexible production technology or other machinery having multiple uses has been analyzed from an options perspective by Kulatilaka[55], Triantis and Hodder[99], Aggarwal[1], Kulatilaka and Trigeorgis[63] and Kamrad and Ernst[46] among others. Kulatilaka[56] values the flexibility provided by an actual dual-fuel industrial steam boiler that can switch between alternative energy inputs (natural gas and oil) as their relative prices fluctuate, and finds that the value of this flexibility far exceeds the incremental cost over a rigid, single-fuel alternative. Baldwin and Clark[6] study the flexibility created by modularity in design that connects components of a larger system through standard interfaces.

In the area of *government subsidies and regulation*, Mason and Baldwin[70] value government subsidies to large-scale energy projects as put options, while Teisberg[96] provides an option valuation analysis of investment choices by a regulated firm. In *research and development*, Kolbe, Morris, and Teisberg[54] discuss option elements embedded in R&D projects. Option elements involved in the staging of *start-up ventures* are discussed in Sahlman[88], Willner[112], and this article. Strategic *acquisitions* of other companies also often involve a number of growth, divestiture, and other flexibility options, as discussed by Smith and Triantis[92]. Other applications of options in the strategy area were discussed in Section I.H. earlier. On the empirical side, Kester[51] estimates that the value of a firm's growth options is more than half the market value of equity for many firms, even 70–80% for more volatile industries. Similarly, Pindyck[84] also suggests that growth options represent more than half of firm value if demand volatility exceeds 20%. In *foreign investment*, Baldwin[4] discusses various location, timing and staging options present when firms scan the global marketplace. Bell[10] and Kogut and Kulatilaka[53], among others, examine entry, capacity, and switching options for firms with multinational operations under exchange rate volatility. Hiraki[39] suggests that the Japanese bank-oriented corporate governance system serves as the basic infrastructure that enables companies to jointly develop corporate real options.

Various other option applications can be found in areas ranging from *shipping* (Bjerksund and Ekern[12]) to *environmental pollution and global warming* (e.g. Hendricks[37]. The potential for future applications itself seems like a growth option.

J. Other Sources and Future Research Directions

Other comprehensive treatments of real options can be found in the articles by Mason and Merton[71] and Trigeorgis and Mason[110], a monograph by Sick[89], an economics review article by Pindyck[85], as well as in a volume edited by Trigeorgis[107] and a book from MIT Press (Trigeorgis[108]). The Spring 1987 Issue of the *Midland Corporate Finance Journal* and a 1991 Special Issue of *Managerial Finance* (Vol. 17, No. 2/3) have also been devoted to real options and capital budgeting. In *Financial Management*, Autumn 1993, the articles by Laughton and Jacoby[65], Smit and Ankum[91], and Kasanen[47] are indicative of an active literature that is evolving in several new directions in modelling, competition and strategy, while the articles by Kemna[49] and Kulatilaka[56] represent recent attempts to implement real options valuation in actual case applications. Clearly, an increased attention to application and implementation issues is the next stage in the evolution of real options.

In addition to more actual case applications and tackling real-life implementation issues and problems, fruitful directions for future research, in both theory and practice, include:

(i)   Focusing more on investments (such as in R&D, pilot or market tests, or excavations) that can 'generate' information and learning (e.g., about the project's prospects) by extending/adjusting option pricing and risk-neutral valuation with Bayesian analysis or alternative (e.g., jump) processes.

(ii)   Exploring in more depth endogenous competitive counteractions and a variety of competitive/market structure and strategic issues using a combination of game-theoretic industrial organization with option valuation tools.

(iii) Modelling better the various strategic and growth options.

(iv)   Extending real options in an agency context recognizing that the potential (theoretical) value of real options may not be realized in practice if managers, in pursuing their own agenda (e.g., expansion or growth, rather than firm value maximization), misuse their discretion and do not follow the optimal exercise policies implicit in option valuation. This raises the need to design proper corrective incentive contracts by the firm (taking also into account asymmetric information).

(v)   Recognizing better that real options may interact not only among themselves but with financial flexibility options as well, and understanding the resulting implications for the combined interdependent corporate investment and financing decisions. In Section III, we take a first step toward recognizing such interactions among real and financial flexibility options.

(vi)   On the practical side, applying real options to the valuation of flexibility in related areas, such as in competitive bidding, information technology or other platform investments, energy and R&D problems, international finance options, and so on.

(vii)   Using real options to explain empirical phenomena that are amenable to observation or statistical testing, such as examining empirically whether managements of firms that are targets for acquisition may sometimes turn down tender offers in part due to the option to wait in anticipation of receiving better future offers.

(viii)   Conducting more field, survey, or empirical studies to test the conformity of theoretical real option valuation and its implications with management's intuition and experience, as well as with actual price data when available.

II. REAL OPTIONS: AN EXAMPLE AND VALUATION PRINCIPLES

This section discusses conceptually the basic nature of different real options through a comprehensive example, and then illustrates some practical principles for valuing such options. To facilitate our discussion of the various real options that may be embedded in capital investments, consider first the following example.

A. Example: An Oil Extraction and Refinery Project

A large oil company has a one-year lease to start drilling on undeveloped land with potential oil reserves. Initiating the project may require certain exploration costs, to be followed by construction of roads and other infrastructure outlays, I_1. This would be followed by outlays for the construction of a new processing facility, I_2. Extraction can begin only after construction is completed, i.e., cash flows are generated only during the 'operating stage' that follows the last outlay. During construction, if market conditions deteriorate, management can choose to forego any future planned outlays. Management may also choose to reduce the scale of operation by $c\%$, saving a portion of the last outlay, I_C, if the market is weak. The processing plant can be designed upfront such that, if oil prices turn out higher than expected, the rate of production can be enhanced by $x\%$ with a follow-up outlay of I_E. At any time, management may salvage a portion of its investment by selling the plant and equipment for their salvage value or switch them to an alternative use value, A. An associated refinery plant—which may be designed to operate with alternative sources of energy inputs—can convert crude oil into a variety of refined products. This type of project presents the following collection of real options:

(i)   *The option to defer investment.* The lease enables management to defer investment for up to one year and benefit from the resolution of uncertainty about oil prices during this period. Management would invest I_1 (i.e., exercise its option to extract oil) *only* if oil prices increase sufficiently, but would not commit to the project, saving the planned outlays, if prices decline. Just before expiration of the lease, the value creation will be $\max(V - I_1, 0)$. The option to defer is thus analogous to an American call option on the gross present value of the completed project's expected operating cash flows, V, with the exercise price being equal to the required outlay, I_1. Since early investment implies sacrificing the option to wait, this option value loss is like an additional investment opportunity cost, justifying investment only if the value of cash benefits, V, actually exceeds the initial outlay by a substantial premium. As noted in Figure 16.1, the option to wait is particularly valuable in resource extraction industries, farming, paper products, and real estate development due to high uncertainties and long investment horizons.

(ii) *The option to default during construction (or the time-to-build option).* In most real-life projects, the required investment is not incurred as a single upfront outlay. The actual staging of capital investment as a series of outlays over time creates valuable options to 'default' at any given stage (e.g., after exploration if the reserves or oil prices turn out very low). Thus, each stage (e.g., building necessary infrastructure) can be viewed as an option on the value of subsequent stages by incurring the installment cost outlay (e.g., I_1) required to proceed to the next stage, and can therefore be valued similar to compound options. This option is valuable in all R&D intensive industries, especially pharmaceuticals, in highly uncertain, long-development capital intensive industries, such as energy-generating plants or large-scale construction, and in venture capital.

(iii) *The option to expand.* If oil prices or other market conditions turn out more favorable than expected, management can actually accelerate the rate or expand the scale of production (by $x\%$) by incurring a follow-up cost outlay (I_E). This is similar to a call option to acquire an additional part ($x\%$) of the base-scale project, paying I_E as exercise price. The investment opportunity with the option to expand can be viewed as the base-scale project plus a call option on future investment, i.e., $V + \max(xV - I_E, 0)$. Given an initial design choice, management may deliberately favor a more expensive technology for the built-in flexibility to expand production if and when it becomes desirable. As discussed further below, the option to expand may also be of strategic importance, especially if it enables the firm to capitalize on future growth opportunities. As noted, when the firm buys vacant undeveloped land, or when it builds a small plant in a new geographic location (domestic or overseas) to position itself to take advantage of a developing large market, it essentially installs an expansion/growth option. This option, which will be exercised only if future market developments turn out favorable, can make a seemingly unprofitable (based on static NPV) base-case investment worth undertaking.

(iv) *The option to contract.* If market conditions are weaker than originally expected, management can operate below capacity or even reduce the scale of operations (by 0%), thereby saving part of the planned investment outlays (I_C). This flexibility to mitigate loss is analogous to a put option on part ($c\%$) of the base-scale project, with exercise price equal to the potential cost savings (I_C), giving $\max(I_C - cV, 0)$. The option to contract, just as the option to expand, may be particularly valuable in the case of new product introductions in uncertain markets. The option to contract may also be important, for example, in choosing among technologies or plants with a different construction to maintenance cost mix, where it may be preferable to build a plant with lower initial construction costs and higher maintenance expenditures in order to acquire the flexibility to contract operations by cutting down on maintenance if market conditions turn out unfavorable.

(v)   *The option to shut down (and restart) operations.* In real life, the plant does not have to operate (i.e., extract oil) in each and every period automatically. In fact, if oil prices are such that cash revenues are not sufficient to cover variable operating (e.g., maintenance) costs, it might be better not to operate temporarily, especially if the costs of switching between the operating and idle modes are relatively small. If prices rise sufficiently, operations can start again. Thus, operation in each year can be seen as a call option to acquire that year's cash revenues (C) by paying the variable costs of operating (I_V) as exercise price, i.e., $\max(C - I_V, 0)$.[2] Options to alter the operating scale (i.e., expand, contract, or shut down) are typically found in natural resource industries, such as mine operations, facilities planning and construction in cyclical industries, fashion apparel, consumer goods, and commercial real estate.

(vi) *The option to abandon for salvage value.* If oil prices suffer a sustainable decline or the operation does poorly for some other reason, management does not have to continue incurring the fixed costs. Instead management may have a valuable option to abandon the project permanently in exchange for its salvage value (i.e., the resale value of its capital equipment and other assets in secondhand markets). As noted, this option can be valued as an American put option on current project value (V) with exercise price the salvage or best alternative use value (A), entitling management to receive $V + \max(A - V, 0)$ or $\max(V, A)$. Naturally, more general-purpose capital assets would have a higher salvage and option abandonment value than special-purpose assets. Valuable abandonment options are generally found in capital intensive industries, such as in airlines and railroads, in financial services, as well as in new product introductions in uncertain markets.

(vii) *The option to switch use (i.e., inputs or outputs).* Suppose the associated oil refinery operation can be designed to use alternative forms of energy inputs (e.g., fuel oil, gas, or electricity) to convert crude oil into a variety of output products (e.g., gasoline, lubricants, or polyester). This would provide valuable built-in flexibility to switch from the current input to the cheapest future input, or from the current output to the most profitable future product mix, as the relative prices of the inputs or outputs fluctuate over time. In fact, the firm should be willing to pay a certain positive premium for such a flexible technology over a rigid alternative that confers no choice or less choice. Indeed, if the firm can in this way develop extra uses for its assets over its competitors, it may be at a significant advantage. Generally, 'process' flexibility can be achieved not only via technology (e.g., by building a flexible facility that can switch among alternative energy 'inputs'), but also by maintaining relationships with a variety of suppliers, changing the mix as their relative prices change. Subcontracting policies may allow further flexibility to contract the scale of future operations at a low cost in case of unfavorable market developments. As noted, a multinational

---

[2] Alternatively, management has an option to obtain project value V (net of fixed costs, I_F) minus variable costs (I_V), or shut down and receive project value minus that year's foregone cash revenue (C), i.e., $\max(V - I_V, V - C) - I_F = (V - I_F) - \min(I_V, C)$. The latter expression implies that the option not to operate enables management to acquire project value (net of fixed costs) by paying the minimum of variable costs (if the project does well and management decides to operate) or the cash revenues (that would be sacrificed if the project does poorly and it chooses not to operate).

oil company may similarly locate production facilities in various countries in order to acquire the flexibility to shift production to the lowest-cost producing facilities, as the relative costs, other local market conditions, or exchange rates change over time. Process flexibility is valuable in feedstock-dependent facilities, such as oil, electric power, chemicals, and crop switching. 'Product' flexibility, enabling the firm to switch among alternative 'outputs', is more valuable in industries such as automobiles, consumer electronics, toys or pharmaceuticals, where product differentiation and diversity are important and/or product demand is volatile. In such cases, it may be worthwhile to install a more costly flexible capacity to acquire the ability to alter product mix of production scale in response to changing many demands.

(viii) *Corporate growth options.* As noted, another version of the earlier option to expand of considerable strategic importance are corporate growth options that set the path of future opportunities. Suppose in the above example, that the proposed refinery facility is based on a new, technologically superior 'process' for oil refinement developed and tested internally on a pilot plant basis. Although the proposed facility in isolation may appear unattractive it could be only the first in a series of similar facilities if the process is successfully developed and commercialized, and may even lead to entirely new oil by-products. More generally, many early investments (e.g., R&D, a lease on undeveloped land or a tract with potential oil reserves, a strategic acquisition, or an information technology network) can be seen as prerequisites or links in a chain of interrelated projects. The value of these projects may derive not so much from their expected directly measurable cash flows, but rather from unlocking future growth opportunities (e.g. a new-generation product or process, oil reserves, access to a new or expanding market, strengthening of the firm's core capabilities or strategic positioning). An opportunity to invest in a first-generation high-tech product, for example, is analogous to an option on options (an interproject compound option). Despite a seemingly negative NPV, the infrastructure, experience, and potential products generated during the development of the first-generation product may serve as springboards for developing lower-cost or improved-quality future generations of that product, or even for generating new applications into other areas. But unless the firm makes that initial investment, subsequent generations or other applications would not even be feasible. The infrastructure and experience gained can be proprietary and can place the firm at a competitive advantage, which may even reinforce itself if learning cost curve effects are present. Growth options are found in all infrastructure-based or strategic industries, especially in high-tech, R&D, or industries with multiple product generations or applications (e.g., semiconductors, computers, pharmaceuticals), in multinational operations, and in strategic acquisitions.

In a more general context, such operating and strategic adaptability represented by corporate real options can be achieved at various stages during the value chain, from switching the factor input mix among various suppliers and subcontracting practices, to rapid product design (e.g., computer-aided design) and modularity in design, to shifting production among various products rapidly and cost-efficiently in a flexible manufacturing system. The next section illustrates, through simple numerical examples, basic practical principles for valuing several of the above real options. For expositional simplicity, we will subsequently ignore any return shortfall or other dividend-like effects (see Section I.D. above for appropriate adjustments).

B. Principles of Valuing Various Real Options

Consider, as in Trigeorgis and Mason[110],[3] valuing a generic investment opportunity (e.g., similar to the above oil extraction project). Specifically, suppose we are faced with an opportunity to invest $I_0 = \$104$ (in millions) in an oil project whose (gross) value in each period will either move up by 80% or down by 40%, depending on oil price fluctuations: a year later, the project will have an expected value (from subsequent cash flows) of $180 (million) if the oil price moves up ($C^+ = 180$) or $60 if it moves down ($C^- = 60$).[4] There is an equal probability ($q = 0.5$) that the price of oil will move up or down in any year. Let S be the price of oil, or generally of a 'twin security' that is traded in the financial markets and has the same risk characteristics (i.e., is perfectly correlated) with the real project under consideration (such as the stock price of a similar operating unlevered oil company). Both the project and its twin security (or oil prices) have an expected rate of return (or discount rate) of $k = 20\%$, while the risk-free interest rate is $r = 8\%$.

In what follows, we assume throughout that the value of the project (i.e., the value, in millions of dollars, in each year, t, of its subsequent expected cash flows appropriately discounted back to that year), V_t, and its twin security price (e.g., a twin oil stock price in $ per share, or simply the price of oil in $ per barrel), S_t, move through time as follows:

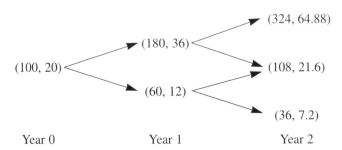

For example, the pair (V_0, S_0) above represents a current gross project value of $100 million, and a spot oil price of $20 a barrel (or a $20 per share twin oil stock price). Under traditional (passive) NPV analysis, the current gross project value would be obtained first by discounting the project's end-of-period values (derived from subsequent cash flows), using the expected rate of return of the project's twin security (or, here, of oil prices) as the appropriate discount rate, i.e., $V_0 = (0.5 \times 180 + 0.5 \times 60)/1.20 = 100$. Note that this gross project value is, in this case, exactly proportional to the twin

---

[3] Trigeorgis and Mason[110] use a similar example to show how options-based valuation can be seen operationally as a special, though economically corrected, version of decision tree analysis (DTA) that recognizes open-market opportunities to trade and borrow.

[4] All project values are hereafter assumed to be in millions of dollars (with 'millions' subsequently dropped).

security price (or the spot oil price). After subtracting the current investment costs, $I_0 = 104$, the project's NPV is finally given by:

$$NPV = V_0 - I_0 = 100 - 104 = -4 \ (<0). \tag{2}$$

In the absence of managerial flexibility or real options, traditional DCF analysis would have rejected this project based on its negative NPV. However, passive DCF is unable to properly capture the value of embedded options because of their discretionary asymmetric nature and dependence on future events that are uncertain at the time of the initial decision. The fundamental problem, of course, lies in the valuation of investment opportunities whose claims are not symmetric or proportional and whose discount rates vary in a complex way over time.

Nevertheless, such real options can be properly valued using contingent claims analysis (CCA) within a backward risk-neutral valuation process.[5] Essentially, the same solution can be obtained in our actual risk-averse world as a 'risk-neutral' world in which the current value of any contingent claim could be obtained from its expected future values—with expectations taken over the risk-neutral probabilities, p, imputed from the twin security's (or oil) prices—discounted at the riskless rate, r. In such a risk-neutral world, the current (beginning of the period) value of the project (or of equityholders' claim), E, is given by:

$$E = \frac{pE^+ + (1 - Ip)E^-}{(1 + r)}.$$

where

$$p = \frac{(1 + r)S - S^-}{(S^+ - S^-)}. \tag{3}$$

The probability, p, can be estimated from the price dynamic of the twin security (or of oil prices):

$$p = \frac{(1.08 \times 20) - 12}{36 - 12} = 0.4$$

Note that the value for $p = 0.4$ is distinct from the actual probability, $q = 0.5$ and can be used to determine 'certainty-equivalent' values (or expected cash flows) which can be properly discounted at the risk-free rate. For example,

$$V_0 = \frac{pC^+ + (1 - p)C^-}{(1 + r)} = \frac{0.4 \times 180 + 0.6 \times 60}{1.08} = 100. \tag{4}[6]$$

In what follows, we assume that if any part of the required investment outlay (having present value of \$104 million) is not going to be spent immediately but in future

---

[5] As noted, the basic idea is that management can replicate the payoff to equity by purchasing a specified number of shares of the 'twin security' and financing the purchase in part by borrowing a specific amount at the riskless interest rate, r. This ability to construct a 'synthetic' claim or an equivalent/replicating portfolio (from the 'twin security' and riskless bonds) based on no-arbitrage equilibrium principles enables the solution for the current value of the equity claim to be independent of the actual probabilities (in this case, 0.5) or investors' risk attitudes (the twin security's expected rate of return or discount rate, $k = 0.20$).
[6] This confirms the gross project value, $V_0 = 100$, obtained earlier using traditional DCF with the actual probability ($q = 0.5$) and the risk-adjusted discount rate ($k = 0.20$).

installments, that amount is placed in an escrow account earning the riskless interest rate.[7] We next illustrate how various kinds of both upside-potential options, such as to defer or expand, and downside-protection options, such as to abandon for salvage or default during construction, can enhance the value of the opportunity to invest (i.e., the value of equity or NPV) in the above generic project, under the standard assumption of all-equity financing. Our focus here is on basic principles for valuing one kind of operating option at a time.

1. The Option to Defer Investment

The company has a one-year lease providing it a proprietary right to defer undertaking the project (i.e., extracting the oil) for a year, thus benefiting from the resolution of uncertainty about oil prices over this period. Although undertaking the project immediately has a negative NPV (of –4), the opportunity to invest afforded by the lease has a positive worth since management would invest *only* if oil prices and project value rise sufficiently, while it has no obligation to invest under unfavorable developments. Since the option to wait is analogous to a call option on project value, V, with an exercise price equal to the required outlay next year, $I_1 = 112.32 (= 1.04 \times 1.08)$:

$$E^+ = \max(V^+ - I_1, 0) = \max(180 - 112.32, 0) = 67.68.$$

$$E^- = \max(V^- - I_1, 0) = \max(60 - 112.32, 0) = 0. \tag{5}$$

The project's total value (i.e., the expanded NPV that includes the value of the option to defer) from Equation (3) is:

$$E_0 = \frac{pE^+ + (1-p)E^-}{(1+r)} = \frac{0.4 \times 67.68 + 0.6 \times 0}{1.08} = 25.07. \tag{6}$$

From Equation (1), the value of the option to defer provided by the lease itself is thus given by:

$$\text{Option to defer} = \text{expanded NPV} - \text{passive NPV} = 25.07 - (-4) = 29.07 \tag{7}$$

which, incidentally, is equal to almost one-third of the project's gross value.[8]

---

[7] This assumption is intended to make the analysis somewhat more realistic and invariant to the cost structure make-up, and is not at all crucial to the analysis.

[8] The above example confirms that CCA is operationally identical to decision tree analysis (DTA), with the key difference that the probabilities are transformed so as to allow the use of a risk-free discount rate. Note, however, that the DCF/DTA value of waiting may differ from that given by CCA. The DCF/DTA approach in this case will overestimate the value of the option if it discounts at the constant 20% rate required of securities comparable in risk to the 'naked' (passive) project:

$$E_0 = \frac{qE^+ + (1-q)E^-}{(1+k)} = \frac{0.5 \times 67.68 + 0.5 \times 0}{1.20} = 28.20.$$

Again, the error in the traditional DTA approach arises from the use of single (or constant) risk-adjusted discount rate. Asymmetric claims on an asset do not have the same riskiness (and hence expected rate of return) as the underlying asset itself. CCA corrects for this error by transforming the probabilities.

2. The Option to Expand (Growth Option)

Once the project is undertaken, any necessary infrastructure is completed and the plant is operating, management may have the option to accelerate the rate or expand the scale of production by, say 50% ($x = 0.50$) by incurring a follow-up investment outlay of $I_E = 40$, provided oil prices and general market conditions turn out better than originally expected. thus, in year 1 management can choose either to maintain the base scale operation (i.e., receive project value, V, at no extra cost) or expand by 50% the scale and project value by incurring the extra outlay. That is, the original investment opportunity is seen as the initial-scale project plus a call option on a future opportunity, or $E = V + \max(xV - I_E, 0) = \max(V, (1 + x)V - I_E)$:

$$E^+ = \max(V^+, 1.5V^+ - I_E) = \max(180, 270 - 40) = 230$$

i.e., expand;

$$E^- = \max(V^-, 1.5V^- - I_E) = \max(60, 90 - 40) = 60 \tag{8}$$

i.e., maintain base scale. The value of the investment opportunity (including the value of the option to expand if market conditions turn out better than expected) then becomes:

$$E_0 = \frac{pE^+ + (1 - p)E^-}{(1 + r)} - I_0 = \frac{0.4 \times 230 + 0.6 \times 60}{1.08} - 100 = 14.5. \tag{9}$$

and thus the value of the option to expand is:

$$\text{Option to expand} = 14.5 - (-4) = 18.5, \tag{10}$$

or 18.5% of the gross project value.

3. Options to Abandon for Salvage Value or Switch Use

In terms of downside protection, management has the option to abandon the oil extraction project at any time in exchange for its salvage value or value in its best alternative use, if oil prices suffer a sustainable decline. The associated oil refinery plant also can use alternative energy inputs and has the flexibility to convert crude oil into a variety of products. As market conditions change and the relative price of inputs, outputs or the plant resale value in a secondhand market fluctuate, equity holders may find it preferable to abandon the current project's use by switching to a cheaper input, a more profitable output, or simply sell the plant's assets to the second-hand market. Let the project's value in its best alternative use, A, (or the salvage value for which it can be exchanged) fluctuate over time as:

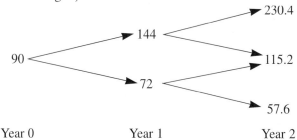

Year 0	Year 1	Year 2

Note that the project's current salvage or alternative use value ($A_0 = 90$) is below the project's value in its present use ($V_0 = 100$)—otherwise management would have switched use immediately—and has the same expected rate of return (20%); it nevertheless has a smaller variance so that if the market keeps moving up it would not be optimal to abandon the project early for its salvage value, but if it moves down management may find it desirable to switch use (e.g., in year 1 exchange the present use value of $V_1 = 60$ for a higher alternative use value of $A_1 = 72$).[9] Thus, equityholders can choose the maximum of the project's value in its present use, V, or its value in the best alternative use, A, i.e., $E = \max(V, A)$:

$$E^+ = \max(V^+, A^+) = \max(180, 144) = 180 = V^+,$$

i.e., continue;

$$E^- = \max(V^-, A^-) = \max(60, 72) = 72 = A^-, \tag{11}$$

i.e., switch use. The value of the investment (including the option to abandon early or switch use) is then:

$$E_0 = \frac{pE^+ + (1-p)E^-}{(1+r)} - I_0 = \frac{0.4 \times 180 + 0.6 \times 72}{1.08} - 104 = + 2.67 \tag{12}$$

so that the project with the option to switch use is now desirable. The value of the option itself is:

$$\text{Option to switch use} = 2.67 - (-4) = 6.67, \tag{13}$$

or almost seven percent of the project's gross value. This value is clearly dependent on the schedule of salvage or alternative use values.

4. The Option to Default (on Planned Staged Cost Installments) During Construction

Even during the construction phase, management may abandon a project to save any subsequent investment outlays, if the coming required investment exceeds the value from continuing the project (including any future options). Suppose that the investment (of $104 present value) necessary to implement the oil extraction project can be staged as a series of 'installments': $I_0 = \$44$ out of the $104 allocated amount will need to be paid out immediately (in year 0) as a start-up cost for infrastructure, with the $60 balance placed in an escrow account (earning the risk-free rate) planned to be paid as a $I_1 = \$64.8$ follow-up outlay for constructing the processing plant in year 1. Next year management will then pay the investment cost 'installment' as planned only in return for a higher project value from continuing, or else it will forego the investment and receive nothing. Thus, the option to default when investment is staged sequentially during construction translates into $E = \max(V - I_1, 0)$:

---

[9] We assume here for simplicity that the project's value in its current use and in its best alternative use (or salvage value) are perfectly positively correlated. Of course, the option to switch use would be even more valuable the lower the correlation between V and A.

$$E^+ = \max(V^+ - I_1, 0) = \max(180 - 64.8, 0) = 115.2,$$

i.e., continue;

$$E^- = \max(V^- - I_1, 0) = \max(60 - 64.8, 0) = 0. \tag{14}$$

i.e., default. The value of the investment opportunity (with the option to default on future outlays) is given by:

$$E_0 = \frac{pE^+ + (1-p)E^-}{(1+r)} - I_0 = \frac{0.4 \times 115.2 + 0.6 \times 0}{1.08} - 44 = -1.33 \tag{15}$$

and the option to abandon by defaulting during construction is:

$$\text{Option to abandon by defaulting} = -1.33 - (-4) = 2.67. \tag{16}$$

or about three percent of project value. This value is of course dependent on the staged cost schedule.

For simplicity, the above examples were based on a one-period risk-neutral backward valuation procedure. This procedure can be easily extended to a discrete multi-period setting with any number of stages. Starting from the terminal values, the process would move backwards calculating option values one step earlier (using the up and down values obtained in the preceding step), and so on. A two-period extension is illustrated in the next section. As the number of steps increases, the discrete-time solution naturally approaches its continuous Black-Scholes-type equivalent (with appropriate adjustments), when it exists.

In the next section, we turn to various financial flexibility options, starting with equityholders' option to default on debt payments deriving from limited liability. A similar financial abandonment option held by the lender can be created through staged financing. Interactions among such financial flexibility and the earlier operating options are explored.

III. INTERACTIONS WITH FINANCIAL FLEXIBILITY

A. Equityholders' Option to Default on Debt (Limited Liability)

So far we have dealt with various operating or real options, implicitly assuming an all-equity firm. If we allow for debt financing, then the value of the project to equity holders can potentially improve by the additional amount of financial flexibility (or the option to default on debt payments deriving from limited liability) beyond what is already reflected in the promised interest rate. We can illustrate how to incorporate the value of financial flexibility by reevaluating the original investment opportunity with project financing (where the firm consists entirely of this oil project). Consider, for example, venture capital financing of a single-project start-up oil company. Suppose initially that venture capitalists (or 'junk' bond purchasers) would be content to provide funds in exchange for contractually promised fixed-debt payments, and require an equilibrium return on comparably risky bonds (that already reflects a premium for equity's option to default) of 16.7%.[10,11]

Specifically, suppose that I_0^D = $44 out of the required immediate $104 outlay is borrowed against the investment's expected future cash flows to be repaid with interest in two years at the promised equilibrium interest rate of 16.7% per year. The balance of I_0^E = $60 is supplied by the firm's equity holders (i.e., the entrepreneurs). Equity holders, of course, have an option to acquire the firm (project) value V — which in the meantime is 'owned' by the debt holders (here, the venture capitalists)— by paying back the debt (with imputed interest) as exercise price two years later. Thus, in year 2, equity holders will pay back what they owe the debt holders (D_2 = 44 × 1.167^2 = 59.92) only if the investment value exceeds the promised payment, or else they will exercise their limited liability rights to default (i.e., surrender the project's assets to debt holders and receive nothing), or E_2 = max($V_2 - D_2$, 0). Thus, depending on whether oil prices move up in both years (++), up in one year and down in the other (+ −) or down in both years (− −), the equity holders' claims in year 2 will be:

$$E_2^{++} = \max(324 - 59.92, 0) = 264.08,$$
$$E_2^{+-} = E_2^{-+} = \max(108 - 59.92, 0) = 48.08,$$
$$E_2^{--} = \max(36 - 59.92, 0) = 0.$$

The value of equity holders' claims back in year 1, depending on whether the oil market was up or down, would then be, according to CCA:

$$E_1^+ = \frac{pE_2^{++} + (1-p)E_2^{+-}}{(1+r)} = \frac{0.4 \times 264.08 + 0.6 \times 48.08}{1.08} = 124.52$$

$$E_1^- = \frac{pE_2^{-+} + (1-p)E_2^{--}}{(1+r)} = \frac{0.4 \times 48.08 + 0.6 \times 0}{1.08} = 17.81$$

Finally, moving another step back to year 0, the present value of the oil investment opportunity (with partial debt financing) is:

$$E_0 = \frac{pE_1^+ + (1-p)E_1^-}{(1+r)} - I_0^E = \frac{0.4 \times 124.52 + 0.6 \times 17.81}{1.08} - 60 = -4. \qquad (17)$$

This (expanded or adjusted NPV) value is the same as the NPV of the all-equity financed project found in Equation (2), confirming that debt financing at the 16.7% equilibrium interest rate (that already reflects a premium for the equity holders'

---

[10] For a good qualitative discussion of venture capital financing arrangements, see Sahlman [88]. Mauer and Triantis [72] present another treatment of dynamic interactions between corporate financing and investment decisions, where they refer to financial flexibility as the ability to adjust the firm's debt level over time (recapitalization).

[11] In addition to contractually fixed debt (or preferred stock) payment (at a high required rate), venture capitalists may want part of their compensation in the form of a percentage ownership of the equity of the firm (or in the form of warrants). Some venture capitalists (especially in an LBO context), however, may prefer to place their funds in the form of debt rather than common equity since they can generally exercise more effective control over their investment through the debt's covenants than through the stock's voting power. The debt principal may also provide a better mechanism for a tax-free recovery of capital for young privately held firms that may not be feasible with stock until the company goes public. Initially we consider here the simpler case of all-debt venture capital financing, but later consider mixed debt-equity financing by venture capitalists.

option to default) is a zero-NPV transaction.[12] Since, in this case, the promised 16.7% interest rate on debt is an equilibrium return, the project's NPV does not change with the introduction of debt financing. The firm compensates the lenders ex ante through a fair default option premium embedded in the promised equilibrium rate in exchange for financial flexibility.

Of course, if lenders were to accept a lower promised interest rate of, say, 12% that did not incorporate fully a fair premium for the option to default, E_0 above would instead be −1.40, resulting in an additional value of financial flexibility to equity holders (resulting from the option to default on debt) of −1.40 − (−4) = 2.60, or about three percent of the investment's gross value. In such a case, potential interactive effects between operating and financial flexibility may further magnify the amount of undervaluation caused by traditional DCF techniques. We next consider the presence of both financial flexibility (deriving from equityholders' limited liability rights to default) and the operating default option analyzed earlier.

B. Potential Interaction Between Operating and Financial Default Flexibilities

Suppose now that $I_0^D = \$44$ were borrowed as before from venture capital sources (or by issuing junk bonds) to be used immediately as an investment start-up cost for infrastructure, while the $60 equity contribution is to be potentially expended (with earned interest) as a second-stage investment 'installment' for building the processing

---

[12] The 16.7% equilibrium return demanded by lenders that takes the firm's option to default into account in pricing the debt can be determined as the promised debt interest rate (r_D) derived from the difference between the face value of the debt to be repaid at the end of the two periods (B) and the current value of the debt ($D_0 = I_0^D = \$44$). The debt face value, B is the amount that satisfies the condition that the discounted expected terminal payoff to the debtholders in each state $i(D_2^i)$ under risk-neutral valuation equals the current debt amount, i.e., $\sum p^i D_2^i/(1+r)^2 = 44$, where the debtholders' terminal payoff is the minimum of the face value of the debt or the value of the firm at default, $D_2^i = \min(B, V_2^i)$. In the above example, at terminal period 2:

$$D_2^{++} = \min(B, 324) = B,$$
$$D_2^{+-} = D_2^{-+} = \min(B, 108) = B,$$
$$D_2^{--} = \min(B, 36) = 36.$$

The value of debtholders' claims back in year 1 then is:

$$D_1^+ = \frac{pD_2^{++} + (1-p)D_2^-}{(1+r)} = \frac{0.4B + 0.6B}{1.08} = \frac{B}{1.08}$$

$$D_1^- = \frac{pD_2^{-+} + (1-p)D_2^-}{(1+r)} = \frac{0.4B + 0.6 \times 36}{1.08}.$$

Finally, moving another step back to year 0:

$$D_0 = \frac{pD_1^+ + (1-p)D_1^-}{(1+r)},$$

or

$$44 = \frac{0.4B + 0.6(0.4B + 21.6)}{1.08^2},$$

resulting in $B = 59.94$. From $D_0(1+r_D)^2 = B$ with $D_0 = 44$, this implies that $r_D = 16.7\%$. The fact that the project NPV remains unchanged with debt financing in Equation (17) confirms that this is the equilibrium rate that fairly prices the default option ex ante.

plant in year 1 (as $I_1^E = 64.8$).[13] Thus, equityholders now have extra operating flexibility to abandon the project (by choosing not to expend the 'equity cost installment,' I_1^E, if it turns out to exceed the project's value) in year 1.

Again, starting from the end and moving backward, the value of equity's claims in year 2 (with debt repayment) remains unchanged, but in year 1 now becomes the maximum of its value in the previous case (in the absence of any outlay for continuing) minus the 'equity cost' I_1^E now due, or zero (if the project performs poorly and equity-holders default), i.e., $(E_1)' = \max(E_1 - I_1^E, 0)$:

$$(E_1^+)' = \max(124.52 - 64.8, 0) = 59.72 \text{ (continue)};$$

$$(E_1^-= \max(17.81 - 64.8, 0) = 0 \text{ (abandon)}.$$

The value of the investment (with both operating and financial default flexibility) is:

$$E_0' = \frac{p(E_1^+)' + (1-p)(E_1^-)'}{(1+r)} = \frac{0.4 \times 59.72 + 0.6 \times 0}{1.08} = 22.12. \tag{18}$$

Thus, the incremental value of the operating default option in the presence of financial flexibility is $22.12 - (-4) = 26.12$ or about one-fourth of gross investment value, for exceeding the three percent value of the equivalent operating option to default under all-equity financing in Equation (16) above. This confirms that the incremental value of an option in the presence of other options may differ significantly from its individual value in isolation, and that financial and operating flexibility options may interact. These option interactions may be more pronounced if lenders accept a lower interest than the fair equilibrium return of 16.7%. For example, had the promised interest rate been only 12%, E_0' would instead be 23.74 and the combined value of the operating option to default on planned cost installments (determined separately to be about three percent in Equation (16)) with the extra financial flexibility to default on debt (separately estimated at about three percent in the preceding section) would be about 28%. This combined value far exceeds the sum of separate option values, indicating the presence of substantial positive interaction (i.e., 28% > (3 + 3)%). Such positive interaction effects are typical in compound option situations such as these.[14]

C. Venture Capitalists' (Lender's) Option to Abandon Via Staged Debt Financing

So far we have focused on the financial option to default on debt payments held by the equity holders (entrepreneurs). The venture capitalists, however, may also wish to generate an option to abandon the venture themselves by insisting on providing staged or sequential capital financing. For example, they could insist on actually providing only half the requested $44 amount up front, $I_0^D = \$22$ (to be repaid at the 16.7% required rate as $29.96 in two years), with the remaining portion (allowed to grow at the eight percent riskless interest rate, $I_1^D = \$22 \times 1.08 = 23.76$) to be provided next year, contingent on successful interim progress. Following a successful first stage, the second stage would be less risky so that a lower 12% rate would be agreeable (with the

---

[13] Notice that this case is identical to the operating default case in Section II.B.4 above, with the only difference being that the initial outlay now comes from borrowed money.
[14] See also Trigeorgis[106] for the nature of real option interactions.

$23.76 to return $26.61 a year later). The equity holders would thus also need to contribute ($I_0^E = 22$) toward the $44 upfront cost for infrastructure ($I_0 = I_0^D + I_0^E = 22 + 22$), as well as ($I_1^E = 41.04$) toward the potential second-stage $64.8 processing plant cost one year later ($I_1 = I_1^D + I_1^E = 23.76 + 41.04$), if the venture at that time appears worth pursuing further.

Suppose that the venture capitalist would choose to provide second-stage financing (at the lower 12% rate) *only* if the first stage is successful (i.e., following a '+' oil price state in period 1), but would otherwise choose to abandon the venture in midstream. In this case, equity holders' value in the intermediate states in year 2 may differ, contingent on first year apparent success. That is, E_2^{+-} would differ from E_2^{-+}, since, in the first case, the venture capitalists would be repaid $26.61 for the second-stage financing they would provide following a successful first stage, in addition to the $29.61 for the second-stage financing they would provide following a successful first stage, in addition to the $29.96 repayment for the upfront debt financing. Thus:

$$E_2^{++} = \max(324 - (29.96 + 26.61), 0) = 267.43$$

$$E_2^{++} = \max(108 - 56.57, 0) = 51.43$$

(while following a '–' state in period 1 only the upfront debt repayment need be made:

$$E_2^{-+} = \max(108 - 29.96, 0) = 78.04$$

$$E_2^{-} = \max(36 - 29.96, 0) = 6.04.)$$

If there were no outlays required in period 1, the value of equityholders' claim would be:

$$E_1^+ = \frac{0.4 \times 267.43 + 0.6 \times 51.43}{1.08} = 127.62$$

(with $\qquad E_1^- = \frac{0.4 \times 78.04 + 0.6 \times 6.04}{1.08} = 32.26).$

Since equity holders would actually need to contribute $I_1^E = 41.04$ in period 1 for the venture to proceed, the correct (revised) value is the maximum of the above value in the absence of any outlays minus the 'equity cost' I_1^E, or zero (if the venture performs poorly and is abandoned in mid-stream), i.e., $(E_1)' = \max(E_1 - I_1^E, 0)$:

$$(E_1^+)' = \max(127.62 - 41.04, 0) = 86.58,$$

but when $(E_1^-)' = 0$, after a disappointing first stage, the venture would be abandoned. Finally, the time –0 value of equity holders' claims becomes:

$$E_0' = \frac{p(E_1^+)' + (1-p)(E_1^-)'}{(1+r)} - I_0^E = \frac{0.4 \times 86.58 + 0.6 \times 0}{1.08} - 22 = 10.07. \qquad (19)$$

Thus, the value of equity's default options, offset by the venture capitalists' option to abandon by refusing to provide second-stage financing, is $10.07 - (-4) = 14.07$ or 14% of gross project value.

This value is less than the 26% equity default option value found in Subsection B above, without the venture capitalists' abandonment option. The venture capitalists should thus be willing to pay a premium of up to $12 (million) to preserve their option to abandon via staged debt financing. Still, the above value (14) is in excess of that in Section III.A., where the full $44 borrowed amount was unequivocally committed upfront. In the present case, venture capitalists are better off via their option to abandon the venture by refusing to contribute second-stage financing in case of interim failure. This, in turn, enables the equity holders to obtain better financing terms, such as saving on debt interest costs.

Indeed, as discussed further below, structuring the financing deal in contingent stages to more closely match the inherent resolution of uncertainty over the investment's different stages can make both parties better off. For example, providing equity financing in stages, rather than all upfront, would not only benefit the venture capitalists via their option to abandon, but may also allow the entrepreneurs to raise equity capital later at a potentially more favorable valuation resulting in less equity dilution. Even following a bad interim state, entrepreneurs (who presumably have more information and may still believe the project is worthwhile to pursue) can prevent abandonment of the venture by the lenders by renegotiating more appropriate second-stage financing terms given the revealed higher risks, thus generating mutual gains by solving the underlying agency or underinvestment problem in this case. More generally, the flexibility to actively revalue the terms of a financing deal to better match the evolution of operating project risks, whether increasing or decreasing, as the project moves into its various stages creates value, compared to a passive alternative where the financing terms are irrevocably committed to from the outset under less complete information. The value created by partially solving this information problem via flexible contingent financing arrangements can be of mutual benefit to both parties.

D. Mixed (Debt-Equity) Venture Capital Financing

Consider now the case where the venture capitalists finance the full $44 start-up cost, half in the form of debt (to be repaid at a 16.7% rate as $29.96 in two years) and the other half in exchange for an upfront 22% equity ownership share.[15] Thus, both the total equity expected return and the risk are divided proportionately (78/22%) among the entrepreneurs and the venture capitalists. The group of equity holders would still make an upfront contribution of $I_0^E = 22$ (using the cash provided by venture capitalists in exchange for the equity share), and may incur a discretionary follow-up equity cost outlay of $I_1^E = 64.8$ if the project proceeds well. In this case,

$$E_2^{++} = \max(324 - 29.96, 0) = 294.04,$$
$$E_2^{+-} = E_2^{-+} = \max(108 - 29.96, 0) = 78.04,$$
$$E_2^{--} = \max(36 - 29.96, 0) = 6.04.$$

In the absence of a period-1 outlay, the value of equity-holders' claims in year 1 would be:

$$E_1^+ = \frac{0.4 \times 294.04 + 0.6 \times 78.04}{1.08} = 152.26$$

$$E_1^- = \frac{0.4 \times 78.04 + 0.6 \times 6.04}{1.08} = 32.26.$$

---

[15] Note that the $22 committed now amounts to 22% of the gross project value of $100, assuming a required 20% return on an equity position of comparable risk.

Adjusting for the $I_1^E = 64.8$ discretionary outlay in case the project is continued,

$$(E_1^+)' = \max(152.26 - 64.86, 0) = 87.46$$

i.e., continue;

$$(E_1^-)' = \max(32.26 - 64.8, 0) = 0$$

since equity holders would abandon the venture. Finally, the time-0 value of the combined equity holder group's claims (with default flexibility) is:

$$E_0' = \frac{0.4 \times 87.46 + 0.6 \times 0}{1.08} = 32.4. \tag{20}$$

The entrepreneurs would receive 78% of this $32.4 net value, or $25.27 (million). This represents an improvement over the $22.12 value of an all-debt capital upfront commitment of Equation (18) (as well as compared to the $10.07 value in the previous case of all-debt staged financing of Equation (19), that gives venture capitalists an option to abandon). Note further that this case of mixed debt-equity financing results in a gross investment value (after adding the 104 costs) of $136.4. Of this total value, 22% or $30 would go to the venture capitalists (in return for their $22 initial equity investment). Venture capitalists are also better off in the case of staged debt financing (compared to an upfront capital commitment) since they would have better control of (part of) their funds, especially in the event of disappointing interim results.

If venture capital equity financing is also provided in stages, the reduced operating uncertainties (as the project proceeds into its later stages) and the higher value to the venture capitalists following a successful first stage can result in less equity dilution for the entrepreneurs. For example, suppose that the venture capitalists again provide the first $22 upfront in the form of debt, but postpone the decision to contribute the rest ($23.76 in a year) in exchange for an equity share to be determined contingent on successful interim progress next year. The year-2 equity values would change only to the extent that now $I_1^E = 41.04$ (since 23.76 of the 64.8 discretionary year-1 outlay will now be provided by venture capitalists in exchange for equity if the first stage is successful). Thus,

$$(E_1^+)'' = \max(152.26 - 41.04, 0) = 111.22 \text{ (continue)},$$
$$(E_1^-)'' = 0 \text{ (abandon)}.$$

If, contingent on first-stage success, venture capitalists can receive a 13.5% equity share in exchange for their $23.76 contribution, the entrepreneurs would then obtain 86.5% of $111.22 for $96.2 in the good state. Thus, the entrepreneurs' time-0 value would be:

$$E_0'' = \frac{0.4 \times 96.2 + 0.6 \times 0}{1.08} - 22 = 13.63. \tag{21}$$

This exceeds the $10.07 value of Equation (19) obtained under all-debt staged financing, with the $3.56 difference representing savings due to the lower equity dilution as a result of the more flexible, contingent arrangement. Thus, staging equity financing sequentially would not only make the venture capitalists better off (by generating an option to abandon), but would also allow the entrepreneurs to raise equity capital later at a potentially more favorable valuation. These results confirm that both parties can be better off if the financing deal is flexibly arranged such that it better matches the evolution of operating project risks and valuation.

IV. SUMMARY, CONCLUSIONS AND EXTENSIONS

Following a comprehensive thematic overview of the evolution of real options, this paper has illustrated, through simple examples, how to quantify in principle the value of various types of operating options embedded in capital investments, both for enhancing upside potential (e.g., through options to defer or expand), as well as for reducing downside risk (e.g., via options to abandon for salvage value or switch use, and to default on staged planned outlays). We have also noted a number of fruitful future research directions, including more applications and implementation problems, empirical and field studies, theoretical extensions combining options theory with Bayesian analysis to model learning, with game theory to model competitive and strategic interactions, with agency theory/asymmetric information to model/correct misuse of managerial discretion, as well as interactions between operating and financial flexibility.

Taking a first step in the latter direction, we extended the analysis in the presence of leverage within a venture capital context and examined the potential improvement in equity holders' values as a result of additional financial flexibility, starting from the equity holders' option to default on debt payments deriving from limited liability. The beneficial impact of staging venture capital financing in installments, thereby creating an option to abandon by the lender, and when using a mix of debt and equity venture capital was also examined. Staging capital financing may be beneficial not only to venture capitalists (by preserving an option to abandon), but also to entrepreneurs as well, since it allows potentially better financing terms in later stages. In later-stage debt financing, for example, better terms may be achieved in the form of lower interest costs. If later-stage financing is to be provided in the form of an equity ownership share based on the project's market value as would be revealed at an interim stage, entrepreneurs could gain by suffering less equity dilution when a higher project value is assessed in reallocating the claims in the good interim state. Even in a bad interim state, entrepreneurs might still gain if they can prevent imminent abandonment of the venture (assuming they still believe it is worthwhile to pursue) by the venture capitalists by renegotiating more appropriate terms given the higher risks (either offering a greater equity share or a higher interest rate). The option to actively revalue the terms of a financing deal as operating project uncertainties get resolved over successive stages is clearly valuable, compared to a passive alternative where the financing terms are irrevocably committed to from the very beginning under less complete information. Building-in flexibility in a financing deal may determine whether the venture will continue and eventually succeed or fail when interim performance does not meet initial expectations.

Thus, contrary to what is often popularly assumed, the value of an investment deal may not depend solely on the amount, timing, and operating risk of its measurable cash flows. The future operating outcomes of a project can actually be impacted by future decisions (by either equity holders or lenders) depending on the inherent or built-in operating and financial options and the way the deal is financed (e.g., the staging of financing or the allocation of cash flows among debt and equity claimants). In such cases, interactions between a firm's operating and financial decisions can be quite significant, as exemplified by the typical venture capital case. These interactions are likely to be more pronounced for large, uncertain, long-development and multi-staged investments or growth opportunities, especially when substantial external (particularly debt) multi-staged financing is involved. Understanding these interactions and designing a proper financing deal that recognizes their true value, while being flexible enough to better reflect the evolution of a project's operating risks as it moves through different stages, can mean the difference between success or failure. Options-based valuation can thus be a particularly useful tool to corporate managers and strategists by providing a consistent and unified approach toward incorporating the value of both the real and financial options associated with the combined investment and financial decision of the firm.

REFERENCES

1. R. Aggarwal, 'Justifying Investments in Flexible Manufacturing Technology,' *Managerial Finance* (May 1991), pp. 77–88.
2. J. S. Ang and S. Dukas, 'Capital Budgeting in a Competitive Environment,' *Managerial Finance* (May 1991), pp. 6–15.
3. C. Baldwin, 'Optimal Sequential Investment When Capital is Not Readily Reversible', *Journal of Finance* (June 1982), pp. 763–782.
4. C. Baldwin, 'Competing for Capital in a Global Environment', *Midland Corporate Finance Journal* (Spring 1987), pp. 43–64.
5. C. Baldwin and K. Clark, 'Capabilities and Capital Investment: New Perspectives on Capital Budgeting', *Journal of Applied Corporate Finance* (Summer 1992), pp. 67–87.
6. C. Baldwin and K. Clark, 'Modularity and Real Options', Working Paper, Harvard Business School, 1993.
7. C. Baldwin and R. Ruback, 'Inflation, Uncertainty, and Investment', *Journal of Finance* (July 1986), pp. 657–669.
8. C. Baldwin and L. Trigeorgis, 'Toward Remedying the Underinvestment Problems: Competitiveness, Real Options, Capabilities, and TQM', Working Paper #93-025, Harvard Business School, 1993.
9. G. Barone-Adesi and R. Whaley, 'Efficient Analytic Approximation of American Option Values', *Journal of Finance* (June 1987), pp. 301–320.
10. G. Bell, 'Volatile Exchange Rates and the Multinational Firm: Entry, Exit, and Capacity Options', in *Real Options in Capital Investment: New Contributions*. L. Trigeorgis (ed.), New York, NY, Praeger, 1993.
11. P. Bjerksund and S. Ekern, 'Managing Investment Opportunities Under Price Uncertainty: from "Last Chance" to "Wait and See" Strategies', *Financial Management* (Autumn 1990), pp. 65–83.
12. P. Bjerksund and S. Ekern, 'Contingent Claims Evaluation of Mean-Reverting Cash Flows in Shipping', in *Real Options in Capital Investment: New Contributions*, L. Trigeorgis (ed.), New York: NY, Praeger, 1993.
13. F. Black and M. Scholes, 'The Pricing of Options and Corporate Liabilities', *Journal of Political Economy* (May/June 1973), pp. 637–659.
14. P. Boyle, 'Options: A Monte Carlo Approach', *Journal of Financial Economics* (May 1977), pp. 323–338.
15. P. Boyle, 'A Lattice Framework for Option Pricing with Two State Variables', *Journal of Financial and Quantitative Analysis* (March 1988), pp. 1–12.
16. R. Brealey and S. C. Myers, *Principles of Corporate Finance*, New York, NY, McGraw-Hill, 4th edition, 1991, Ch. 21.

17. M. Brennan, 'The Pricing of Contingent Claims in Discrete Time Models', *Journal of Finance* (March 1979), pp. 53–68.
18. M. Brennan and E. Schwartz, 'Finite Difference Methods and Jump Processes Arising in the Practice of Contingent Claims: A Synthesis', *Journal of Financial and Quantitative Analysis* (September 1978), pp. 461–474.
19. M. Brennan and E. Schwartz, 'Evaluating Natural Resource Investments', *Journal of Business* (April 1985), pp. 135–157.
20. M. Brennan and E. Schwartz, 'A New Approach to Evaluating Natural Resource Investments', *Midland Corporate Finance Journal* (Spring 1985), pp. 37–47.
21. D. Capozza and G. Sick, 'Risk and Return in Land Markets', Working Paper, University of British Columbia, 1992.
22. P. Carr, 'The Valuation of Sequential Exchange Opportunities', *Journal of Finance* (December 1988), pp. 1235–1256.
23. K. Chung and C. Charoenwong, 'Investment Options. Assets in Place, and the Risk of Stocks', *Financial Management* (Autumn 1991), pp. 21–33.
24. G. Constantinides, 'Market Risk Adjustment in Project Valuation', *Journal of Finance* (May 1978), pp. 603–616.
25. T. Copeland and J. F. Weston, 'A Note on the Evaluation of Cancellable Operating Leases', *Financial Management* (Summer 1982), pp. 60–67.
26. J. Cox and S. Ross. 'The Valuation of Options for Alternative Stochastic Processes,' *Journal of Financial Economics* (January 1976). pp. 145–166.
27. J. Cox, S. Ross and M. Rubinstein, 'Option Pricing: A Simplified Approach', *Journal of Financial Economics* (September 1979), pp. 229–263.
28. J. Cox, J. Ingersoll and S. Ross, 'An Intertemporal General Equilibrium Model of Asset Prices', *Econometrica* (March 1985), pp. 363–384.
29. J. Dean, *Capital Budgeting*, New York, NY, Columbia University Press, 1951.
30. A. Dixit, 'Entry and Exit Decisions Under Uncertainty', *Journal of Political Economy* (June 1989), pp. 620–638.
31. R. Geske, 'The Valuation of Compound Options', *Journal of Financial Economics* (March 1979), pp. 63–81.
32. R. Geske and H. Johnson, 'The American Put Option Valued Analytically', *Journal of Finance* (December 1984), pp. 1511–1524.
33. R. Geske and K. Shastri, 'Valuation by Approximation: A Comparison of Alternative Option Valuation Techniques', *Journal of Financial and Quantitative Analysis* (March 1985), pp. 45–71.
34. J. M. Harrison and D. M. Kreps, 'Martingales and Arbitrage in Multiperiod Securities Markets', *Journal of Economic Theory* (June 1979), pp. 381–408.
35. R. Hayes and W. Abernathy, 'Managing Our Way to Economic Decline', *Harvard Business Review* (July–August 1980), pp. 66–77.
36. R. Hayes and D. Garvin, 'Managing as if Tomorrow Mattered', *Harvard Business Review* (May–June 1982), pp. 71–79.
37. D. Hendricks, 'Optimal Policy Responses to an Uncertain Threat. The Case of Global Warming', Working Paper, Harvard University, Kennedy School of Government, 1991.
38. D. Hertz, 'Risk Analysis in Capital Investment', *Harvard Business Review* (January–February 1964), pp. 95–106.
39. T. Hiraki, 'Corporate Governance. Long-term Investment Orientation, and Real Options in Japan', in *Real Options in Capital Investment: New Contributions*. L. Trigeorgis (ed.), New York, NY. Praeger, 1993.
40. J. Hodder. 'Evaluation of Manufacturing Investments: A Comparison of U.S. and Japanese Practices.' *Financial Management* (Spring 1986), pp. 17–24.
41. J. Hodder and H. Riggs, 'Pitfalls in Evaluating Risky Projects. *Harvard Business Review* (January–February 1985), pp. 128–135.
42. J. Hull. *Options, Futures, and Other Derivative Securities*. Englewood Cliffs, NJ. Prentice-Hall, 1989, Ch. 9.
43 J. Hull and A. White, 'The Use of the Control Variate Technique in Option Pricing'. *Journal of Financial and Quantitative Analysis*. (September 1988), pp. 697–705.
44. J. Ingersoll and S. Ross, 'Waiting to Invest: Investment and Uncertainty', *Journal of Business* (January 1992), pp. 1–29.

45. H. Johnson, 'Options on the Maximum or the Minimum of Several Assets', *Journal of Financial and Quantitative Analysis* (September 1987), pp. 277–284.
46. B. Kamrad and R. Ernst. 'Multiproduct Manufacturing with Stochastic Input Prices and Output Yield Uncertainty', in *Real Options in Capital Investment: New Contributions*. L. Trigeorgis (ed.), New York, NY, Praeger, 1993.
47. E. Kasanen, 'Creating Value by Spawning Investment Opportunities', *Financial Management* (Autumn 1993), pp. 251–258.
48. E. Kasanen and L. Trigeorgis, 'A Market Utility Approach to Investment Valuation', *European Journal of Operational Research* (Special Issue on Financial Modelling), 1993.
49. A. Kemna, 'Case Studies on Real Options', *Financial Management* (Autumn 1993), pp. 259–270.
50. J. Kensinger, 'Adding the Value of Active Management into the Capital Budgeting Equation', *Midland Corporate Finance Journal* (Spring 1987), pp. 31–42.
51. W. C. Kester, 'Today's Options for Tomorrow's Growth', *Harvard Business Review* (March–April 1984), pp. 153–160.
52. W. C. Kester, 'Turning Growth Options Into Real Assets', in *Capital Budgeting Under Uncertainty*. R. Aggarwal (ed.), Englewood Cliffs, NJ, Prentice-Hall, 1993, pp. 187–207.
53. B. Kogut and N. Kulatilaka, 'Operating Flexibility, Global Manufacturing, and the Option Value of a Multinational Network', *Management Science*, forthcoming 1993.
54. A. L. Kolbe, P. A. Morris and E. O Teisberg, 'When Choosing R&D Projects, Go with Long Shots', *Research-Technology Management* (January–February 1991).
55. N. Kulatilaka, 'Valuing the Flexibility of Flexible Manufacturing Systems', *IEEE Transactions in Engineering Management* (1988), pp. 250–257.
56. N. Kulatilaka, 'The Value of Flexibility: The Case of a Dual-Fuel Industrial Steam Boiler', *Financial Management* (Autumn 1993), pp. 271–280.
57. N. Kulatilaka, 'The Value of Flexibility: A General Model of Real Options' in *Real Options in Capital Investment: New Contributions*, L. Trigeorgis (ed.), New York, NY, Praeger, 1993.
58. N. Kulatilaka, 'Operating Flexibilities in Capital Budgeting: Substitutability and Complementarity in Real Options', in *Real Options in Capital Investment: New Contributions*. L. Trigeorgis (ed.), New York, NY, Praeger, 1993.
59. N. Kulatilaka and A. Marcus, 'A General Formulation of Corporate Operating Options', *Research in Finance*, JAI Press, 1988, pp. 183–200.
60. N. Kulatilaka and A. Marcus, 'Project Valuation Under Uncertainty: When Does DCF Fail?', *Journal of Applied Corporate Finance* (Fall 1992), pp. 92–100.
61. N. Kulatilaka and S. Marks, 'The Strategic Value of Flexibility: Reducing the Ability to Compromise', *American Economic Review* 1988, pp. 574–580.
62. N. Kulatilaka and E. Perotti, 'Strategic Investment Timing Under Uncertainty', Working Paper, Boston University, 1992.
63. N. Kulatilaka and L. Trigeorgis, 'The General Flexibility to Switch: Real Options Revisited', *International Journal of Finance*, December 1993.
64. V. S. Lai and L. Trigeorgis, 'The Capital Budgeting Process: A Review and Synthesis', in *Real Options in Capital Investment: New Contributions*. L. Trigeorgis (ed.), New York, NY, Praeger, 1993.
65. D. G. Laughton and H. D. Jacoby, 'Reversion, Timing Options, and Long-term Decision-Making', *Financial Management* (Autumn 1993), pp. 225–240.
66. W. Lee, J. Martin and A. Senchack, 'The Case for Using Options to Evaluate Salvage Values in Financial Leases', *Financial Management* (Autumn 1982), pp. 33–41.
67. J. Magee, 'How to Use Decision Trees in Capital Investment, *Harvard Business Review* (September–October 1964).
68. S. Majd and R. Pindyck, 'Time to Build, Option Value, and Investment Decisions', *Journal of Financial Economics* (March 1987), pp. 7–27.
69. W. Margrabe, 'The Value of an Option to Exchange One Asset for Another', *Journal of Finance* (March 1978), pp. 177–186.
70. S. P. Mason and C. Baldwin, 'Evaluation of Government Subsidies to Large-scale Energy Projects: A Contingent Claims Approach', *Advances in Futures and Options Research*, 1988, pp. 169–181.

71. S. P. Mason and R. C. Merton, 'The Role of Contingent Claims Analysis in Corporate Finance', in *Recent Advances in Corporate Finance*, E. Altman and M. Subrahmanyam (eds.), Homewood, IL, Richard D. Irwin, 1985, pp. 7–54.

72. D. Mauer and A. Triantis, 'Interactions of Corporate Financing and Investment Decisions: A Dynamic Framework', Working Paper, University of Wisconsin-Madison, 1992.

73. J. McConnell and J. Schallheim, 'Valuation of Asset Leasing Contracts', *Journal of Financial Economics* (August 1983), pp. 237–261.

74. R. McDonald and D. Siegel, 'Option Pricing When the Underlying Asset Earns a Below-Equilibrium Rate of Return: A Note', *Journal of Finance* (March 1984), pp. 261–265.

75. R. McDonald and D. Siegel, 'Investment and the Valuation of Firms When There is an Option to Shut Down', *International Economic Review* (June 1985), pp. 331–349.

76. R. McDonald and D. Siegel, 'The Value of Waiting to Invest', *Quarterly Journal of Economics* (November 1986), pp. 707–727.

77. R. McLaughlin and R. Taggart, 'The Opportunity Cost of Using Excess Capacity', *Financial Management* (Summer 1992), pp. 12–23.

78. R. C. Merton, 'Theory of Rational Option Pricing', *Bell Journal of Economics and Management Science* (Spring 1973), pp. 141–183.

79. R. Morck, E. Schwartz and D. Stangeland, 'The Valuation of Forestry Resources under Stochastic Prices and Inventories', *Journal of Financial and Quantitative Analysis* (December 1989), pp. 473–487.

80. S. C. Myers, 'Determinants of Corporate Borrowing', *Journal of Financial Economics* (November 1977), pp. 147–176.

81. S. C. Myers, 'Finance Theory and Financial Strategy', *Midland Corporate Finance Journal* (Spring 1987), pp. 6–13.

82. S. C. Myers and S. Majd, 'Abandonment Value and Project Life', *Advances in Futures and Options Research*, 1990, pp. 1–21.

83. J. Paddock, D. Siegel and J. Smith, 'Option Valuation of Claims on Physical Assets: The Case of Offshore Petroleum Leases', *Quarterly Journal of Economics* (August 1988), pp. 479–508.

84. R. Pindyck, 'Irreversible Investment, Capacity Choice and the Value of the Firm', *American Economic Review* (December 1988), pp. 969–985.

85. R. Pindyck, 'Irreversibility, Uncertainty, and Investment', *Journal of Economic Literature* (September 1991), pp. 1110–1148.

85A. L. Quigg, 'Empirical Testing of Real Option-Pricing Models', *Journal of Finance* (June 1993), pp. 621–640.

85B. L. Quigg, 'Optimal Land Development' in *Real Options in Capital Investment: New Contributions*, L. Trigeorgis (ed.), New York, NY, Praeger, 1993.

86. K. Roberts and M. Weitzman, 'Funding Criteria for Research, Development and Exploration Projects', *Econometrica* (September 1981), pp. 1261–1288.

87. M. Rubinstein, 'The Valuation of Uncertain Income Streams and the Pricing of Options', *Bell Journal of Economics* (Autumn 1976), pp. 407–425.

88. W. Sahlman, 'Aspects of Financial Contracting in Venture Capital', *Journal of Applied Corporate Finance* (1988), pp. 23–36.

89. G. Sick, *Capital Budgeting With Real Options*, Monograph, New York University, Salomon Brothers Center, 1989.

90. D. Siegel, J. Smith and J. Paddock, 'Valuing Offshore Oil Properties with Option Pricing Models', *Midland Corporate Finance Journal* (Spring 1987), pp. 22–30.

91. H. T. J. Smit and L. A. Ankum, 'A Real Options and Game-Theoretic Approach to Corporate Investment Strategy Under Competition, *Financial Management* (Autumn 1993), pp. 241–250.

92. K. W. Smith and A. Triantis, 'The Value of Options in Strategic Acquisitions', in *Real Options in Capital Investment: New Contributions*, L. Trigeorgis (ed.), New York, NY, Praeger, 1993.

93. G. Stensland and D. Tjostheim, 'Some Applications of Dynamic Programming to Natural Resource Exploration, *Stochastic Models and Opinion Values*, in D. Lund and B. Oksendal (eds.), Amsterdam, North-Holland, 1990.

94. R. Stulz, 'Options on the Minimum or the Maximum of Two Risky Assets: Analysis and Application', *Journal of Financial Economics* (July 1982), pp. 161–185.

95. E. Teisberg, 'Methods for Evaluating Capital Investment Decisions Under Uncertainty', in *Real Options in Capital Investment: New Contributions*, L. Trigeorgis (ed.), New York, NY, Praeger, 1993.

96. E. Teisberg, 'An Option Valuation Analysis of Investment Choices by a Regulated Firm', *Management Science*, 1993.

97. S. Titman, 'Urban Land Prices Under Uncertainty', *American Economic Review* (June 1985), pp. 505–514.

98. O. Tourinho, 'The Option Value of Reserves of Natural Resources', Working Paper No. 94, University of California at Berkeley, 1979.

99. A. Triantis and J. Hodder, 'Valuing Flexibility as a Complex Option', *Journal of Finance* (June 1990), pp. 549–565.

100. L. Trigeorgis, 'A Conceptual Options Framework for Capital Budgeting', *Advances in Futures and Options Research*, 1988, pp. 145–167.

101. L. Trigeorgis, 'A Real Options Application in Natural Resource Investments', *Advances in Futures and Options Research*, 1990, p. 153–164.

102. L. Trigeorgis, 'Valuing the Impact of Uncertain Competitive Arrivals on Deferrable Real Investment Opportunities', Working Paper, Boston University, 1990.

103. L. Trigeorgis, 'Anticipated Competitive Entry and Early Preemptive Investment in Deferrable Projects', *Journal of Economics and Business* (May 1991), pp. 143–156.

104. L. Trigeorgis, 'A Log-Transformed Binomial Numerical Analysis Method for Valuing Complex Multi-Option Investments', *Journal of Financial and Quantitative Analysis* (September 1991), pp. 309–326.

105. L. Trigeorgis, 'Evaluating Leases with a Variety of Operating Options', Working Paper, Boston University, 1992.

106. L. Trigeorgis, 'The Nature of Option Interactions and the Valuation of Investments with Multiple Real Options', *Journal of Financial and Quantitative Analysis* (March 1993), pp. 1–20.

107. L. Trigeorgis (ed.), *Real Options in Capital Investment: New Contributions*. New York, NY, Praeger, 1993.

108. L. Trigeorgis, *Options in Capital Budgeting: Managerial Flexibility and Strategy in Resource Allocation*, Cambridge, MA, The MIT Press, 1994.

109. L. Trigeorgis and E. Kasanen, 'An Integrated Options-Based Strategic Planning and Control Model', *Managerial Finance* (May 1991), pp. 16–28.

110. L. Trigeorgis and S. P. Mason, 'Valuing Managerial Flexibility', *Midland Corporate Finance Journal* (Spring 1987), pp. 14–21.

111. J. Williams, 'Real Estate Development as an Option, *Journal of Real Estate Finance and Economics* (June 1991), pp. 191–208.

112. R. Willner, 'Valuing Start-Up Venture Growth Options', in *Real Options in Capital Investment: New Contributions*, L. Trigeorgis (ed.), New York, NY, Praeger, 1993.

Index